AF600319

THE COURT AND ITS CRITICS

Anti-Court Sentiments in Early Modern Italy

The Court and Its Critics

Anti-Court Sentiments in Early Modern Italy

Paola Ugolini

UNIVERSITY OF TORONTO PRESS
Toronto Buffalo London

Toronto Buffalo London
utorontopress.com

ISBN 978-1-4875-0544-8 (Cloth)
ISBN 978-1-4875-3212-3 (EPUB)
ISBN 978-1-4875-3216-1 (PDF)

Library and Archives Canada Cataloguing in Publication

Title: The court and its critics : anti-court sentiments in early modern Italy/Paola Ugolini.
Names: Ugolini, Paola, 1974– author.
Description: Includes bibliographical references and index.
Identifiers: Canadiana 20190188146 | ISBN 9781487505448 (hardcover)
Subjects: LCSH: Italy – Court and courtiers – History – 16th century. | LCSH: Italy – Social life and customs – 16th century. | LCSH: Satire, Italian – History and criticism.
Classification: LCC DG447 .U36 2019 | DDC 945/.07 – dc23

University of Toronto Press gratefully acknowledges the financial assistance of the Lila Wallace-Reader's Digest Publication Fund of the Villa I Tatti Harvard Center for Italian Renaissance Studies, Florence, in the publication of this book.

University of Toronto Press gratefully acknowledges the financial assistance of the University at Buffalo College of Arts and Sciences, Julian Park Fund in the publication of this book.

University of Toronto Press acknowledges the financial assistance to its publishing program of the Canada Council for the Arts and the Ontario Arts Council, an agency of the Government of Ontario.

Canada Council for the Arts Conseil des Arts du Canada

Funded by the Government of Canada | Financé par le gouvernement du Canada | Canada

Contents

Acknowledgments vii

Introduction 3

1 The Courtier 13

2 The Lady 50

3 The Satirist 84

4 The Shepherd 145

Afterword 181

Notes 187

Bibliography 253

Index 275

Acknowledgments

It is a great pleasure to thank the people and institutions that have provided me with support and guidance in the writing of this book. I am indebted to the outstanding scholars I have been lucky to have as mentors during my years at New York University and beyond. Virginia Cox's thorough comments on every page I wrote, her professional generosity and availability to discuss with me the fascinating intricacies of early modern culture have been an invaluable source of intellectual stimulation. Jane Tylus first introduced me to the world of the early modern pastoral, igniting a fascination that would accompany me over the years that followed. Her feedback and conversation, her respect for my work, and her kindness have been a constant source of motivation. Daniel Javitch further encouraged me to pursue this project (also in the name of our mutual passion for the works of Ludovico Ariosto) and broadened my scholarly horizons by teaching me to see the Italian Renaissance from a pan-European perspective.

As this book project started to take shape, many friends and colleagues were kind enough to read it in its earliest form. I am indebted to Sarah G. Ross, Giuseppe Gerbino, Paolo Savoia, Aileen A. Feng, and Marco Faini for offering precious feedback on my manuscript. Lindsay Eufusia helped me with her unbeatable proofreading and editing skills, and Anna Wainwright was a fantastic interlocutor in bringing the translations of quoted text into shape. The two anonymous reviewers at the University of Toronto Press provided thoughtful and meticulous feedback, which has greatly improved the quality of this book.

This book would not have been possible without the generous support of Harvard University's Villa I Tatti. The academic year I spent at Villa I Tatti was memorable in many ways, human and professional. I would like to thank the I Tatti staff and the many friends I met there, during both my fellowship year and my later research trips to the astounding Berenson Library; they all continue to be irreplaceable sources of intellectual exchange. My thoughts go in particular to Francesco Lucioli and Martina Piperno, Sarah G. Ross, Mary Vaccaro, Laura Moretti, Jessica Goethals, Alessandro Polcri, Paolo Savoia, Dario Brancato, Aileen A. Feng, and Cory Gavito. I am also indebted to Villa I Tatti for supporting the publication of this book through the Lila Wallace-Reader's Digest Publication Subsidy.

My colleagues at the Department of Romance Languages and Literatures at the University at Buffalo have been a continual source of support for me. I want to thank in particular David Castillo, Amy Graves-Monroe, Stephanie Schmidt, Henry Berlin, Colleen Culleton, and Maureen Jameson. Very special thanks, of course, to the "Dream Team" of the Italian program: Laura Chiesa, Emanuela Pecchioli, Andrew Serio, and Maria Cimato-Cirulli. I also acknowledge the University at Buffalo for awarding me the Julian Park Publication Fund.

My old and new friends in different parts of the world – in New York City, in Buffalo, in Modena – have kept me grounded and offered encouragement, conversation, and entertainment. Special thanks go to Elena Bellina, Erika Mazzer, Vincenzo Rochira, Elisabetta Pederzini, and Wendy Quinton.

My family has been a constant source of immeasurable support and love: my parents, Franco Ugolini and Maria Concetta Montermini, who taught me to pursue my passions and goals, to work hard, and to never give up in the face of adversity; my uncle Gabriele Ugolini and my aunt Vanna Fontana, who taught me to love art and encouraged me to travel the world; and my Montermini family, who are a constant reminder that there is nothing wrong in not conforming.

Finally, my greatest thanks go to Marco Faini: first-class scholar, superb pastry chef, gifted rock guitarist, tennis player, and goalkeeper – a man of so many talents that had he only been born in the sixteenth century, he would have proved to the world that Castiglione's perfect courtier was indeed possible. To him – for his intelligence, kindness, integrity, elegance, and sense of humour; for never doubting me even when I doubt myself – this book is dedicated, with admiration and love.

THE COURT AND ITS CRITICS

Anti-Court Sentiments in Early Modern Italy

Introduction

courtier, *noun*.

1 gentleman living at court: *Il Cortegiano* (*The Book of the Courtier*), title of a dialogue by Baldassar Castiglione (1478–1529); "Cortigiani, vil razza dannata," first verse of an aria from *Rigoletto* by Giuseppe Verdi (1813–1901)
2 (*figurative*) flatterer; scheming hypocrite.[1]

Present-day dictionaries of Italian define the word "courtier" by breaking it down into two different but related interpretations, as exemplified here by the *Dizionario Garzanti della Lingua Italiana*. The literal definition of the courtier as a gentleman making a profession of life at court is paired with a figurative sense reminding the reader of the most common vices associated with that profession: flattery, hypocrisy, deviousness. This figurative use of the word "courtier" given by current Italian dictionaries is not at all a modern interpretation, nor are the anti-court invectives of Rigoletto's aria the product of a Romantic portrayal of early modern society. On the contrary, they parallel the depictions of courts as hell on earth and of those living at court as servile, ambitious sycophants, all common features of early modern writings on courts, which can be encompassed under the general category of anti-courtly sentiments. An exploration of anti-courtly sentiment in early modern Italy could lead to a hypothetical sixteenth-century version of the entry in the Garzanti dictionary, obtained by conflating the two definitions into one:

> **courtier**, *noun*: gentleman living at court, and, *as such*, flatterer, scheming hypocrite.[2]

The centrality of the court in Renaissance society has often been underscored by scholarship. The second half of the twentieth century, in particular, witnessed the emergence of research that expanded the field of investigation of court studies: while for a long time the court had been explored merely in relation to habits of sumptuousness, public representation of grandeur, and conspicuous consumption, more recent studies have concentrated on the court as a pivotal social and political centre.[3]

In spite of this renewed scholarly interest, the court has remained a vast and complex topic that resists any attempt at being circumscribed by a univocal definition. Such complexity is fostered by the fact that the term "court" in the Renaissance encompassed a variety of meanings. The court consisted first and foremost of the group of people who assisted and accompanied the *Signore* in his different activities, both private and public. The first meaning of the term "court" is, therefore, a network of interpersonal relations. It was within this network that delicate matters such as a person's promotion or fall from favour were dealt with on a daily basis.

During the Renaissance the court ceased to be the travelling entity that it had been in the Middle Ages, progressively acquiring instead the character of an institution set in a definite place. The term "court" thus came also to define a location: the place of residence of the prince and his entourage. It is hard not to think that this additional meaning acquired by the term "court" may have had a direct consequence for writings on courts. The physical presence of the court in a specific place made it possible to identify it as a tangible entity and to discuss that entity – to praise it, or, as is the case with the documents analysed in this book, to criticize it as well as its inhabitants – by having in mind an exact point of reference.

At the same time, historians examining court milieus have pointed out the "frustratingly elusive" nature of the Renaissance court – scholars have debated who composed the court, whether courtiers had any specific functions, and whether there was a definable court culture – so that the Renaissance court appears to possess a "chameleon-like character."[4]

Such a chameleon-like and difficult-to-define nature also results in readers of early modern writings on courts – especially those writings that are critical of the court – being confronted with the puzzling vagueness of most of these writings, which leaves them with many unresolved questions. Are writers referencing a particular court when they condemn "the evils of the court"? Or should readers assume that every court is equally to blame? Do writers have a specific court in mind when they contrast such evils with the "good courts" of an unspecified past? When investigating anti-courtly sentiments, how much weight should be attributed to a given author's potentially unhappy firsthand experience with court life? And what to do with those writers who, despite lacking any significant direct interaction with the world of the court, still engage in anti-court writing?

The general sense that can be inferred from writings against courts and courtiers is that the court was invested with a highly symbolic value, to the point of transcending place and time, as Paola Vecchi Galli has aptly described: "[M]ore than a place, the court is [...] a conceptual *crux*, a myth (often projected in a non-existing past), or a literary meta-place (at the border with utopia or with dystopia)."[5] In a vast number of writings on courts, the abstract meaning of the court and its role as a symbol can be said to surpass its concrete value.[6] As a consequence, although a good number of complaints against courts and courtiers can be traced back to the authors' biographies and their experience with courtly life, such writings need to be explored while also keeping in mind that they present not so much a realistic representation as a contrived picture, either in a positive or in a negative way. Remarking on the mythical character of the court in writings on courts and courtiers does not, however, deprive reflections on courtly life from their value as documents for interpreting their contemporary culture. On the contrary, they are key to understanding the relevance that the court and all that was associated with it had for the Renaissance mind.

The importance of the early modern court also resided in its being the space that witnessed new forms of identity negotiation and prestige, the definition of masculinity and gender-specific roles, as well as the birth of modern politics and a modern ethics based on merit and individual self-interest. Anti-court discourse, by casting itself as a rejection of court culture, entails a reflection on all of the fundamental themes listed above.

This study employs the term "anti-courtliness" to refer to the sentiments of dissatisfaction, regret, negativity, scepticism, and mockery aimed at the court as an institution, at the kind of life one might lead at court, and at those who inhabit it (i.e., the courtiers and their prince) that are a widespread feature of early modern Italian culture. The flourishing of anti-court and anti-courtier sentiments in the Renaissance was a far-reaching European phenomenon rooted in a medieval moralistic tradition and revised in the early modern age, with increasing influence from Latin and Greek satires.[7] The commonality of topics and themes among critics of the court has led scholars to identify recurring sets of topoi of anti-court critique. Such negative representations are responsible for the dissemination of the image of the court as a school for wickedness and the courtier as nothing more than an assemblage of the most hideous vices: ruthless ambition, envy, deceitfulness, and toadyish servility; abject subjection disguised in vain under expensive clothes and manicured appearance.

A striking aspect of anti-courtliness is its pervasiveness. Indeed, it often goes so far as to appear a sort of obsession. Critiques of courts and courtiers were widely disseminated to the point that there seems to be not one single literary genre or artistic medium that was not touched by them. The scholar of early modern Italy is inevitably bound to run into anti-courtly sentiments in all kinds of genres (dialogues, *novelle*, satires, early examples of novels, pastoral dramas), in different media (not only literary texts but also emblems and paintings, music and dance), and across the social spectrum (from noble-born courtiers to ambitious social climbers).

Early modern Italian anti-court writings range from complaints about the condition of the court to the laments of unhappy courtiers to explicitly satirical representations of the court as a hell on earth. What all such stylistically variegated texts have in common is that the court is constantly described as a devilish place that hides a reality of squalor and suffering under a splendid surface. Life at court means living in a world of simulation, artificiality, and deceit, in a theatre where everyone is forced to always be on stage. Courtly language is a distorted form of communication: every word is deviousness, falsehood, flattery. Everything at court is under the dominion of Fortuna; virtue and worth, far from constituting the path to success at court, are often counterproductive. The perfect alter ego of the court is Lady Folly, and thus the jester and the buffoon become the only truly successful figures there: the incarnation of the spirit of a system that is now the antithesis of the values it once represented.[8]

Tomaso Garzoni's *La piazza universale di tutte le professioni del mondo* (1585) offers – in keeping with the book's intended exhaustiveness – a sample of the anti-court topoi in Renaissance Italy. Garzoni's chapter "Dei cortigiani e delle donne di corte insieme" (On Both Courtiers and Court Ladies) begins with a general overview of courts and courtiers that includes both classical sources and the most recent manuals of courtliness (quoting Antonio de Guevara's 1539 *Aviso de favoriti*)[9] and provides what may appear a neutral judgment on courts and courtiers. Yet the text soon switches tone, moving to a completely negative portrayal of the world of the court, presenting a perfect sample of the proliferation of anti-courtly sentiments in Renaissance Italian culture. In the resulting picture the court becomes the dystopian embodiment of a world turned upside-down, where vices prosper and virtues are shattered:

> [N]owadays many courts are nothing but a gathering of depraved men, an assembly of cunning foxes, a theatre of wicked satellites, a school of depraved mores and a refuge of the most dishonest felonies [...]. Envies,

> malevolences, badmouthings, bad deeds, passions of the soul, disdains, outrages, revenges, and all shame convene at court. Here pride rises, presumptuousness is exalted, arrogance flies high, rapacity has no restraint, lust has no limitation, perfidy is not corrected, gluttony guzzles, wrath leaps, envy sways, and all vices have a home, a dwelling, and a shameful bed inside the court. Here rapes, abductions, adulteries, fornications, harlotries, pimpings are the games and pleasures of courtiers and noble men; where there is a shipwreck of all virtues, an oppression of all goodness; where the simple are tricked, the just are persecuted, the presumptuous and the insolent are favoured. Here can prosper only flatterers, gossipmongers, spies, traitors, accusers, defamers, the good-for-nothing, evil tongues, crooks, inventors of evils, mischief-makers, and other kinds of criminals [...]. And so it seems that all the bestiality of the world is collected in the flock of courtiers as in a body [...]. Here you can find violent centaurs, dangerous Chimeras, insane satyrs, dirty harpies, wicked sirens, Scyllas with two forms, monstrous Medusas, multifarious Proteuses, horrible ostriches, greedy griffins, terrible dragons, and all the strange and frightening monsters that nature has ever created against its will. Here every kind of virtue suffers its torturers and tyrants. And, to conclude, all the calamities and all the evil in the world are to be found at court.[10]

Books of emblems offer intriguing examples of pictorial translations of the anti-court topoi enumerated by Garzoni. Different editions of Andrea Alciato's emblem *In aulicos* (On courtiers) include variations on the same theme: the image of a refined and elegantly dressed courtier, whose legs, however, are trapped in stocks.

The inscription underneath the emblem further underscores the idea of courtly life as captivity: *Vana Palatinos quos educat aula clientes, Dicitur auratis nectere compedibus* (The court, so full of vanities, supports the palace entourage but binds them with fetters of gold, it is said).[11] The stocks that bind the courtier's legs are symbolic of his lack of liberty – of his being a slave in spite of his rich clothes – and the emblem very effectively conveys the notion of courtiership as the antithesis to personal freedom.

Amid such a vast array of critiques, Baldassar Castiglione's masterpiece, *Il libro del Cortegiano* (*The Book of the Courtier*, 1528), offers a partly dissonant voice. In its attempt to create a perfect courtier who will, in addition, be endowed with the noble mission of becoming his prince's trustworthy and just counsellor, the *Book of the Courtier* offers – at least in theory – a path toward correcting such dismal pictures of the court. The *Book of the Courtier* itself, however, is not devoid of the presence of anti-courtly sentiments, which insinuate themselves under the apparently serene atmosphere of the court represented in its pages.

Figure 1. On courtiers. Andrea Alciato, *Emblemata* (Lyon: Macé Bonhomme for Guillaume Rouille, 1551), 94. *A well-dressed courtier whose legs are trapped in stocks, as a symbol of his lack of liberty.*

Castiglione's manual of courtliness was destined to become one of the most influential works of Renaissance literature and as such, to become in the years that followed its publication the object of critical attention as well, with either a nostalgic or a bitter tone. The critiques concerned in particular the figure of courtier put forward by the *Book of the Courtier*, an ideal that was already problematic at the time of its creation and that with the passing of time came to be perceived as more and more unattainable. In taking the figure of the perfect courtier as theorized by Castiglione as a point of reference, this book argues that anti-courtliness acted as crucial testimony to the growing discomfort toward the model of subjectivity and self-fashioning – a term made familiar through Stephen Greenblatt's seminal work

Renaissance Self-Fashioning (first published in 1980) – represented by the courtier.

My use of the notion of self-fashioning is also informed by Mario Biagioli's application of the same concept in *Galileo, Courtier: The Practice of Science in the Culture of Absolutism*, in which he analyses Galilei's construction of his identity as a particular type of court philosopher. Biagioli clarifies that the portrait of Galileo he is presenting "is not that of a 'slave to the system' – of somebody who fit himself within received roles and expectations in order to receive legitimation." He also specifies that in emphasizing the notion of self-fashioning, he does not "assume either an already existing 'Galileo' who deploys different tactics in different environments and yet remains always 'true to himself,' nor a Galileo who is passively shaped by the context that envelops him." Biagioli wants to highlight instead the way Galileo "used the resources he perceived in the surrounding environment to *construct* a new socio-professional identity for himself."[12] The courtiers and critics of the court whose lives and works are explored in this book likewise cannot be defined as "slaves to the system," passively adapting to the requirements of court culture and court life. Rather, just as Galileo the courtier-scientist depicted by Biagioli did, these courtier-writers strived to employ any resource available to construct for themselves an identity that, in some intriguing cases, both matched and opposed the requirements of courtliness.

John Jeffries Martin has further investigated the Renaissance self in connection with issues concerning prudence and sincerity, and in terms of the "myth of Renaissance individualism." I am referring here to Martin's eponymous monograph and essay,[13] wherein he puts forward the notion of a plurality of coexisting Renaissance selves. Moreover, in "Inventing Sincerity, Refashioning Prudence: The Discovery of the Individual in Renaissance Europe,"[14] Martin has brought to bear Jacob Burckhardt's very influential and yet much-debated notion of the discovery of the individual in Renaissance Europe upon the New Historicist formulation of the concept of self-fashioning.[15] Martin underlines how Greenblatt's scholarship – which defines self-fashioning as being not "an epiphany of identity freely chosen" but instead "a cultural artifact," according to which the human subject is considered "remarkably unfree, the ideological product of the relations of power in a particular society"[16] – represents the strongest opposition to Burckhardt's theory of the discovery of the individual.

Martin's investigation of selfhood, as well as his analysis of the concepts of sincerity and prudence in the Renaissance, paves the way for a renewed view of the issue of individual subjectivity in the Renaissance, one that introduces into the concept of self-fashioning a form of agency that is mostly absent in Greenblatt's original formulation. In particular, Martin re-addresses the focus on oppositional and dissenting voices, and explores the possibility of rebellion on the part of Renaissance men and women against those very same structures by which they were shaped and constrained.[17] What is especially relevant to this study is that Martin's investigations identify the presence of a layered quality in the Renaissance self, growing anxieties about personhood, as well as what he defines as the experience of a "divided self" – the notion of "a person who was frequently forced to erect a public façade that disguised his or her convictions, beliefs, or feelings."[18] My reading of anti-courtly discourse as a dissenting voice against the constraints of the institutions that modelled the Renaissance self and as representative of anxieties about the self is indebted to Martin's analysis.[19]

The discomfort with the court and the figure of the courtier increased in the second half of the sixteenth century, resulting in a reaction against the idealization of courtly self-fashioning and a search for alternative models. The satirist and the shepherd of pastoral dramas are here investigated as attempts to fashion a new, distinctly non-courtier self for the court intellectual. As a consequence, the exploration of anti-courtly discourse also sheds light on the emergence of a notion of personal identity based on achieved (rather than ascribed) characteristics and on the idea of a changeable, performative self.

The first chapter of this book, "The Courtier," investigates books of advice to prospective courtiers in order to establish the legacy of literary conversations about the courts, as well as the legacy of anti-court attitudes running through those conversations. In this context, the court is analysed as a society whose members are always on stage, their success depending on their ability to fashion a protean, ever-changing self, adapting to the continuous challenges of such forced performance. In exploring the notion of courtliness and the figure of the courtier in the most important conduct manuals of the time, this chapter highlights how both were subjects of harsh debate; that is to say, they were not so much taken for granted but were in constant flux and under construction.

In the second chapter, "The Lady," the intertwining of anti-courtliness, misogyny, and masculine identity is explored, starting with Castiglione's configuration of the court lady and then moving to defensive or satirical responses to that model. A section of this chapter is devoted to satirical works that represent the court as a woman, pointing out how "Lady Court" takes on the characteristics of figures who are often employed in the misogynistic works of the period, notably the cruel mistress and the harlot who subjugate and emasculate their suitors.

The third chapter, "The Satirist," centres on some of the most renowned verse and prose satires of Renaissance Italian literature (such as those authored by Ludovico Ariosto, Pietro Aretino, and Cesare Caporali). In these satires, the court is portrayed as a system that fosters the worst kind of conformity, and the figure of the courtier is represented as the product of a de-individualizing experience. By contrast, adopting the persona of the satirist – outspoken, unsophisticated, but genuine and true to one's self – becomes the way to reaffirm one's individuality in opposition to the depersonalization of the court.

Works that juxtapose the miserable life of the court with the quiet, simple, but happy life in a pastoral dimension are considered in the fourth chapter, "The Shepherd." The pastoral is here analysed as an attempt at negotiating a space different from the courtly one, while at the same time being inextricably conjoined to the world of the court, thus paradoxically representing both an idealization of the court and a critique of it. The figure at the centre of pastoral works, the shepherd, becomes a utopian synthesis of the refined courtly persona and the genuineness of the satirist.

This study aims to redress the long-standing neglect of sources reflecting the expression of anti-courtly sentiments in Renaissance Italy, arguing instead for their centrality to the culture of the time. In doing so, it also intends to show that anti-courtly discourse furnished a platform for discussing some of the most pressing questions of Renaissance Italian society, such as subjectivity and self-fashioning, gender and identity, social mobility, the possible role of the intellectual in the political and social spheres, and a sense of anxiety related to foreign occupation of the Italian peninsula. By devoting attention to details of historical context, this study also hopes to bring together literary and historical explorations of Renaissance court culture.

The dismissive attitude toward anti-court literature may (at least for what concerns the field of Italian studies) find its roots in Benedetto Croce's essay "Libri sulle corti," a brief, general sketch of anti-courtliness in sixteenth- and seventeenth-century Italian texts. In this essay Croce voices a bitter critique of what he sees as the disengaged nature of anti-court writings, considering them only the product of an escapist attitude. According to Croce, anti-court sentiments "result in nothing but yearning for the countryside and rustic life and relinquishing ambitions, that is, social struggle, and being content with little."[20] Croce seems unable to forgive what he perceives as the failure of works expressing anti-court sentiments to propose an alternative to a situation of subjection – a feature that he appears to consider a long-standing malaise of the Italian *literatus*. Hence his implicit advice is to ignore anti-court texts because of their fundamental lack of substance.[21]

The almost obsessive appearance of anti-court motifs in early modern documents, however, leads necessarily to re-evaluating their importance in their contemporary culture – or, at least, to questioning such a recurrent presence. Anti-court writings, after all, deal with common, easily relatable experiences and emotions: the desire to showcase one's talents, ambition, and commitment in order to improve one's socio-economic position, the will to succeed in a tricky professional environment, disappointment in seeing one's deeds unrecognized, uncertainty over one's future in a rapidly changing world, peer rivalry, envy, frustration, feelings of dispossession, and yearnings for recuperation and independence. The peculiar features of Renaissance Italy – the social, political, and cultural upheavals that gave the period its richness and complexity – made these themes particularly relevant at the time, but the universality of such matters also calls for a reconsideration of anti-courtly sentiments in our present-day society.

Chapter One

The Courtier

A new manual for a new profession

In the same years that witnessed the development and dissemination of anti-courtly sentiments, the courts were becoming established as the dominant institution in early modern society. Increasingly, courts were centres that emanated both power and culture, thanks to what Lauro Martines has defined as their brilliant marriage of "power and imagination."[1] Surprisingly, courtiers – the new, progressively more professionalized figures who populated such centres of political and cultural dominance – suffered for a considerable time from the lack of any general representations other than the unflattering satirical portraits popularized by anti-courtly stereotypes.[2]

Sydney Anglo has pointed out that one of the major novelties of Baldassar Castiglione's *Book of the Courtier*, and one of the main reasons behind its success, was precisely that it met the needs of those who were engaging in this profession by offering them both advice on their chosen career path and a mirror for their identity as courtiers.[3] Yet Castiglione's consciousness of the newness of his project has not been fully underlined. Such awareness can be corroborated by the *prima redazione* (first draft) of the *Book of the Courtier* in a passage, later removed in the definitive version, where Castiglione acknowledges a new climate in the relationship between princes and courtiers:

> Among the other things born during the times past the point for which we have information, and not so far from our own centuries, we see becoming widespread the sort of men whom we call courtiers, [the art of] which is now practised all over Europe. Despite princes and great lords having at

> all times been obeyed by many servants, some of whom they always held dear, some less so, some clever, some foolish, some cherished for their valour in arms, some in letters, some for the beauty of their bodies, many for no such thing but only for a certain obscure conformity of nature, no one has ever before, but only just recently, turned – one could say – this courtiership into a profession, and made of it almost an art and a discipline, as one can see now.[4]

Castiglione's programmatic statement not only informs us of the author's awareness of the novelty of the profession of courtier and of his own book, but also points out one of the most controversial topics of the entire text: the irrationality of princely favour. By remarking that some favourites are in this position not because of any specific accomplishments but simply because of an inexplicable "conformity of nature," the passage hints at the discomfort in seeing unworthy men move up the ladder of *grazia* and recognition at court, thus alluding to one of the most common complaints one can find in anti-courtly critiques.

Anglo has also brought the *Book of the Courtier* into productive conversation with earlier writings on courts and courtiers, and has identified the *Book of the Courtier*'s most original contribution as being the first text to present a picture of the courtier that was not the aggregate of vices it had been until then, but a positive figure centred on what Anglo calls "the apotheosis of dilettantism," a "scaled-down version of the omnicompetent Renaissance prince."[5] Anglo's suggestion paves the way for a reading of the *Book of the Courtier* and its "forming in words" the perfect courtier as a reaction against the deconstruction of the courtier figure enacted by prior negative representations of courts and courtiers. Such a reading is also useful for casting light on the largely unexplored relationship between the *Book of the Courtier* and anti-court literature.

In Anglo's opinion, the *Book of the Courtier*'s relationship with the antecedent anti-court tradition is peculiar: while Castiglione condemns all the vices traditionally associated with courts and courtiers, he also "contrives to ignore the great mass of earlier anti-court writings."[6] Through a close reading of some of the most controversial passages of the *Book of the Courtier*, I argue, however, that Castiglione does not actually ignore anti-courtliness. Rather, the treatment of anti-courtly sentiment in the *Book of the Courtier* corresponds to a dynamic that Harry Berger Jr has defined as "conspicuous exclusion": a way to simultaneously hide and highlight potentially threatening features, which then turn out to be not missing, but "*present-as-missing*."[7]

The legacy of anti-courtly sentiments

The impression of Castiglione's complete silence in relation to critiques against courts and courtiers could be strengthened by comparison with how an earlier book on the subject dealt with the same topic. Diomede Carafa's *Dello optimo cortesano,*[8] written in 1479, collects the author's reflections at the end of his long and successful career as statesman and diplomat at the Aragonese court.[9] Born in Naples in the early fourteenth century to a family that had strong ties with the Aragonese court, Carafa entered the service of King Alfonso as a child. He was able to become one of the most influential figures at court and held a prominent position until the end of his life. *Dello optimo cortesano* may thus be considered the memoir of a prosperous life spent in service at court, but Carafa does not shy away from recounting the less flattering aspects of courtly experience. Part of the second chapter of *Dello optimo cortesano* is devoted to explaining that princes can have very different natures. The courtier who is serving a righteous one must be grateful to God, while those who have the misfortune of encountering a wicked prince deserve all our sympathy, because "no one, may he be burdened by poverty or by ill health or by imprisonment, should be pitied more than a wise and good man subjected to a wild and reckless lord."[10] Carafa does not hide the fact that there are also courts where princes arouse envy and rivalry among their courtiers with the aim of maintaining control over them and of improving their performance:

> And there are lords who really enjoy such competitions and disparities in their households, and one can also find those who not only enjoy them but also work on them, saying that [...] both [courtiers] serve better when they are envious.[11]

Carafa then refers to his own experience by expressing gratitude for not having had to deal with such a ruler, "since places where there are no such ways of living look like angelic houses, while the others are infernal lives."[12] Even in such angelic houses, however, a courtier's life cannot be expected to be idyllic. The first chapter of *Dello optimo cortesano* opens with a testimony to the inevitability of court envy for those who manage to succeed in gaining princely favour. The exhortatory and confident tone of the text, which urges the young courtier to aspire to the highest positions at court, is balanced by warnings that the most gifted and successful courtier will be the object of the harshest envy:

> And the first thing that a young man who wants to serve at court needs to do is to prepare and to strive and to make up his mind to serve in such

> a way so as not to be one of many, but with the intention to be, if not the first, at least the second or third or fourth. And one must notice that at court jealousies are greater the more one is known to be committed and virtuous, to the point that he has to be careful not only to do nothing that is wrong, but to do nothing that even appears to be wrong.[13]

In addition, Carafa's prince shares with his counterparts in anti-court writings a substantial fickleness and a potentially tyrannical attitude. The most difficult task at court is not gaining princely favour but maintaining it.[14] In order to be successful, the courtier is urged to "love and fear his lord as he does his beloved"[15] and "always give way and surrender to his lord," since "whoever wants to win at all cost with his lord, plays to lose";[16] most of all he must always remember to behave alongside the lord as someone who "is near a terrible lion."[17]

While an anti-court background plays a key role in Carafa's advice to courtiers, it is remarkable that Castiglione's *Book of the Courtier* devotes no space to a direct discussion of anti-courtly sentiments. This lack of any explicit mention of anti-courtliness is the result of an act of authorial self-censorship. When comparing the *seconda redazione* (second draft) and the *terza redazione* (third and final edition) of the *Book of the Courtier*, one is struck by the absence in the final version of a large section of the prologue to Book 2 aimed precisely at confronting critiques of the court. The second book begins with an attack against the nostalgic attitude of the older men, who "praise bygone times and denounce the present."[18] In criticizing present times, the old men are also said to juxtapose past courts and their supposed virtue and harmony with the vices of contemporary courts:

> Of courts therefore they speak as of all else, declaring those they remember to have been far more excellent and full of outstanding men than those we see nowadays. And when such discussions get under way, they begin at once to extoll with boundless praise the courtiers of Duke Filippo or of Duke Borso; and they recount the sayings of Niccolò Piccinino, and remind us that in those days there were no murders (or rarely), no fights, no ambushes, no deceits, but only a certain loyal and kindly good will among all men, and a loyal trust; and that in the courts of that time so many good customs prevailed along with such goodness, that the courtiers were all like monks; and woe unto him who spoke a bad word to another or so much as paid some less than honorable attention to a woman. And, on the contrary, they say that everything is the reverse these days, and that not only have the courtiers lost that fraternal love and that sober manner of life, but that in the courts nothing prevails save envy, malevolence, corrupt

> manners, and a most dissolute life given over to every kind of vice – the women lascivious and shameless, the men effeminate.[19]

Castiglione quickly dismisses this negative attitude as unrealistic: it is not likely, in his opinion, that the present times are richer in vice than the past the old men yearn for, since in every time and society good and evil are and always will be there in equal measure.

Immediately after these considerations of old men's attitudes toward the present, the *seconda redazione* proceeds to challenge

> another sort of men who, in order to seem like philosophers, condemn all courts in general, the present and the past ones, and praise freedom, and say they cannot be endowed with living in court and serving, as one does, ambition and a thousand other vices no less than their lords. But we think that we have given these people a proper reply by making our courtier first and foremost a good man.[20]

The revised prologue to the second book of the *Book of the Courtier* omits these remarks on court criticism and instead voices critiques of present-day courts only through the old men's misty-eyed view of bygone courts and courtiers. The *terza redazione* thus conflates anti-courtliness with old men's yearnings for the past, almost to the point of making court criticism appear as nothing more than the nostalgic attitude of discontented elderly courtiers.

In the *seconda redazione*, anti-court speakers are also denounced for their readiness to do a volte-face and convert into admirers of courts and courtiership whenever it might be convenient:

> And these severe arbiters have a habit, every time they can stick their noses in the courts, of completely immersing themselves in those same passions that they criticize in others. When their own words reprimand them as well, they change their words and start talking about the excellence of the lords and the great princes, and declare them sacred and elected by God, as Homer says, and their greatness and dominion over different peoples, and their victories, and fame, and triumphs, to be divine things; and since God made them superior to other men, it makes sense that all should revere and respect them; and in addition to other evidence that they are held in high esteem by the Heavens, they add signs and foretellings that often appear at the times of their births or deaths, and say that Aristotle resided in Alexander's court and that he taught Calisthenes, his disciple, almost to flatter him, that Plato lived for some time as a courtier in the courts of the kings of Sicily, as many other philosophers, and

> this happened because they knew that in the courts so many noble and different minds came together, that one could learn just as well there as one could in school. To these, then, since they answer to themselves, we will say no more. It is enough to us to have shown that the courts of today are no less worthy of praise than the ones that these old men praise so much. We will occupy ourselves with the discussions held about the courtiers and with our games.[21]

Against the defeatist attitude of those who criticize the court but do not hesitate to go against what they themselves have preached, Castiglione puts forward an attempt to deal with the current situation of courtly life. This proposal, however, is by no means linear, painless, or free from doubts and inconsistencies.

The game and its space

Scholarship has underscored how the *Book of the Courtier* was adopted in its contemporary culture as a coherent, confident, and absolute model, in spite of being a contradictory and sceptical text, lacerated by internal ambiguity and evasiveness.[22] Yet the reasons behind the text's complicated nature have not been fully explored. The *Book of the Courtier* has also enjoyed a long-lasting reputation as a portrayal of courtly utopia. While it is undeniable that the *Book of the Courtier* constructed a somewhat idealized version of the Urbino court,[23] one must also resist the temptation to read the dialogue and its creation of an ideal courtier as an idealizing retreat into a protective and secluded dream-like dimension. The *Book of the Courtier* owes most of this reputation to its unique setting. When compared with other sixteenth-century writings on courts, the *Book of the Courtier* is striking for its discussion of the court from its core, represented by the enclosed and protected frame of the Urbino court of the early 1500s, a distinctive reality that Thomas Greene has compared to a maternal space.[24] Greene has also detected a sense of enclosure and of strong physical containment in the *Book of the Courtier*, and has characterized the courtly space of Castiglione's Urbino as a community turned inward, existing only in its circumscribed self-sufficiency.[25]

Wayne Rebhorn has noted how Castiglione's representation of the Urbino court shows some characteristics of a pastoral world, thus motivating a reading of the Urbino court as some sort of civic Arcadia.[26] Greene's and Rebhorn's visions of the court society of the *Book of the Courtier* have the merit of calling attention to the harmoniously restrained, well-defined, and ordered space that allows the construction of the ideal courtier. Yet contemporary readers would have remembered the stark reality behind such an idyllic scenario. During the years that the *Book of the Courtier* was set, the Urbino court was going through one of its darkest moments. Dwindling finances, the duke's declining health and lack of direct heirs, and the recent memory of Cesare Borgia's invasion contributed to a sense of downfall. The *Book of the Courtier*'s harmonious world, in other words, could appear as such only by excluding any potentially troubling aspects.

Greene has highlighted as well how a dynamic of rejecting possible disruptions is in place at the moment of choosing the game. His analysis of Urbino's maternal space is part of a broader discourse concerning the meaning of the game enacted at the Urbino court, in opposition to the rejected games and their potential values.[27] All the rejected games – Fra Serafino's and Unico Aretino's "non-proposals in bad faith," Gasparo Pallavicino's game on lovers' self-deceptions, Cesare Gonzaga's game on folly, Ottaviano Fregoso's game on scorn, and Pietro Bembo's game on ladies' anger – deal, in Greene's opinion, with "the socially aberrant, private passions, imbalances and blindnesses which could threaten the harmony of the group" by suggesting "the presence of the potentially dangerous,"[28] that is to say, the presence of self-deception, cruelty, folly, and hostility. By contrast, the remaining four games are structured to function as a form of healing and to contain antisocial deviations.[29]

The rejected games also point to a vision of courtly life as full of emotional tensions. More significantly, being aimed at a minute, potentially destructive analysis of essentially hostile circumstances and dynamics, the games might have carried the dialogue along a path not too dissimilar from that of most complaints on courtly life. It is significant, therefore, that such games and their potential anti-courtly implications are met with silence by the authority figures, the duchess and Emilia Pio, who simply ignore them and leave the word to the next speaker. Juxtaposed with the rejected games is Federico Fregoso's successful proposal: a formational game where the participants are immediately granted the opportunity to contradict the speaker,[30] but where the opportunity for open contradiction is a further tool for both highlighting and strengthening the fraternal harmony of the group that the author has pointed out just a few pages earlier.[31]

Dynamics of reticence similar to the duchess's silence on the rejected games often surface during the chosen game in the very moments of contact with the most risky undersides of its proposed plan. Potentially threatening issues are hinted at in fractured and contradictory passages, often to be left suspended or quietly dismissed. Nuances of anti-courtliness pervade the first half of the *Book of the Courtier*'s narrative by being simultaneously invoked and then left unresolved, undermining the project's facade of assertiveness in forming the perfect courtier in words.

Unhappy birds born in some miserable valley

One meaningful example is Ludovico da Canossa's explanation of the importance of first impressions, which he deems powerful to the point that "dull-witted and maladroit" men have been able to maintain, for a certain amount of time, the reputation of being excellent courtiers. Such an undeserved reputation cannot, however, be entirely considered the courtiers' fault, since the princes themselves have a great part in this: "and there are various causes of such errors, one being the judgement of princes who, thinking to work miracles, sometimes decide to show favor to one who seems to them to deserve disfavor."[32] The princes portrayed by Canossa begin to look suspiciously like the capricious tyrants often portrayed by anti-court writings.

The courtier designed by Canossa must also take into account the power of Fortuna. The reflection on the power of Fortuna is brought forward by Gasparo Pallavicino in an attempt to oppose Ludovico da Canossa's emphasis on the courtier's nobility. As Gasparo puts it,

> I say that to me this nobility of birth does not seem so essential. And if I thought I was uttering something not already known to us all, I would adduce many instances of persons of humble birth who, through their virtue, have made their posterity illustrious. And if what you said just now is true, that there is in all things that hidden force of the first seed, then we should all be of the same condition through having the same source, nor would one man be more noble than another. But I believe that there are many other causes of the differences and the various degrees of elevation and lowliness among us. Among which causes I judge Fortune to be foremost; because we see her hold sway over all the things of this world and, as it seems, amuse herself often in uplifting to the skies whom she pleases and in burying in the depths those most worthy of being exalted.[33]

Castiglione's view of Fortuna, as expressed through the words of Gasparo, mirrors the treatment of the same topos in anti-court literature: Fortuna is presented as the overwhelming force in courtly dynamics, bringing a man to the highest honours only to immediately throw him down in disgrace. Significantly, Canossa finds no better reply to Gasparo's remarks than referring to one more anti-court topos, the princely flaw of raising to favour unworthy men while neglecting faithful and deserving servants.

A similar yet far more dramatic impasse happens in the second book of the *Book of the Courtier*, when Federico Fregoso addresses an extremely delicate issue within court culture: how to ask for – and how to be sure to obtain – benefits from the prince. Fregoso here makes a point of putting forward a meritocratic vision, according to which "to receive favors from princes, then, there is no better way than to deserve them."[34] To Fregoso's optimistic perspective, Vincenzo Calmeta (a minor speaker, who would have been known to contemporary readers for his past problems with the court)[35] counters with a harsh reality that he – as well as, we may speculate, most of his interlocutors – has witnessed in person:

> Here Vincenzio [Vincenzo] Calmeta said: "Before you go any further, if I well understood, I believe you said a while ago that the best way to get favors is to deserve them; and that the Courtier ought to wait until they are offered to him rather than seek them presumptuously. Now I greatly fear that this precept is of little effect, and I believe experience shows us quite the contrary. For nowadays few indeed enjoy the favor of princes, except those who are presumptuous; and I know you can testify to the fact that some who found themselves in small favor with their princes have managed to please them only through presumption; but, as for there being those who have risen through modesty, I for my part do not know of any; and I will even give you time to think on this, but I believe you will discover few."[36]

In the face of Calmeta's objections, Federico at first defends contemporary princes but is eventually forced to confess the significant impotence of the virtuous courtier stuck with an evil prince:

> "But do not say this," messer Federico then rejoined; "for that would be too plain an argument that the princes of our day are all corrupt and bad – which is not true, because there are some who are good. But if our Courtier happens to find himself in the service of one who is wicked and malign, let him leave him as soon as he discovers this, that he may escape the great anguish that all good men feel in serving the wicked."[37]

The virtuous courtier stuck with an evil prince has no other option but to leave his service as soon as possible – which brings Calmeta to evoke the courtly hells described in the anti-court tradition:

> "We must pray God," replied Calmeta, "to grant us good masters, for, once we have them, we have to endure them as they are; because

> countless considerations force a gentleman not to leave a patron once he has begun to serve him: the misfortune lies in ever beginning; and in that case courtiers are like those unhappy birds that are born in some miserable valley."[38]

The dialogue here does not allow Calmeta, or any other speaker, to further explore the unhappy fate of such unhappy birds born in a miserable valley or to find other remedial strategies for coping with an evil prince, apart from the troublesome prospect of finding a worthier patron.[39] The only follow-up to Calmeta's gloomy picture is Federico's brief reply that in his opinion, such a courtier "has a right to quit, and ought to quit, a service which in the eyes of all good men is sure to disgrace him,"[40] where Federico's convoluted subordinate clause (most evident in the original Italian) linguistically marks his own scepticism about the proposed solution.

As Virginia Cox has shown, insinuations that all is not as it should be in the courts are already present in Fregoso's speech, and Calmeta does nothing but make them bluntly explicit. Even more significant is Fregoso's inability to counter Calmeta's gloomy picture with a convincing alternative, and to provide answers to pressing questions from other speakers concerning the courtier's moral status. Cox has also identified in Fregoso's speech a shift from the straightforward moral standards that one finds in a text such as Carafa's *Dello optimo cortesano* toward a sort of ethical flexibility.[41] This shift in moral standards proceeds from the necessity of having to deal with the far-from-ideal reality of present courts. Cox has highlighted as well how the perspective of the second book of the *Book of the Courtier* differs from that of the first book: it is in the second book that the ideal courtier envisioned by Canossa is brought in touch with the actuality of contemporary courtly life.

It may be useful to add that the second day of the dialogue (recorded as Book 2) happens in the presence of the heir to the Urbino court, Guidubaldo's nephew Francesco Maria della Rovere, who at the end of the first night of discussion had burst into the duchess's chamber unannounced and accompanied by his guardsmen. In the text Francesco Maria is praised for his wisdom and intellectual vivacity while his misdeeds go unmentioned,[42] and the reader is left with the impression that his abrupt arrival at the end of the first night has literally invaded the secluded space of the drawing room. Most importantly, Francesco Maria's violent character could have not been a sharper contrast to the educated and wise Guidubaldo. The change of tone from the first to the second book of the dialogue also matches a change of tone in the life of the duchy, with Francesco Maria's self-imposed presence symbolizing the controlling gaze of a potentially despotic ruler – the kind of prince who would need to be addressed with all the carefulness that the courtly arts could provide. Unsurprisingly, it is in the subsequent pages of the *Book of the Courtier* that anti-courtliness makes its most prominent appearance.

The anti-courtly nuances that were suggested in the first book of the *Book of the Courtier*, come, in the second book, dangerously close to upsetting the entire structure of the dialogue. When Fregoso states his desire that the courtier love and please his prince in the best way possible ("I would have the Courtier devote all his thought and strength of spirit to loving and almost adoring the prince he serves above all else, devoting his every desire and habit and manner to pleasing him"),[43] Pietro da Napoli is ready to bring up the issue of courtly flattery ("nowadays you will find many such courtiers, for it strikes me that you have, in few words, sketched a noble flatterer").[44] To Pietro's objection, Federico can find no other response than to appeal to the courtier's true love for his master, thus leaving the burden of sincerity versus flattery completely to the courtier's judgment:

> "You are quite wrong," replied messer Federico, "for flatterers love neither their prince nor their friends, which I wish our Courtier to do above all else; and it is possible to obey and to further the wishes of the one he serves without adulation, because by wishes I mean such as are reasonable and right, or those which in themselves are neither good nor bad."[45]

However, Federico's solution is doubly debatable: first, because the distinction between the devoted courtier and the base flatterer is a subjective one and also non-verifiable; and second, because the reasonable and right wishes that are neither good nor bad in which the courtier should fully second his lord remain unspecified.

Federico is caught in a similar impasse when Canossa wonders whether the courtier should obey his prince in all sorts of things, even in things that are "dishonorable and disgraceful."[46] Federico seems to feel, now, almost forced to defend a morally correct position by insisting, as he does, that we should obey no one in morally reproachable matters. Nonetheless, he is also compelled to specify that "many things that are evil appear at first sight to be good, and many appear evil and yet are good."[47] Federico's act of courtly prudence – carefully avoiding condemning an order coming from a prince as immoral – has the side effect of undermining the courtier's independent judgment, his own ability to tell right from wrong.

The importance given here to the courtier's independent discernment is also counterbalanced by the remark that "it is a quite dangerous thing to depart from our superiors' commands, trusting more in our own judgment than in theirs, when in reason we ought to obey."[48] The various contradictions in the passage, where the courtier's discernment and independence of thought are appealed to only to be denied shortly thereafter, have the effect of further reinforcing a scenario in which there can be no fixed moral boundaries, where what can be defined as righteous by one person might well be thought immoral by another, and where the dividing line between agency in matters of morality and the duty of obedience are constantly blurred.[49]

Conspicuous exclusions

One could not, by any means, argue that the text is allowing anti-courtly sentiment to invade what Harry Berger has defined the "second world" of the Urbino court.[50] The dialogic structure of the text and its courtly setting call for a more indirect attitude: allusions to anti-court criticism are limited to hints the reader is guided to. The result, at least in the first two books, is a contradictory relationship of acknowledgment and evasion of anti-courtliness, where quickly dismissed critical elements and threatening signs manage to attract the characters' as well as the reader's attention, forcing both parties to question the picture of harmony before their eyes.

Analysing Vermeer's *Allegory of the New Testament*, Berger has noted how in Vermeer's idyllic garden every sign of evil or danger has been reduced to a tiny dragon, pierced through the middle and lying on the ground. According to Berger, in this way the danger is chastened and dismissed in the figure of an insignificant toy dragon. At the same time, however, the artist stresses this very incongruity by making the image appear too good to be true, thus forcing us to question the yearning to exorcize evil through a non-threatening symbol. Berger names this mechanism of pastoral representation "conspicuous exclusion" and defines it as the poetic mechanism that allows the artist to purge the presence of evil and danger from his artistic creation by exorcizing those forces into small, unthreatening tokens, while at the same time leading the viewer's attention toward these very symbols. In Berger's words, "conspicuous exclusion makes us attend to what has been left out: the omitted item is not merely missing but *present-as-missing*."[51] Conspicuous exclusion directs our attention to the omitted item by "purging its world of darker shadows so that we take note of their absence, hence presenting a world that seems excessively overordered and idyllic, and that displays incongruities – tokens of what has been purged – similar to the toy dragon in the redeemed garden."[52] I maintain that this dynamic of simultaneously highlighting and denying critical and potentially disruptive elements is precisely what is in place in the first half of the *Book of the Courtier* regarding everything that concerns anti-courtly sentiment.

Berger has also applied the concept of conspicuous exclusion to Castiglione's notion of *sprezzatura,* which he considers a "figuration of anxiety" proceeding from the courtiers' awareness of their disempowerment in a culture dominated by despotic princes,[53] and from Castiglione's denial of the painful realities of history in his nostalgic and idealized depiction of the Urbino court.[54] In framing exclusions in the *Book of the Courtier,* Berger has underscored the determining importance of two absences in the text: the absence of the duke, and the absence of the author.[55] I claim that there is also a third, even more conspicuous absence that informs the dialogue: that of the body of anti-court writings that represented a significant portion of coeval writings on courts. These Castiglione conspicuously excludes from the *terza redazione* of the *Book of the Courtier,* leaving the more easily managed figures of the nostalgic old courtiers and their futile *laudatio temporis acti* as the only polemical target.[56] Still, the presence of anti-courtly sentiments continues to linger over the Urbino court. The dramatic issues put forward by Pallavicino, Fregoso, and Calmeta are quickly bypassed before their anti-court potential is fully realized, and yet they successfully disturb the harmony of the text and of its courtly community just as the toy dragon intrudes on Vermeer's pastoral garden – small but still powerful presences that attract the reader's attention, acting as signposts of a structural fragility. Like the secluded drawing room into which Francesco Maria della Rovere makes his threatening, almost disruptive entrance, the fraternal harmony of the Urbino court and the text's ambitious program of forming the perfect courtier are revealed as unable to provide a completely safe space.

The courtier-counsellor

An even more delicate situation surfaces in the *Courtier*'s fourth and final book, when Ottaviano Fregoso proposes an audacious attempt to carve out some kind of influence for the ideal courtier under the restraints of princely despotism.[57] Throughout the first half of the fourth book, Ottaviano presents his portrait of the courtier with the goal of further improving the model presented in the first two days of the dialogue. It is worth remarking that Castiglione gives such a difficult task to a character coming from the Genoese republican environment (who would later become Doge of Genoa) and who therefore could embody a good point of view from which to articulate a possible critique of the court system. Ottaviano's talk, in fact, also takes the form of a *speculum principis*: while explicitly flattering, it is implicitly critical, as it simultaneously presents to the eyes of the prince/reader a picture of what he should aspire to be, alongside an often unflattering image of the actual state of court life.

Ottaviano begins his speech by going straight to the heart of the problem with the courtier as constructed in the first two days of the dialogue: the risk of triviality.[58]

> For indeed if by being noble of birth, graceful, charming, and expert in so many exercises, the Courtier were to bring forth no other fruit than to be what he is, I should not judge it right for a man to devote so much study and labor to acquiring this perfection of Courtiership as anyone must do who wishes to acquire it. Nay, I should say that many of those accomplishments that have been attributed to him (such as dancing, merrymaking, singing, and playing) were frivolities and vanities and, in a man of any rank, deserving of blame rather than of praise.[59]

Clearly, according to Ottaviano, the picture of the virtuous courtier realized in the first two books of the dialogue is not enough to redeem the man of court from negative clichés. As he points out,

> [T]hese elegances of dress, devices, mottoes, and other such things as pertain to women and love (although many will think the contrary), often serve merely to make spirits effeminate, to corrupt youth, and to lead it to dissolute life; whence it comes about that the Italian name is reduced to opprobrium.[60]

It is precisely in order to save the courtier from effeminacy and triviality that Ottaviano will construct his courtier as a moral figure who can act as a wise counsellor to his prince.

The potentially effeminizing and deceiving arts of the courtier are morally justified by being explained as necessary tools to educate the prince through the means of a "salutary deception" ("inganno salutifero").[61] Courtly amusements become a way for the courtier to "captivate the mind of his prince" ("adescar ... l'animo del suo principe")[62] and to veil the wisdom and moral integrity through which he will eventually lead the prince to love morality. Courtly arts also serve as a means for the courtier to turn his position of disempowerment at court into an indirect, disguised form of influence on the prince.

It is evident that the subtext to Ottaviano's insistence on salutary deception is an unflattering notion of contemporary princes, who are then portrayed as almost irreparably corrupted by the false praise of sycophants as well as by their own arrogance:

> [B]esides never hearing the truth about anything at all, princes are made drunk by the great license that rule gives; and by a profusion of delights are submerged in pleasures, and deceive themselves so and have their minds so corrupted – seeing themselves always obeyed and almost adored with so much reverence and praise, without ever the least contradiction, let alone censure – that from this ignorance they pass to an extreme self-conceit, so that they become intolerant of any advice or opinion. And since they think that to know how to rule is a very easy thing, and that to succeed therein they need no other art or discipline save sheer force, they give their mind and all their happiness and all their thoughts to maintaining the power they have, deeming true happiness to lie in being able to do what one wishes.[63]

Even more intriguing is the fact that Ottaviano diverts onto princes the vices of unmanliness and emptiness hidden by misleading appearances of charm that traditionally plagued the image of the courtier.[64] Ottaviano compares princes to

> the colossi that were made last year at Rome on the day of the festival in Piazza d'Agone, which outwardly had the appearance of great men and horses in a triumph, and which within were full of tow and rags.[65]

Most importantly, he also advises the courtier to lead the prince through the austere path of virtue,

> adorning it with shady fronds and strewing it with pretty flowers to lessen the tedium of the toilsome journey for one whose strength is slight; and now with music, now with arms and horses, now with verses, now with discourse of love, and with all those means whereof these gentlemen have spoken, to keep his mind continuously occupied in worthy pleasures, yet always impressing upon him also some virtuous habit along with these enticements, as I have said, beguiling him with salutary deception; like shrewd doctors who often spread the edge of the cup with some sweet cordial when they wish to give a bitter-tasting medicine to sick and over-delicate children.[66]

The prince here becomes a frail and vain figure whose life revolves around graceful, trivial enchantments, while the courtier – his deceptive guiles now redeemed by the righteous moral function concealed behind their charming allures – comes to be the cautious doctor able to cure rulers of their tendencies toward immorality and despotism. Ottaviano converts the widespread image of the powerless trivial courtier into the morally respectable figure of a severe philosopher who nonetheless still hides behind the courtly mask of a pleasant entertainer. The logical implication of Ottaviano's speech is that courtly grace enables the courtier to deceive his prince in the name of virtue and lead him along the path of goodness and morality.[67] Ottaviano's proposal hence not only reverses the picture of the courtier but also vindicates his pleasant deception, thanks to the moral aim concealed beneath it.

But how seriously can readers take Ottaviano's proposal, when even Ottaviano himself freely admits that if he were to actually try this approach on a prince, he would most likely lose the prince's favour? The *Book of the Courtier* offers no clear answer to this question. Rather, many critical issues in the text seem to work in the background to undermine Ottaviano's plan. This impression is reinforced by the incipit of the fourth book, where the author nostalgically remembers the participants in the dialogue who died before the *Book of the Courtier* was published. The mournful tone of these pages brings to mind the prologue to the book – the letter to Miguel De Silva – and the author's confession of the sadness that pervaded him when he recalled that "the greater part of those persons who are introduced in the conversations are already dead."[68] To pay homage to their memory, Castiglione famously declares his intention to send out his book "as a portrait of the Court of Urbino."[69] However, Castiglione's refusal to mention the difficulties that the court was undergoing during those same years results in an abstract portrait of Urbino – or, one may even argue, in a portrait of a court that never really existed. The consciously utopian atmosphere in the depiction of the Urbino court inevitably has an effect on the entire dialogue, and particularly on its boldest part, Ottaviano's proposal of a courtier-counsellor, which could then begin to look implicitly self-critical. Such self-criticism and conscious utopia become especially visible when one takes into account the recurring fractures that underlie Ottaviano's speech.

Ottaviano's virtuous courtier is met with scepticism by Giuliano de' Medici, who raises the objection that a courtier who is more virtuous than his prince would be extremely inappropriate, since it would logically imply that such a courtier would possess more dignity than his own lord:

> You cannot say, signor Ottaviano, that the cause which gives a certain quality to an effect does not always have more quality than its effect has. Thus, the courtier, through whose instruction the prince is to become so excellent, would have to be more excellent than the prince, and in this way he would also be of greater dignity than the prince himself, which is most unseemly.[70]

Ottaviano's response to this objection is that while the courtier might be the one who instructs his prince in justice, liberality, and magnanimity, only the prince is entitled to put these ideals into practice:

> [I]t is neither impossible nor surprising that the Courtier should lead the prince to many virtues, such as justice, generosity, magnanimity, the practice of which the prince can easily realize and so acquire the habit of practicing them; and thus the prince, led to virtue by the Courtier, can become more virtuous than the Courtier.[71]

In order to defend his courtier, Ottaviano is forced to admit his substantial disempowerment.

Readers will also not have forgotten that the stratagem of the "inganno salutifero" was created as a necessary tool to deal with modern-day princes, spoiled by flatterers and corrupted by bad habits and by their own misguided self-awareness:

> [S]ince the princes of today are so corrupted by evil customs and by ignorance and a false esteem of themselves, and since it is so difficult to show them the truth and lead them to virtue, and since men seek to gain their favor by means of lies and flatteries and such vicious ways – the Courtier, through those fair qualities that Count Ludovico and Messer Federico have given him, can easily, and must, seek to gain the good will and captivate the mind of his prince that he may have free and sure access to speak to him of anything whatever without giving annoyance.[72]

Ottaviano is here addressing a dramatic present reality. Princes are spoiled, overconfident, and whimsical creatures, and have to be approached with extreme caution. The fine qualities that Ludovico da Canossa and Federico Fregoso had assigned to the courtier are here transformed into protective mechanisms that will allow the courtier to approach the potentially threatening prince in a safe way.

Ottaviano and his interlocutors are well aware that such a prescription is not guaranteed to work in every case. There are princes who are too corrupt to be healed by the courtier's medicine, and Ottaviano eventually lapses into admitting the irreparable moral turpitude of some rulers:

> I did not hold that the Courtier's instruction should be the sole cause of making the prince such as we would have him be, so every care and every exhortation on the part of the Courtier would be in vain: even as the labor of any good husbandman would also be in vain if he were to set about cultivating and sowing sterile sand of the sea with excellent seed, because such sterility is natural to it [...]. Thus, there are many princes who would be good if their minds were properly cultivated; and it is of these I speak, not of those who are like sterile ground, and are by nature so alien to good behavior that no training can avail to lead their minds in the straight path.[73]

This grim picture is shortly thereafter contrasted with a successful model of the courtier-counsellor: the philosopher Aristotle. Ottaviano recounts that

> Aristotle so well knew Alexander's nature and encouraged it so cleverly and well that Alexander loved him and honored him more than a father. [...] Aristotle instructed him in the natural sciences and in the virtues of the mind so as to make him most wise, brave, continent, and a true moral philosopher, not only in words but in works [...]. And Aristotle was the author of these deeds of Alexander, employing the methods of a good Courtier: which is something that Calisthenes did not know how to do, even though Aristotle showed him; for he wished to be a pure philosopher and an austere minister of naked truth, without blending in Courtiership; and he lost his life and brought infamy instead of help to Alexander.[74]

Here, the reference to Alexander the Great would have called to the mind of some readers not only Aristotle and his fortunate experience as preceptor and counsellor, but a contemporary prince as well, often celebrated as the new Alexander: the Duke of Urbino, Guidubaldo da Montefeltro.

The comparison of Guidubaldo with Alexander was a recurring theme of the encomiastic literature produced at the Montefeltro court.[75] The young Duke of Urbino was often equated to the Greek prince for his valour on the battlefield, his impressive education, and his physical prowess.[76] Yet Guidubaldo was also known to be affected by a severe form of gout that left him progressively impaired (in Castiglione's words, "one of the fairest and ablest persons in the world was deformed and marred to a tender age")[77] and eventually led to his death at the age of thirty-six. Guidubaldo was also notoriously impotent,[78] and his lack of any direct offspring forced him to adopt his nephew Francesco Maria della Rovere.

The prince who presided over the Urbino court at the moment when, according to Castiglione's portrait, that court was a haven of harmony and grace – the appropriate setting for the creation of the perfect courtier – was an ideal prince, yet only in the abstract. Guidubaldo may have represented the perfect prince to match the perfect courtier, yet early modern readers were aware that in actuality that prince was sick, impotent, and disfigured. In other words, although Guidubaldo was still alive, in his capacity as the perfect prince he was as good as dead; as Bembo put it, "his condition resembled more that of the dead, than that of the living."[79]

Furthermore, Ottaviano's reference to the education of Alexander the Great reminds us that even in the case of princes who do not lack the qualities that may enable the courtier to instil virtue in their hearts, caution is necessary. The ghost of Calisthenes, who paid with his life the price for not being able to mix the "naked truth" with the sweetness of courtliness, is evoked to remind courtiers of the fate reserved for those who are not careful enough in dealing with princes.[80] Ottaviano points out again that even the most virtuous and wise among courtiers can do little when confronted with a tyrant, as Plato's experience shows:

> By this same method of Courtiership, Plato taught Dion of Syracuse; and later, when he found the tyrant Dionysius like a book full of defects and errors and in need of complete erasure rather than of any change or correction (since it was not possible to remove from him that color of tyranny with which he had been stained for so long), he decided not to make use of the methods of Courtiership with him, judging that they would all be in vain; which is what our Courtier ought also to do if he chances to find himself in the service of a prince of so evil a nature as to be inveterate in vice, like consumptives in their sickness; for in that case he ought to escape from such bondage in order not to incur blame for his prince's evil deeds and not to feel the affliction which all good men feel who serve the wicked.[81]

Just as Federico Fregoso came to a dead end when confronted by Calmeta, so has Ottaviano. Courtiers faced with a tyrannical prince have no option but to attempt to escape, like birds fleeing a miserable valley.

In lauding the courtiership of Aristotle and Plato, Ottaviano is echoing the passage in the *seconda redazione* where words in praise of the two court philosophers were expressed by champions of anti-courtly sentiment and denounced as one of the clearest signs of the moral ambiguity of such a sentiment. Although the stratagem of having anti-court speakers praise Aristotle and Plato in order to account for their reconversion to courtliness was removed from the final edition of the *Book of the Courtier*, it is likely that the most perceptive readers would have recognized that Ottaviano's mention of the two philosophers in their role as courtiers was echoing an argument traditionally employed by those who tried to justify their involvement with the court despite their awareness of its evils. Paradoxically, the reference to the two ideal models of courtier-counsellors would risk undermining Ottaviano's proposal, further disclosing the anti-courtly subtext that the numerous critical nuances in his speech had already evoked.

It would be reductive, then, to state that the *Book of the Courtier* ignores anti-courtly sentiment. The image of the dysfunctional, ill court popularized by anti-courtly writings is removed from the peaceful setting of the discussion and relegated to a hidden space, just like Urbino's sick, disfigured prince. But unlike Guidubaldo, anti-courtly sentiment keeps resurfacing throughout the dialogue.

Mutable selves

Tracing the presence of anti-courtliness in the *Book of the Courtier* can also help understand the book's paradoxical reception[82] – that is to say, how in spite of being praised by moralists, it may also have been a starting point for the increasingly cynical trend in Italian manuals of courtliness. To solve this issue in the reception of the text, Cox has argued for a reading as flexible as the text, one that can pay justice to the text's complexity.[83] Such complexity does not involve matters of morality alone but is reflected in the selfhood of the courtier formed in the dialogue as well. In Book 2, Federico Fregoso points out that the courtier should be able to switch between serious and trivial matters when talking to his prince, and consequently, Fregoso wants him to be able to don a different persona whenever the circumstances may require it.[84] The courtier, in short, must be flexible to the point of performing a complete change of character at will. The book's indetermination over key matters is also reflected in the constant shape-shifting of the character that it creates. In this way, the dialogue generates not one courtier but many courtiers in one. The courtier's self-fashioning, in other words, must include multiple selves, none of which is definitive – neither the pleasant entertainer nor the wise counsellor.

This constant mutability is related to the structure of the early modern Italian court as inherently theatrical and to courtly life as implying, in one way or another, some form of acting. Scholarly analysis has frequently highlighted how Renaissance society, particularly in its courtly form, was structured as a performative society whose members were always on stage.[85] This performativity is linked to the system of panoptical control that the court implied. Not only, as Rebhorn has noted, "[was] scarcely anyone [...] ever alone in the palaces, town-houses, and humble cottages of Renaissance Europe,"[86] but the court in particular appears to have been a structure based on constant evaluation by one's superiors as well as one's peers, where a false step with potentially ruinous consequences was always possible.[87] Success at court depended on the capacity to fashion a protean, ever-changing self, able to adapt to the continuous challenges of such forced performance.[88] For this reason, Castiglione's key notion of *sprezzatura* has also been defined as an ironic behaviour, implying a mismatch between what the courtier really is and what he wants to show.[89]

Such mutability is not simply an accessorial feature of the courtly persona but constitutes one of the main features of the Renaissance self at large. In John Jeffries Martin's definition, "the Renaissance self [...] was a protean thing."[90] Though studies agree in pointing out this quality, the potential discomfort it implies has not yet been investigated. The Renaissance protean self, especially when taking the form of a courtly self, is often presented matter-of-factly, with the risk of giving the impression that such a feature of identity was experienced with almost no complications at all. However, writings against the court and courtiers and books on courtliness alike show an evident discomfort toward a protean self. This discomfort comes to a sort of breaking point in anti-court texts;[91] yet it is traceable as well in manuals of conduct at court and constitutes one of the many signs of the conflicted relationship that court writers had with the world they were portraying.

The evolution of manuals of conduct at court

The sixteenth century witnessed a change in the conditions of court elites: new socio-historical conditions led to the development of a specialized bureaucracy at court that resulted in an increasingly rigid definition of the role of every court member. Scholars have pointed out that beginning in the 1530s, courtly elites – especially court *literati* – experienced a redefinition of their position at court that reduced their autonomy and decreased their opportunity to exert any active role or influence over the prince.[92] Tasks at court grew progressively more technical, and the *literati* were forced to turn into specialized figures, as testified by the development of literature on the role of secretary that reached its maximum expansion toward the end of the century.[93] An eloquent example of the difference between this professional figure and the courtier-counsellor imagined by Castiglione is offered by Battista Guarini's *Il segretario* (first published in 1594), where it is clearly stated that a secretary and a counsellor hold very different, rarely reconcilable roles.[94] In the secretary, the protean qualities already theorized for the courtier reach their maximum expansion: the secretary should "be able to do with his pen what Proteus was able to with his person, transforming it into all possible forms and mutating it according to what needs require."[95] The secretary, it is later stated, must follow his lord in all matters: "It is not sufficient that the secretary conform to his lord in matters of the intellect if he does not conform to him in matters of will, and in mores as well."[96]

The traditional scholarly view of the relationship between courtly elites and princely power, associated with Norbert Elias's pioneering work on court society, maintained that the growth of absolutism resulted in a progressive disempowerment of the nobility.[97] In the past decades, however, Elias's theory has been subject to revision. Some scholars now maintain that the rise of the absolutist court did not produce a loss of power for the court nobility; it did involve an increased need to master the art of courtly performance, which became the foundation for gaining and retaining power and which no one at court, including the prince, could ignore.[98] Courtly arts became even more important in power struggles and for social mobility at court: "those who could crack it [courtly performance] found the way open to higher status."[99]

Manuals of conduct at court reflected such changes by switching from depicting a multifaceted figure such as the courtier fashioned by the *Book of the Courtier* to conveying a set of precepts aimed at providing ambitious courtiers with practical advice on climbing the social ladder at court, or, in the less cynical and more optimistic cases, at helping courtiers safely navigate the increasingly dangerous waters of courtly life.

Carlo Dionisotti has identified a period of expansion in Italian literature beginning around the 1530s and lasting until the 1560s. This expansion, favoured by the developing print industry, brought to the literary scene groups of *homines novi* whose presence determined a significant change in the production of and audience for written works.[100] If the author and the first readers of the *Book of the Courtier* belonged to the same social group – that of the minor nobility looking for patronage from more powerful families – later in the sixteenth century a significant number of those looking for advice on how to pursue a career at court, as well as those publishing collections of such pieces of advice, were new men who may have found themselves having little or even nothing to do with the ideal courtier fashioned in the pages of Castiglione's text, and who might, as a result, have looked for a different approach to courtliness.

This is not to say that the *Book of the Courtier* became an outdated text. The history of its printed editions clearly indicates the contrary. As Robert Muchembled has pointed out, the *Book of the Courtier* reached its greatest success (with fifty editions and translations) between 1528 – the year of its publication by Aldo Manuzio – and 1550, peaking in the 1540s and remaining very popular until the 1590s.[101] According to Peter Burke, the real decline in interest in the *Book of the Courtier* happened only in the 1650s.[102] As a consequence of such success, it is not uncommon to find references to Castiglione's text as the ultimate masterpiece on courtliness in later manuals of conduct at court. Yet such admiration did not prevent misreadings and oversimplifications. There is an undeniable tendency in later manuals of courtliness to propose a simplistic view of the *Book of the Courtier*, more specifically, one that refused – consciously or not – to adequately highlight the many contradictions in the text, often reducing it to a set of precepts to either endorse or oppose.[103]

Anti-court sentiments play an important, if hitherto underappreciated, role in such manuals. Authors do not shy away from unflattering portrayals of courts and courtiers. Mid- and late-sixteenth-century manuals of behaviour at court make no attempt to glorify the courtly milieu or represent it as the congregation of the best, nor do they offer an idealistic representation of the court as a contrast to negative, satirical portrayals. On the contrary, the court is now openly recognized as a "dangerous sea,"[104] populated by envious detractors who act like the rocks ("scogli") on which it is easy to shipwreck,[105] or at least as an environment where falling is extremely dangerous – and extremely likely.[106]

Anti-courtliness and the *Book of the Courtier*'s epigones

The influence and dissemination of the *Book of the Courtier* prompted the emergence in Italy and abroad of many other treatises that tried to replicate its success.[107] The change in tone in later writings on courts, however, is significant, and concerns first and foremost the representation of the court, especially in terms of social interaction with one's prince and with one's peers. Later writings on courts make explicit the anti-courtliness that lurks in the *Book of the Courtier* and explore in much greater depth the vices of the court, which often results in a grim tone that recalls contemporary anti-court satires. The *Book of the Courtier*'s epigones, from Pellegro Grimaldi Robio's career-oriented *Discorsi* to the "chilling cynicism" of Lorenzo Ducci's *Ars Aulica* (*Arte aulica*),[108] openly dwell on the courtly milieu's moral corruption, hypocrisy, and ruthless ambition, not in order to discourage prospective courtiers or call for a reform of the court but to point out the necessity of playing according to these rules in order to succeed in the quest for princely favour. Unsurprisingly, the ambitious proposal of the courtier-counsellor voiced in the fourth book of the *Book of the Courtier* did not have a legacy in court manuals.[109]

The production of advice manuals addressed to courtiers peaked in the sixteenth century, continued in the seventeenth century (with influential works such as Matteo Peregrini's 1624 *Che al savio è convenevole il corteggiare*), and was still happening in the early eighteenth century. Yet the only book on courtliness that rivalled the popularity of the *Book of the Courtier* was Stefano Guazzo's *Civile conversation* (*La civil conversazione*).[110] Guazzo's dialogue, first printed in Brescia in 1574, was featured in many Italian editions and different translations over the course of the sixteenth and seventeenth centuries.[111] Another successful piece of writing was Agostino Nifo's 1534 *De re aulica*, which was translated into Italian by Francesco Belloni and reprinted in 1560 with the title *Il cortigiano del Sessa*. Other manuals of advice on behaviour at court were similarly republished in Italy and also translated and disseminated across Europe. Lorenzo Ducci's *Arte aulica*, printed in Ferrara in 1601, was reprinted in 1615 but had been already translated into English by Edward Blount in 1607, and appears to have been highly popular in seventeenth-century England. A court manual by an author who is almost unknown nowadays, *Discorsi ne' quali si ragiona compiutamente di quanto far debbono i gentilhuomini ne' seruigi de lor signori per acquistarsi la gratia loro*, by Pellegro Grimaldi Robio, appeared in 1543 and was later republished in 1544, 1583, and 1584.[112] Giovan Battista Giraldi Cinzio's *Discorso intorno a quello che si conviene a giovane e nobile e ben creato nel servire un gran principe* was printed only once, in 1569,[113] but undoubtedly had a great influence on Torquato Tasso's *Malpiglio, overo de la corte* (1581).[114] Even a text that was never printed, Giovanni Francesco Commendone's *Discorso sopra la corte di Roma* (most likely written around 1553–4), appears to have circulated widely in manuscript form.[115]

Apart from the Genoese Grimaldi Robio, for whom biographical details are scarce,[116] all the authors of these manuals are known for having had some direct experience with the court or at least with private households: both Giraldi Cinzio and Tasso were courtiers of the Ferrara court; Ducci arrived in Ferrara as the secretary of Cardinal Giovan Francesco Biandrate di San Giorgio; Commendone spent some years at the Roman court, where Nifo himself seems to have been well received in the years of Leo X's papacy; Guazzo was born into a family that held a close relationship with the Mantua court.

Unlike the *Book of the Courtier*, none of these writings is set in a courtly environment; nevertheless, three of them – Commendone's, Giraldi Cinzio's, and Grimaldi Robio's – are structured as responses to requests for advice from a prospective courtier. The opening lines of Commendone's *Discorso* present the text as a reply to a request from the "most illustrious Sir Ieronimo" (identified by Cesare Mozzarelli as Gerolamo Savorgnan), asking for the author's opinion on his return to court. Giraldi Cinzio's *Discorso* is described as having been written at the behest of his son, Lucio Olimpio, who in turn had been asked for a book of this sort by Pietro Battista Lomellini of Genoa (the commander of the ship on which Lucio Olimpio had fought in Lepanto). Grimaldi Robio's *Discorsi* is a dialogue between the author's brother Pierfrancesco and his young friend Battista, who is about to become a courtier in the service of the Marchese del Vasto. Battista is presented as the reason for the discussion: worried about his upcoming entrance at court, he yearns to hear more about courts and courtiers, since – as he admits – he has read many books on the topic, including the *Book of the Courtier*, but has found little practical advice in any of them.

Tasso's *Malpiglio* stages a similar request for advice in a conversation between Tasso's alter ego, the Forestiero Napoletano, and the young Giovanlorenzo Malpiglio, the son of his acquaintance Vincenzo Malpiglio and an enthusiastic aspiring courtier who has long wanted to meet with the Forestiero, precisely to discuss everything that concerns courts and courtiers. Guazzo's *Civile conversation*, on the other hand, performs the reconversion to courtliness of the author's brother, Guglielmo, who had receded from public life to improve his health.

As a consequence of their being structured as responses to a pressing occasion – someone's entrance or re-entrance at court – all such texts possess an urgency that is absent from the *Book of the Courtier*. The distance from Castiglione's masterpiece, or more precisely, the authors' intention to distance themselves from it, is most evident in the critical glance that they often cast on the *Book of the Courtier*. The *Book of the Courtier*'s lasting success and influence was, in fact, accompanied by an increasing number of critiques.[117] Late sixteenth- and early seventeenth-century books of advice to courtiers often combine praise for the *Book of the Courtier* with a dismissal of the figure of the courtier proposed by Castiglione, now seen as an unattainable ideal. The impression on the modern reader is that of an oscillation between a fascination with Castiglione's masterpiece and a generalized mistrust toward its core principles that in some cases is also combined with nostalgia for the courts of the past. This attitude is perfectly exemplified by Tasso's *Malpiglio*, a text that claims for itself the role of the "new *Book of the Courtier*" for new times: no longer addressing an ideal courtier in an ideal court, but a manual that takes into account the actual reality of the courts of its time.[118] Interestingly enough, none of the later manuals of courtliness seems to acknowledge the conflicted relationship of the *Book of the Courtier* with critical attitudes toward the court, or the nuances of anti-courtliness that pervade it.

The will of subsequent authors to distance themselves from the *Book of the Courtier* may be explained as, among other things, a marketing strategy aimed at promoting their message as more suited to contemporary courts. However, it is crucial to point out that such an attitude was also a by-product of the evolution in the structure of the court; at its core lay the awareness that, as the Forestiero Napoletano's interlocutor Vincenzo Malpiglio declares, "courts change with the times."[119] The bleak picture of contemporary courts that these texts present is well exemplified by the topos of court life as a voyage in a stormy sea, where it is very easy to shipwreck.[120] Further anti-court commonplaces featured in these texts – such as the court as place of cut-throat competition among peers, and unabashed flattery as the only way to gain a prince's favour – are also paired with an increasingly mercantilist view of courtliness and with a conversion of *sprezzatura* into an art of self-defence.

Grimaldi Robio explains the uneasiness of life at court as resulting from the continuous proximity that the court requires of men of "different complexions" ("differenti complessioni"), but also from the omnipresence of envy, "which seems to always have had, and having today more than ever, its own residence here," and from the "desire, that anyone is shown to possess, of being among the first in the grace of their lord."[121] Last but not least, one must consider the whimsical nature of princes and the arbitrariness of their favour. All of these features contribute to rendering the court a slippery place ("luogo [...] sdrucciolevole"), to the point that there is no place where one could more dangerously fall ("ove più perigliosamente si cada").[122] In the *Discorso*, Giraldi Cinzio gives an even more brutal account of court life through the myth of Momus. The personification of blame, Momus is said to have wed Envy and generated Wickedness and Slander, which in turn married Hate and Venom and had many children who now live and prosper in the courts. In this mythical portrayal, courtiers become the "new Momuses" ("nuovi Momi") who are always waiting for a chance to damage someone.[123] As Walter Moretti has pointed out, Giraldi Cinzio had good reasons to be wary of fellow courtiers and to hold a grudge against competitors for princely favour: the *Discorso* was written shortly after his humiliation at the court of Ferrara, when he lost his positions as ducal secretary and as professor of rhetoric to his former friend Giovan Battista Pigna.[124] The presence on the *Discorso*'s frontispiece of the emblem of the Hydra, the sea monster killed by Hercules, and the motto *Virescit vulnere virtus* (Virtue is strengthened by injuries) are also significant.[125] The court assumes the features of the mythical seven-headed serpent, while the man who is able to confront such a monster without being tarnished becomes a hero whose virtue is equal to that of Hercules.

The most intriguing – and probably also the most problematic – account of court life is provided by Guazzo's *Civile conversation*, thanks to its connection between courtliness and illness. The *Civile conversation* stages a debate between two characters, the doctor Annibale Magnocavalli and the author's brother Guglielmo Guazzo, a former courtier. Guglielmo, as we learn from the preface, is unwell and has receded from public life to try to recover his health in the quiet of the paternal home. Guglielmo's illness is, however, not a physical one. Guglielmo has come to the point of refusing conversation because it makes him too tired, and he feels that solitude is the only thing that can restore his spirits. Guglielmo's discontent with company and conversation is directly related to court life: more precisely, his abandonment of society demands to be read first and foremost as a disavowal of court life.[126] The *Civile conversation* depicts courtly interaction as potentially negative for the health of its members: as Guglielmo points out, the court exhausts him to the point that he feels he is losing his vital spirits to the benefit of his prince.[127] Thus, the *Civile conversation* elaborates and authenticates the intertwining of courtliness and illness and the idea of the court as needing medical help, ideas already present and well developed in the *Book of the Courtier*.[128] It is also significant that Annibale Magnocavalli, the interlocutor of the disaffected courtier Guglielmo Guazzo, is a doctor. Guglielmo himself highlights the connection between courtiership and sickness by asking Annibale to provide advice for courtiers in medical style: "I would it might please you to observe the order of a diligent Phisition, who besides the receytes of other Phisitions, wil be sure to minister to his patient somwhat of himselfe."[129]

The doctor's reply is particularly significant, since it continues the medical metaphor and also underlines the strategy most commonly recommended by late sixteenth-century court manuals: a wary attitude characterized by prudence and dissimulation. In Annibale's words,

> I give to a Courtyer this receyte, that the Prince being [...] a God on earth, it behoveth him to doe him honoure as to a sacred thing [...]. Beholde the first receipte. The other is compounded of two drugs which I have fetcht out of the shoppe of an excellent Philosopher, the one of whiche or both, the courtier using, may long time maintaine himself in his princes favour: These are abstinence, or else suger soppes.[130]

To Guglielmo's request for further explanations about these "due medicamenti," Annibale responds with two lines:

> Before their Prince let Courtiers silent be,
> Or let their words be saust with pleasaunt glee.[131]

The tone of Annibale's pithy summary recalls the quality of self-defence that characterizes *sprezzatura,* which scholarship has often underlined, defining it as a protective irony motivated by the constraints of despotism and by cut-throat competition among peers in the quest for princely favour.[132] This aspect of *sprezzatura* is dramatically enhanced in later writings on courts, however, where all the courtly arts seem designed first and foremost for the purpose of protecting oneself. Giraldi Cinzio's notion of *gentile ironia* (gentle irony)[133] as the main courtly virtue makes such a shift in the purpose of courtly arts particularly evident. The idea of courtliness proposed in Giraldi Cinzio's *Discorso* appears in fact to be structured mainly as a set of norms for defending oneself against the dangers of court life, and the semantic distance between the concept of *gentile ironia* and that of *sprezzatura* is a clear demonstration of this feature. *Sprezzatura* is a form of irony, but is semantically linked to a sense of disdain and carelessness. *Gentile ironia,* on the other hand, makes the ironic, dissimulative, and defensive dimension usually implicit in court behaviour immediately explicit.

The picture of court life as a constant struggle reaches its apogee in Tasso's *Malpiglio,* where interaction between peers is represented as a wrestling match:

> [T]he man who enters a discussion at court with a desire to win by any means against everyone, without consideration of time or place, is more attracted by intellectual glory than by courtly honor. For not only in debate but in every activity, the courtier must compete by yielding, like certain

> expert fighters who give way when attacked and by a supple trick they throw their opponent more easily to the ground.[134]

The *Malpiglio*, too, is the product of bitter disillusionment with court life, having been written after the author's disagreements with his patron, Duke Alfonso II d'Este, which resulted in his expulsion from the court and imprisonment in the hospital of Sant'Anna. According to Cox's definition, the *Malpiglio* can be considered the new *Book of the Courtier* for the new times precisely by virtue of its refusal to portray an ideal courtier in an ideal court. With the *Malpiglio* Tasso intends, rather, to devise a manual that can take into account the reality of the courts of its time.

Again, one essential step in the creation of a new art of courtliness is the incorporation of the topoi of anti-courtliness. Flattery, the ultimate evil of the court, is transformed into a prudent behaviour by emphasizing that a courtier's role is primarily to please his prince and execute his commandments. In referring to the theme of courtly flattery, and especially in commending it instead of condemning it, Tasso is drawing on Nifo's *De re aulica* and its notion of *affabilitas*, a specific form of courtly sweet talk.[135] In *De re aulica* Nifo declares his intention to go against those who want the courtier to have many different abilities and many different virtues.[136] By contrast, the courtier portrayed in *De re aulica* is a pleasant entertainer whose function is "to provide pleasure and amusement to his prince, especially after those affairs that are known to have made him weary."[137]

Such an entertainer clearly needs to be skilled in the art of pleasing his prince. Nifo's treatment of flattery aims for a conciliatory position that intends to redeem the courtier from the anti-court stereotype of the sycophant but that nonetheless reaffirms the necessity of flattery in courtly life, and tries to achieve a difficult balance between blunt truthfulness and overt adulation. In striving for such balance, however, it is recommended that the scale tip toward flattery: as Nifo points out, "[A]ffable men are received at court, and sycophants, and flatterers as well, and difficult men are chased away."[138]

Thanks to such cleverly ambivalent statements, writings on courts offer a practical demonstration of the prudence that is now recommended as the principal virtue of the successful courtier. Courtiers are advised to hide any outstanding qualities they might possess, since these would not gain them any honour or praise but only generate annoyance and suspicion. Tasso is particularly keen to emphasize that a courtier should always make sure to prove himself inferior to his prince, avoiding any conspicuous display of excellence that could provoke the envy of both his fellow courtiers and his prince. The focus on courtly prudence and the structure of writings on courts as examples of prudent behaviour explain why a text such as the *Malpiglio*, in spite of its evident anti-court undertones, could become one of Tasso's tools for winning the favour of the future Duke of Mantua, Vincenzo Gonzaga, who would eventually grant the poet's release from the hospital.[139]

Shaped as a way to prudently navigate the troubled waters of court life and removed of any mentoring purposes with regard to the prince, service at court takes one further step away from any moral concerns by acquiring a businesslike tone as well. This change of attitude reflects the new audience of court manuals: ambitious young men from the emerging classes who relied on service at court to climb the social ladder. This was certainly the situation for Giovanni Francesco Commendone, the son of a Venetian doctor who entered the Roman court to overcome the career obstacles that a non-noble birth posed for him in his homeland.[140] It may also have been the case for Lorenzo Ducci, whose *Ars Aulica* never fails to impress scholars with its ambitious tone and wherein courtliness is reduced to issues of "good" ("bene"), "commoditie" ("interesse"), and "profit" ("utilità") between the courtier and the prince.[141] Courtliness becomes a matter of gaining and losing, and success at court a question of having a killer instinct in the ruthless competition among peers. In this scenario, the Renaissance topos of the struggle between *virtù* and Fortuna finds a new narrative. The court becomes the embodiment of Fortuna, and court manuals are structured as ways to provide their readers with the correct form of *virtù* to fight the battle against Fortuna.[142] Nifo goes so far as to identify a peculiar form of virtue that he names "courtly virtue" ("virtù cortigiana"). The property of this type of virtue is that it must be restricted to the profession of courtliness alone, without involving the moral sphere:

> courtly virtue does not embrace all other virtues: because courtly virtue is a certain peculiar virtue thanks to which a man becomes a courtier: and it is not consequent that due to the same virtue he is also generous, just, and strong.[143]

The vision of service at court as a struggle against Fortuna leads in some cases to a different attitude toward anti-courtly sentiments, now seen as the mark of a defeatist attitude that cannot be tolerated in the ruthless competition for success at court. Grimaldi Robio is very keen to point out that interaction at court is complicated by the forced cohabitation between men of different natures, by the omnipresence of envy, by the unceasing competition to be among the prince's favourites, and by the whimsicality of the prince's desires.[144] Yet he has no sympathy for those who vent their discontent toward the court or blame their disgrace at court on peer envy, on their prince's ingratitude, or especially on the mutability of Fortuna. Fortuna is just the scapegoat for the losers,

> the refuge of those who are of little worth, and by unloading onto her that which is nothing, or, even if it is something, has little force on us, when we are able to hold ourselves together well, the cause of all their difficulties, and of other people's prosperities, they appear to be excused of their faults.[145]

According to Ulrich Langer, in the *Book of the Courtier* (and, presumably, in the genre of writings on courts at large) Fortuna stands for a prince who is both absolute and fickle: "Fortune is a product of despotism, for the whimsicality of the prince is precisely a sign and a proof of his absolute power."[146] By refusing to accept justifications of failure at court based on the power of Fortuna, conduct manuals such as Grimaldi Robio's *Discorsi* actually refuse to surrender to arbitrariness and whimsicality, thus making Fortuna – and success at court with it – conquerable by those who can recognize and apply the correct behavioural tactics. Nonetheless, an interpretation of Grimaldi Robio's career-oriented activism as optimistic would be a simplistic reading. Coming to the point of giving actual advice on effective behaviour at court, Grimaldi Robio is unable to provide more than a "negative theology" of court conduct: his examples involve only what should not be done at court and what should be avoided to prevent the loss of the prince's grace.

Surprisingly, given the text's reputation for unabashed career-oriented cynicism, Lorenzo Ducci's *Ars Aulica* is pervaded by the same negativity. Ducci's most frequent model of courtly behaviour is Sejanus, the emperor Tiberius's favourite, who is praised with the title of "great Master in the Courtiers arte."[147] An expert reader, however, would have remembered Sejanus's eventual downfall and execution (also quoted in Enea Silvio Piccolomini's anti-court masterpiece *De curialium miseriis*) as a clear example of the unreliability of success at court, an issue which is also briefly recalled by Ducci himself in the chapter on the difficulty of maintaining the prince's favour after having conquered it. Moreover, Ducci maintains that the *arte aulica* is utterly under the dominion of chance and is therefore included among those arts "the which not by necessitie, but contingently, and as it were by fortune or chance, obteine their desired ends."[148] In spite of the attempts at developing a courtly virtue that could withstand the power of Fortuna, the scale eventually tips back to the side of chance and unpredictability. The impression one draws is that even the most enterprising, self-confident, and opportunistic writings on courts seem unable to break free from the scepticism and pessimism of anti-court texts. In a court now explicitly recognized as a stormy sea wherein a shipwreck is always likely, the self-promoting cynicism of texts such as Ducci's *Ars Aulica* is thus more problematic than it may seem at a first reading.

Langer has identified one of the major contradictions of books on courts as their demanding an ideal courtier while at the same time refusing to give definitive rules by which all aspiring courtiers may be able to attain success at court.[149] Langer's observation can be supported by referring to the "negative theology" of courtliness into which many manuals of courtliness fall when having to provide actual behavioural advice to courtiers. In analysing the inability of these books to keep their promise of providing the reader with a constructive and universal model, it may be useful to refer to Michel de Certeau's notion of strategies as opposed to tactics. De Certeau defines a strategy as "the calculation (or manipulation) of power relationships that becomes possible as soon as a subject with will and power [...] can be isolated."[150] A tactic, on the other hand, is an "art of the weak" that has the space of the other as its only space and is therefore forced to play only on the terrain imposed by an external power. Tactics do not include the inherent opportunity to plan general strategies or guarantee independence but must always depend on opportunities provided by an external entity. While strategies can master place to the point of making panoptic practices possible, tactics, because of their ability to act only within the enemy's territory, are arranged as a way to play on time and on those opportunities that present themselves. The court – shaped as a definite space whose structural panopticism is evident in the call for continuous performance in its perennial theatre, a call often pointed out by writings on courts – can be easily read as an embodiment of strategic practices managed by the prince. Courtly arts are, by contrast, organized as ways to play on opportunities, as an art of the weak forced to resort to deception and trickeries. The inability of courtiers to realize a universally valid and everlasting set of rules is then genetically inscribed in their tactical nature, in their being unable – as de Certeau explains – to keep to themselves in a position of "withdrawal, foresight and self-collection"[151] and thus devise strategies from a position of even relative power. Thus instead of being defined only as morally unscrupulous guiles for self-advancement, ironic courtly practices can be also explained as a set of tactics developed as the only way to cope with the strategies of a despotic power.

Courtly morals

It is important to keep underscoring the extent to which such courtly tactics are progressively removed from any moral concerns. The second book of the *Book of the Courtier* already contained hints that could have been developed by less scrupulous writers into a morally neutral science of human behaviour, according to a process that Cox has defined a "rhetoricization of ethics."[152] Ducci even comes to the point of excusing ethically ambiguous behaviour at court on the basis that the duty of obedience to the prince relieves the courtier of any responsibility in matters of morality:

> [T]o the dutie of service so much is pardonable, as may for the pleasure and service of his Prince bee done in some things, if not honorable, at least without such note of infamy; as in a person at full liberty could not be born out without passing censure or incurring blame.[153]

In the previous chapters of his text, Ducci had briefly covered some of the most controversial aspects of court life, such as ambition, flattery, the artificiality of courtly life and behaviour at court, and the necessity to always conform to the nature and the inclinations of the prince. This explicit insistence on the evils of the court is one of the main features that give manuals such as the *Ars Aulica* their peculiar cynical tone. Yet it must also be noted that the same detailed depictions of the vices of court life also contribute to creating an image of rectitude for the author. By denouncing the court as corrupt and by warning prospective courtiers about the nature of their peers, these texts place their authors in a position of moral superiority to the courts and courtiers they are exposing in all of their faults. The moralizing condemnation in court manuals of the evils of the court offered the authors the chance to redeem their courtly persona – which was potentially compromised, given the corruption of court life they are so eager to point out. It also gave them the opportunity to fashion it as a moral persona, even as a heroic one, as the references to courtiers as Herculean figures suggest. In court manuals, however, such redemption is only indirect, and compromised by the authors' implication in the very same system they condemn.

Golden chains

The emblem *In aulicos* (On courtiers) by Andrea Alciato briefly analysed in the introduction was printed in many different editions that slightly diverge from each other in a few details. Among the different versions of the emblem, one element is of particular interest: some French editions of the text (those printed in Paris in 1534, 1539, and 1542, and the one printed in Lyon in 1556), feature the elegantly dressed courtier in stocks wearing an ostentatious golden chain around his neck, just like the emblem analysed earlier. A couple of these editions also include commentaries that address precisely the topic of the courtier's golden chains.

> Against Courtiers
>
> Serving the court nicely dressed, eating well and drinking likewise, being surrounded by fine talk, being full of long-awaited hope makes the less wise very happy, as one who is bound by a golden chain: from which he never tries to get free, and such a prison he finds pleasant.[154]
>
> Those who are educated and fostered in the courts of princes and kings live splendidly, eat and drink sumptuously, dress magnificently, walk boldly, and their life seems most happy. Yet they are not masters of themselves and cannot be defined as free, but instead are bound by golden ties. They are reprimanded by Seneca, who deems foolish those who love their chains, however golden; therefore the condition of courtiers became proverbially known as golden chains.[155]

Both commentaries contrast the courtier's luxurious life with the lack of freedom that the chains embody. Giving golden chains as a reward was an ancient custom that was revived and popularized in the early modern period. As Julius S. Held has underlined, the golden chains were "symbols of both eminence and servitude"[156] since they represented luxury and power yet were also a reminder of the power of the giver and the inferior status of the recipient. Thanks to evidence from Anton Francesco Doni, we know that even Pietro Aretino, the notorious scourge of princes, was prompted to keep in mind that chains stood for servitude when he received a golden chain from Francis I of France. In his *Nuova opinione*, Doni quotes a letter from Francis I warning Aretino to make careful use of his proverbial *malalingua*, or else Francis's gift would become proof of Aretino's servitude to the king ("unless the golden chain that I send you as a courtesy transforms into shackles of servitude").[157]

The most fascinating aspect of the commentaries on Alciato's emblems is that they underline the attachment that the courtier feels toward his golden chains. The captivity portrayed in the emblems is not only physical but also mental, and the golden chains become representative of the courtier's inability to break free psychologically from the court. Even some of the texts that criticize the court more harshly sometimes

Figure 2. *Against courtiers.* Andrea Alciato, *Les emblems* (Paris: Chrestien Wechel, 1542), 241, emblem 111. *The courtier in stocks with a golden chain around his neck.*

betray signs of a feeling of dependence, or of residual attraction for its world. This is well exemplified by the final passages of the third book of Guazzo's *Civile conversation*. One of the most interesting features of the *Civile conversation* is precisely the inability of both speakers to completely forsake the court in spite of the undoubtedly anti-court tone

Figure 3. Andrea Alciato, *Emblematum libri II* (Lyon: Jean de Tournes and Guillaume Gazeau, 1556), 184, emblem 111. *A variant on the subject of the courtier's stocks and golden chain.*

that pervades the dialogue, resulting in a dynamic that Daniel Javitch has defined as "courtly anti-courtliness."[158] The character of Guglielmo Guazzo, in particular, seems stuck in a contradictory fluctuation between his anti-court attitude and his affiliation with the world of the court. Throughout the dialogue, Guglielmo is often on the point of becoming something very similar to a character from an anti-court satire: an experienced yet disillusioned courtier who regrets his involvement with the world of the court. Yet when confronted with the possibility of openly expressing an anti-court critique, Guglielmo backs down and launches into a declaration of his attachment for the court.

Analysing the conversation between masters and servants, Annibale Magnocavalli points out that he sees no real divide between noble-born courtiers and simple servants: the only difference is that "the chaynes or Fetters of the baser sort, are of yron, and those of the Gentlemen, of Golde."[159]

Guglielmo agrees with such a definition and adds that in his opinion, the courtier's golden chains are tighter than the servant's iron ones.

However, he disagrees with the doctor's opinion that "common Servingmen hate both their Mayster and the Chayne, where the other love their Maysters, but cannot away with the chayne."[160]

Noble courtiers enter the court not because they are compelled by indigence but to pursue glory, and therefore cannot hold their golden chains in contempt. At this point, Guglielmo refers to his own experience and suddenly abandons his previous anti-court attitude to state his affection for the court:

> [W]hen I shall live in rest at my fathers house, I shall be no more than others of my neighbours are, and I shall take my selfe to be as unprofitable to the world, whereas being about that Prince, I am in case every hower to pleasure a number of persons, to get friendes daylye, and to make my selfe honoured of the most honourable in the court: by reason whereof, I curse my infirmitye, whiche will not suffer mee long to be bound in this chayne of Gold, which I like above all things in the world.[161]

By declaring himself unfit to retreat to the villa – such a retreat being the author's ultimate goal in many anti-court writings – and by professing his longing for the court, Guglielmo highlights the vacillation between praise and blame that characterizes writings on courts.

Such contradictory feelings can be further complicated by personifications of the court as a female figure and by the use of Petrarchan love metaphors to describe this conflicted relationship, while in satirical writings these dynamics of attraction and rejection also become connected to the satirist's attempt to forsake his courtly identity and to fashion for himself a new kind of persona.

Chapter Two

The Lady

Women, anti-feminism, and anti-courtliness in the Italian Renaissance

The novelty of the *Book of the Courtier* is not limited to its elaboration of the figure of the perfect courtier: it also owes a good part of its originality to being the first Italian codification of rules of conduct for the court lady. The importance of the figure of the court lady as a necessary companion to the courtier is signalled by the progressive expansion of the section dedicated to the *querelle des femmes* and to the qualities of the *donna di palazzo* in the different versions of the text, eventually coming to the point of giving this discussion a book of its own, the third in the *Book of the Courtier*.[1] The very presence of women as interlocutors of the dialogue is remarkable, in spite of their minor role as speakers.[2] Even more remarkable is the discussion's setting in what has been defined the "feminine enclosed space" of the duchess's private apartments.[3]

The examination of the figure of the court lady and her relationship to the courtier, of the female characters featured in the dialogue and their interaction with the more prominent male speakers, and of the treatment of the *querelle des femmes* in the *Book of the Courtier* is part of a larger debate on the role of women in the early modern period. For a long time the prevailing interpretation of women's status in early modern society was the one set by Joan Kelly-Gadol in her seminal essay, "Did Women Have a Renaissance?" According to Kelly-Gadol, women endured subjection to a patriarchal male order even during the cultural renewal of an otherwise "progressive" Renaissance. Recent scholarship has been moving away from Kelly-Gadol's pessimistic perspective. Over the past few years, scholars have focused on the spaces reserved for women to exercise power or cultural influence. Although it is unquestionable that women had fewer opportunities for political and cultural influence than their male counterparts had, studies have underscored how over the course of the sixteenth century elite women became prominent as advisors to their spouses and children, as regents of states, as patrons of the arts, as consumers of cultural artefacts, and as writers and artists. Most literary scholars stress how the court, as the site of political power and a locus for cultural production, played an important role in the emergence of women as protagonists.[4]

Early modern Italian courts also allowed close interaction between their male and female members that might be considered unprecedented in its extent and features. Scholarship has offered different interpretations of the activities and functions of women at court, either as the male courtiers' audience for their performance of courtliness and therefore as judges of men's behaviour, or as an effeminizing presence that contributed to a lack of manliness in court men. Court women have additionally been seen as the enforcers of a "civilizing process" that eventually led to the domestication of a class of former warriors, transforming them into refined courtiers: theories based on Norbert Elias's work have explained the courtiers' discontent as the malaise of warriors who witness themselves being tamed by a female-dominated and emasculating court.[5]

The new relevance for women that was allowed and supported by the rise of court culture did not mark the end of the secular tradition of Aristotelian theories that defined women as nothing more than an imperfect version of men – as testified by the anti-feminist outbursts by Ottaviano Fregoso and Gasparo Pallavicino that are juxtaposed with Giuliano de' Medici's praise of female virtues in the *Book of the Courtier*.[6] The dispute between the proto-feminist Giuliano and the ranting misogynist Gasparo dramatizes the debate about the nature of women and their role in society, but the *Book of the Courtier* is not the only early modern Italian text to offer contrasting views of women's nature and opinions on their role in society in a way that modern readers often find puzzling. Very different pieces of writing, ranging from Teofilo Folengo's mock epic *Baldus* (first published in 1517) to Matteo Bandello's *Novelle* (published in different editions in the second half of the sixteenth century) similarly shift between pro- and anti-women attitudes and eventually leave the question of their authors' opinions on women unresolved. Furthermore, the few texts that – in the wake of the *Book of the Courtier* – deal with the fashioning of a perfect court lady, offering testimony to the relevance of a female presence at court, at times also betray an underlying anti-feminism. An example of this stance is represented by the second section of Agostino Nifo's *De re aulica*, titled "De muliere aulica," later translated into Italian by Ludovico Domenichi with the title *La donna di corte* (1564). In the end, in spite of their often contradictory attitudes toward women, all these texts provide evidence that it was no longer possible to deny women a place in the sophisticated mixed society of sixteenth-century Italian courts.[7]

An investigation of the connection between anti-feminism anti-courtliness must therefore take into account the anxieties associated with the extremely refined and unprecedentedly mixed court society, anxieties that are revealed by the contrasting attitudes toward women expressed by the literary works of the time. These anxieties concerned, first and foremost, the very presence of women at court, and in particular the opportunities for exercising certain forms of influence that the court offered to women. The rise of courts as centres of power, culture, and patronage provided many women of the elite classes with the opportunity to act as patrons of artists and writers. When not directly responsible for distributing allowances, women were powerful intermediaries who could recommend aspiring protégés to their spouses.[8] Wives of rulers of early modern Italian courts could also directly experience leadership on numerous occasions, when acting in place of their husbands when the men were away at war, or as regents for their minor children and as dowagers after the death of a spouse. The influence of such women, as well as the honest admiration that many of them could inspire for their erudition and for their administrative abilities, was counterbalanced by the persistence of misogynist notions grounded in Aristotelian biology that saw women as unfit for leadership because of their childlike, underdeveloped nature, and their psychological instability that made them easy prey to passions and whims.

The scholarly tradition has highlighted a persistent concern in the *Book of the Courtier* about the threats that court life poses to the courtier's masculinity. Ottaviano's speech in Book 4 reacts not only to the triviality of courtly arts but also to their perceived capacity for feminization;[9] one more reason court life became the target of satirical attacks was precisely such a potentially emasculating effect. The notion of the possible emasculation of the courtier has also been linked to the female presence at court, related to the courtiers' abandonment of military pursuits and their all-male environment in favour of the refined ways of courtliness, and to their need to integrate in the mixed court society wherein women were often depicted as invested with the role of evaluators of men's behaviour.

In an influential article, David Quint has shed new light on the anti-feminist sentiments uttered in the *Book of the Courtier* by arguing that the expressions of resentment against the ladies can be read as actually directed against the prince. According to Quint, women – already the focus of a century-long misogynist tradition that described them as fickle and vain, and depicted by Petrarchan conventions as cruel and unrequiting, keeping their faithful suitors in a state of perennial dissatisfaction – became an easier target for courtiers' venting of the anger they felt toward princes they perceived as capricious in their favours, often rewarding unworthy courtiers over the loyal and virtuous ones.[10] Quint's innovative reading of the third book of the *Courtier* paves the way for a wider exploration of the bonds that tie together anti-feminist and anti-court sentiments in early modern Italian culture. The connection between anti-feminist and anti-court sentiments results in a complicated picture wherein anxieties over the affirmation of women in the courtly scene, over the perceived progressive feminization of a subjugated Italy and of powerless courtly elites, and over *la Corte* personified as a witch-like figure that can simultaneously repulse and attract her subjects all intertwine, with intriguing consequences for the cultural sphere. In the context of this explosive mixture, anti-feminism and anti-courtliness together become ready-made, easily available, and easily understandable languages to explore and express discontent in early modern Italian society.

The courtier's anxious masculinity

The game that constitutes the heart of the *Book of the Courtier* carries, from the very beginning, polemical value. The dialogue can actually be considered a statement with a positive, constructive purpose as much as a counter-statement specifically aimed at suppressing the fallacious opinions of "the many fools who in their presumption and ineptitude think to gain the name of good courtiers."[11] The game takes the shape of both an offensive and a defensive move, explicitly directed at challenging those who usurp the name of the good courtier. Among those usurpers are, first and foremost, those who transgress the border between the elegance that is required of a good courtier and an unwelcomed effeminacy. In the first pages of Book 1, Ludovico da Canossa voices a harsh critique of such a transgression:[12]

> I would have our Courtier's face to be such, not so soft and feminine as many attempt to have who not only curl their hair and pluck their eyebrows, but preen themselves in all those ways that the most wanton and dissolute women in the world adopt; and in walking, in posture, and in every act, appear so tender and languid that their limbs seem to be on the verge of falling apart; and utter their words so limply that it seems they are about to expire on the spot; and the more they find themselves in the company

> of men of rank, the more they make a show of such manners. These, since nature did not make them women as they clearly wish to appear and be, should be treated not as good women, but as public harlots, and driven not only from the courts of great lords but from the society of all noble men.[13]

The picture evoked by Canossa borrows heavily from the portraits of vain, effeminate courtiers in satirical writings. The satirical invective against the un-masculine courtier is exemplified by the scorn for the "Ganymedes with purple cheeks" ("Ganimedi con le guance d'ostro") who manicure their hair and body "as if they were a beloved bride and diva" ("come sposa fusse amata e diva") voiced by Pietro Aretino in the anti-courtier pasquinade *Lamento de uno cortigiano già favorito in palazzo, et hora in grandissima calamità*.[14] The central character of the *Lamento* is a once-successful, now impoverished and repentant courtier whose life mission is to disabuse prospective courtiers by denouncing the evils that the court hides under its facade of opulence. In doing so, the failed courtier confesses to having been, in his years at court, the image of vanity itself, obsessed as he was with clothes, jewels, perfumes, and everything that pertained to the world of appearances:

> I am one who did not deign to touch rubies with his fingers and now my clothes are richly adorned with lice. In my grandeur I held pompous feasts in scorn and turned up my nose at the smell of civet and all perfumes; now I would buy the plague with my own life.[15]

Ludovico da Canossa and Federico Fregoso thus juxtapose satirical portraits of supercilious and excessively manicured courtiers against the positive ideal of a serious, restrained, and sober gentleman.

Studies on masculinity have identified in early modern writings a variety of models of manhood that were constructed and discussed, such as the prince, the Roman orator, and the captain.[16] Yet the speakers in Urbino attempt to create their courtier not only as the ideal model for a new profession but as an additional model of manhood, to be added to the existing set of available types. The *Book of the Courtier* could thus provide those who intended to become a courtier – and for whom, of course, models of manhood such as the prince or the soldier could not work – with an example after which to fashion the manliness of their courtly persona. Such a model was much needed, not only because the fairly recent profession of courtier had to be defined in all of its features but also because from the point of view of masculinity – as the example of Aretino's anti-courtier satire makes clear – the courtier was a potentially problematic figure.

Scholarship on the *Book of the Courtier* agrees that effeminacy was an indubitable concern of the participants in the dialogue. The fact that masculinity was the object of disquiet may not come as a surprise: as Mark Breitenberg has pointed out, masculinity is inevitably surrounded by anxiety.[17] In the case of the courtier, however, such anxiety was additionally fuelled by the requirement for exquisite manners and elegant appearance at court, and by the courtier's feminine-like posture of subordination to the dominant figure of the prince. In the case of the speakers in the *Book of the Courtier*, such feminization can be seen as extended by their subjugation to the female authority figures represented by the Duchess Elisabetta and her lady-in-waiting Emilia Pio.

Gerry Milligan has called attention to the politically charged quality of the discourse of masculinity in the *Book of the Courtier*. According to Milligan, the discussions of potentially problematic areas for the courtier's masculinity such as music, dance, and dress are part of a larger rhetorical strategy during the period that witnessed the progressive subjugation of the peninsula to foreign powers, wherein gender shaming and accusations of effeminacy become tools for awakening a political conscience among Italian elites. With this in mind, Milligan has also argued for the need to "nuance the critical tradition of the 'effeminate courtier.'"[18] In particular, Milligan wants to offer a corrective to the theories that see the relationship of male courtiers to female authorities, or even the simple presence of women within the courtly environment, as necessarily causing feminization. Milligan argues instead that court women have a relevant role in the construction of courtiers' masculinity, and aligns such a formational role with women's capacity to shame men into political and military action. Thus the masculinity of courtly elites is called into question not because of the courtiers' subjugation to women or because of women's relevant presence in court society, but because of their subjugation to foreign rule. The notion that capitulation to foreigners may be key to understanding the anxieties surrounding the looks and habits of Italian courtiers could also explain the satirical portrayal of Aretino's manicured courtiers quoted above, where courtiers are additionally ridiculed for "straightening their hair like the French" ("lisciarsi la chioma a la franzese") and speaking in "Spanish sighs in a slow voice" ("sospiri spagnoli in voce lenta").[19]

Was the courtier really un-masculine? As Milligan has convincingly argued, in investigating issues of courtliness and masculinity, we must not fall into an "ahistorical interpretation wherein Renaissance courtly activities [...] may seem un-masculine by modern gender standards."[20] Kenneth Gouwens has similarly pointed out how early modern notions of masculinity, especially in reference to martial activities, encompassed a broader range of qualities than we may imagine, not being limited to fortitude but including resilience and patience as well.[21] Yet despite reconsideration in the light of such historical correctives, the courtier – even the restrained gentleman proposed by the speakers of the *Book of the Courtier* who makes arms his first profession – hardly seems a successful model of masculinity. If courtly activities did not necessarily render the courtier un-masculine by the standards of the time, and if women's presence at court did not immediately imply a loss of masculinity among their male counterparts, different reasons must be found for the courtier's masculinity becoming a satirical target in anti-courtier critiques, and for the failure of the courtier figure to become completely acceptable as a model for masculinity. One explanation may be found in the notion of the courtier as constantly shaping his manners, his appearance, and even his body to please his courtly audience (first of all his prince). The imitation of others' virtues that the courtier is advised to pursue, like a bee ("pecchia") flying to different flowers,[22] and the notion of having to shape his tastes and interests according to those of his prince contribute to an image of the courtier's persona as mutable and perfectible – an image thus opposed to the Aristotelian notion of men as fully formed perfection and instead closer to a woman's imperfect nature.

Yet the courtier's elegant body nourished anti-courtier sentiments for another reason as well, one that is, intriguingly, only apparently related to the courtier's masculinity. The hostility toward the courtier's manicured appearance needs to be investigated also as representative of different anxieties that target not so much the courtier as an individual as the nature of the court as an institution. The repentant courtier portrayed in Aretino's *Lamento de uno cortigiano* is keen to disabuse young prospective courtiers, whom he considers dazzled by the luxurious aspect of the court to the point of having become blind to the court's real nature. His wake-up call, "But can the Heavens allow this / O excellent youth / are you so blinded by the court / that you cannot see its shortcomings?,"[23] is a plea to look beyond appearances. Courtiers are satirized for their narcissism, their obsession with dress and cosmetics, their invented noble ancestries, their counterfeit Tuscan accent, their artistic pretences, their constant showing off of riches when they actually live in poverty. Critics attacked courtiers, in short, for fostering a world where illusions rule and for falling in love with the court to the point of letting themselves be blinded by its – or better, *her* – deceptive charms.

All such features played their part in the intertwining of scenarios representing court life with ones involving misogynistic commonplace figures of seductresses, such as the cruel mistress, the evil sorceress, or the shrewd harlot, whose suitors are often represented as powerless and emasculated.

The court is a woman

Nuancing the notion of the effeminate courtier and the idea that the presence of women at court was a threat to masculinity does not call into question the intertwining of anti-courtliness and anti-feminism, or, more precisely, the fact that anti-court sentiments were often channelled through anti-feminist expressions. The reason anti-feminist language could be employed in the apparently unrelated field of anti-court complaints becomes clear when one considers that, as Cesare Caporali points out in the *capitolo* titled *La corte*, the court itself is a woman:

> The court is depicted as a matron,
> with a gaunt face and perfumed hair
> with a hard back and a soft body,
> who goes around costumed in a green cloth.
> Although she drapes across her body, just like Hercules,
> a large cloak made of a donkey's skin.
> Around her neck hang harsh chains,
> due to her ineptitude, or her inability
> to free herself from them, and leave all pain behind.
> She dons a regal crown of mirrors and whips,
> and sits on a layer of straw,
> with one foot in a brothel and the other in a hospice.[24]

Cesare Ripa, in his *Iconologia* – a book of images derived from ancient and contemporary sources – quotes Caporali's personification of the court as a woman and offers another portrait of the court in female attire:

> A young woman, with a beautiful hairstyle, dressed in green, shimmering tones, who, with both hands, lifts the front hem of her dress, revealing her knees, and carrying in her lifted dress various garlands of diverse flowers. In one hand she will also hold some hooks tied with thread made of green silk; she will have at her feet a small statue of Mercury, upon which she will lean, and on the other side a pair of golden fetters: that is to say the shackles that are usually put on both feet, and with these, chains, also in gold. The earth, upon which she lies, will be covered in stones, but also in the flowers that fall from her dress, and on her feet she will have shoes made of lead.[25]

Ripa's description makes explicit the sexual allure of the young woman representing the court by her lascivious gesture of lifting her skirt to reveal her knees. The *Iconologia* provides, as well, a detailed explanation of the visual symbolism associated with the court. In this section, Ripa presents his own credentials for the task of depicting the court: he maintains he is the right person for this task by virtue of "the time I spent there from my childhood until now."[26] Despite such extensive personal expertise – which, we may assume, might lead the author to present a different, mostly unflattering, picture of the court – Ripa declares that he will report only

> the encomium of those who say that the court is the highest majesty of human living, the foundation of elegance, the measure of eloquence, the theatre of honours, the measure of magnificence, and the open forum of polite conversation and friendships; that it knows everything and understands everything, in all the most honourable and worthy fields in the entire structure of the world upon which our every operation and understanding is founded.[27]

In accordance with an encomiastic vision of the court, the garlands are said to stand for "the fragrant qualities to which she gives birth" ("quest'odorifere qualità che essa partorisce"). And yet, it is pointed out that these fragrant gifts come at a price, as many courtiers live in risk of losing their money or even their honour, and in constant anxiety of falling from grace, burdened by the inexorable passing of time, "which can be seen by her knees, naked almost to the point of showing her shameful parts, and in the shackles that restrain and avoid that."[28] Similarly, the shimmering green colour of her dress illustrates the court's changeable nature, the ease with which she can grant favour and quickly take it away.

The court is a witch

The account of the court offered by the *Iconologia* is stuck in the impasse created by the author's declared intention to offer an encomium of the court, on the one hand, and by his reticent allusion to a very different picture that he may have chosen to present, thanks to his direct experience of courtly life, on the other. His Lady Court well represents the ambivalence of the court's charms and the threats hidden underneath them. Ripa's personified court is tainted with anti-court nuances, yet Renaissance literature offers much more disquieting images of female figures who can be connected to the court: settings wherein male characters are rendered powerless and imprisoned in a court-like world of illusions that is under the power of one or more female characters. The realm of Alcina in Ludovico Ariosto's *Orlando Furioso*, the kingdom of the witches in Teofilo Folengo's *Baldus*, and Armida's garden in Torquato Tasso's *Gerusalemme Liberata* all depict court-like scenarios pivoting around dangerously beautiful women who possess the magical power to create fictional worlds where they hold men prisoner. The association between female characters and worlds of enticing appearances is not surprising when one considers the tradition that invested female beauty and its ability to enchant men with a devilish power.[29] In anti-feminist satires, moreover, women often stand accused of being able to conceal monstrous ugliness under a beauty artificially created through the use of makeup – the *lisci* and *belletti* that are frequently attacked in writings on women.[30]

In Folengo's *Baldus* – a macaronic poem that presents a parodic combination of the *Aeneid* with the *Orlando Furioso* and narrates the adventures of the titular hero from his birth to his final mission to destroy the Kingdom of Hell – the anti-court sentiments reflect the author's notion of the court as corrupted. Teofilo Folengo, a Benedictine monk, regarded the world of the court as the epitome of corruption in the upside-down contemporary world, which had strayed from Christian values.[31] This theme is exemplified in the depiction of the realm of the witch Gelfora in the twenty-third book of the poem.[32] Gelfora's world (which Baldus needs to destroy in order accomplish his mission)[33] is a perfect courtly utopia: within golden walls and under golden roofs, in rooms decorated with the most expensive fabrics, and amid lovely perfumes, exquisitely dressed young men (whose real nature Baldus recognizes as diabolical) perform elegant dances. The court ladies, on their part, apply makeup to their cheeks, curl their hair, pluck their eyebrows, and stuff their bodices to make their breasts look bigger:

> The rooftops shine with gold, the walls, floors, benches, and the various layers of bedcovers and beds are made of silver, satin, samite, shot-silk and velvet. Baldo observes youth here joking around the girls: elegant in their movements, with handsome and charming faces, well-dressed, agile, always seen dancing. As soon as he sees them, Baldo judges them to be devils that have put on human heads and manly manners. I won't describe their golden clothes and velvet hats and their purple stockings and fine linen shirts. And likewise I'll omit the precious jewels, the musk, the perfumes, and little vials of civets and orange essence. He feels rising to his nose spirals of storax and rose, with which the palace is often doused. Floral draperies decorate the walls of porphyry, on which mirrors hang to give light all around. In that place pathetic girls stand about admiring themselves and put makeup on their cheeks and foreheads and necks.

> They make their precious lips seem the color of coral; they curl their hair with irons and trim their eyebrows, plucking out stray hairs, and with rags and straw they pad their shoulders and enlarge the breasts on their chests. So what we think to be the image of Pallas Athena is a sack of straw or one of those scarecrows we place in an orchard to chase away birds.[34]

Anti-court sentiments are voiced first of all as a denunciation of the womanly tricks used to conceal ugliness under fake beauty. In the following book of the *Baldus*, the criticism will be structured as a mockery of the courtiers' lack of manliness. There, the witch queen will try to fight Baldus and his comrades with the help of her entire court, but her refined courtiers will, predictably, prove themselves useless in battle. The arrival of Gelfora's court provides the occasion for a denunciation of contemporary courtiers:

> There was never a queen more pompous then she [...]. A long line of men follows: perfumed with civet, they claim to be refined courtiers; but if you were to examine them with an objective eye, you would say that they are not virile men, but harlots. A true courtier existed back in the olden days, when that valiant king, the most excellent King Arthur, held an illustrious court and Round Table. Back then, the face of a courtier was able to please and soften the heart of a stern lady when it was bathed only in the sweat of a helmet, or blackened by dirt under a burning sun. But in this day and age of ours, ye gods, only with various perfumes and the scent of civet, only with manes that are styked or trimmed and with velvet hats and caps of gold, with gold brocade and emblems and medallions and a thousand other decorations on trousers and coats, do we seek the precious seed of a shitty love. And so it is now, while Gelfora whips her rapid coach, and five other carts of cows follow behind her, darling courtiers accompany them as if they were nymphs, divas and lovely ladies, and speak to them of I don't know what dreams seen the night before. And they go bustling along on quick little mules, gnawing smooth little sticks with their teeth and reporting phony passions and reciting sonnets quite poorly strung together and telling a thousand fibs and uttering idiotic twaddle about their own loves. Baldo had witnessed all this at a distance from a high mound and, laughing, spoke thus to his friends: Note, companions: among all those thousands, I don't see one real man, not one who might know how to unsheathe a wooden sword, much less make a thrust. They are the kind that only a beard shows to be men; otherwise they are like women suited to the spindle.[35]

Folengo's picture of the dishonourable courtiers echoes the critique uttered by Ludovico da Canossa in the *Book of the Courtier*. And as in the *Book of the Courtier*, ineptitude on the battlefield is cited and the language of gender shaming is employed to remind contemporary courtiers of their military failure, contrasted with the valour of their counterparts from the glorious past. It is important to point out that Folengo's description of the noble courts of the past does not fail to recognize the relevance of a female presence there. Rather, the example of an ideal court is that of "the great king Arthur," which, a few lines later in the text, will be defined as the court of "the beautiful Guinevere" as well. In such a court, virtuous ladies rewarded men who proved their military valour. The Arthurian court is praised for having both a masculine and a feminine soul, embodied by Arthur and his valour, on the one hand, and by Guinevere and her graces, on the other.[36] The degenerate court of the *Baldus* is guilty of having lost both its masculine valour and its feminine grace. The courtiers, for their part, have sworn loyalty to a court that is no longer a virtuous lady but a witch, whose depravity has tainted their spirit as well. In this panorama of utter decadence, men and the failure of manliness, represented by military ineptitude, embody the failure of the court in the public sphere, while the vain and falsely beautiful women embody its (maybe more disquieting) power of extending corruption into the sphere of selfhood.

In a similar vein, some of the most famous episodes of the *Orlando Furioso* and the *Gerusalemme Liberata* see Ruggiero and Rinaldo, respectively, capitulate to powerful and disquieting female figures. While the general correlation between these two episodes is well known, scholars have not attended to the fact that both Alcina's and Armida's worlds offer a gloomy metaphor of court life in epitomizing a reality where every charm and appeal is a forgery. Gelfora's and Alcina's courts are also closely related, as is evident from the figure of the witch who hides her true, repulsive self under a counterfeit beauty, and from both courts being built as places where everything is an enchantment masking the most dangerous captivities. In Alcina's court, every lover and favourite is transformed into a beast or a plant as soon as Alcina gets tired of him.[37] Yet to the naive Ruggiero, Alcina's court looks like "the most splendid and delightful palace to be seen in the whole wide world."[38]

In such a splendid setting, the warrior is welcomed by the ruler Alcina and by her ladies-in-waiting in perfect courtly fashion. Moreover, the palace is rendered so magnificent thanks to the quality of its courtiers and ladies:

> What was remarkable about the splendid palace was not its opulence (unrivalled though it was) so much as its inhabitants – the most attractive, courteous people in the world. For youth and comeliness there was little to judge between them all; only Alcina outstripped them every one in beauty, as the sun is more radiant than any star.[39]

In Alcina's palace, Ruggiero forgets his chivalric duties and his commitment to his beloved Bradamante. Only the intervention of the sorceress Melissa, who reminds him who he really is, will rescue him from his oblivion. It is also worth recalling that Melissa finds Ruggiero completely mutated and depersonalized by Alcina's court, to the point that he is no longer himself, but just a name:[40] "all about him was sickly, all but his name; the rest was but corruption and decay. Thus was Ruggiero discovered, thus changed from his true self by sorcery."[41] Melissa is able to bring Ruggiero back to his self-awareness by taking the shape of the wizard Atlante, Ruggiero's adoptive father, which reminds Ruggiero of his military past – the battles he was raised for and the greatness that awaits him – and with it, his true identity.

Ruggiero's downfall was caused by his neglecting the advice of the paladin Astolfo, one of Alcina's former lovers, whom Ruggiero had met upon his arrival on the island and who had been transformed by Alcina into a myrtle bush.[42] Alcina's main characteristic is, in fact, her fickleness: she constantly seeks new lovers, whom she exalts to the highest honours as long as her infatuation with them persists, only to turn them into plants or animals as soon as they fall out of her grace.[43] This dynamic again recalls the whimsicality of the court, where a man can go from rags to riches and back again in the blink of an eye.[44]

Alcina and her court can be read as representing the court's deceits and the mutability of fortune within its realm, while Armida's garden in the *Gerusalemme Liberata* exemplifies the bewitching charms and the factitious beauty of the courtly milieu. This is a beauty that overcomes natural beauty – or better, that distorts it into excessive perfection.[45] Armida's garden is depicted as being completely flawless and so cleverly created that it appears entirely natural:[46] the sorceress's perfect use of *sprezzatura* ensures that "the art that fashioned it did not appear."[47]

The paladins Carlo and Ubaldo, on a mission to bring Rinaldo back to the battlefield, find him entirely forgetful of his role as a warrior, lost in the paradise created by the sorceress and in his love for her. Like Ruggiero, Rinaldo will be awakened from the spell only by a shocking experience aimed at reminding him of his true self: the battle shield/mirror that Carlo and Ubaldo put in front of his eyes to confront him with what he has become.

Love and courtliness

It is particularly relevant that in the episodes of Alcina and Armida the references to court life are intertwined with love scenes. The identification of the court with a lady – and, most importantly, a lady that is the object of one's love – was further fostered by the commutability of the language of courtly love and the language of patronage, as pointed out by David Quint and by Lauro Martines (among others).[48] In their studies, both Quint and Martines have underlined how the language of love poetry, with its offers of service and praise in exchange for favour, matches the language and the structure of patronage. Such a similarity is also strengthened by the fact that, as Quint puts it, "not only does the lover serve the lady he loves, but the courtier is to love the prince he serves."[49]

In writings on courts, the analogies between the language of love and the language of patronage result in complex patterns that become a precious tool for exploring the dynamics of enchantment with the court, bitter disappointment with it, and residual attraction to it in spite of all the disillusion, which can be found in anti-court documents. This attitude is perfectly summed up in a passage by Matteo Peregrini in the last chapter of his *Difesa del savio in corte* (1634):

> All those who cursed the Court were part of it all the same. And all those who are part of it, curse it. [...] It is a custom of those in love who, the more they curse, the more they love. Such denigrations are denigrations that come from the tongue, and not from the heart. Otherwise they would leave once and for all what they constantly condemn. The curses on the Court in the mouths of a Courtier are the curses of a Lover, not of an Enemy.[50]

The most eloquent testimony to the attraction that the court could exert on prospective courtiers and repentant former courtiers alike comes from a masterpiece of anti-courtly sentiment. In addition to expressing the growing disappointment of early modern courtiers, Tasso's *Malpiglio* presents in the figure of Giovanlorenzo Malpiglio the perfect specimen of a young man fascinated by a romanticized vision of the court. So powerful is Giovanlorenzo's passion for the court that one could advance doubts about the effectiveness on him of the Forestiero Napolitano's advice. In his analysis of the *Malpiglio*, Dain A. Trafton has hypothesized a twofold audience for the text: one group standing behind Giovanlorenzo, and the second behind his courtier father, Vincenzo. According to Trafton, the first group of readers understands only those ideas that agree with their own infatuation, while the second group is not only experienced enough to follow the Forestiero's irony but also prudent enough not to reveal the thoughts they have been led to think.[51]

Trafton's depiction of Giovanlorenzo as a representative of the larger group infatuated with the court is indeed compelling. Giovanlorenzo appears bewitched by the court, in a manner not dissimilar to Rinaldo imprisoned in Armida's enchanted garden. Tasso demonstrates his awareness of such enthralment with the court by having the Forestiero Napolitano tell Giovanlorenzo Malpiglio that he is not surprised by his love for the court:

> It is no wonder, then, Signor Gianlorenzo, that you are in love with the court. It gathers to it the best, or nearly the best, of everything, not only from cities but also from whole nations and kingdoms. It seeks perfection and strives to make perfect whatever comes to it.[52]

The Forestiero's use of the expression "being in love" (*invaghirsi*) and – in the original Italian – of the ambiguous feminine personal pronoun *lei* ("her," instead of a neutral pronoun *essa*) directly recalls the personifications of the court as a charming, bewitching female figure.

The *Malpiglio* is a cleverly ambiguous document, a critique of the court dissimulated as a set of precepts for prospective courtiers, via the autobiographical voice of a court writer who has experienced falling from grace at court in the hardest way possible. Yet one can hear underneath the pungent irony of the Forestiero's praise of the court Tasso's awareness of the power of courtly charms and the tenacity of such an infatuation.

In analysing the connections between love and courtliness, it is also important to stress that the role of lover and the role of courtier are alike in their both being based on a disparity between the one who can grant favour (the beloved or the prince) and the one who assumes a posture of self-abasement in order to request such favour (the lover or the courtier).[53] The interplay of the language of love poetry, dynamics of power, and the issues concerned with the courtier's masculinity has led Quint to reassess the role of female figures and their relationship to male courtiers in the general economy of the *Book of the Courtier*, and to review the widespread interpretation of the book that sees courtiers and court ladies as sharing a common destiny of powerlessness, their role at court being reduced to a merely ornamental function. In Quint's opinion, the structure of the *Book of the Courtier*, by investing its female protagonists with the power of controlling and correcting the behaviour of male courtiers, eventually "aligns the court lady not with the disempowered courtier, but with the prince who has power over him."[54]

This parallelism between the court lady and the prince opens the path to further analysis concerning not only the public dimension of courtly life but also the courtier's selfhood. The investigation of the courtier's self and identity in relation to issues of gender roles at court becomes relevant when one considers that, as Guido Ruggiero has pointed out, "court ladies [...] were the officially recognized group that disciplined and recognized the identity of male courtiers as true courtiers and lovers."[55] Furthermore, according to Virginia Cox, Cesare Gonzaga's defence of the relevance of a discussion of the court lady in the third book of the *Book of the Courtier* affirms the centrality and the structural necessity of the presence of women for the court. In Cox's reading, women patrons as dedicatees of poetry were a way for male poets to profess their allegiance to "the ideal of courtliness and ultimately to the power system that underlay it."[56] If court ladies are to be understood as the structural core of the court, and as responsible for conferring on a man the identity of courtier and lover, it comes as no surprise that a rejection of courtliness and of one's courtly identity would also imply a reaction against the figure considered foundational to the former and in charge of the latter. Scenarios where a woman in possession of devilish charms embodies the court and its allures, such as the palace of the witch Gelfora or the artificial paradises created by Alcina and Armida, illustrate cases in which courtiership becomes a nightmare and the identity of courtier and lover is converted into a de-individualizing prison. For Ruggiero, in particular, his identity as a member of Alcina's court and as a lover of the court ruler becomes a complete negation of his former identity ("[a]ll about him was sickly, all but his name"),[57] everything else about him having been wiped out by the seductions of his golden prison.

Court ladies and courtly power

The disquieting, overpowering, and de-individualizing female figures portrayed in epic poems recall a recurring feature of misogynist discourse: the fear of women holding a position of power. Seen as weak bodies hosting whimsical minds, women were considered naturally unfit for legal and political authority or responsibility. Using a female figure to portray a dystopian realm, therefore, was rooted in a tradition that saw "female rule in itself as a perversion of natural order."[58] The court, already the object of satirical representations that depicted it as a world turned upside-down (*mondo alla rovescia*) could also appear as a suspicious reversal of the natural order for the significant role that its environment could grant to women, and hence become the epitome of the disastrous consequences of subverting such order as well.

In representations of contemporary life at court, the anxieties surrounding women in a position of power result in scenarios wherein the evils of the court proceed from an influential female figure whose misdeeds unleash all sorts of suspicions, jealousies, and vengeances, with disastrous consequences for virtuous members of the court. An eloquent example is novella 6, part 4 in Matteo Bandello's *Novelle*:[59] the story of the cruel Duchess of Burgundy. The wanton duchess, unworthy wife to a just and generous duke, is stricken with desire for her husband's favourite courtier, the noble Carlo, and repeatedly tries to seduce him. When Carlo rejects her advances, protesting his faith to his prince, the duchess gives way to a spiral of jealousy and slander that leads the duke to do wrong to his faithful courtier and that eventually concludes with Carlo's death, after the duchess has turned a harmonious court environment into one of the courtly hells described by anti-court satires.

The uneasiness that surrounded the relative prominence and influence that the courtly environment could grant to women explains how it was possible, even in the peaceful courtly society depicted by Castiglione, for the role of authority granted to two otherwise praised and respected female figures such as the duchess and Emilia Pio to put them at risk of being resented by the same courtiers who professed love and admiration for them. In opposition to these potentially conservative, unspoken nuances surrounding the representation of women and the definition of their role in society, scholarship has also pointed out that women are pivotal to the "civil conversation" that is the foundation of courtliness.[60] The court lady configured in the *Book of the Courtier* needs to possess a "pleasing affability" ("affabilità piacevole") that will make her able to "entertain" ("intertenere") her interlocutors in a decorous way and to be the fulcrum of courtly conversation.[61] Despite the fact that rulers' consorts did counsel their spouses, and could themselves be de facto rulers for significant periods of time, the idea of a court lady who becomes an advisor to her *Signora* is introduced only as a mere suggestion. The possibility that a court lady could ever act as an advisor to a male ruler is completely excluded.[62]

Court ladies and courtly competition

In spite of the frequent mention of cut-throat competition among male courtiers, early modern Italian texts very rarely transferred the same topic to court ladies. Yet one can easily infer that the rivalry and envy that plagued the life of male courtiers affected court ladies with no less intensity.[63] A clear evidence of such rivalry can be found in a novel set at court, bearing the intriguing title *La pazzesca pazzia degl'huomini e donne di corte innamorati, ovvero il cortigiano disperato*.

La pazzesca pazzia, published in Venice in 1592 by Giulio Somasco,[64] is the work of Gabriele Pascoli da Ravenna, a Lateran canon who mainly authored religious works. The narrative – a story of jealousy and love quarrels at court – revolves around the events that follow the discovery of a distressed young man named Gioseffo wandering in a forest. He is later revealed to be a former courtier at the Barcelona court who has fled after having been let down by both his prince, who opposed his love interest in a court lady named Panfilia, and by the lady herself, who broke off their engagement as soon she was informed of the prince's disapproval. In Gioseffo's eyes, prince and lady are allies who disregard and refuse to reward their faithful suitor and servant, and Gioseffo's resentment toward both of them epitomizes the conflation of anti-courtly and anti-feminist sentiments. With the help of Gregorio, the gentleman who has found him in the forest and who has become his closest friend, Gioseffo will take revenge on Panfilia, deceiving her with fake love letters with the forged signature of another courtier, making her lose her honour in front of the whole court, and leading, finally, to her dying of shame.

In spite of the novel's pro-masculine stance – the conclusion is centred on a praise of friendship among men, defined as the only honest relationship possible – the most complex character is the court lady Panfilia. Both a product and a victim of the system, Panfilia's narrative epitomizes the court as the receptacle of all evils, a corrupt environment that the novel contrasts with the healthy environment represented by male extra-courtly friendship. Tormented by the envy of her fellow court ladies, Panfilia vents her unhappiness over being in love and over living at court in a lamentation wherein courtly love is depicted as the ally of a tyrannical courtly power:

> O adverse fate of mine, you have doubled my suffering [...]; that is being both a lady of the Court, and a Courtesan of Love, two servitudes which are equal in their unhappiness [...]: as court lady I am repaid with ingratitude, as a lover I am rewarded with tears and pain, as a court lady I am the object of envy, as a lover I am fooled and derided by my rivals. As a court lady I am to serve the Gentlewomen, as a lover I surround my beloved with infinite praise, without realizing that I stain myself many times with infinite blame.[65]

Despite the clever gender role reversal represented by Panfilia's outburst – a female lover is here seen as the victim of Love's cruelty – the lady's tragic fate seems to be unavoidable. Panfilia is doomed by her "service" to Love and by her service at court, and courtly rivalry and envy eventually kill her when it becomes evident that her love for a successful courtier is unrequited and that she has lost the prince's favour. The male courtier Gioseffo is instead saved by his decision to forsake the court and courtly love with it, in favour of the sincere affection of his male friend Gregorio. The conclusion of the novel sees Gioseffo and Gregorio return together to their hometown (Ravenna),[66] cementing their bond by marrying each other's sisters. By contrast, *La pazzesca pazzia* leaves no hope for those who remain at court, especially for a young lady such as Panfilia, who is forced to live, as she laments,

> without any protection [...] with no father or mother, under the rule of the ladies of the Court, where you are exposed to a thousand perils, in addition to the torment of the evil tongues of gossiping court ladies, and of courtiers who are never done with you.[67]

Given the picture of life at court for young ladies presented by texts like Pascoli's *Pazzesca pazzia*, it makes sense that in contemporary conduct literature we also sometimes encounter parental anxiety. For a father who had invested much time and money in preparing a gifted daughter for a career as court lady, the steps his daughter would need to take in order to succeed in such a vicious environment could unsettle him to such a point that he might decide to send her to court with a detailed set of instructions on almost every aspect of her life.

Training a successful court lady

Written in the winter of 1585 and published in 1586, Annibale Guasco's *Ragionamento a Donna Lavinia sua figliuola, della maniera del governarsi ella in Corte; andando per Dama alla Serenissima Infante Donna Caterina, Duchessa di Savoia*[68] belongs to the group of texts that take inspiration from the *Book of the Courtier* and strive to adapt its model courtier to the environment of the Italian courts of the second half of the sixteenth century. Conceived as a private set of instructions for a talented child who has been groomed from early infancy for success at court, Guasco's text discloses a picture of female courtiership that is as riddled with hidden obstacles and potential dangers as any late sixteenth-century writing on courts addressed to a male audience.

Guasco's *Ragionamento* is exceptional in being a manual of conduct specifically envisioned for a court lady alone: the unoriginality of Ludovico Domenichi's *La donna di corte* – nothing more than a translation of the second part of Agostino Nifo's *De re aulica*, a text that mainly deals with the male courtier – makes the *Ragionamento* unique in the Italian panorama. As the work of an ambitious father who wants his brilliant daughter to shine at court, Guasco's *Ragionamento* also represents a reverse trend to the Nifo/Domenichi text, as the latter often appears to downsize the role of women within the courtly environment.[69]

Annibale Guasco (1540–1619) was a renowned intellectual born into an important family in Alessandria.[70] For a gentlemen of his time, having a child holding a position at an important court would have meant establishing a network of connections that would benefit the entire family. Lavinia, the most gifted among Guasco's male and female children, was trained for the court due to her extraordinary talents: able to read by age four, Lavinia also revealed aptitudes for music, dance, and calligraphy. Realizing his daughter's uncommon potential, Guasco – as we learn from the *Ragionamento* – devised an intensive educational program uniquely for her and spared no expense to provide her with the best teachers, all with her eventual placement at court in mind. The marriage in 1585 of Carlo Emanuele of Savoy with the Infanta Caterina of Spain and the establishment of their court in Turin represented the long-awaited opportunity for Lavinia to begin her career at court. Caterina's court, independent from that of her husband, was substantial, including more than one hundred people employed in different roles.

Eleven-year-old Lavinia was accepted among the new ladies-in-waiting hired by the Infanta upon her arrival in Turin. The *Ragionamento* is presented as having been written on the occasion of Lavinia's departure from the paternal house and entrance at court, and it is structured as a rulebook for her to refer to in every situation of her life at court. It includes a range of instructions, from how to preserve and refine her skills to how to manage her possessions, from dealing with her princess and fellow ladies-in-waiting to how to treat her personal staff. The *Ragionamento* belongs to the popular early modern genre of conduct manuals for women, meant to provide instructions for every possible situation in the life of a woman, while always reminding her of the importance of chastity and of preserving her honour.[71] Yet this text intriguingly combines references to traditional womanly virtues such as humility and modesty with the career-oriented references appropriate for a manual of conduct at court.

Guasco's *Ragionamento* is, after all, the *Book of the Courtier* turned from theory into practice.[72] The tireless educational process that Guasco had devised for his daughter and the careful instructions intended to address all possible issues of her new life attest to an attempt to shape the perfect court lady not only in words but in also in reality. In Lavinia's case, this attempt turned out to be very successful. Her accomplishments received recognition, and she was able to secure a stable position at the court of the Infanta Caterina. One is tempted to wonder, however, whether this realization of the model envisioned in the *Book of the Courtier* can be defined as successful precisely by virtue of Lavinia's gender: as an attempt at shaping a court lady, whose involvement in politics would in any case be more limited – or at least more indirect – by the fact that she was a woman, the delicate issue of the courtier's actual role raised in the fourth book could be put aside.

Yet Guasco's *Ragionamento* seems to have been read by contemporaries as something more than a conduct manual for court ladies – or at least, this is the impression that one gets from a letter to Guasco by Stefano Guazzo, in which Guazzo defines Guasco's instructions for his daughter as an attempt to reform courts and courtiers.[73] In the letter, Guazzo thanks Guasco for having praised his work in the *Ragionamento*, and he thanks Lavinia for having decided to print the manuscript of the text her father had given her as a parting gift,[74] so that its precious advice can be a benefit to everyone. More interestingly, Guazzo also reads the *Ragionamento* as a dissimulated attempt to reform courts and courtiers under the pretext of instructing Lavinia and praises the virtuous stratagem ("il virtuoso artificio") that Guasco has employed "in threatening one and wounding one hundred" ("nel minacciar uno, et nel ferir cento"), since "in instructing his daughter, he has instructed and reformed all Courtiers" ("istruendo la figliuola, ha instrutti, et riformati i Corteggiani").[75]

Guazzo's reading of the *Ragionamento* as an attempted reform of the court is surprising, since there is no statement to that end anywhere in the text. The image of the court there presented is, as in many other manuals of court conduct of the time, anything but flattering. Courtly life is depicted as a ruthless competition for favour, wherein the only form of defence is – as the Forestiero Napoletano told Giovanlorenzo Malpiglio – lying low to avoid attacks. Tasso expressed this concept through a comparison with wrestling; Guasco depicts court envies as furious beasts ("fiere rabbiosissime"),[76] and recommends humility as the only effective weapon, "for not even wild bears attack a prostrate prey."[77]

Despite the advice to resort to humility to protect herself from envy,[78] Lavinia, unlike Giovanlorenzo Malpiglio, is never advised to hide her talents. On the contrary, she must constantly search for opportunities to shine, especially in front of her princess's eyes. Showcasing her multiple talents, Guasco believes, is Lavinia's key to success at court. Lavinia's superior talent and hard work will – he seems to imply – sooner or later be noticed, and he appears convinced that someone equipped with such rare gifts will eventually be rewarded.

Courtly competition and the court *virtuose*

Guasco's hopes for a bright future for his exceptional child might have been supported by the awareness that accomplished young women such as Lavinia were increasingly sought after at court. Early modern Italy saw the rise of the phenomenon of the *virtuose*: women with multifaceted artistic talents who became real sensations within courtly environments. Because of their talent and success, progressively acquiring fame as writers, artists, and musicians in their own right,[79] these women became for their male counterparts simultaneously an audience to please, interlocutors for intellectual confrontation, and potential rivals. As rivals, they may have been considered threatening competition to male courtiers for patronage, and this suspicion also reinforced the connection between hostility against the court environment and hostility toward women.

Not only the status of *virtuosa* but the term itself was potentially problematic. As Fredrika Jacobs has pointed out, the term *virtuosa* challenged early modern gender standards. A *virtuoso* was a man of exceptional talent, moral qualities, and good looks. The denotation of *virtuosa*, however, was complicated by the fact that the traditional feminine virtues of passivity and silence contrasted with the public dimension implicit in an artistic profession.[80]

The most interesting case study involving *virtuose* at court is the celebrated Ferrarese *concerto delle donne*.[81] Created in the 1580s by Duke Alfonso II and his third wife, Margherita Gonzaga, the *concerto delle donne* was the duke and duchess's main interest in this period – even "a sort of obsession," according to Anthony Newcomb.[82] As soon as its fame was established, imitations of the sensational *concerto* started to appear in the principal courts of Italy, such as Rome, Florence, and Mantua. The *concerto delle donne* in Ferrara evolved from an amateur group of courtiers and court ladies with singing skills to a professional ensemble composed of the renowned women singers Laura Peperara, Livia d'Arco, and Laura Guarini (and according to some sources, Tarquinia Molza as well), who were brought to court primarily by virtue of their musical talent and were formally designated ladies-in-waiting to the duchess.[83] During the *concerto*'s first period of activity, the ensemble included a male voice as well, the temperamental gentleman, soldier, and bass singer Giulio Cesare Brancaccio, who, as in the case of the ladies, held an official appointment as a courtier.

The extraordinary visibility to which the court ladies/singers participating in such ensembles were exposed could easily have given rise to the harshest envy of fellow courtiers, who were also competing for the spotlight at court. The prestige held by the ladies who formed the *concerto delle donne* also clashed with the views of those who deemed women unable to achieve excellence at court. An example of this attitude can be found in Nifo's *De re aulica*. Nifo, who supported the Galenic view of women as perpetual children and therefore incapable of any noteworthy deeds,[84] approved of the presence of women at court only as a concession: since the court was divided into two parts, one for the prince and one for his wife, it was necessary for a princess to have her own entourage of ladies.[85] Highly successful figures such as the *virtuose* who formed the Ferrarese *concerto* were a living contradiction of similar conservative theories on the role of women at court. Furthermore, the status of *virtuosa*, perceived as inappropriate in terms of gender roles, reinforced an idea of the court as a female-dominated *mondo alla rovescia*, where traditional manly occupations and virtues were held in less consideration.

The warrior who sang with court ladies

The figure of Giulio Cesare Brancaccio and the story of his troubled relationship with the Ferrarese court are an eloquent example of the additional issues that the rise of the court *virtuose* introduced to the already complicated gender dynamics at court. Brancaccio, born into the Neapolitan nobility, was known for having taken part in numerous military campaigns and for his extraordinary bass singing voice.[86] After some tumultuous experiences in armies and at courts in Italy and abroad, Brancaccio seems to have joined the Este court in the late 1570s,[87] most likely hoping to obtain recognition for his military expertise.[88] He was soon to be disappointed. By 1580, Brancaccio must have realized that the duke's main interest in his presence at court lay not in his military prowess, and not even in his courtly skills, but in having him sing together with the *donne*. In a resentful letter to Alfonso II, Brancaccio accused the duke of considering him lacking in courtly manners to the point of seeming afraid that he could be an embarrassment to guests, and stated that he considered himself underestimated not only as a soldier but also as a courtier.[89] In his mid-sixties at the time, eager to be recognized as a military expert thanks to his commentary on the *De Bello Gallico* and notorious for his arrogance, Brancaccio might have appeared to the court as the reincarnation of the boastful soldier evoked in the first book of the *Book of the Courtier* who is lectured by a lady on the appropriate behaviour to follow at court. At court there is no room for those who refuse to ever leave their armour behind,

> for to such as these one may rightly say what in polite society a worthy lady jestingly said to a certain man (whom I do not wish to name) whom

> she sought to honor by inviting him to dance, and who not only declined this but would not listen to music or take any part in the other entertainments offered him, but kept saying that such trifles were not his business. And when finally the lady said to him: "What then is your business?" he answered with a scowl: "Fighting." Whereupon the lady replied at once, "I should think it a good thing, now that you are not away at war or engaged in fighting, for you to have yourself greased all over and stowed away in a closet along with all your battle gear, so that you won't grow any rustier than you already are"; and so, amid much laughter from those present, she ridiculed him in his stupid presumption.[90]

The role of singer posed two issues for Brancaccio, one related to his identity as a noble-born courtier and the other to his masculinity. Duke Alfonso's court differed from other courts for its treatment of music in relation to courtiership: instead of limiting the performance of music to a private activity practised by and for noble-born courtiers, Alfonso hired professional musicians, arranged their marriages with gentlewomen to have them acquire noble status,[91] and then had his singers give public performances that a gentleman such as Brancaccio may have found inappropriate.[92] The anti-court discontent of someone in Brancaccio's position was hence more dramatic than the discontent of the *literatus* turned courtier: while the latter could complain (as Ariosto did in his *Satire*) of having little time to dedicate to the pursuit of literary glory, Brancaccio saw his identity as a nobleman, as a man of arms, and as a courtier – an identity that seemed the realization of what the *Book of the Courtier* advocated – denied, and witnessed his status reduced to that of a lowly professional musician. At the same time, the treatment that Brancaccio received from the duke – who, although holding Brancaccio in high esteem, made him perform against his will on several occasions – is also a testimony to the increasingly absolutistic attitudes of princely figures in the late sixteenth century.

In addition, Brancaccio's military pride was, as in the case of the self-important soldier quoted in the *Book of the Courtier*, wounded through the company of women, and his role as a male singer in an otherwise all-woman ensemble may have been a further source of discontent. Or at least his position appeared problematic to Torquato Tasso, who, in a poem dedicated to Brancaccio, represents him as endangered by the "siren voices" of the lady singers. Tasso must have seen a kindred spirit in this fellow Neapolitan troubled by difficult relations with the duke and the court. In one of the three poems he dedicated to Brancaccio in the early 1580s,[93] Tasso laments the harsh destiny ("dura sorte") that led Brancaccio away from his homeland and describes his own similar condition as a wandering pilgrim ("peregrino errante").[94] As already pointed out by Richard Wistreich, Tasso's representation of Brancaccio in a poem titled "A Giulio Cesare Brancaccio per il concerto de le dame a la corte di Ferrara" echoes the passage in the *Gerusalemme Liberata* where the paladins Carlo and Ubaldo (on their mission to rescue Rinaldo from Armida's garden) are tempted by the sirens' songs but are ultimately able to render themselves deaf to the temptation.[95] Brancaccio is, in fact, advised likewise to close his ears to the sweet voices of the *donne*:

> Sir, Love has found you
> Among new sirens,
> Such that our arenas may never have heard.
> Oh, close your ears to this sound
> And open your eyes to sleep.[96]

Despite the similarity with the episode of the paladins rescuing Rinaldo, it is important to point out one major difference. While Carlo and Ubaldo were tempted by sirens when travelling through a faraway land, the sirens threatening Brancaccio inhabited the core of the court. By presenting the Ferrara court as populated by sirens, Tasso offers a depiction of it as a feminized space, where masculine valour is constantly under the attack of feminine guiles. The poem also portrays the concerted singing of Brancaccio and the ladies as a quarrel between Phoebus Apollo and Love, where Phoebus is championed by the male singer and the ladies are Love's emissaries. Brancaccio is represented as difficult prey for Love's poison, owing to his disdain of foolish pleasures ("piacer folli") and feminine wit ("feminino ingegno"). But Love is set on conquering him and defeating Phoebus, and only hardening his *sdegno* or running away will save him:

> [F]light and oblivion
> Are safer wherever Love sings or smiles.
> Flee, or Disdain will harden you
> And make of you such hard fibre
> That sweet pleasures will not be able to soften your heart.[97]

In the final lines of the poem the two gods are each proclaimed victor over the other, and thus are both losers; similarly, Brancaccio's song overcomes that of the ladies, but he is won over by their eyes and imprisoned in sweet chains. The poem ends on a conciliatory note, yet the injunction to "flee" ("fuggi"), uttered by a poet who was undergoing the most difficult period of his relationship with the courtly milieu, leaves the reader with a disquieting feeling about courtly life in Ferrara.

The representation of the Ferrara ladies as sirens, furthermore, is cleverly set to pay apparent homage to the enchanting quality of their voices while at the same time introducing some less flattering insinuations about their femininity (echoed in the reference to the pleasures that Brancaccio holds in disdain). The condition of women singers in the Renaissance was indeed problematic. According to Bonnie Gordon, the status of women singers was controversial during the Renaissance, a perception rooted in a sexualized vision of the female voice. The reason was based, once again, in the contemporary understanding of female anatomy: the body parts related to singing – the mouth, the throat, and the tongue – were associated with a woman's sexual and reproductive organs.[98] Even in the case of women singers who were noble born, and also respectable by virtue of their marriages of high rank, their musical activity could raise suspicions about their status and their chastity. In a society obsessed with women's chastity, an activity that involved such association could easily prompt concern or disapproval. Singing, as well as dancing, also involved putting one's body on display, another feature that contradicted prescriptions for chastity. A further complication was the association between music and courtesans. Courtesans, in fact, were famous for using musical performances as part of their practice of seduction.[99] Through music, a respectable *donna di palazzo* might find herself associated with the infamous *cortigiana*. The connection to courtesans, however, was not an issue for the court lady alone: despite the gender difference, the courtesan was a haunting presence for the courtier as well.

Cortigiano, donna di corte, cortigiana

The early modern period also saw the emergence of *cortigiane* (courtesans), women of mostly humble origins who were in some cases able to attain literary fame and considerable wealth while at the same time embodying a total rejection of the dogma of female chastity. The use of periphrases such as *donna di corte* (court lady) or *donna di palazzo* (lady of the palace) in court manuals to refer to the female counterpart of the *cortigiano* instead of the feminine *cortigiana* was a prudent way to avoid the ambiguities implied in a term that had come to designate high-class prostitutes. The term *cortigiana* is, clearly, semantically derived from *corte* as is the masculine *cortigiano*: specifically, it originated from the Roman papal *corte*, where it was used to refer to the sexual companions of prelates.[100] Hence *cortigiane* were immediately relatable to courts and courtiers. The risks associated with this semantic analogy are pointed out by Sperone Speroni, who, in his *Orazione contra le cortigiane* (1575), recounts how a certain honourable gentleman ("qualche onorevole cavaliere") that is, Baldassar Castiglione, was forced to resort to the term "donna di palazzo" to avoid any correlation between the socially respectable court lady and the despicable courtesan.[101]

Speroni's caution in distancing the *cortigiana* from the *donna di corte* hints at the disquieting notion that some may see these two figures as not totally unrelated. As pointed out by Adriana Chemello, the courtesan was at the same time a "downgrade" of the chaste court lady and an actualization of the capacity for love, which in the case of the court lady was to be limited to the idealized sphere of the conventions of courtly love. The intellectual and social virtues of the court lady – elegance, wit in conversation, refined education – remained the same.[102]

If the courtesan could represent a disturbing figure for the court lady, she was an even more disquieting mirror for the male courtier. Courtiers and courtesans alike, in fact, relied on the ability to ingratiate potential patrons by making a show of themselves and their qualities. Both shared anxieties about upward social mobility: dreams of being rewarded by their patrons and nightmares of falling from grace. The rapid rise and at times dramatic fall of these women has prompted scholars to draw a parallel between the fate of the courtesan and that of the courtier. These studies read misogynist anti-courtesan satires as the reaction of disabused courtiers against the subjection and the loss of dignity that the courtier and the courtesan have in common.[103]

The similar destiny of courtiers and courtesans has been thoroughly investigated over the past few years.[104] In particular, Margaret Rosenthal has analysed texts such as Sperone Speroni's *Orazione contra le cortigiane*, Pietro Aretino's *Sei giornate*, and the anti-courtesan satires authored by Lorenzo and Maffio Venier to show that Venetian satirists used courtesans as the target of their satires in order to differentiate themselves and their own patronage-seeking techniques from the supposedly immoral and shameful techniques of the courtesan.[105] Rosenthal argues that since Venetian "freedom" actually required a measure of prostituting oneself to powerful urban patrons and political leaders,[106] the frequent anti-feminism of Venetian satirical writings finds an explanation in the male authors' uneasiness about their relationship to patronage.[107]

Aretino's *Sei giornate* – six dialogues featuring prostitutes and *ruffiane*, set in Rome but written and published in Venice between 1534 and 1536 – and Speroni's oration (1575) stand in sharp contrast to each other for their authors' attitudes toward courtesans, and for their reactions to the link between *cortigiana, cortigiano,* and *corte.* Speroni's *Orazione* is a call for repentance addressed to an imaginary interlocutor. In denouncing the sins of courtesanship, Speroni also refuses any associations between the *cortigiana* – defined as "devoid of any good, and always replete with all the vices that could ever be in a bedeviled human heart"[108] – and the *corte* and *cortigiano,* since

> the court is the abode of courtesy, and courtesy is virtue, or is not without virtues, rather it is composed of many virtues, as electrum is composed of gold and silver; especially of generosity, and mercy, and discretion, and modesty, all prudently gathered in those who make up the household of a valiant lord.[109]

Speroni acknowledges that the term *cortigiana* may have been introduced with the intent of flattering courtesans, or (and even worse) of blaming the court, but he wants to underscore that in fact no relationship whatsoever exists between courts and courtesans. To prove this point, Speroni states that

> these sinners hold court in many places throughout Italy where there is no court, but where there are certainly houses and palaces; and where there are a prince and a court, harlots serve not only courtiers, but also the general populace.[110]

Speroni's *Orazione contra le cortigiane* was written at the request of the Roman Inquisition, at the time when Speroni's *Dialoghi* were under examination after an anonymous denunciation.[111] The vehement anti-courtesan tone of the *Orazione* is not surprising in post-Tridentine Rome, when the popes were actively trying to reform city morals and were taking particularly harsh measures against prostitution.[112] Similarly, its pro-court defence may be explained by referring to the author's intention to establish connections with the papal court of Rome, where Speroni was intending to relocate from his native Padua. What is surprising is for such a text to have been written by the same author who had portrayed the famous courtesan Tullia d'Aragona as one of the main characters of his *Dialogo d'amore,* a fact that raises doubts about the sincerity of its anti-courtesan invective. Whether a genuine expression of the author's mind or simply intended to curry favour with the Inquisition and the papal court, the *Orazione contra le cortigiane* is striking in its effort to separate courtiers from any association with courtesans, thus providing a testimony to how common such an association was in contemporary culture.

Unlike Speroni's *Orazione*, Aretino's dialogues show undeniable sympathy on the part of the author for his less-than-honourable characters. In addition, there is no attempt to distance courtiers from courtesans; rather, there are continuous remarks that they are "on the same scales" ("in una medesima bilancia"),[113] whether semantically or socially. Courtesans behave just like courtiers – the courtesan Nanna explains – and this should not be a surprise: courtiers have given courtesans their name, and so "it was necessary that they also gave us their face."[114] Courtier and courtesan are both faces of a society – the Rome of the papal court – that is ruthless and individualistic, one whose inhabitants are forced to resort to fraud in order to survive; as Nanna states, "The whores of today look like the courtiers of today, in that they need to steal for their own well-being: otherwise they would die of starvation."[115] True to her word, Nanna will prepare her daughter Pippa for courtesanship by teaching her to steal ("mariolare"), to please, to flatter, to deceive – in short, to use every possible means (just as courtiers do)[116] to win her clients' favour and extort as much as possible from them.

The *Sei giornate* has been compared to formational manuals describing the path to accomplishment in one's profession, such as the *Book of the Courtier*, which the *Sei giornate* is considered both to imitate and to satirize.[117] The harshest parody of Castiglione's dialogue in the *Sei giornate* is to be found not only in its converting the formation of the perfect (and moral) courtier into the creation of the perfect (immoral) courtesan, but also in its exposing some of the more problematically nuanced moral positions of the *Book of the Courtier* and taking to the extreme some of its potentially ambiguous pieces of advice. Alessandro Piccolomini's *La Raffaella, ovvero Dialogo della bella creanza delle donne* (1539) – a dialogue wherein the old procuress of the title persuades the young, neglected wife Margarita to cheat on her husband – shares the same irreverent and morally questionable perspective. Throughout the dialogue the *ruffiana* (procuress) Raffaella captivates her interlocutor, just as the courtier is advised to do with his prince, and yet the goal, in this case, is to lead Margarita everywhere but on the path of virtue. Likewise, the dissimulating techniques that were suggested in the *Book of the Courtier* with an ultimately noble end in mind are here converted into the tricks of adulterers. Also meaningful is Raffaella's warning to Margarita that the advice she is about to receive from her may seem like a peccadillo ("peccatuzzo") and yet, given the circumstances, is totally sensible. And most of all, the important thing is that everything be done with dexterity ("destrezza") and wit ("ingegno") so that one's name is not stained by dishonour.[118]

Texts like the *Sei giornate* and *La Raffaella* evoke the moral dilemmas and the "rhetoricization of ethics" present in the *Book of the Courtier*,[119] and reinterpret them in an unscrupulous guise in order to distort morality in the sphere of marriage and sexuality. The individualism and the dubious morals of these texts are the signs of a society that, after the crises of the Sack of Rome and of the Protestant Reformation, was led more and more toward safeguarding individual interests rather than investing in higher ideals.[120] Once again, misogynistic stereotypes, especially the commonplace polemical targets of the adulteress and the prostitute, provide useful figures to depict a crisis of traditional morals. Intriguingly, anti-court and anti-courtier sentiments are now included – a sign that courts and courtiers had also come to represent the popular face of a society that was perceived as increasingly meretricious.

The connection between the courtesan and the courtier is developed in depth in a text featuring both figures as its main characters: Michelangelo Biondo's *Angitia cortigiana: De natura del cortigiano* (1540).[121] The Venetian-born Biondo was a doctor who had studied in Naples under the supervision of Agostino Nifo and later moved to Rome and joined the papal court.[122] In the last years of his life he went back to his native Venice, where he was among Pietro Aretino's circle of friends.[123] The date of publication of the *Angitia*, following shortly after the publication of the second part of Aretino's *Sei giornate*, suggests a correlation between the two texts.[124] Like the *Sei giornate*, Biondo's dialogue has a courtesan (the eponymous Angitia) as one of its main speakers, seen in conversation with the old courtier Aristeo. Their conversation is imagined as having happened during a trip to Rome, where Angitia is headed to seek better fortune in her profession.[125] The *Angitia* is divided into two parts: the first explores the relationship between the courtier and the courtesan, while the second focuses on the courtesan and the notion of courtesy. Scholarly analysis of the *Angitia* has often pointed out its strict moralistic tone (coherent with the author's traditionalist and anti-feminist mentality), which is particularly evident in the condemnation of courtesans.

What is fascinating in the *Angitia*, however, is that the author's condemnation incorporates the courtier as well, and that the courtier and the courtesan are portrayed as two complementary figures – literally as each other's half. Biondo quotes the myth of the androgyne from Plato's *Symposium* to portray courtiers and courtesans as two parts of the same entity, constantly seeking each other's embrace to restore their lost unity.[126] There is nothing flattering to courtiers and courtesans, however, in Biondo's reference to the Platonic myth. The two figures are equated for being vicious, untrustworthy, and for constantly playing tricks on each other for the sake of their own interests. Aristeo, on the one hand, warns Angitia against trusting courtiers, since a courtier "thinks of nothing but fraud, deceits, harms, and rapes,"[127] and further reminds her that "those who cheekily occupy the profession of Courtier are the most miserable, the most unhappy, the dirtiest, the filthiest and the most perverted of men, and are like a wall that has been whitewashed."[128] On the other hand, he defines the courtesan as "the universal plague, the inextricable ruin and the indelible stain of those who mingle with her,"[129] and as "the haze that covers the true and largely illuminates the false."[130] Both, in the end, are equally disgraced, as evident from the name they share: "Oh how unhappy is the fate of the Courtier, though I hear that you are miserable too, since you and the Courtier are adorned with the same name."[131] And, consequently, their destinies are connected: as Aristeo tells Angitia, "[N]o other fortune turns your wheel, Courtesan, than that of the Courtier, and in the opposite direction."[132] In the *Angitia*, anti-courtier and anti-courtesan sentiments merge with a clarity that is not found in any other work: anti-courtesan allegations mirror anti-courtier ones almost word for word. Both, in Biondo's opinion, live the most immoral of lives, and both are doomed to eventual ruin.

Tomaso Garzoni's "De' cortigiani e delle donne di corte insieme," in the *Piazza universale*,[133] similarly expands the condemnation of the meretricious behaviour of courtiers to include court ladies. In Garzoni's text, in fact, there seems to be no difference at all between court ladies and courtesans. Completely corrupted by the false values of "the courtly books of love ("i libri cortigiani d'amore") and by old matrons who instruct young women in all wrongdoing, the *donne di corte* are intent only on grooming their appearance with clothing, makeup, and perfumes, all with the purpose "to seduce, to steal, to plot, to enchant, to bewitch their lovers, the [...] womanly arts being nothing other than deceits, frauds, spells, and the falseness of enchantments."[134] The concluding sentence might lead the reader to consider these critiques against court ladies as inspired by traditional misogynist stereotypes alone, and therefore as attacking court ladies more as women than as members of a court. Yet once again, male courtiers are likewise accused of meretricious behaviour. More precisely (as already pointed out by Rosenthal),[135] Garzoni's text constitutes one further example where courtiers are depicted as having exactly the same vices as courtesans: flattery, duplicity, treachery, and greed.

The parallel between courtiers and courtesans provided by texts such as Biondo's *Angitia*, Aretino's *Sei giornate*, and Garzoni's *Piazza universale* has been employed by recent scholarship primarily to explain satirical attacks against courtesans. Yet this connection also sheds light on the reasons behind the growing uneasiness with the figure of the courtier. One of the most common accusations against the courtesan is that she has no high purpose in mind: all she wants is money, favours, commodities. According to anti-courtier satires, so does the courtier: all the statements concerning his role as an advisor to his prince or his dedication to art and culture are lies used to hide his greed. Equally false are the courtesan's declarations of love for her paramours and the courtier's affection for his prince. The courtier and the courtesan are similarly unable to love: as Aretino's Nanna points out, "[i]t is impossible that those who submit themselves to everyone love anyone."[136] With the sole aim of satisfying their greed, the courtier and the courtesan renounce what everyone should hold most dear: independence and control over one's own persona. Both are constantly performing, and both are ready to become whatever their patron wants them to be. Both, furthermore, seem to have put aside any shame to achieve their interest. The courtesan was notorious for her status as a shameless public woman. Deanna Shemek has pointed out that the courtesan's supposed lack of discomfort at being looked at made her body available for display and public performances, which could also include rituals of public shaming.[137] Just like the courtesan, the courtier made a spectacle of himself: he needed to make himself visible to his prince and be eager to perform for his prince's eyes. Through tourneying and dancing, or simply through a display of his refined manners and his exquisite clothes, the courtier was expected to put any shame aside and offer his body to the other's gaze. One further reason for the omnipresence of anti-courtier satire in early modern Italian culture can thus be found in the courtier's appearing to be a "public man" as much as the courtesan appeared a "public woman," and in his resulting availability (like the courtesan's) for being gazed at and for being shamed.

Anti-court texts also offer an explanation for this meretricious behaviour on the part of courtiers. The courtier is an analogue to the courtesan because court society has degenerated from its role as the haven of courtesy to instead become the cradle of whoredom: according to the picture offered by Garzoni in the *Piazza universale*, when a princely court visits a city, at the court's departure one finds the city disfigured, its aspect "changed like the face of a harlot."[138]

The court is a whore

Whoever wants to know what exhaustion and Death are
Can read my lines while I describe
The misery and the dangers of the Court.
A burial and prison for the living man
is what this Circe is, or, better, she transforms a man
from his own true being, as soon as he gets there.
[...]
The court is exactly like a whore,
Who looks pretty on the outside, but on the inside
Has no part that is not corrupted.[139]

The satire *Della corte,* written by Gabriello Simeoni (a Florentine who had been a courtier at Francis I's court in France and at Cosimo I's court in Florence), sums up the allusions to the court's bewitching charm and the innuendos to the meretricious strategies of courtly life by straightforwardly defining the court as a Circe and a whore. Here, the personification of the court as a female figure is taken much further than the figure of the matron offered by Cesare Caporali's *capitolo.* In addition to misogynist stereotypes, the embodiment of the court as a whore evokes an image of an environment structured according to laws that could have been devised by someone like Nanna. Just like the immoral, insolent, but brilliantly successful whore portrayed in the *Sei giornate,* the court devises clever strategies to entice desire, takes as much as she can from those who are naive enough to think they can conquer her, and then discards them when they are no longer of use.

Most importantly, in Simeoni's satire the court resembles a whore in seeming healthy only in its external appearance, while in reality it hides an infectious internal decay. Anti-courtesan satires denounced courtesans as carriers of syphilis (*malfrancese*), the disfiguring and often fatal disease that the sex trade was spreading in early modern cities.[140] The court, in Simeoni's *Della corte,* becomes the agent of an equally infectious plague that, just like the *malfrancese,* deforms whoever is affected by it:

But let us just mention how this court
changes anyone, both in mores and his very skin
be he unaccustomed to vice, or to virtue.[141]

But while the disease transmitted by the courtesan infects just the body, the one transmitted by the court goes to a deeper level, corrupting a man in his morality. Since the court is – once more, like a whore – entirely made of deceit and fraud (as Simeoni puts it, "The Court is filled with envies and deceits / with a brow decorated with roses and violets"),[142] anyone who wants to preserve himself from its corruption or who tries to present himself as non-corrupted must focus on the antithesis of the court's elegant frauds: that is to say, an unpolished truthfulness. The figure of the satirist, who makes coarse sincerity his own trademark, thus becomes the only antidote to the depravity of the court's meretricious techniques.

Chapter Three

The Satirist

A paradise for satirists

According to the Roman satirist Juvenal, satire was not at all difficult to write. On the contrary, given the conditions of the Rome he was living in, it was hard *not* to write it.[1] Juvenal's motto surely spoke to Renaissance Italian court writers. Not writing satire seems to have been hard for them, too – at least, if we are to believe the picture of court life they present to readers.

As an institution with a recognizable power structure, the court had been a common polemical target much earlier than the period we now call the Renaissance. Yet critics of the court flourished particularly during this period. The sycophants, parasites, buffoons, and ambitious social climbers of all sorts that populated the courtly milieu, together with the perceived effeminacy of its courtiers and the wantonness of its ladies, made the court an ideal target for whoever wanted to denounce the moral decay of society. As the vogue for satire spread, the court became a subject that one could expect to find in any work titled "Satire" or "Capitoli piacevoli."[2] In such works, the court, portrayed as the epitome of corruption and the antithesis to morality, stood as the ideal foil to the figure of the satirist, who became the embodiment of rectitude.

It is necessary, however, to ask how trustworthy this picture of both the satirist and the scene that surrounded him could be. Given that in early modern sources negative depictions of life at court overwhelm any positive ones, one may be tempted to take the representations of the court offered by satiric writings at face value.

Certainly, the ruthless competition among peers and the rapid changes of fortune that characterized court life lend some reliability to the picture of the court as a stormy sea wherein one could very easily be shipwrecked – to refer to one of the most common metaphors of court life. Confronted with such a reality, and in an age when the possible role of the intellectual in society and his relation with those in power was being widely discussed, the court *literatus* could likely have felt the call to become a critical conscience of the world around him. Nevertheless, some caution is necessary when dealing with the pictures of the speaker and his milieu offered by satiric writings. As Alvin Kernan has pointed out in *The Cankered Muse*, the figure saying "I" in satire should be understood as a poetic device employed by the author. Although this poetic device – the "I" of satire – could be varied to suit different purposes, it invariably draws on a set of fixed features that were established by the satiric tradition; in spite of their presentation as truthful self-portraits of a single author in a specific moment of his life, all self-representations offered by satirists inevitably share some predetermined common features.[3] Specifically, the satirist inevitably tries to present himself as "a blunt, honest man, with no nonsense about him."[4] In keeping with this persona, the satirist stresses his lack of style and his use of an everyday plain language. The scene of the satire, the background for the reflections of the satirist, is similarly constituted by a series of recognizable features: a chaotic and crowded place where vices appear to prosper.[5]

The flocks of ambitious courtiers from many different backgrounds that populated Renaissance courts, their being forced to live in close quarters, their often frantic quest for favours and promotions, the efforts to display magnificence and splendour, and the antics of some princes rendered the court the perfect setting for satire. Anyone who regretted his experience at court could easily feel an affinity with the persona of the honest satirist and expose through the satirist's voice the shortcomings of the courtly milieu that he had experienced. Satire, in this way, became an outlet for frustration and payback in verse against those who had wronged its author. Still, the popularity enjoyed by anti-court satire in this period suggests that contemporary interest in the topic and the seeming fascination with the figure of the satirist may have gone beyond a simple desire to vent one's misfortune and use verse as a form of denunciation. The satiric persona in Renaissance Italy, that is to say, especially in its anti-courtier form, seems to have been invested with a peculiar significance that may help explain its stunning popularity. The purpose of this chapter will be to investigate which characteristics of the satiric persona and of the satiric setting were emphasized in early modern Italian anti-court satires, and the specific functions such characteristics assumed in the context in which the satires were written.

This chapter analyses satires (both in prose and in formal verse) specifically directed against courts and courtiers and considers them a specific group in the panorama of satiric writings – a set of works with peculiar features that distinguish them from the related set of satires against tyrants or against political corruption in general. In fact, satires that can be labelled "anti-court satires," despite minor differences regarding the specific socio-historical context in which they were written and the authors' biographies, constitute a surprisingly homogeneous category. These features can be summed up as, first of all, the will on the part of a courtier/writer-turned-satirist to distance himself from the reality surrounding him in his daily life at court and to highlight that despite his status as a (current or former) insider to the court system, he is and has always has been an outsider. The outsider perspective that the court satirist assumes (often with an ostentatious tone) enables him not only to reflect on the reality of the court and on his condition as a courtier, and to profess his innocence with respect to the court's crimes, but also to construct for himself a new status and a new persona, which is portrayed as cleansed from the evils that in contrast taint the persona of the courtier. As a consequence, this process of refashioning the courtier-satirist's persona also has repercussions in the sphere of individual identity.

Classical and medieval sources

Greek and Roman satires – mostly the works of Juvenal himself and of Horace – through their representations of flatterers and fortune hunters offered a model for satirizing the behaviour of most courtiers. Moreover, as the Horatian model became the dominant model for satire writing, writers began to reflect on the distance separating their condition from that of the classical poet and the gratitude he felt toward his patron, Maecenas. The Renaissance Italian court and the status of courtier hence became a foil to the serenity professed by the classical poet. In addition to the model theorized by Horace, the figure of Juvenal's spokesperson Umbricius – the moral man proclaiming his otherness to a corrupt environment – became an influential specimen for the self-fashioning of early modern satirists.[6] Renaissance Italian court writers found in Juvenal a kindred soul, thanks to his depictions of the decline of patronage in his time. The indignation of the Juvenalian satiric persona was thus combined in Renaissance Italy with the more intimate but equally moral Horatian one. In general, Roman satire, both in its Horatian and in its Juvenalian forms, was influential precisely for its inherent "stance of the estranged observer who knows he is reluctantly a part of what he is observing,"[7] a stance that clearly was particularly appealing to court writers wanting to distance themselves from the evils of the court.

Similarly influential for the genre of prose satire was the work of the Greek satirist Lucian.[8] Lucian's works, which contained vehement attacks against the flattery and servility of social climbers, became a model for satire against courtiers across Europe, thanks to the numerous Latin and then vernacular translations.[9] In particular, as pointed out by Pauline M. Smith, Lucian established the model for the genre of satirical eulogy – a genre further revived by Erasmus's *Encomium Moriae* – and for satires wherein one of the speakers gives another pieces of advice meant to be read ironically.[10]

If the vogue for the classics that characterized the Renaissance influenced the recuperation of the genre of satire and satiric motifs from classical models, anti-courtliness was not alien to medieval literature, and the legacy of that period also made its mark on the genre's evolution during the Renaissance. The importance that the courts and their associated culture progressively assumed in the Middle Ages throughout all Europe had its counterpart in the rise of anti-court sentiments. Mindful of the motto expressed by Lucan in his *Pharsalia* – *Exeat aula, qui vult esse pius* (Let him, who wants to be good, leave the court)[11] – medieval anti-court critiques targeted the court as a haven for corruption and stressed the dichotomy between the toadying servility, ruthless ambition, and attachment to material goods typical of the courtly milieu, and the Christian values of simplicity and sincerity.[12] A large part of medieval anti-court critiques addressed the papal court and the members of the clergy who opted for a secular career at court instead of pursuing Christian values. Terms such as *corte* or *curia* in medieval anti-court writings almost inevitably refer to the Roman papal curia, which is blamed for betraying the Christian values upon which it was founded. Although the papal court would continue to play a fundamental role as a subject of anti-court writings, in the Renaissance the term *corte* can refer equally to the court of Rome, or to a secular, princely court.

Peter Damian's *Contra clericos aulicos* (ca 1072) was one of the most well known among such invectives.[13] The tradition of critique of the court flourished in particular in twelve-century England, thanks to the works of John of Salisbury (ca 1120–1180), Peter of Blois (ca 1130–ca 1203), Nigel of Longchamps (d. ca 1200), and Walter Map (ca 1140–ca 1208). Salisbury – considered by some critics as the founder of medieval anti-court satire – was, with his *Policraticus*, an important point of reference for Enea Silvio Piccolomini's *De curialium miseriis epistola* (1444),[14] as was Peter of Blois, who fathered the lexical phrase *miseriae curialium* that gave the title to Piccolomini's work. Blois attacked members of the clergy who devoted themselves to the secular interests of the court, decried the lack of temperance in eating and drinking seen among courtiers, and depicted the squalor of the court *tinelli* (the modest communal dining rooms, separate from the princes' banquet halls, where most of the members of a court or a household had their meals). Nigel of Longchamps also condemned clerics involved in the court, seeing them as a receptacle of vices and a source of unhappiness for the virtuous man. Although the papal court was the main target of medieval satire, secular courts were soon addressed as well: an eloquent example is Walter Map's *De nugis curialium,* wherein King Henry II's court is depicted as a hell on earth. The medieval satirist juxtaposes the topsy-turvy world of the court with a picture of himself echoing the basic Christian virtues as personified by Christ himself: simple piety, humility, honest poverty.[15]

Kernan has noticed a significant change in the persona of the satirist in England at the end of the sixteenth century, when "plodding medieval humility"[16] is replaced by an educated satiric persona who makes use of elevated rhetoric and vents his rage at patrons who favour unworthy men and base poetasters instead of virtuous men and accomplished poets. Interestingly, Kernan also links the change in the English satiric persona to the development of the Italian genre of the pasquinade.[17] In Italy, however, and as far as the specific genre of anti-court satire is concerned, the appearance of a rhetorically accomplished and secularized satirical persona occurs much earlier and can be traced back to Enea Silvio Piccolomini's *De curialium miseriis.*

De curialium miseriis and the onset of "modern" anti-court sentiments

Written in the form of a letter addressed to a friend, the jurist Ioannes Haich, and dated 30 November 1444, *De curialium miseriis* is a complaint about life at court based on Piccolomini's direct experience as a courtier.[18] The narrator begins his anti-court epistle with a self-portrait that will become a paradigm for anti-court texts: the ambitious but naive young man who enters the court attracted by its splendours, in spite of advice to the contrary from his own father, who had tried life at court and then left after realizing that happiness can be found only in private life. The father's praise of *optima vita apud privatos* is contrasted with a depiction of courtly life, minutely deconstructed through a detailed analysis of the different discontents that await the courtier-to-be. Ambition is given as the only reason why men tolerate so many vexations. Instead of devoting themselves to the salvation of their soul, men hunt for fame and privilege and put up with anything in order to acquire them.

The theme of the pursuit of salvation as an antidote to courtly ambition is a trope of medieval satires, yet the tone of the remarks on men's earthly aspirations in *De curialium miseriis* is not one of moralistic condemnation but of sympathetic understanding. In this regard, *De curialium miseriis* marks the transition from medieval anti-court sentiments to the more concrete and earthly perspective of early modern anti-court satires. While in medieval anti-court writings the court is rejected as the antithesis to Christian ideals and a distraction from the service of Christ, early modern texts denounce the court as a place of fallen hopes, where the worthless are rewarded while the worthy and virtuous are denied well-deserved honours and material gains. *De curialium miseriis* represents a watershed between the two different phases of the same genre, underscoring at times how court life and its pursuit of material goods contrasts with God's commandments, while simultaneously giving voice to the frustration of those who feel denied the riches and honours they should rightfully expect for their service at court. Heir to the medieval anti-court tradition, Piccolomini innovates by imbuing it with a new perspective: a more worldly and mundane viewpoint that understands ambition without condemning it per se, that stresses the importance of material compensation for one's service, and that is concerned by the court's corruption of morals as much as by its corruption of sensory pleasures. Piccolomini's work also represents a watershed in that while he speaks of "the court" in general, it is very likely that he was referring to the secular courts (or more precisely, the imperial court where he had lived) rather than the Roman papal curia that was often the target of medieval invectives.

Four main aspirations are presented as capable of persuading a young man to enter the court: honour, power, riches, and pleasure. Piccolomini states that he believes that all who enter the court do it in search of material gains; yet he also admits that some may believe they will gain salvation by exposing themselves to the hardships and perils of the court (although immediately he also asserts that he has never known anyone who would join the court for any other reason than mere earthbound interests). But even those trying to acquire virtue from living at court would be, in his opinion, mistaken. The text then proceeds to prove the courtiers' inevitable *stultitia* by taking such hopes down one by one. Piccolomini's scrutiny of honour is aimed at disabusing those who look for upward social mobility, reminding them that at court honours are given not to the virtuous but to the wealthy and powerful.[19] Similarly, riches go to the rich just as waters flow to the sea, and those who dwell in the illusion of attaining wealth by court service give up their liberty without any profit.[20] The hope of gaining power is equally a chimera: the power one can acquire in court is ephemeral, and those who are the most prosperous are more prone to failure. To prove this point, Piccolomini quotes the notorious example of Sejanus, abruptly ruined by his own immoderate ambition.[21] Finally, the pleasures of the court – the powerful troops, the elegant courtiers and beautiful ladies, the splendid palaces and the horses, the garments, the sculptures, the games and pastimes – are delightful solely to those who look at them from the outside, while those who are subjected to the court take no pleasure from them at all. Courtiers cannot help but stumble across something that will embitter their day and deprive them of any possible pleasure.[22]

It is in refuting the idea of courtly life as a possible source of sensory pleasure that *De curialium miseriis* reaches the climax of its critical exposé, analysing all the annoyances of courtly life in relation to each of the five senses and proving in detail how no possible delight could ever come from it. Everything at court that offends the eye is listed first, then everything related to hearing, touch, smell, and taste. In the paragraphs dedicated to pleasures, *De curialium miseriis* collects all the most common anti-court themes of depictions of the evils of court life that would be further developed by later anti-court satires: the squalor in which most courtiers are forced to live, the endless lies of flatterers, the noisy fights among courtiers, and the rancid food, sour wine, and foul smells of the *tinelli*. The hypothetical group of those who think that the tribulations of life at court will make them virtuous is the last one to be addressed. For them, Piccolomini reserves his harshest piece of advice: so many are the vices of the court that no man is virtuous enough to resist. Everyone will be corrupted eventually and dragged away from the right path like a ship brought to shipwreck by a stormy sea.

Through the image of the virtuous man dragged to his ruin, *De curialium miseriis* introduces one more theme that will be central to early modern Italian anti-court satires: the image of a court that becomes a totalizing and uncontrollable force, capable of changing a man's individuality to the point of enslaving him forever in courtly chains. No man can stay virtuous at court, because the court dictates that everyone change his nature to adapt to the needs of courtly life. The courtier cannot be master of his own time, nor even of his own feelings: his meals, his sleep, and his waking hours depend on the often-capricious will of his prince; he must force himself to feel sad when all around him are sad, and happy when all are happy. The courtier is, in other words, deprived of the very basis of his selfhood.

After his painstaking deconstruction of the court, Piccolomini concludes his letter with an exhortation to his friend as well as to himself to leave the stormy sea of the court for a different life.[23] However, in the letter's first pages Piccolomini had openly confessed his inescapable dependency on the court system. Courtiers are compared to husbands who repent having married but who, when their wife dies, immediately get married again; men, in fact, are addicted to the life they have been living to the point of being unable to change it, even when they recognize it is an unhappy life. The very last lines of the text repeat the confession of ineluctable attachment to the court when Piccolomini greets the dedicatee of the letter by calling him a prudent man – if it were not for the fact that he, too, is a courtier.[24] Thus at the very moment of its conclusion, the text seems to distance its author and dedicatee, as well as its readers, from its previous *exeat aula* statements.

This text's complexities, moreover, bear out John Woodhouse's reading of it as a useful manual for one who aims to pursue a career at court, a practical guide for the ambitious.[25] In this regard, *De curialium miseriis* might have had a "homeopathic" function for the prospective courtier, both warning him about and readying him for the evils of court life, and at the same time exorcizing those evils by presenting them in hyperrealistic detail.

The ambiguities in *De curialium miseriis* become more understandable if one considers that Piccolomini's work has a likely precedent in the equally ambiguous dialogue – although its title is openly pro-court instead of against it – by Lapo da Castiglionchio titled *De curiae commodis* (1438).[26] The diametrical opposition that the two works show already in their titles is confirmed by the way some sections of the texts overlap in reversed tones. The most meaningful example is the analysis of the *curia* according to its effects on the five senses: while *De curiae commodis* enumerates the sensorial delights the *curia* can offer to its inhabitants, in *De curialium miseriis*, as shown above, the same theme is a way to express the harshest anti-court invective. In a similar reversal, while *De curialium miseriis* ends on a note of continued attraction to the court, *De curiae commodis* is not devoid of anti-court sentiments. In Castiglionchio's text, as in *De curialium miseriis*, such sentiments are expressed through a denunciation of the vices that one can find at court (especially gluttony and lust), and also through the distaste of the author – a Florentine nobleman from an impoverished family – for men of low birth who manage, thanks to the court, to be upwardly mobile.

One of the features that make Castiglionchio's *De curiae commodis* particularly intriguing is its ability to walk a fine line between straightforward praise and satire. In fact, the most recent scholarly exploration of *De curiae commodis*, Christopher Celenza's modern edition, presents a convincing reading of the text as non-satirical.[27] The destiny of the author is as murky as his satirical intentions may be, as it is not known with certainty whether he eventually left the *curia* or continued his career as a courtier.[28] According to Celenza, Castiglionchio never left the court, and in spite of his evident disillusionment with the reality of life at court, he still considered it praiseworthy – at least in theory.[29] Castiglionchio's position, in short, is that of a man who considers the court in positive terms but who is enraged by its present shortcomings, owing to the presence of a few corrupt men amid the courtly entourage.[30]

Despite the fact that Castiglionchio still praised the court in the mid-fourteenth century, and that even the speaker and the addressee of Piccolomini's caustic satire ultimately cannot leave it behind, any optimism about the possibility for upward social mobility offered by the court – especially an upward mobility fostered by hard work and talent, and not by the mere occurrence of Fortuna – appears to waver more and more. This weakened optimism would eventually lead to the straightforward pessimism of sixteenth-century writings, wherein anything pertaining to courtly life is seen as subject to the mercy of a capricious Fortuna. While manuals of conduct at court often strived to develop a set of weapons to be used against the upheavals of Fortuna, anti-court satires offer testimony to the futility of putting up such a fight.

Satire/satirist/satyr

Jacob Burckhardt first saw in the Italian Renaissance the birth of a distinctive spirit of wit and satire. Drawing on Burckhardt's suggestion, W. Scott Blanchard has underlined the public nature of satirical writings and identified in the "deeply public dimension" of civic life in the Italian city states a fertile terrain for the growth of satire.[31] Blanchard proceeds to define satire as a mode that could be flexible, experimental, and even avant-garde, and that therefore could become particularly appealing. Furthermore, according to Ejner J. Jensen, early modern satire not only encouraged innovation and experimentation but also offered more attractive features to young writers, such as a limitless range of subjects and the opportunity to exploit one's knowledge of classical models.[32]

In Italy, the popular genre of verse satire became systematized and formalized in the second half of the sixteenth century, thanks to two essays and the anthologies they prefaced: Francesco Sansovino's "Discorso sulla materia della satira," in his own *Sette libri di satire* (1560),[33] and Lodovico Paterno's "Lettera di M. Lodovico Paterno sopra la materia della satira," in Mario degli Andini's *Satire di cinque poeti illustri* (1565).[34] Through their prefatory essays, both texts establish the structure and function of satire, and the features of the satirical persona. Through the satirical poems included, the two anthologies also set out the most common satirical targets: human vices, women, the city (as opposed to the countryside), warfare, and of course, the court.[35] While Andini's text exists only in its 1565 edition, Sansovino's collection was reprinted over three decades (1563, 1573, 1583) and most likely enjoyed editorial success, given the number of copies that can be found in libraries throughout Italy and abroad. These anthologies also help in identifying further reasons for the dissemination of the satirical spirit in early modern Italy.

Sansovino and Andini alike are very keen on defending the value of satire, both from the literary and from the moral point of view. In his prefatory letter (addressed to Camillo Porzio) Sansovino states that he put his collection into print with the precise purpose of benefitting everybody.[36] According to Sansovino, the primary aim of all poetry is to "remove men from vice [...] directing them toward the good order of nature."[37] Satire in particular has a leading role in the pedagogical mission of poetry, since, Sansovino explains,

> good men have always held satiric matters dear, as things that do not only move but also have a direct effect on people's hearts, since as these matters are free in their quality, they are also severe chastisers in all that is not good.[38]

Mario degli Andini, in turn, begins his letter "Ai lettori" by pointing out the widely known beneficial function of satire and by affirming that it is for this very reason that he has resolved to collect the satirical works of the five poets included in his collection.[39]

Both texts also narrate the birth of the satirical genre in order to support claims for its pedagogical role and the image of the satirist as a moral man acting for the good of society. In the "Discorso sulla materia della satira," Sansovino presents satire as a spin-off from the genre of comedy, specifically developed to better chastise the vices of humankind through satyrs, who, Sansovino specifies,

> are feral Gods, who delight in lasciviousness, and are impudent. Hence, just as in our time, it is common for those who fear talking openly to cede to buffoons, fools and drunkards who will say what they themselves want to say, and in this manner speak their minds, so in that time, those who dared not recount the ugliness of those times ceded to the Satyrs.[40]

Satire must therefore be humble in style and "imitating nature: because it is sufficient for the Satirist to explicitly reprimand the errors of others, with no other artifice."[41] The characters in satirical poems are to be similarly plebeian. Satire, that is to say, is antithetical to refinement and artifice, since it requires only "the truth, naked and explicit."[42] The satirist must always maintain a harsh, caustic style and make his words appear as motivated by his insuppressible rage over the vices of humankind:

> Satirists do not begin with an invocation, or with astonishment, but with disdain, or in another similar manner, as if, being provoked by the multitude of vices of humankind, they act disdainfully and with anger to reprimand them, having reached a point where they cannot be silent anymore.[43]

Paterno's "Lettera sopra la materia della satira" remains similarly faithful to the etymological link of satirist and satyr. The satyrs, he explains, were employed in ancient times in satirical writings to scold human wrongdoings. Like Sansovino, Paterno warns against the potential excesses coming from satire's licence to attack and denounce the vicious. Nevertheless, the social importance of satirists is reasserted by pointing out that "these bizarre minds have much in common with doctors, who with irons, and with fire, either awaken the slumbering limbs, or cut away the ill and gangrenous ones."[44]

Paterno's idea of the social value of the satirist is a variation on the topos of the man of letters being a doctor for the community. Interestingly enough, the figure invested with the power to cure the moral infirmities of society is no longer the polished courtier-intellectual advocated by Ottaviano Fregoso in the last book of the *Book of the Courtier*, but the uncouth and "artless" satirist. Confronted with a court society that appeared more and more corrupt, and wherein careers seemed increasingly at the mercy of princely whims, it may easily have appeared that the court was in need of a stronger medicine than that suggested, with ambiguous optimism, in the *Book of the Courtier*. Within the specific genre of anti-court satires, moreover, the medicinal properties of satire seem to extend to the writer himself. Anti-court satires often were also a means of release for the malaise of an author who was confronting – or had confronted for a period of time – the grim reality of life at court, and who had to don a courtly persona.

What is intriguing in these anti-court satires written by court insiders (or former insiders) is the degree to which having to don a courtly persona is increasingly perceived as a source of malaise, which in some cases almost reaches the stage of an existential crisis. In anti-court satires, the court is represented as a system that fosters only the worst kind of conformity and produces depersonalization. Anti-court satire and the voice of the uncouth, blunt satirist become a way to reclaim the possibility for the individual to fashion an identity outside the conformity of the court. The persona of the satirist, which in anti-court satires is fashioned as radically opposed to that of the courtier, allows the courtier-writer to strip off his identity as a courtier, thus providing – at least momentarily – some relief for his malaise.

Anti-court satire par excellence: Ludovico Ariosto's *Satire*

When they first appeared in print in 1534, Ariosto's *Satire* had most likely already been privately circulating in manuscript form among Ariosto's acquaintances[45] or orally performed within private circles.[46] The reason for this discreet circulation is immediately evident: the *Satire* contain numerous critical reflections on the contemporary Ferrarese court. In the years that followed their composition and circulation, Ariosto's *Satire* would prove to be extremely influential, to the point of becoming the foundation of early modern Italian prose satire.[47] By the example of Ariosto's *Satire*, the Italian *capitolo satirico* is set as being mostly Horatian in style and tone – quietly ironic, witty, and measured – thus moving away from the moral and political invective that characterized earlier examples of the genre.[48] Yet the Horatian inspiration does not exclude the darker nuances provided by the model of the angry speaker persona of Juvenalian satire, which is also intertwined with echoes from Dante.[49]

Piero Floriani has identified in Ariosto's *Satire* the expression of the need to give a new form and sensibility to traditional themes, a need that reflects a moment of relevant historical and social transformations.[50] The themes developed by Ariosto in the *Satire* are indeed diverse, ranging from marriage to the best education for a son. Yet the centrality of the theme of the court and of the relationship with those in power cannot be overestimated.[51] The *Satire* owe most of their popularity to their being a reflection on court life written by the ultimate insider, a court poet fully involved in courtly activities. Ariosto's *Satire*, in fact, establish the satirical *capitolo* as the preferred means of expression of anti-courtly sentiments in early modern Italy. Moreover, the *Satire* also establish the features of the speaker of the anti-court *capitolo*: a quiet-loving, often self-debasing speaker who professes his otherness from the overcomplicated and often duplicitous manners of the court. It is precisely when the expression of anti-courtly sentiments and reflections on the status of the court *literatus* and on the relationship with a patron, in particular, become the focus of a satire that echoes of the outraged Juvenalian satiric persona and his despondent perspective on the current status of patronage become evident. This feature represents the main element of continuity between Ariosto's *Satire* and earlier anti-court literature, which often returned to Juvenal as a source of inspiration (thanks especially to the invective against flattery and duplicity contained in Juvenal's third satire) in addressing the evils of court life.[52]

The topic of the court is directly addressed in Ariosto's first and third satires, but the collateral themes of the whimsicality of the powerful, of Fortuna, and of the longing for a simple and quiet life as opposed to the anxiety of searching for success all recur throughout the *Satire*. It is precisely an anti-court sentiment – subsequent to an act of anti-court insubordination – that inaugurates the volume. Ariosto's rupture with his patron, Cardinal Ippolito d'Este, which followed the poet's refusal to accompany the cardinal on a trip to Hungary, generates the occasion for the first satire – and consequently, appears to give impetus to the entire collection.

In the incipit of *Satira I*, the speaker expresses interest in learning from his addressees what the reactions at court were to his disobedience toward his patron, and then vents his anti-court sentiments:

> I wish to hear from you, Alessandro, my brother, and Bagno, my dear friend, whether at the court there lingers any recollection of me; whether my lord continues to revile me; whether a comrade rises to defend me and explains why I am staying here while everyone else is leaving; or whether you are all schooled in sycophancy (that art among us studied and revered) and help him blame me beyond reason. Mad is the man who would contradict his lord, even if he were to say he had seen the day full of stars and at midnight the sun. Whether he praise a man or disgrace him, suddenly one hears a concert of as many voices as he has around him in accord; and he who has not for meekness the courage to open his mouth applauds with all his face and seems to yearn to say, "I too agree." But blame me though you must in other respects, you should at least praise me, because I declared openly, without deception, that I wanted to stay.[53]

In pure anti-court satirical fashion, Ariosto paints a gloomy picture of toadying courtiers eager to please the prince in every possible way, among whom any form of solidarity is inherently impossible. In contrast, the satirical speaker presents himself as a different kind of man, as someone who is not afraid to speak the truth – or more precisely, as the last champion of truthfulness in a world of falsity and hypocrisy.

Ariosto returns to the issue of his truthfulness with equal vehemence in his third satire. To his friend Annibale Malaguzzi, who enquired about Ariosto's new position under his new patron, Duke Alfonso d'Este, the satirist replies that his condition has neither worsened nor improved, and he is aware that such a response will cause his friend to most likely consider him nothing more than a lazy, worn-out horse, a jade with a broken back:

> Now tell me I have a broken back, and, if it pleases you, tell me I am a jade and tell me worse. In short, I do not know what to be if not truthful.[54]

Ariosto-the-satirist portrays this veracity as the reason for his otherness to courtiership and for his inability to adapt to court life. It is precisely in order to better illustrate such veracity that the satirist likens himself to vile beasts: the "reluctant jade" ("rozzon lento") of *Satira III*, the ravenous donkey that gets trapped by his own voracity in *Satira I*, and the little mouse in the same satire that advises the donkey that the only way to free himself is to vomit all the food he has gobbled up. In the third satire, the animal metaphor is extended to a self-representation of the poet as a magpie, once loved by its owner in times of prosperity but aware of being considered useless now that a drought forces the household to define priority among its members.[55]

Fables where speaking animals prompt reflections on human mores are a common feature of satires and of comic writings at large that stems from classical literature.[56] Still, Ariosto's use of this literary topos to give voice to anti-court sentiments is remarkable: Ariosto's animal metaphors directly recall representations of the court as a Circe who transforms all of those who come in contact with her into beasts. Behind the amused resignation of the courtier-poet disappointed by all of his patrons, the praise of mediocrity and quiet, and the understated "Ludovico, or on tranquillity" ("Ludovico della tranquillità"),[57] the anti-courtly sentiments expressed in Ariosto's *Satire* are every bit as upsetting as the ones expressed in more outspoken anti-court satires such as Simeoni's or Caporali's, leading the reader to a dimension where "the corruption of the Court [...] extends to the entire world, especially to the interior one."[58]

The themes of interiority and subjectivity are particularly relevant in connection with anti-court writings. With regard to Ariosto, the *Satire* have been rightfully read as a defence of the poet's self. Cesare Segre spoke of their general "apologetic system,"[59] and Eduardo Saccone defines the *Satire* as "the defence, and the apology, of an 'I' that precisely in opposition to the other [...] finds certainty and self-awareness,"[60] while

Giulio Ferroni underlines how the *Satire* differ from the *Orlando Furioso* by expressing an "explicit opposition between the rights of the self and the constrictions imposed by contemporary powers."[61] The notion of satiric writings as the forum for defending an interiority and a self that appear threatened by the burdens of social constraints (an attitude already noticeable in earlier examples of satiric writings) will become, thanks to the example set by Ariosto's *Satire*, one of the leitmotifs of sixteenth-century satire dealing with the world of the court. One of the main novelties of Ariosto's *Satire* resides precisely in how they establish the prototype for satires as a defence of interiority against the threats represented by the contemporary notion of courtly life. Ariosto's peculiar characterization of the persona of the satirist as a discontented intellectual who yearns for tranquillity and genuineness makes that persona a quintessentially anti-court speaker. The satirist as set by Ariosto, that is to say, is first and foremost an anti-courtier.

Throughout the *Satire*, Ariosto-the-satirist undertakes a project of self-fashioning that appears to oppose the very notion of courtliness.[62] This is particularly evident in *Satira I*, where Ariosto refers to his service to Ippolito as "my wretched servitude " ("la mala servitude mia")[63] – which he professes to hold responsible for the scarce rewards he has obtained from the cardinal – and where he exhorts the brother who has agreed to follow Ippolito to Hungary to "serve for the both of us, and make good my errors" ("servi per amendua, rifà i miei danni").[64]

The speaker's professed otherness to courtliness results in a self-portrayal as the ultimate simple and genuine man – someone, that is to say, who could very well have existed "when men lived on acorns" ("quando viveano gli uomini di giande").[65] It is important to underline how this self-portrayal, while incorporating the basic features of the satiric persona, is also the perfect foil to the sophisticated and well-groomed courtier. Intriguingly, the model of the anti-courtier theorized in Ariosto's *Satire* is developed in the very same years that witness the formation of the perfect courtier in Castiglione's *Book of the Courtier*.[66] As such, they testify to two equal and opposite impulses of the same cultural climate. Moreover, ambiguities that pervade both the *Satire* and the *Book of the Courtier* – residual attraction to the court when expressing anti-courtly sentiments, and nuances of anti-courtliness while forming the perfect courtier, respectively – make them intertwined with one another. The anti-courtliness developed by Ariosto contrasts with the notion of courtliness as contemporarily theorized by Castiglione by presenting an idea of courtliness as primarily a distortion of the self. Later satires further expand on this notion, criticizing and satirizing a notion of forming (*formar*) the perfect courtier that becomes synonymous not only with masking and artifice, but also with an alteration of one's true nature that goes so far as to appear de-individualizing.

In Ariosto's *Satire*, furthermore, the speaker's otherness from the condition of courtier is structured to give proof of his status as a poet, of his pertinence to the dimension of poetry, and of the pertinence of poetry itself – a dimension here seen as structurally opposed to the activity of courtiership. When examining the *Satire* from the point of view of the status of court *literati* in Renaissance Italy, and of anti-court writings at large, it becomes evident that Ariosto-the-satirist's often-stressed, sometimes over-emphasized longing for quiet (*quiete*) is not so much the candid confession of an idle and easily contented personality as it is the self-conscious claim of a committed courtier-poet striving to defend the value of his literary works, and of intellectual practices at large, in an increasingly bureaucratized environment. Such an emphasis on creating for himself the character of the anti-court intellectual is a key to understanding the author's real problem with the court system. Ariosto-the-satirist, just like every anti-court satirist, certainly enumerates the physical discomforts of life at court. Yet a close reading of the *Satire* reveals that such discomforts are in most cases a poetic device used to draw attention to the author's main concern: his *Signore*'s intellectual shortsightedness. In creating for himself the persona of the "new Horace" of early modern Italian satirical writings, Ariosto cannot help but utter his most bitter lines when he observes that the man that should be the Maecenas to his Horace is unable to prove himself worthy of that name. As he points out in *Satira I*, Cardinal Ippolito

> does not consider his praises, composed by me, as work worthy of any thanks, but to be a galloping postman is worth a reward.[67]

The speaker's demand for poetic *otium* shows his unwillingness to abandon his defence of his role as a poet and his reclaiming the value of intellectual production in the power-obsessed and increasingly bureaucratized courtly context. In this light, it is not surprising to see, toward the conclusion of *Satira I*, Ariosto-the-satirist confess that in spite of his previous disavowal of service at court, he would be ready to resume his service under Ippolito d'Este if the cardinal proved himself willing to employ him as a poet, and as a poet only:

> If he wishes to make use of me with ink and quill, and not budge me from my firm resolve, tell him, "My lord, my brother is yours." Dwelling here, I will with a shining clarion make his name ring out higher perhaps than ever flew a dove.[68]

The avian metaphors present in the *Satire* – a self-comparison in *Satira III* with the swallow that, if kept in a cage, "will go mad and die in a single day" ("in un dì vi mor di rabbia"),[69] and then with the cherished but eventually forgotten magpie – reverse his previous identifications with base animals and stress the poet's desire to identify himself with the freedom of birds and not the subjugation of beasts of burden. It is interesting that the same kind of metaphor is applied in canto 35 of the *Orlando Furioso* to distinguish proper poets (whose art will make their patrons' names immortal), portrayed as noble white swans flying high in the sky, from the vile crows, ravens, and vultures that stand for the mass of sycophants and parasites populating the courts and laying claim to the name of poet.[70]

The image of swans versus croaking birds is featured in the same canto where Saint John shows how much a poet worthy of such a name can achieve in terms of exalting his patron as a man of great deeds. In Saint John's words, however, the good poet is revealed to be not the most truthful one but the one who can better fashion for his patron fame as a man of exceptional achievements and virtues. Every writer lies, Saint John declares, and all the great men of history were not really so great: their only merit was to invest in writers who created their eternal fame.[71] It is therefore striking that the use of a similar metaphorical field – the image of the poet as a bird – is realized through two opposite speakers: the blunt anti-court satirist who boasts of his sincerity, on the one hand, and the skilled court poet who knows how to embellish reality in order to praise his patron, on the other.[72] But in each case, the common ground is a critique of a courtly world that neglects talent and intellectual work, and praises vulgar flattery instead.

The strenuous defence of the value of intellectual practices in a courtly context, combined with the contradictory image of the anti-court satirist ready to forsake the truthfulness of satire for the artifice of courtly poetry, is a particularity of Ariosto's *Satire* that has no precedent in earlier anti-court writings in verse. It will, however, represent one of Ariosto's most compelling legacies to later anti-court satires.

Italian anti-court verse satire: Early examples and leitmotifs

Ariosto's role as an innovator in the field of Italian satiric writings in verse can hardly be overstated.[73] Yet it is also important to point out that if on the one hand, Ariosto established the persona of the Renaissance Italian satirist, and the *capitolo* in *terza rima* as his privileged form of expression on the other hand, he was also, in his anti-court and anti-courtier sentiment, heir to a tradition that continued medieval critiques of the court and also incorporated the more secularized tone introduced by Piccolomini in his *De curialium miseriis.* In particular, the topos of the court as a topsy-turvy world filled with every kind of vice, a feature Ariosto carried forward from medieval complaints against the corruption of the Roman curia, is revisited in fourteenth- and fifteenth-century sonnets that extend this topos to involve secular courts as well.

A particularly eloquent example is offered in a sonnet by Niccolò Postumo da Correggio (1450–1508), lord of the eponymous small town in Northern Italy and a courtier at the Este court in Ferrara, which he describes a "pasture for vices" and a "cup full of poison":

> Pasture of vice, cup full of poison,
> hospice of pain that is named court,
> guarantor of envies, of hates and of grudges,
> full of death in every corner and up to the roof,
> he who grows old at your ungrateful doors
> truly sows seeds in a barren terrain
> and he whom you applaud more and keep closer to your bosom
> always meets with an unhappier fate.
> You behave like the eagle with the tortoise
> raising them high and suddenly throwing them down,
> the greater your pleasure the more they deceive each other.
> Within you, oh house of error, one lives continuously
> between water and fire, hammer and anvil,
> cursed be my every step in your direction.[74]

A similarly dystopian depiction of the court is expressed in a sonnet by Serafino Aquilano (1466–1500), "Invida corte, d'ogni ben nimica":

> Envious court, enemy of every good,
> devoid of faith and full of impiety
> school of betrayals and of falsehood
> and poor and empty of every other virtue.
> Hell on earth, and source of strain,
> root of misery and of misfortune,
> abundant river full of spite,
> always adverse to a happy fate.
> Oh when will it be, that from the heavens
> Vulcan's fierce arrows will fall,
> to expose so many frauds, so many deceits?
> But if I die before growing white hair,

I hope to see you at the bottom, although it will be late,
with all your disciples and your wicked tyrants.[75]

This sonnet, first published in 1502, is quoted by Smith as possibly the first relevant example of Italian anti-court satire.[76] However, an even earlier example has been identified by Vittorio Cian in the sonnet "Io ho provato che cosa è amore," attributed to Antonio Beccari da Ferrara (1315–71/74?):[77]

I have experienced what love is,
and I have felt the pain of toothache
I have suffered the death of a close relative
and rule by minor orders;
I have had many other pains in my heart
that are not to be mentioned to everyone;
a deadly fever ... All are nothing
compared to having to obey a lord.
If you ask me – Tell me, how do you know this? –
I would reply that I have experienced it,
and day and night it gave me trouble.
So I would like to see flayed
whoever takes pleasure in having a lord.
I thank God for having freed me from that.[78]

The "doglia" (pain) that Beccari claims to have experienced so intensely at court is left unspecified, yet the message is clear: no happiness can ever await those who enter the service of a *Signore*. Correggio's anti-court sonnet makes the reason for such sorrow explicit: those who live at court are constantly between water and fire, hammer and anvil. No quiet can ever be attained at court; courtly life is a futile search for success and happiness that results only in constant misery.

In anti-court satires the torments of life at court are often epitomized in the tragicomic scene of the terrible dinner in the *tinello*. A theme directly inherited from classical authors (especially Juvenal, Martial, and Lucian), the scene of the bad dinner of rotten food, served on dirty tableware in the spare room reserved for the humblest among the courtiers is one of the most common dystopian depictions of courtly life.[79] The topos was so popular that it was employed by an author of high social status: Enea Silvio Piccolomini devotes many pages of *De curialium miseriis* to describe the less-than-appetizing foods and wines served to courtiers. A vivid portrayal in verse of a meal in the *tinello* is also offered in a poem by an acquaintance of Correggio's, the poet

Antonio Cammelli, known as Pistoia (1436–1502), wherein the speaker tells a friend about his previous night's dinner at court:

> Dining, O my Fedele, yesterday night at court
> Serafino and Galasso set for me
> a tablecloth that had been washed in grease
> and that showed the table through its holes.
> And then the dishes set in front of me –
> ill-dressed salad, oh alas!
> fuzzy bread, harder than stone,
> and the wine flowed fast for fear.
> They gave me Boetius's mother first,
> wrapped around the bone, which still had
> the scum of the broth all around it.
> I put my teeth on that hard leather
> (one was weary, and the other shaken)
> with my butt on the stall and my feet on the wall.
> And then I said: – I do not care
> for eating much of these victuals,
> as I am not used to brushing oakum –
> And then I turned my back on them
> and said, whoever is destined to the court
> either dies a saint, or dies miserable.[80]

In presenting his account of the dinner as a chronicle of the previous evening, Cammelli, just like Aquilano, Correggio, and Beccari, is eager to prove that he speaks from firsthand experience of the court – that he has, as Beccari puts it, "provato" the pain of life at court on his own skin. Despite their different social backgrounds – Cammelli was the son of a *priore* of his hometown, Aquilano's family belonged to the minor nobility, Correggio was heir to a small estate under the influence of the Ferrara court, while Beccari was most likely the son of an artisan – all four authors seem equally to have experienced the hardships and frequent disappointments of courtly life, and had lived through its upheavals.[81] Cammelli travelled through many courts, most notably Ferrara and Mantua, obtaining national fame as a poet, but – if we are to trust Aretino's *Ragionamento delle corti* – without ever acquiring economic stability.[82] Intriguingly, his introduction to the courtly world – for once, a positive experience – seems to have occurred precisely at the Correggio court of Niccolò.[83] Niccolò da Correggio, himself a *Signore* in his own small court, was nonetheless forced to adapt to the life of a courtier (although one of a privileged background) when serving the more powerful Este at the Ferrara court.

Aquilano's case is the most representative of the diverse fates that could befall anyone who attempted a career at court. A courtier in Naples and then in Rome at the service of Cardinal Ascanio Sforza, Aquilano became extremely popular as a poet and musician – to the point that he could allow himself to distribute anti-court sonnets all over Rome by tying them to the collars of the cardinal's dogs. Yet he must have pushed his luck too hard, if it is true that the pastoral anti-court eclogue "Dimmi Menandro mio, deh dimmi sozio" was the cause of his expulsion from the cardinal's court. Aquilano, like many other court *literati* of the time, thus tasted the fickleness of favour at court. No wonder, then, that one of the leitmotifs of Renaissance anti-court writings was precisely courtly Fortuna: a force that – as Correggio's sonnet depicts – can bring one up high in the sky only to drop him down to his ruin, just as an eagle does to break the shell of a turtle it has captured.

The courtier also had one more insidious obstacle to overcome that was not an abstract and remote force such as Fortuna, but something very definite and concrete: the ruthless competition of his peers. A description of the dynamics of courtly competition can be found in another sonnet by Pistoia, which begins "Questi signor fan come piace a loro" and wherein the poet praises his patron for holding his loyal poet in high esteem ("my lord has the habit / of praising a nightingale more for his harmony / than the Barb horse that carried the Messiah")[84] and imagines the resentment of his fellow courtiers. The bitterest portrait of relationships among peers at court, however, belongs to a sonnet by Aquilano from 1502, which presents the court as a game in which every courtier is constantly trying to improve his position at the expense of the others:

> The court is like the game of *quadrelo*,
> each one chases the other from his seat and post,
> not for a reason, but only because of greed,
> since there is much more money than brains.
> One night you'll see without a cape
> a big kid standing like a lost owl
> the next morning you'll see him dressed in silk and gold
> so that you'll say: he's not the same person.
> When he has risen as far as he can go
> some random countryman shows up, and ruins his luck
> and makes him fall down on the wheel of fortune
> and become a page boy once again.
> How accurate that old saying is:
> the shadow of a lord is a fool's hat.[85]

No relationships other than competitive ones seem to be possible at court. In a world where everything is unreliable, and where everyone must strive to defend himself against constant treachery, no honest communication is possible either. The court is only a school of betrayals and lies; nothing can be learned there besides falsehood and treachery. The words used at court, although erudite and polished, are employed only to alter reality, curry favour, and slander. Nothing can be more different from the plain, often blunt, and yet truthful words of the satirist.

In its disenchanted reflection on the cut-throat competition of the court and in presenting it as a game, Aquilano's 1502 sonnet seems to anticipate the late sixteenth-century cynicism of Alonso de Barros's *Filosofia cortesana* (1588), a Spanish-Italian board game structured as a Game of the Goose and set at court, where in order to achieve victory the players need to overcome all the *perigli* of the sea of suffering that is the court.[86] Barros's courtly Game of the Goose is a witty metaphor of the dynamics of courtly life, but anti-court satires, by insisting on the constant upheavals of life at court, also reveal something more: no player was ever completely safe. For those who chose to play the game of the court, even for those who thought they were winning, the only option was to keep playing forever. No game piece could ever be said to have reached the final space on the board and achieved victory.

It would seem that only a crazy man could think of spending all his life at court. Since the time spent at court was always spent in vain, the court stole the years of a man's life without ever giving him anything back. An additional theme of anti-court writings captures this sentiment, featuring the figure of a man who has grown old at court, always hoping over the years to get recognition and security, and who now reproaches himself for having wasted his life in pursuit of an unattainable goal. Another work by Pistoia, the play *Filostrato e Panfila* (a romantic tragedy inspired by novella 4.1 from Boccaccio's *Decameron*) offers a fascinating example.[87] The play tells the story of the unhappy love between the princess Panfila and the courtier Filostrato, both eventually killed by the king who disapproves of his daughter's love for a subordinate. The play's most significant innovation with respect to the *Decameron* is the introduction of the figure of Tindaro, an old and disappointed courtier. In presenting a picture of the court as a site of cut-throat competition among peers, Tindaro blames himself for not having left the court when he was still young ("Crazy is the one who grows old at court")[88] and also inveighs against his prince, who has betrayed him by stealing the years of his life ("I can say that the king has betrayed me / by stealing my time").[89]

The expression of anti-courtly sentiments in Beccari's, Correggio's, Aquilano's, and Pistoia's sonnets relies on almost obsessive enumeration of the evils of the court. Such evils, which pertain both to the physical realm – learning to tolerate many discomforts – and to the moral one – having to confront envy, lies, and ruthless competition among peers – together build the image of the court as hell on earth. By contrast, Ariosto's configuration of the satirical *capitolo* on the court employs similar topoi (for example, the humorous references in *Satira I* to the "feet" ["piei"], "armpits" "ascelle"], and "belches" ["rutti"][90] that the speaker is forced to smell when dining at court, or his suspicion that his former companions may now indulge in gossiping about him as a way to flatter the prince) with extreme parsimony, focusing instead on the incompatibility of his satiric persona with the environment of the court. Later sixteenth-century Italian anti-court *capitoli* revive the topos of the "courtly hell" and express it through the words of a satirical persona that is very often indebted to the one created by Ariosto. It is precisely the contrast between the discontented and sardonic *literatus*, on the one hand, and the physical discomforts and the moral corruption of the court, on the other, that becomes the trademark of sixteenth-century anti-court satiric *capitoli*.

The court in satires

What is Court? A greedy Courtesan
who gives brief pleasures and prolonged pains
a theatre, where the scenes keeps changing
and every character learns to play multiple parts.
A palace, which looks like smoke, and temple, and altar
a galley where you are always in chains,
a ladder that you need to climb, and often it happens
that she unites in one a throne and a coffin.
Within her walls you see a Belisarius blinded
Seneca killed, and she leads to prison
the chaste Joseph, who barely escapes.
Because of her Aman was hung on a fatal gibbet,
Peter set foot inside and lost his faith,
John spoke, and lost his head.[91]

In bringing together many anti-court topoi, this anonymous and undated sonnet, held in the Vatican library,[92] also reveals an important feature of the court as portrayed in early modern Italian satirical writings. The court is immediately identified with the misogynist stereotype of the greedy courtesan who will only cause suffering and never give pleasure. The definition of the court as a theatre, wherein all are constantly acting but also need to play more than one part at the same time, underlines the utter lack of sincerity of all courtly interactions and also evokes the Baroque image of the "theatre of the world." Traditional negative definitions of the court as a place of fictional pleasures, as the opposite of freedom, and as a mirage for those seeking success are expressed in images of the court as a realm of smoke, a galley ship, and a ladder, while the references to figures from antiquity and from scripture reinforce the theme that at court the good are endangered – when not corrupted – while evil men prosper.

The handwriting style and the references to the court as a theatre suggest that the sonnet was most likely written in the late sixteenth or early seventeenth century.[93] Along with no identification of the sonnet's author, there is also no reference to a specific court that may be identified as the precise target of this invective. The court in question may very well be the papal court in Rome, and yet there are no elements within the text that support this claim – but neither are there any elements to exclude it and relate the sonnet to any particular secular court in Italy or abroad. Far from being a limitation, however, this feature represents one of the most interesting aspects of this piece of writing, and of anti-court satires at large. "The court" portrayed in most anti-court satires is very rarely identifiable as a specific court, with possible scholarly identifications (e.g., the Ferrara court of the Este dukes as opposed to the Roman court of the pope) being based only on the author's biography. Anti-court invectives written by an author known for having been a courtier in Rome must refer to his disappointment with the corruption of the papal court, while the same lament authored by a *literatus* employed in a secular court is interpreted as depending on the author's dissatisfaction with his particular *Signore*.

In the case of anonymous sonnets such as "What is Court? A greedy courtesan" ("Che cosa è Corte? Cortigiana avara"), the specific object of the anti-court sentiments uttered in the text is destined (at least for the moment) to remain unknown. Just as all satirical personae share basic characteristics – all satirists are rustic, truth-speaking, moral men disgusted by the corruption around them – so do the worlds upon which they gaze. The scene of satire, as Kernan has pointed out, is "always disorderly and crowded."[94] The courtly hell depicted in anti-court satires becomes one more scene of satire with its precise set of characteristics. What is important to highlight is that in anti-court satires, conformity to the common characteristics of the scene of satire produces the impression that all courts are virtually undistinguishable from each other. But this feature of satirical writings was distinctly at odds with the reality of the courts of the Italian Renaissance.

Renaissance Italy was home to a variety of courts, each very different from the other in terms of geographic location, rulers, dimensions, riches, and political allegiances. Yet anti-court satires appear not to bear any traces of such a complex reality. In anti-court satirical writings, all the existing courts represented are conflated into the general and abstract notion of "the court." Large or small, wherever it may be located and whoever may be its ruler, the court is always hell; within it all lords are fickle and unrewarding and all courtiers are backstabbers and flatterers. The court in satires, therefore, is not a real place so much as it is a concept, an abstract notion that takes the shape of a *dystopia* (at times opposed to the equally unrealistic *utopia* represented by the courts of the past).[95] The court in satires is, ultimately, anonymous.

One reason for such anonymity may be found in the desire of satirists to protect themselves from any repercussions from their *Signore*, or even their peers. While the court was a common and accepted satirical target (as were women and friars), any direct critiques of one's lord or of the court where one was employed might have resulted in retaliations. Still, anti-court satires' grouping of all distinctive courts into the general concept of "the court" conveys to readers the idea that no matter the characteristics that distinguished one court from the other, all courts were fundamentally the same and life at court had the same dynamics everywhere.

One partial exception was the papal court of Rome, which continued to be the target of satires and invectives addressed specifically against it. The reasons for the Roman court being singled out are found in the legacy of medieval invectives against the corruption of the clergy and the secularization of the papacy (denunciations against the hypocrisy of the papal court as the embodiment and official seat of Christian values while the actual behaviour of its members often stood in stark contrast to those values), in its being one of the biggest, richest, and most visible courts in the Renaissance, and in the rapidity of changes in entourages, favours, and Fortuna that often accompanied the death of a pope and the ascent of his successor. All of these factors made of the court of Rome the negative paradigm for every early modern court in satirical writings.

Once we acknowledge that "the court" is more of an archetype than a real place in satires – and that the court being criticized in a given satire both is and is not the actual court of Ferrara, Mantua, or even Rome – it also becomes clear that anti-courtliness comes to be a codified and universal language for expressing discontent with some of the most controversial aspects of contemporary society. The court becomes everything the satirist loathes and feels is other from himself and from his mores and values.

Moreover, since anti-court sentiments have a common language, and since satiric personae share common features even though the specific reasons that may have prompted a given individual to express his discontent toward the court (such as disagreements with one's lord or peers, frustration, perceived lack of recognition for one's merits) may be different from case to case, the spokesperson and the stylistic features of anti-court satires tend to be homogeneous. A series of consolidated leitmotifs – which are already noticeable in the early examples of vernacular anti-court verse, and include themes such as courtly language as distorted communication, cut-throat competition among peers, the futility of time spent at court, to name just a few – recur throughout the literary productions of authors from different cities of origin, social backgrounds, and careers over the period of a few decades.

Courtly Fortuna

The first challenge that the prospective courtier has to confront in his career at court is coming to terms with the constant uncertainty of his condition: a courtier should never forget that he may fall from grace at any moment, as eloquently pointed out in Simeoni's *Della corte*:

> The sky does not change so frequently
> at the most beautiful time of its first age
> or in between the summer and the icy weather
> as does the Courtier who rises high, and then
> falls down. At one moment he has plenty of servants
> and at the next, you find him alone on the streets.
> Today you'll see him dressed in scarlets,
> and tomorrow he'll be in rags; today he's clean and fat,
> and tomorrow he'll be shabby, scrawny and pale.
> Today you'll see him walking with his lord
> like an equal, and tomorrow locked in a cell,
> disgraced, and sentenced to death.[96]

The frequent upheavals of life at court made it the perfect background for reflections on the power of Fortuna that played such a central role in Renaissance Italian culture. In a sonnet by Niccolò da Correggio, the court is defined as the only apt residence for something as fickle and unreliable as Fortuna:

> Fortune, whoever painted you with hair only in the front,
> naked and fleeting, was not mistaken:
> whoever does not tie you down while he has your favour,
> has only himself to blame if you then attack and offend him.
>
> You have polished one who dirties the water in springs,
> to the point that the sun, next to him, loses its splendour,
> but then you deprive a great man of any honour,
> so that he is reduced to praying in a hermitage.
> Sometimes I wonder where you hold your seat:
> I think of heaven, but no evil ever comes from there,
> if in the abyss, then you would bring unceasing death.
> But upon seeing that, after having done to a poor man
> the worst that you can do, then you do him some good,
> your residence can be nowhere but at court.[97]

Classical notions of Fortuna, and the related idea that virtue is needed in order to overcome fortune's blows, were revived in early Renaissance thought.[98] The optimism in the possibility of overcoming fortune thanks to virtue was a characteristic of humanistic thought.[99] Yet the culture of the later Renaissance, in a Europe ravaged by wars and upset by profound social and political crises, evolved toward an increasingly pessimistic view of the power of virtue to counter fortune.[100] According to Mario Santoro, it was precisely the shock created by the French invasion of Italy in 1494 that gave way to a shared feeling of there being an uncontrollable dominion of irrational forces over human life. This revelation, in turn, created renewed interest in the topic of the power of fortune, but with a very different feeling from the humanistic faith in the resources of human *virtù*: sixteenth-century cultural elites became "increasingly worn down by the sense that they were living in an age in which *virtù* and *ragione* were no longer capable of parrying the blows of fortune."[101]

With their frequent reflections on the ephemeral character of any favourable outcome at court, anti-court satires offer an even clearer testimony to the loss of faith in virtue's power against Fortuna.[102] Anti-court satires are, in fact, pervaded by awareness of the chanciness of princely favour, on which a courtier's fate depended entirely. The increasingly absolute nature of the lord's power and will resulted in a notion of princely grace that more and more resembled divine grace, and in the perception that the favour that could be granted to a courtier was becoming progressively more erratic and unsteady. Castiglione's *Book of the Courtier* had warned prospective courtiers that the power of fortune over human affairs could result in the inexplicable event that an accomplished courtier might "find little favor with the prince, and [...] go against the grain; and this for no understandable reason,"[103] which would in turn prompt the entire court to scorn such a courtier and eventually result in his being denied the favour he would otherwise deserve. In anti-court satires, the already pessimistic view of Castiglione's *Book of the Courtier* is transformed into a sense of the complete unpredictability of one's career at court, even at the moment of one's greatest success.

Courtly payoffs

In a court perceived as being completely under the dominion of Fortuna, where success and failure are determined by chance, any time spent striving to foster one's career could easily be perceived as time totally wasted chasing an impossible dream. The court steals a man's lifetime, without ever giving enough in return, as Francesco Berni stated: "The court borrowed / sixteen years of turmoil and struggles from me / and from her I received four hundred *ducati*."[104] The destiny that awaits those who spend their lives at court is described in a satirical reworking of Petrarch's *Movesi il vecchierel canuto et bianco* authored by the Sienese Lattanzio Benucci (1521–98):

> The old courtier takes his leave, white-haired and pale,
> of the *tinello* where he filled out his age
> and leaves the household, bewildered
> to see vigour and time disappear;
> and suddenly unable to drag his limbs
> without struggling and ending his life,
> he tries as much as he can to go back,
> to his home, tough, broken and weary,
> once he gets there, he no longer has any desire
> to spend his days serving the one
> whom he now hopes to see one day destroyed.
> Just so, alas, I keep learning
> at my own expense, and through the example of others, that the Court is only pure and real Death.[105]

The reflection on time that was so central to Petrarch's poetics is reinterpreted by Benucci (who had experience serving in courts and households in France, Rome, and Naples) in completely courtly terms.[106] Benucci's poem also features the pun *Corte/Morte* (Court/Death) in its last line, another common topos of Italian anti-court satires that would be made popular by Aretino's *Ragionamento delle corti* but that is already visible in the first quatrain of Niccolò da Correggio's sonnet "Pascul de vizii, pocul di veneno,"[107] and later featured in the opening lines of Gabriello Simeoni's *Della corte*. According to Aretino's *Ragionamento delle corti* and Lodovico Paterno's *Satira III* (included in Mario degli Andini's *Satire di cinque poeti illustri*), *Morte* was the original name for *Corte*, and only later was the *M* was changed to a *C* to mitigate the scary effect of such a name.[108] The topos *Corte/Morte* was also employed (from the very first lines, again) in Cesare Caporali's *La corte*: "at Court [...] where life / is registered in the book of Death."[109] The ease of the pun *Corte/Morte* should not mislead the reader and prompt an interpretation of such a play on words as a facile comic trick. *Corte* is *Morte* not simply because of the challenges it requires – the physical exhaustion, the stress of constant peer rivalry – but because courtliness becomes the negation of the basis for living in a community, and of the foundations of selfhood.

Courtly interactions

Entering the court means, first and foremost, undergoing a process of irreparable transformation. It is useful to recall Simeoni's definition of the court as a Circe who transforms a man into something else. Like the mythical sorceress of ancient epic, the court can strip a man of his humanity. No one can hope to go through the experience of life at court unaltered; as Simeoni goes on to clarify, neither the most virtuous nor the most vicious among men can escape the tarnishing power of the court.[110]

In a world where men are possessed and shaped by the toxic environment that surrounds them, just as Circe's suitors were transformed into beasts, no normal human interaction is possible. The perverted system of the court and the constant striving to succeed over one's peers in conquering the lord's favour emphasize peer rivalry to the extreme and make cut-throat competition omnipresent.

In addressing his *Satira III* to a friend who is about to become a courtier, Lodovico Paterno is aware that depicting the evils of the court will most likely not suffice to dissuade his friend. Paterno decides instead, therefore, to devote his satire to providing useful advice (based, once more, on the author's direct experience at court) for surviving among its perils.[111] A substantial part of such advice concerns not placing one's trust in anyone: not in one's lord, whose love "is like wine / that today tastes like yesterday, but tomorrow is different,"[112] and most importantly, not in one's peers, who are to be considered enemies at all times:

> Have no trust in your dear fellow servants,
> think that they have no trust in you.
> Be double-faced: and use your blood, bones, flesh and nerves
> to this end, and your chest, and hands, and tongue, and feet.
> If you do not believe me, you will be no safer
> than if you were fighting a thousand men, on foot;
> alas, once you are old, and no longer at court,
> you will regret your lack of judgment greatly.
>
> They are enemies to you, and you to them,
> cease, and do not ask, O brother, for a reason.
> The round table, and its ruler Arthur
> are beyond the field held by Elijah.[113]

Courtly language

Paterno's advice to use duplicity in all things draws attention to one further feature of courtly life: at court, everything is two-faced. Consequently, communication is always distorted, and words never match reality. Courtly words are spoken with ulterior motives in mind, either to distract, flatter, or deceive. To this twisted and cynical use of language, the satirist wants to juxtapose plain and honest speech that shows things for what they are, without manicuring reality. The satirist's truthfulness as opposed to the lying and flattering chorus of the court is already a theme of Ariosto's *Satire*, developed in particular in his first and third satires, wherein the author offers a picture of himself as a man unable to lie.[114] This theme is then developed with particular depth in Luigi Alamanni's tenth satire, which centres precisely on the courtly distortion of language.

The Florentine Alamanni (1495–1556) is the best-known Italian satirist after Ariosto.[115] The styles and sensibilities of the two writers are, however, very different, and equally different was the reaction of contemporary critics to their work. Alamanni's thirteen satires were likely written between 1524 and 1527, after the author had experienced exile due to his republican, anti-Medici political ideals and his involvement in the failed plot to assassinate Cardinal Giulio de' Medici (the future Pope Clement VII). Twelve of them were first published in France, where the author had taken shelter, between 1532 and 1533.[116] Alamanni abandons

Ariosto's colloquial and ironic Horatian style in favour of the Juvenalian model of the indignant speaker – a choice that was criticized by contemporary critics: Sansovino considered Alamanni's satires to be written in an excessively elevated style, and Andini regarded their tone as too harsh ("spiacevoletto").[117] Alamanni's satires are, in fact, heavily saturated with political and social topics and mostly revolve around criticism of contemporary rulers and denunciation of the vices of the time.[118]

In *Satira X* (addressed to Alamanni's fellow expatriate in France, Tommaso Sertini), the author's indignation is directed toward the art of praising the powerful. Alamanni sets himself outside the group of those who can easily turn language away from truth to make it more gratifying to the ones in power, proclaiming instead his inability to deviate from sincerity: "I would not know, O Sertino, how to set aside / the truth, praising incessantly the one / who goes farther from good by harming others."[119]

The statement "I would not know" ("non saprei") is repeated throughout the satire to provide evidence of the poet's discomfort with courtly language. He would not know – he claims – how to hide thorns under fake flowers when speaking ("nel parlar covrir le spine / con simulati fior"),[120] or how to blame the just and applaud the vicious, or eulogize tyrants and condemn those who fought for freedom. He would not be able to call a coward brave, a violent man just, a flatterer courteous, a slanderer honest, or a cruel man righteous. Through the anaphora of "I would not know," Alamanni develops anti-courtliness as a sort of language of negation that quotes the language of courtliness in order to deny it and to proclaim the satirist's extraneousness to such a practice.

The satirist wants to counter this perversion of language with communication that restores correspondence between words and reality, between the verses of the author and what he truly feels in his mind. In the case of Gabriello Simeoni's *Satire alla berniesca*, the satiric impulse for sincerity becomes a programmatic declaration at the very beginning of the collection:

> The Book speaks. Not to please the offenders, nor to badmouth them,
> but to defend the good, by writing the truth;
> a pure and sincere heart birthed me,
> whose desire is not for any mortal thing.
> *Quis vetat dicere verum?*[121]

If the satirist can speak only sincerely, and if language at court is only a mystification, then whoever has the spirit of a satirist is by definition unable to be instructed in the courtly arts and adapt to life at court, no matter how hard he tries. In the case of Girolamo Fenaruolo – a clergyman from Brescia who lived in the second half of the sixteenth century,[122] and who had four satires included in Sansovino's collection – the author's habit of talking honestly becomes the reason adduced to turn down an invitation (from the satire's addressee, Vettor Ragazzoni) to join the Roman court:

> I always speak the way one speaks here
> and I call the bread "bread," and the wine "wine"
> [...]
> When I sweat, I want to say that I am sweating
> when I shiver, that I am shivering
> and I want to call that which is cooked "cooked," and that which is raw "raw."[123]

Such a character and such an attitude toward language would be unfit for a courtly speech that requires denying any sincere expression of feelings and thoughts in order to tell the *Signore* only what he wants to hear.

Courtly malaise

According to Cesare Caporali, courtliness was born precisely out of a distortion of language. In the second part of his *capitolo* on the court, Caporali depicts an uncorrupted golden age that knew no slander, no flattery, and no lies. But then Nature created "some mute Effects / that were confusedly negotiating among each other" ("certi Effetti muti / Che fra lor negoziavano in confuso"), and after that "Excellencies" ("l'Eccellenze") were created, together with honorific titles that were applied even to porters.[124] That is when courtliness was born, and language was corrupted:

> And with them, at the same time, courtiership was born
> which was the end to our native freedom,
> and which corrupted every freedom of speech.[125]

The distortion of language is only the first sign of the complete deformation of reality that happens at court. By this view, the court is a topsy-turvy world where everything is falsified and perverted, where the rules that regulate the world have no place: only at court "the fool will be called a sage / and the sage a fool, since the Prince's will / goes against every law and rule of Nature."[126]

The peculiar malaise experienced by courtiers is expressed with particular vehemence in the poems of Alessandro Allegri (Florence, 1560–1629), a self-described "Scholar, Courtier, Soldier, and Priest,"[127] who in his collection of *Rime piacevoli* (1605) also professes to have left the court after the bitter disappointments of his career as a courtier.[128] Interestingly, Allegri depicts the courtly malaise as a disease with both physical and psychological symptoms:

> Living at court and being ill,
> seem to me – how can I say it? – like brothers by blood
> so much is one condition like the other.
> [...]
> And just as a sick man goes from the bed to the toilet
> to throw up undigested bitter roots,
> in various ways, whenever he can,
> the courtier – who is troubled inside – secretly pours out
> what gives him grief.[129]

If courtliness is a disease, the court, hence, is nothing more than

> a hospital,
> which collects and tends to anyone,
> where – I believe – no one goes who is
> not sick in his body or soul.[130]

In a *capitolo* written to teach a lesson to his friend Pandolfo N. (who, according to the author, has put on an attitude since having become a courtier), Allegri underlines the distance separating the courts and courtiers of his time from the court of Urbino as depicted by Castiglione, when courtliness still was a noble art. Castiglione's courtier was "divine" ("divino"), while Allegri's courtier is "a goose" ("un'oca"). The fault is in the court of Allegri's time itself: "the barrel / of the present is not what it was in Urbino,"[131] and becoming a courtier means being ruined economically and – most importantly – morally. The friend's hope of not being affected by the court's evils by limiting himself to doing his best in serving the lord and attending to his own business is destined to be frustrated: as Allegri points out, "[W]hen would you find that white / rubbing with black, does not become gray?"[132]

Allegri's wistful reference to Castiglione's *Book of the Courtier* is testimony to the persistence of the ideal of a "healthy" courtier and a "salubrious" court, even in the pages of someone who considered courtliness "a too-common disease among gentlemen" ("un mal troppo frequente ne' galantuomini")[133] Such an observation paves the way for the question of whether anti-courtliness needs to be understood as a refusal of courtiership tout court, or as a more restricted complaint about the present conditions of the court. Anti-court texts, nevertheless, do not offer a definite reply to this question, being characterized by a continual oscillation between rejection and regret.

One further question is whether the label of "political satire" can be applied to anti-court writings. Piero Floriani has underscored how the distinctive quality of sixteenth-century satire is its predominately private and psychological tone. This feature, Floriani points out, is typical of both writers who are involved with the court and those operating outside of it. Alamanni's satires, with their substantial political tone, are, in this sense, an exception. The political topic, when present, however, is only secondary: a consequence of the satire's being a reflection on the everyday life of its author, wherein politics is involved only as part of such daily reality.[134] Floriani refers to Ariosto's second satire as a relevant example of such an attitude, it being "rich in precisely political judgments on the Roman Curia [...] and yet, the point of view is strictly private, and the tone strictly psychological."[135]

Contrary to what one might expect, the private and psychological dimension, and not the political one, needs to be recognized as the predominant dimension of anti-court satire. The modern reader who looks for politics as the main theme of anti-court writings or expects anti-court satires to conform to the standards of political satire as we know it risks engaging in an anachronistic interpretation. The malaise expressed in anti-court satires, and in anti-court sentiments in general, demands to be read first of all in private and psychological – one could almost say existential – terms. What anti-court writings deal with, in fact, is not so much the court as an institution but the effect that courtliness and courtly life have on individuality, or on the courtier's sense of self.

The courtly self

> The Golden Age must have been beautiful,
> O Trifone, when everyone was his own courtier,
> and each one lived in his own decorum
> without having other courtiers around,
> except for two hands, and two feet that
> promptly did what they were commanded to do.[136]

This golden age described by Caporali is structured as a time that was – contrary to what one may expect – not devoid of courtliness, but where courtliness was reserved to oneself: everyone was his own courtier, and as such his own *Signore* as well. What was so disquieting about the sixteenth-century art of courtliness to make a poet dream of such a golden age? What strikes the reader is that the notion of "being one's own courtier" ("corteggiare se stesso") in the golden age depicted by Caporali actually meant having control over one's will and one's body. Clearly, such a mastery of one's own self was not to be taken for granted in the world of the early modern courts.

At court, the *Signore* alone was in charge of everyone's time and had the last word over everyone's desires and needs. In Simeoni's opinion, this was the worst aspect of life at court, since it concerned matters of one's own life and death:

> One more thing I see at Court,
> which – since it involves a man's
> life and death – seems worst of all.
> It is that, in the day, if you feel hungry,
> or are sleepy at night, neither of those
> will be satisfied according to your needs,
> unless you pay of your own pocket,
> because, until the Lord has eaten,
> your belly will be filled only with rage.
> You could die for lack of sleep,
> for if the Lord does not go to sleep first,
> it would be a disgrace to leave him alone.
> If [a courtier] is sick, or about to die,
> the Lord will say, full of anger and disdain,
> that he is trying to avoid his chores.[137]

In spite of all the horrible meals in the *tinelli*, all the lies and flattery, all the cut-throat competition with one's peers, the real discomfort of life at court, as Simeoni describes it, is always having to submit one's will to another's desires in every minute detail. Following the same train of thought, Allegri deems the life of the courtier even worse than that of the prisoner, remarking that the latter has more autonomy and fewer constrictions: "It is sweeter, I believe, being in the dungeons / where one can at least nap on the bench / and sleep until the Sun shines on the window bars."[138] As further contrast to life at court, Allegri asserts the freedom he enjoys since having left it: "How, and when I want, I sit, and stand / I put my hat on and take it off / and to my will I soften and anger."[139]

The defence of individual autonomy is also the main theme of a satire by Giovanni Agostino Caccia, written in response to an invitation at court coming from an unspecified *Signore*, and published as part of his *Satire e capitoli piacevoli* in 1549. Caccia's satire is original in featuring a series of precise conditions set by the author in order for him to accept a position at court. These requests are incredibly detailed and cover almost every aspect of his potential daily life at court. He refuses to be employed either as a page or an emissary; he has no intention of dining in a *tinello* and insists on having his meals alone; he demands to have his meals at a time he determines; he does not want to be forced to go hunting early in the morning and wants to be in control of when he wakes up each day; he insists on being able, when he is tired, to withdraw to his room, which he refuses to share with another courtier; he demands – with an allusive tone – a *garzone* all for himself; and finally, he even includes details on the kind of wine and food that should be granted to him. Caccia then proceeds to further affirm his individuality by fashioning for himself an anti-court persona that clearly shows the legacy of the satiric character developed in Ariosto's *Satire*:

> You will tell me: "Maybe you reveal yourself
> to be a lazy man, a good-for-nothing:
> it would be wiser to hide your shortcomings."
> Because of this, I worry – and it is better to say out loud
> that I am not made to be at court
> for sincerity is too much a friend of mine.[140]

Caccia's conditions for acceptance may seem trivial, but such requests actually serve to defend his autonomy in a courtly space that is perceived as de-individualizing. To his prospective patron's possible objection concerning the necessity of abandoning one's comforts at court, the satirist's reply (which is, again, reminiscent of Ariosto's *Satire*) states that he values his freedom and his autonomy more than any honour he may receive at court:

> You may say: "You are looking for
> too many things to reach an agreement,
> when I give some thought to this.
> But you are greatly mistaken, if you think
> that you can live as you wish and be at court
> and still get all the things that you want"
> [...]
> And I reply that I will not spend any more time

making pacts with you, and I thank you
for having alerted me in advance.
I have already had enough of the court
and I do not intend to come and torture myself
with the hope of gaining profit.
Whatever I have left to live, be it a little or a lot,
I intend to spend it in freedom and in peace,
in my native humble abode;
and if I have to struggle, struggle I will
in my own home, without being a slave
to those who silently enjoy another man's suffering.[141]

In the conclusion to the satire, Caccia offers the compromise of trying service at court for a month, but keeping the option of going back to his previous life should he dislike court life:

But in order to be better informed about this
I will come to serve at court for one month, and if I like it
I will stay, but if do not, I want to leave
and be able to return by my own path.[142]

The alternative to defending one's autonomy is depicted in a sonnet by Francesco Berni, centred on a courtier whose entire identity has become one with the court:

Sir Cecco cannot be without the court
and the court cannot be without Sir Cecco;
and Sir Cecco needs the court
and the court needs Sir Cecco.
He who wants to know who Sir Cecco is
must reflect on what the court is:
this Sir Cecco looks just like the court
and the court looks just like Sir Cecco.
And the court will live as long
as Sir Cecco's life will last,
because Sir Cecco and the court are one and the same.[143]

Berni's Cecco,[144] a man whose complete existence depends on his identification with the court, is the epitome of the renunciation of individual needs demanded by courtliness. The effect that such an abdication had on the courtier's sense of self is what appears most to worry the authors of anti-court writings. To understand why the requirements of court life appeared to pose such a threat to individuality, and to better illustrate why anti-court satires need to be recognized as a defence of selfhood, it is important to also consider the changes to the notion of selfhood happening in this period and take into consideration how the Renaissance sense of self was constructed.

For some time, scholarship has questioned Jacob Burckhardt's notion of the discovery of the individual in the Renaissance. Scholars of the Middle Ages have rejected the claim that no notion of individuality existed before the Renaissance, and historians of the Renaissance have called attention to the continued relevance of collectivity in the early modern period.[145] As pointed out by John Jeffries Martin, "[I]t is no longer possible to tell the story of the Renaissance discovery of the self as a straightforward and heroic narrative that lays the foundations for the more 'modern' forms of individualism seen as characteristic of the Enlightenment, the Romantic period, or even modern life in general."[146] Despite contesting the "heroic" narrative of the development of the individual, Martin still considers the early modern period extremely relevant to the evolution of selfhood. Instead of seeing it as a straightforward process, he casts light on the complexities and contradictions of the early modern self, explaining how it was shaped within the tension between two concepts in early modern society: prudence and sincerity. Prudence, understood as the ability to conceal one's inner thoughts under an acceptable facade, was a needed feature in a society that placed so much significance on decorum and codified behaviour. The same society, nevertheless, also experienced "a new emphasis on inwardness or the idea of an interior self as the core of personal identity," as well as "a growing moral imperative to make one's feelings and convictions known" and a "desire to connect speech with feeling."[147] The result was that the early modern self was characterized by what Martin describes as a "layered quality"; it was also a divided self, torn between the necessity to maintain a public facade and the opposite impulse to be true to one's inner feelings and to express them.[148]

Martin has identified different kinds of self that Renaissance men and women could experience, and that were often present in the same individual.[149] The dominant type of self was the "communal self," or the way in which a collective or group identity defined an individual's sense of his or her place in society. Another type was the "porous self," reflected in the notion that the body was itself porous and possibly influenced by spiritual forces (instead of the modern notion of one's soul being enclosed in one's body). The typology of self that is most relevant to courtliness and anti-courtliness is what Martin calls the "prudential" or "performative self." This type reflected the increased awareness of the need for the individual to assume different roles in different contexts, and its development, Martin explains, was especially fostered by the rise of the early modern court.[150] Martin underlines how courtly life was constantly "studied and self-examined," and how in the courtly context men and women found the arts of prudence, self-reflection, and dissimulation necessary for survival.[151] It is precisely this prudential self that was the antithesis to the emerging urge for sincerity, and that pressured those living at court to seek spaces where they could offer a sincere image of themselves.[152]

The urge for sincerity was connected to the will to safeguard one's private dimension, and with it one's individuality: the desire to be sincere became the mark of the desire to be true to oneself and to discard the disguise imposed by courtliness.[153] It is precisely within this context that discourse about the satirist's sincerity and the idea of staying true to oneself expressed in anti-court satires come into play. The exploration of anti-court satires becomes relevant precisely because of the insistence on honesty, the opposition to dissimulation, and the desire to see one's individual agency and freedom respected that can be found in such texts.

In addition, the investigation of anti-court writings sheds light on a significant issue concerning the prudential or performative self, which may help further explain the reason why many men and women of the Renaissance, in particular those living at court, may have had a conflicted relationship with such a model of selfhood. Chapter 1 illustrated how a defining feature of the prudential or performative self, especially in its courtly embodiment, was its distinctively protean character: a constant need to change in order to thrive in different environments and to please different kinds of people. With their insistence on authenticity and genuineness, anti-court satires investigate precisely the uneasiness that resulted from such an imperative for protean flexibility.

The courtier as Proteus

In 1562, Ludovico Domenichi published a collection of dialogues revolving around a variety of themes that most likely constituted hot topics at the time: love, true nobility, fraternal friendship, remedies for lovesickness, emblems, fortune, printmaking, and, of course, the court. The *Dialogo della corte* is based on Ulrich von Hutten's 1518 *Misaulus sive de aula*.[154] Domenichi's rewriting is rather faithful to the original,[155] introducing only minor variations to adapt it to an Italian setting: the identities of the speakers are changed from the original fictional names of Castus and Misaulus to Andrea Lario and Francesco Sardo, respectively.

The two interlocutors have roles that are a common feature of anti-court dialogues: one is an experienced courtier, the other a young man fascinated by the court, and the progression of the dialogue sees the young man enlightened about the real nature of the court. The *Dialogo della corte* opens with Andrea Lario stopping the courtier Francesco Sardo to compliment him on his clothes and the elegance of his appearance. Sardo, however, immediately begins to disabuse his interlocutor: he actually misses his old indigence, since it meant freedom. Those who spend their lives at court, he states, are not really free; all their silk, gold, and honorific titles are nothing more than tangible signs of their subjection.[156] Court life, Sardo goes on to say, is not even real life, only an image of it. The courtiers' elegance is, in fact, merely proof that courtiers are "banished from the real occupations of life."[157] Lario, moreover, cannot imagine the obligations that courtly servitude entails. Sardo depicts for him a state of total abnegation of one's own needs and desires and a complete dependence on the prince's will. As he puts it, "[S]o little am I Lord and master of myself, that I am entirely dependent on others' orders and desires."[158] What could be more humiliating than

> having no place, no time for oneself? every single thing according to someone else's will? living at another's table? turning pale at every meeting with the Prince? blushing? running away? occasionally being afraid and astonished? simulating and dissimulating many things? often bending one's knee, and bowing? almost always being bareheaded? doing everything as a slave, and with humility? never being master of oneself?[159]

What, in conclusion, can be more disquieting than having no mastery over oneself? What could be worse than being forced to "never say a thing that you mean, but only that which suits you? [...] to despise oneself? to have every thing under someone else's control? [...] and many times, against your own nature, to conform to the others?"[160]

What makes Domenichi's dialogue particularly relevant to the meaning of anti-courtliness, and to the relation of anti-court writings to the early modern sense of self, is that it explains with particular clarity how the courtier's identity seems almost to become the lack of any identity. In order to survive at court, the courtier has to become an eternal shape-shifter, someone able to adapt to ever-changing tasks, environments, lifestyles, and customs, just like the notorious Alcibiades, and to become even more variable than the mythological Proteus:

> And yet everyone who puts his neck under this yoke must start imitating Alcibiades. Because just as he lived in a different way in Athens, and in

> Lacedaemon, and in Thrace, and in Persia, always using different habits according to the flavour of the place, so it is necessary that a courtier adapt in every way to the habits of those with whom he lives, and that he be by nature mutable at every occasion; in all things double and astute; and in short much more changeable than was said of Proteus.[161]

There is a difference separating the reading of the protean mutability necessary for a courtier given by Domenichi's anti-court dialogue from the meaning assigned to the same feature in Castiglione's *Book of the Courtier*. For Castiglione, the courtier's protean flexibility was an essential part of his *grazia*; it is the quality that distinguishes him from the lack of adaptability of the soldier and the buffoon, the skill that will enable him to eventually conquer the confidence of his prince.[162]

Castiglione's idea of the courtier's protean qualities goes back to early modern readings of the figure of Proteus as the symbol for human artistic creativity and potential for learning. However, as A. Bartlett Giamatti points out, the figure of Proteus in the Renaissance had a negative side as well, associated with deception and misleading evil. The positive image of Proteus was based on a view of the mythological figure as a foundational agent in the civilizing process of humankind.[163] However, the dark side associated with protean mutability was equally influential in the Renaissance imagination. The infinite potential of the protean man could just as well become a curse, as Giamatti explains: "[I]f a man is Proteus, capable of all shapes [...] then he is also at the mercy of vanity and emptiness."[164] Proteus's ability to alter reality, furthermore, brought him dangerously close to the figure of a sorceress, such as the mythological Circe and the related Renaissance figures of Alcina and Armida. Possessing such a protean quality meant deceitfulness and duplicity at the least, and even emptiness and loss of meaning.

The sincerity advocated by the satirist becomes an antidote against this dark side of protean mutability. To the potential emptiness, meaninglessness, and loss of any individualizing characteristic that resulted from infinite potential, sincerity opposed its own quality as an "ethics of difference": something that allowed subjects to discover and to express the innermost part of themselves, what set them apart from all other individuals.[165] The sincere mode of expression advocated by satire, styled as proof of the author's otherness to courtliness, and the enumeration of the author's idiosyncrasies, which served the purpose of proving how the satirist was unfit for the demands of courtly life, all provide useful testimony to the uneasiness that surrounded the protean self of the courtier. In an age that saw "a new awareness of the self as subject, as an individual," as well as the emergence of an "ethic of individualism" that led the individual "to see him- or herself as a unique entity,"[166] the protean shape-changing required by courtliness, which contrasted – or even menaced – the sense of the individual as unique, could easily become a source of anxiety.

Anti-court satires and Renaissance society

Scholarly analysis has long sought an explanation for the success and dissemination of anti-court satires. The genre has been dismissed as repetitive and meaningless, voicing only the futile complaints of a class that could not find a way to oppose its subjection to an increasingly authoritarian power. However, the correlation between anti-court satires and issues concerning the early modern self can shed light on the reasons behind the popularity of the genre and the appeal that anti-court writings had for Renaissance authors and their public, despite the genre's purported triviality. Such a perspective also clarifies possible doubts concerning the veracity of the experiences of life at court recounted in anti-court writings, and to what extent such writings should be considered a reliable source of biographical and historical information.

The most telling case is that of Giovanni Agostino Caccia. Giuseppina Stella Galbiati has pointed out that despite employing anti-court motifs in his satires, Caccia never had any substantial relationship with the court.[167] Stella Galbiati also supposes that the addressee of Caccia's second satire – the unnamed *Signore* who intended to hire the author into his service – was purely fictional.[168] Similar observations show the extent to which anti-court writings could be an author's honest depiction of existing conditions, as well as a motif that little had to do with the author's biography.

Recognizing the presence of elements in anti-court writings that go beyond the life facts of their authors does not diminish their relevance in the panorama of Renaissance society. On the contrary, it means recognizing a general value in anti-court discourse. Anti-court sentiments, that is to say, appear as much more than personal complaints voiced as a consequence of an unhappy experience. The reasons and meanings behind anti-court sentiments and their expression in satirical writings need to be sought not in single facts concerning one person's life experience but in more extensive matters involving more than one subject. By authoring anti-court texts, both those who had actual experience with courtly life and those who, like Caccia, had never been employed as a courtier could employ a common language in anti-courtliness, for the expression of themes that were deeply relevant to contemporary men and women, and that transcended individual biographical experiences.

The most compelling definition of the function of anti-court writings in Renaissance society is offered by Amedeo Quondam, who has spoken of an "antiphrastic function" ("funzione antifrastica") of anti-court texts.[169] In Quondam's view, while they unmask the risks and the servitude of courtly life, anti-court writings transform the act of choosing the court into choosing freedom, and ultimately preach the necessity of becoming a courtier. Writings against the court thus end up celebrating the court, representing it as "the site of a really exceptional virtue, of a peculiar fortune, of an heroic practice."[170] Quondam concludes that anti-court discourse is nothing more than a part of courtly discourse, ultimately just one of its "power effects" ("effetti di potere").[171] Quondam's analysis is extremely significant, as it underscores relevant features of anti-court writings: the persistence of feelings of attraction to the court, and the possible use of anti-court texts as cynical pieces of advice on how to survive at court, as seems to have been the case for Piccolomini's *De curialium miseriis*. Following Quondam's train of thought, Stella Galbiati emphasizes that anti-court production, being mostly practised by court writers, needs to be subjected to an "antiphrastic decoding" ("decodifica antifrastica"): only the court could provide *literati* with the funds they needed to pursue their intellectual *otium*, and by praising such *otium*, anti-court writings ultimately reinforce the idea of the court as the only place of employment for the early modern *literatus*; as a result, the autonomy endorsed in anti-court satires appears a contradiction in terms.[172]

A reading of anti-courtliness as dealing with not only matters concerning intellectuals' independence from power but also issues pertaining to the early modern sense of self allows for additional interpretative perspectives on anti-court writings. While it is undeniable that anti-court writings assert the court's centrality to early modern culture even while denigrating it, when we take into account questions of selfhood and individuality, it can be argued that such writings have broader significance than being exclusively a reflection on the court.

When one considers the mask of the satirist, with its insistence on honesty and artlessness, as part of a search for models of self-fashioning other than the exemplar of the courtier, anti-court writings appear not only as a reinforcement of the discourse of courtliness; they also reveal an attempt to develop a different discourse concerning, if not society and the court, at least the dimension of selfhood. For most anti-court writers, such a search for an alternative model of self-fashioning remained, in fact, confined to the private dimension. Ariosto constructed for himself the persona of the genuine and easygoing satirist, opposed to his guise of the refined court writer and skilled functionary (who was assigned delicate tasks like acting as commissioner for the rebellious province of Garfagnana).[173] Caccia is representative of one more tendency: the intellectual who was able to reject the court and live on his own, withdrawing to his own villa.[174] The sixteenth century also saw, however, quite a different model: the celebrated satirist who succeeds in leaving the court behind and fashioning for himself a persona diametrically opposed to that of the courtier without having to withdraw into a private dimension but becoming instead a very public figure.

The whore, the virgin, and the satyr

When Pietro Aretino – the notorious scourge of princes ("flagello dei principi") and the most outspoken representative of anti-courtly sentiments in early modern Italy – first took up residence in Venice in 1527, thus exchanging courtly servitude for Venetian freedom, he considered it only a temporary arrangement.[175] The son of a cobbler from Arezzo, Pietro, like many ambitious young men of his time, had moved to Rome, seeking fortune at the papal court.[176] Although the exact date of his arrival in the capital is unknown, he certainly was able to quickly immerse himself in the chaotic, carnivalesque, and yet potentially propitious atmosphere of the city under the papacy of Leo X.

His first patron in Rome was the rich banker Agostino Chigi. According to Paul Larivaille, Aretino's role in the Chigi household can be described as a hybrid between courtier and secretary, with different and changing tasks. Thanks to the many banquets and feasts that took place in the palace, the Chigi household also offered Aretino the opportunity to network with the most influential members of the papal court. Aretino's innate talent for witty conversation soon allowed him to reach the spotlight he craved.[177] In addition, Aretino made the most of his talent for poetry by writing Petrarchan poems, like many of his contemporaries did, but also – and most significantly – satires.

Aretino's Roman years are, in fact, the years that mark his "discovery" of Pasquino. Aretino did not invent the figure of Pasquino – a mutilated statue where people would hang anonymous poems criticizing institutions and society, and that came to embody the voice of popular discontent – but he was able to exploit the popularity of the figure to such a point that his name became synonymous with Pasquino.[178] Thanks to the mask of Pasquino, Aretino quickly acquired a reputation as a witty and caustic satirist, a figure to be respected and feared lest one feel the bite of his satiric invention.

Testimony to the fame Aretino earned in papal court circles is offered by an anonymous poem titled *Farza*. The poem has been alternatively ascribed to Aretino, and although most critical studies tend to reject such an attribution,[179] it remains a revealing document of the status Aretino had attained at the Roman court in the late 1510s and early 1520s. Most likely written in 1519–20,[180] the *Farza* stages two characters: the older and successful Calandro, "an expert in the court" ("pratico in corte"); and the young and naive Neapolitan shepherd Silvano, who has been promised a place at court. To the young aspiring courtier, the seasoned courtier Calandro has no better advice to offer than to recommend that he makes sure to have Pietro Aretino on his side; Aretino is so popular and powerful that "he is a bad enemy to whoever becomes such."[181] The last verse of the poem praises Aretino's verbal power: "May God protect all from his tongue!"[182]

Pasquinades and the mask of Pasquino garnered Aretino fame in Rome, but he also strove to create a name for himself as a refined man, a connoisseur of the arts, a skilled *literatus*, and a clever conversationalist. Yet these attainments were still not the extent of Aretino's aspirations, for his worst nightmare – as the portrait of struggling courtiers in his play *Cortigiana* illustrates – was to be just one of the many low-level courtiers who populated the court of Leo X. Perhaps surprisingly for a man who was to become the living embodiment of anti-court sentiments and who was to author a comedy that parodied the *Book of the Courtier*, starting with its title, Aretino's main goal was very much inspired by Castiglione's masterpiece on courtly manners. He aimed, in fact, to become the wise counsellor that the *Book of the Courtier* presents as the highest possible achievement of a courtier's career.[183] Aretino's aspirations, at least in Rome, were destined to be frustrated, and such frustration is expressed in both versions of the *Cortigiana*, the play that immortalized the image of the papal court of Rome as a whore-like figure.

In spite of depicting the court – and especially the papal court – with whorish features, Aretino was not ready to end his love affair with it. The decision to settle down in Venice and support himself through his literary work came only later, when all possible sources of patronage in Rome had been exhausted.[184] Aretino's departure from the Roman court, in fact, was the result of a tragic incident. After the death of Leo X, Aretino joined the supporters of Cardinal Giulio de' Medici and used the voice of Pasquino to denounce the corruption of the 1522 conclave that elected Adrian VI; this poetic activity resulted in a huge hike in Aretino's popularity. The election of the Dutch pope, however, was unfavourable to Aretino, and he left Rome. After brief stays in Bologna, Arezzo, and Florence, he finally moved to the court of Federico Gonzaga in Mantua, where he received a very positive reception. Yet unwilling to settle down in what was, after all, a minor court, in 1523 he joined the military camp of Giovanni dalle Bande Nere, stationed in Reggio Emilia at the time.[185] Aretino and Giovanni seem to have developed an immediate affinity, but the allure of the Roman court was still strong for Aretino, and he returned to Rome a few months later, after Adrian VI's death and the election of Giulio de' Medici as Pope Clement VII.

Aretino's return to Rome was, however, destined to a bitter end. He soon found himself involved in the hostilities between the two parties (pro-France and pro-Spain) that divided the Roman court. His involvement in the scandal that surrounded Marcantonio Raimondi's prints of Giulio Romano's *I modi*, sexually graphic images for which Aretino composed the licentious *Sonetti lussuriosi*, and the growing animosity between Aretino and powerful members of the papal court resulted in an assassination attempt carried out in 1525, which left Aretino wounded by stabbings and fighting for his life. The episode represented Aretino's first great disillusion with the world of the court, where he had a prominent role at the time and whose intrigues he might have underestimated.

For a second time, Aretino found refuge in the camp of Giovanni dalle Bande Nere, at whose side Aretino was finally able to perform the role of counsellor to which he aspired. Yet Giovanni's untimely death in 1526 put Aretino on the move again. He was briefly in Mantua, but for reasons yet to be ascertained,[186] he shortly thereafter moved to Venice, the city celebrated in his later works as the symbol of freedom in contrast to the abject servitude of the court, the Virgin that was a foil to the Whore representing the papal court of Rome. Over the years – especially after the Sack of Rome, which Aretino interpreted as rightful punishment for Roman corruption – Aretino's eulogizing of Venice would assume the features of a *translatio Romae*, with Venice becoming the new Rome and only heir to the glory that Rome had forsaken.[187]

The shift from the role of courtier – although one often critical of courtly life – to his new life in the Venetian republic also entailed for Aretino a change of character. In the years that followed, Aretino invested more and more in his self-presentation as the critical conscience of his age, the *acerrimus virtutum ac vitiorum demonstrator* (fierce presenter of virtues and vices) who would raise his voice to praise the worthy and fearlessly denounce the vicious. Aretino would increasingly declare himself the voice of truth, in pure satiric style, and even adopt a mask that took the notion of satiric blunt sincerity to the extreme: that of the satyr.

The popular Renaissance etymology of "satire" from "satyr" fostered the reading of the satiric persona as a coarse but truthful speaker. Raymond B. Waddington has investigated Aretino's association of his own public image with the figure of the satyr, and according to

Waddington, the satyr becomes the *impresa* that Aretino "chose to justify his profession of satirist through the satyr's legendary sexuality and truthfulness."[188] Waddington sees a parallel between Aretino's self-presentation as the natural, artless satyr and Castiglione's key concept of *sprezzatura*, the art of concealing one's art.[189] Aretino's carefully constructed anti-courtly persona thus becomes the highest embodiment of the primary courtly skill. Such conflicting dynamics well reflect Aretino's complex relationship to the courtly environment and its most prominent figures.

Ambition, success, and failure

For someone like Aretino – ambitious and conscious of his talent, but also very aware of being a new man overcoming barriers of class and rank[190] – a career at court represented a distinct possibility for upward social mobility, and yet also a position where the spectre of sudden disgrace and failure and the fear of losing in a moment everything that had been conquered with much effort were always present. These anxieties are expressed from the time of his early years in Rome, in the eloquently titled *Lamento de uno cortigiano già favorito in palazzo, et hora in grandissima calamità*.[191] The lamentation uttered by the eponymous failed courtier was most likely composed in 1522 and performed live during Carnival festivities,[192] and it can be considered an early hint of the crisis that would later turn Aretino from a brilliant prospective courtier (although one able to look critically at the institution) to the most vehement anti-court voice of the Italian Renaissance.[193]

The anxiety over a courtier's uncertain condition is voiced from the opening lines of the poem:

> Oh insolent hopes of the Court
> favour drunk on capricious smoke
> oh cowardly, lying, and dishonest fate.[194]

The rhyme *Corte/sorte* (Court/fate) immediately conjures the image of the court as the embodiment of Fortuna, against which even the wisest among men have little power. The once thriving but now derelict courtier is paying the price for having believed himself immune to the upheavals of Fortuna, and his present dishonour is also a warning to those who are, like he was, overly confident in their capacity to achieve and maintain success at court.

Marco Faini has identified the speaker with a historical figure, Giovanni Lazzaro de Magistris, known as Serapica. Of humble origins,

Serapica became one of the attendants and intimates of Leo X. His fortune came to an abrupt end with the death of the pope, when he was accused of theft and imprisoned.[195] It is significant, however, that the speaker of the *Lamento de uno cortigiano* is not singled out by even a geographic reference, and that both the scenario and the historical references in the text are too general to allow for anything more than speculations on the identity of the protagonist. Setting aside any attempts at identifying the speaker, then, the *Lamento de uno cortigiano* is noteworthy for the possible universal validity of its main character and the destiny that he embodies. The fact that the protagonist of the *Lamento de uno cortigiano* lacks any distinguishing biographical marks makes him just one courtier among many, whose destiny might as well be that of any of his peers.

In Aretino's vision, all courtiers share a sort of original sin: a hubris that leads them to dwell in the illusion that the luxury and privilege they have obtained will never falter, and that the "stalle" they come from can be forgotten forever. The failed courtier is well aware that his advice, addressed especially to young and naive prospective courtiers, will not be listened to. At the conclusion of the text he simply suggests the courtiers participate in Carnival, while he – having finished preaching his "vangelo" – wanders away in search of food:

> Place a mask on your face
> since Carnival is here anyway
> which has already made everyone silly from games.
> Set your comedies and meals
> call Trascin to entertain you
> and throw away one hundred *scudi* at once.
> [...]
> Now I want to go, with this new bag
> after having read my epistle and gospel
> to buy some cabbage, if I can find any.[196]

The references to Carnival festivities and, more precisely, to participating in such festivities in spite of the failed courtier's tirade, conjures an attitude that combines harsh critiques of the court and its shortcomings with a vital and somewhat joyous participation in its chaotic, carnivalesque dynamics. This attitude also informed the first version of Aretino's play about the court, the *Cortigiana.*

The 1525 draft of the *Cortigiana* does not construct a radical opposition to court life but instead immerses itself in the babelic atmosphere of the early sixteenth-century Roman court.[197] The play – whose title is clearly a pun on Castiglione's *Book of the Courtier* and can be understood as either "the courtly play" or "the courtesan" – stages two simultaneous plots, both involving a relationship with the court. The first plot follows the gullible Maco da Coe, who arrives in Rome in the hope of becoming a cardinal. He is approached by Maestro Andrea, who convinces Maco to hire him as a tutor by promising to make him a superb courtier, since he is a master in making them ("maestro di farli"),[198] and persuading him, finally, to take a bath in a hot-water boiler and be beaten with wooden sticks in order to make him "courtier in form" ("cortigiano ne le forme").[199] The second plot concerns a self-important Neapolitan gentleman named Parabolano who is pursuing the affections of a Roman lady (significantly named Laura) with the help of two servants: the virtuous and underestimated Valerio; and the scheming Rosso, who tricks Parabolano into meeting a courtesan disguised as his beloved lady.

In the first version of the *Cortigiana*, the author's point of view often coincides with that of Valerio, who becomes (as Giulio Ferroni has pointed out) a representative of "those subordinate courtiers to whom Aretino feels close."[200] Valerio is the character who shows the most awareness of the spirit and dynamics of the relationship between the subordinate and the powerful. He knows that the often-blamed tyranny of Fortuna at court is nothing more than a metaphor for the capriciousness of the powerful in rewarding loyal service, and he does not refrain from telling his master, Parabolano, that "Fortune is you lords, you lords are fortune, who raise ignorance and vice from stables and stirrups to high honours, and relegate instead virtue to stables and stirrups."[201] Yet Valerio is also able to partake in Fortuna's courtly reign and seize the opportunities that might come from it.[202] His dynamism, characterized by his openness to the opportunities potentially offered by Fortuna, contrasts with the more traditional and defeatist attitudes of his fellow courtiers Flaminio and Sempronio.[203]

The residual optimism that still pervades the play, in spite of many aspects of court life being objects of ridicule, becomes evident at the end when Valerio's virtue and wisdom are recognized by Parabolano. When Parabolano openly confesses to having mistreated his only faithful servant and asks for forgiveness, Valerio does not hesitate to rebuke his master directly, blaming "the nature of you lords, who let yourselves be easily fooled by the malicious and the flatterer, refuse to hear the reasons of one who has been accused in his absence, and exile any just man from your grace."[204] To this lament, the contrite master only replies, "[N]evermore!" ("non più!").

From amusement to invective

Aretino's attitude toward the Roman court began to change immediately after he fled the city. In a sonnet most likely written in December 1526, he reflects a much different attitude toward his time at the Roman court: no longer amused participation in the court's perennial Carnival, but bitter condemnation and regret for the time spent there fruitlessly:

> Seven traitor years I have wasted,
> four with Leo and three with Sir Clemen*dacious*[205]
> and I am made the people's enemy
> more for their sins than for mine
> and I have scarcely two ducats of income
> and I am worth less than Gian Manente,
> so that, if one gives some thought to this,
> all the hopes of such papacies – I have them up my ass.[206]

In the sonnet Aretino depicts himself as a neglected virtuous servant – a Valerio without his *Signore*'s final recognition. The pope, Clement VII, is cast as the quintessential unrewarding patron, one who does not hesitate to lie to and betray those who served him faithfully, as the styling of his name – "Chemente," the one who lies – makes clear.

Yet even his life at the court of Mantua, where Aretino was welcomed with the sincere admiration of Duke Federico, was not without disappointment. Aretino's conflicted relationship with Federico is expressed in the 1533 play *Il Marescalco*, set at the court of Mantua and centred on a joke played by the duke himself on the stablemaster of the title. The eponymous character, notoriously misogynist and averse to marriage, is drawn into despair when he is told that the duke wants him to marry. Having no other choice than to submit to the will of his lord, the *marescalco* unwillingly accepts, but everything is revealed to be only a *beffa* the duke has played on his servant for his own amusement. Through the theme of a prince who arrogates to himself the power of being in charge of the private lives of his subjects, the *Marescalco* performs an analysis of the mechanisms of courtly power. The most perceptive reading of the play belongs to Deanna Shemek, who considers the *Marescalco* Aretino's revenge against Federico Gonzaga, since when the text was being written and performed, Federico himself was being forced into an unwanted marriage.[207] The courtly *beffa*, although orchestrated by the prince, eventually turns against him: the character of the duke can be in charge within the plot and is free to have fun at his subjects' expense, but it is the author who eventually has the upper hand, and who can sneakily turn the mockery onto the prince himself with the play and its public performance.

Aretino had already left Mantua for Venice when, in the summer of 1527, news of the Sack of Rome started reaching the rest of Italy. Aretino's reactions to the Sack range from sorrowful and heartfelt laments to harsh satire that depicts the devastation of the city as appropriate retribution for the corruption of the papal curia.[208] What both reactions have in common is the idea that the atmosphere of perennial carnival that had characterized Rome under the two Medici popes – the same atmosphere that gave life to the chaotic background of the first *Cortigiana* – was gone forever. This change in tone, which is intertwined with Aretino's progressive "conversion" to Venice and will lead to the complete condemnation of the Roman court in the *Ragionamento delle corti*, is reflected in the 1534 revision of the *Cortigiana*.

The first noticeable difference is the retrogression of the character of Valerio. The character who in the first version acted as spokesperson for the author now becomes a marginalized figure and is indirectly criticized for not being able to ever free himself from a courtly mentality. Instead it is Flamminio,[209] a character who only had a few lines in the first version of the *Cortigiana*, who now expresses the most elaborated reflections on the court.

Flamminio is revealed to be a writer – more precisely, a satirist – and as the author of anti-court satires, someone who has denounced the court "as a heretic, a forger, a traitor, as insolent and dishonest."[210] It is Flamminio who voices the harshest critiques of the court throughout the play: in his exchanges with Valerio, whom he tries in vain to turn to the cause of anti-courtliness; and especially in his conversation with an old man named Sempronio, whom he successfully persuades not to send his son to court. Sempronio is, in this version, representative of a lost golden age of courts, when they really embodied the breeding ground for "virtue and decorum,"[211] and when courtiers were respected by the *Signore* and respected each other. The court of present times described by Flamminio is the complete reversal of this picture, even worse than hell, because "the soul is tormented in Hell, but at court are tormented both the body and the soul."[212]

Flamminio's anti-court invective is paired with his equally vehement praise of Venice, the city where he plans to find the respect he is denied in court:

> I may go to Venice, where I have already been; and I will enrich my poverty with Venetian freedom; because there, at least, no favourite (either male or female) has the power to murder a poor innocent; because only in Venice are the scales of Justice kept even; only there does the fear of someone

> else's disgrace not force you to worship someone who just yesterday was covered in lice. And whoever doubts the worth of Venice should consider how Venice is blessed by God; and certainly this is the Holy City, and Heaven on earth.[213]

Larivaille describes Aretino's praise of Venice as "courtier-worthy."[214] It would not be completely wrong to see in the second version of the *Cortigiana* traces of an ambivalent attitude toward the court, in spite of the vehemence of its anti-court invective. Again in conversation with Valerio, Flamminio launches himself into praise of the king of France that rivals his eulogy of republican Venetian freedom, and professes he is ready to move to the French court, being too accustomed to servitude to be able to leave the court behind: "[H]aving been accustomed, over the course of so many years, to serving at court, I cannot be without it, and I hence resolve to go to the court of His Majesty."[215] The reference to the French court is related to Aretino's hope that King Francis I, who had been showing him appreciation and providing him with financial support (although not as much or as often as Aretino wished), would eventually invite him to join his court.

Yet in spite of this residuum of courtly ambition, Aretino's attitude toward the court was beginning to change radically, as was his attitude to anti-court satire. Evidence of this latter shift is found in the character Valerio's loss of prestige. Valerio, as in the first edition of the *Cortigiana,* still utters passionate denunciations of the evils of the court, blaming especially the lords' ingratitude. Yet he proves himself utterly incapable of ever imagining an alternative lifestyle to the courtly one, since he ultimately switches to defending the court and the *Signori* during his dialogue with Flamminio.[216] While the character of Flamminio reflects Aretino's attempt to play both sides – praising the Venetian republic as heaven on earth and the only antidote to the hell of the courts, but still flirting with influential princes – Valerio is relegated to reiterating formulaic anti-court complaints, while at the same time confessing his inextinguishable attachment to the court.[217] Valerio's loss of credibility reflects Aretino's evolving attitude on anti-court laments coming from insiders to the court system and on their effectiveness, an attitude that would further be developed in his anti-court masterpiece, the *Ragionamento delle corti.*

Aretino's new anti-courtliness

Aretino's detachment from courts and courtliness became increasingly pronounced during the 1530s, paralleling his growing integration into Venetian society and his ability to find additional ways to support himself without having to return to courtly service. Aretino's "conversion" to Venice is expressed in an undated letter to Doge Andrea Gritti, where Aretino repudiates the court and professes eternal loyalty to Venice, which is described as the antithesis of the court and its evils:

> But I, who in the freedom of such a great state have managed to learn to be free, refuse the Court forever, and I here I build a perpetual tabernacle to the years that I have left, because here betrayal has no place, here favour cannot do an injustice to what is right, here the cruelty of prostitutes does not reign, here the insolence of the effeminate does not command, here one does not steal, does not rape, does not murder.[218]

Understanding that staying in Venice was his best alternative, Aretino started planning a diverse set of strategies to secure financial support. From 1527 until their final rupture in 1531, he had been able to obtain support from the Duke of Mantua in exchange for writing a chivalric poem designed to continue the plot of the *Orlando Furioso* and which would have brought prestige to the court of Mantua. The poem, *Marfisa disperata*, was never completed,[219] but it represented a crucial step in Aretino's life: the moment when he understood that he could live off his literary works.[220]

Aretino's strategy would include first of all a sagacious balance of praise and criticism of the powerful, thanks to his mastery of the opposite genres of encomium and satire. This strategy has been accurately described by Larivaille as consisting of "practising paid encomium protected by the tacit menace of Pasquino, set aside as an instrument for putting reluctant patrons under pressure."[221]

In addition, in 1534 Aretino, overcoming some initial perplexities regarding the status of the printing press,[222] began a fruitful collaboration with the printer Francesco Marcolini that paved the way for his successful career as a *poligrafo*.[223] Although Aretino's career was not without its highs and lows, his strategy proved to be effective, so much so that the son of an obscure cobbler from Arezzo was able to live in an elegant residence on the Canal Grande and maintain a sumptuous lifestyle. In the years that followed, Aretino would become a model for many more *literati* who would try to follow in his footsteps and live independently, supporting themselves with their literary activity.

Aretino's growing self-confidence and sense of independence would give rise to a new anti-courtliness that represents a summary of all his previous writings against courts and courtiers, but taken to more radical conclusions. The *Ragionamento delle corti*, published in 1538, is thus heir to the reflections on the nature of the court and the status of the courtier that Aretino started with the *Lamento de uno cortigiano*, as well as, more broadly, to the tradition of anti-court satires in both verse and prose forms.[224] Its peculiar Venetian perspective, though – in being written not by a court writer but by a former insider who had found shelter in the freedom of the Venetian republic – makes it a unique piece of work.[225]

The *Ragionamento delle corti* has its origins in a few letters written in 1537, the year before its publication, all of which discuss Aretino's rejection of the court in favour of Venetian freedom.[226] Aretino depicts his life in Venice as the embodiment of the mastery over oneself that is often longed for and portrayed as lost in anti-court satires; in Venice, he says, "all the hours belong to my free will."[227] One letter is particularly relevant, since it is addressed to Francesco Coccio, one of the characters in the dialogue, and it stages Coccio's abandonment of courtly aspirations. In the letter, Aretino congratulates Coccio for having come to reason and abandoning the idea of becoming a courtier, deciding instead to devote his life to his studies.

The *Ragionamento delle corti* depicts the process of Francesco Coccio's conversion to anti-courtliness. The *poligrafo* Lodovico Dolce, to whom Coccio has disclosed the intention of giving up his studies to enter the court, recruits two speakers whose task is to open Coccio's eyes to the real nature of the court. The first speaker is Pietro Piccardo, a former member of the Roman court, who instructs Coccio on the nature of the papal court. The second speaker, Giovanni Giustiniano, a man of letters, has the task of describing princely courts.[228] At first reading, the *Ragionamento delle corti* may simply look like a further development of an already stated view on courts and courtliness, or even nothing more than a virtuosic piece that reiterates all the conventions of anti-court satire. However, when one confronts the *Ragionamento* with Aretino's other ventures in the genre of anti-court critique, especially in reference to the figures of courtiers who act as spokespersons for critiques of the court, the *Ragionamento* appears to be more of a reconsideration of Aretino's approach to anti-courtliness, or even a way of rethinking anti-court satire in general.

The courtier Piccardo starts right away by enumerating the many evils of the court:

> The Court, good Sirs, is the hospice of hopes, the graveyard of lives, the governess of hatred, the root of envy, the bellows of ambition, the trading place of trickeries, the seraglio of suspicions, the prison of peaceful accords, the schoolhouse of sneakiness, the homeland of flattery, the heaven of vices, the hell of virtues, the purgatory of good deeds and the limbo of delights.[229]

Piccardo continues by naming other common evils of the court – such as ambition, envy, and flattery – and by pointing out how, in spite of its perverse nature, the court can still attract many young men drawn by the hope of a quick rise to fame and wealth. In the explicitly polemical and satirical passages that form Piccardo's speech, Aretino consciously revives traditional anti-court discourse and renews it through the infusion of new, powerful, and controversial topics such as the unnaturalness of courtly life, exemplified by the monstrous figures of bearded children ("fanciulli barbuti") and white-haired youths ("giovani canuti") that can be found only at court.[230] The rest of Piccardo's disquisition takes the form of an overview that addresses the archetypal anti-court topoi one by one. Piccardo accurately points out how the court forces men of very different natures to live side by side, how it is pervaded by envy and grudges, how it imposes every kind of physical hardship without ever rewarding the virtuous, and how easy it is to fall from grace and never recover.

Piccardo's anti-court tirade is probably the most eloquent and incisive critique of the court ever written during the Italian Renaissance. Yet despite its satiric intensity, it is not effective in converting Coccio to the cause of anti-courtliness.[231] A close reading of the *Ragionamento* reveals in fact that Coccio's eventual disillusionment is not really a consequence of the blunt anti-court position presented by Piccardo. Coccio appears still very much attracted to the court, even after hearing such an unforgiving anti-court invective. Piccardo's picture of the court as hell on earth is at risk of functioning antiphrastically, reinforcing in the aspiring courtier a heroic view of court life. By contrast, the point of no return – Coccio's conversion to anti-courtliness – comes later, as a result of Giustiniano's nuanced and less uncompromising speech.

Piccardo's invective is an example of a critique of the court coming from one of its members. The undeniable amusement and sympathy that the old, disenchanted courtier Piccardo provokes is accompanied, on several occasions, by suggestions that undermine him as a persuasive anti-court narrator. Coccio seems to react in a sceptical way to the vehemence of Piccardo's bitter outbursts, calling him "possessed" ("spiritato")[232] and even defending the princes' liberty in raising or demoting whomever they want.[233] Furthermore, the dialogue makes clear that Piccardo is and always will be part of the world that he is criticizing. Piccardo is ready to confess the meretricious strategies that he has developed as a courtier to please his patrons,[234] and while the remarks on Piccardo's undeniable affiliation with the court give his speech the credibility of direct experience, they nevertheless cast an unquestionable shadow of scepticism over the truthfulness and persuasiveness of an anti-court lecture from someone admittedly so skilled in courtly deception, mystification, and subterfuge. Such scepticism explains why Coccio does not hesitate to accuse him of exploiting the system he is criticizing: "Whoever twisted your arm a little would make you confess how you have smuggled some profits out of the hands of the Court, which you now enjoy while shitting all over the Court!"[235]

What is significant in Coccio's reaction to Piccardo's anti-court lecture at the end of the first part of the *Ragionamento* is that Coccio remains faithful to his proactive view of the court as the embodiment of Fortuna, considering it a source of opportunities for the ambitious and persistent. At the end of the first day of the dialogue, Coccio is not discouraged from entering the court but is instead very ambivalent. He accepts Dolce's offer to meet with Giovanni Giustiniano on the following day, stating that "I will either abandon the resolution to enter the court, or I will immediately put it into effect."[236] And most significantly, to Dolce's additional anti-court remarks he eventually replies, "[T]hen the Court is right for me, if one gains happiness from action there."[237]

The second day of the dialogue centres on Giustiniano's speech, which, unlike Piccardo's completely negative picture of the court, negotiates exceptions by referring to some virtuous courts and proposes strategies on how to deal with the powerful. It is only thanks to this approach that Coccio's courtly aspirations come to an end. The ambiguous position, in other words, succeeds where the direct critique had failed. Instead of replicating the traditional topoi of anti-courtliness, Giustiniano – alerted by Dolce that Coccio is "voracious" ("ingiottonito") for the court, and that he is not frightened by what he has heard – demolishes one of Coccio's most resilient hopes: that of achieving social mobility at court. Giustiniano demonstrates that the court denies any real upward social mobility by consistently refusing to reward the talented. He shows that, on the contrary, at court there is no respect for them.[238] Reworking a point already expressed by Piccardo – the ability of the court to drive mad even the wisest among men[239] – Giustiniano shows that there is no way of effectively confronting the court with the weapons of virtue and rationality, since nothing at court amounts to more than unpredictable folly. The lack of reward for the talented in search of upward mobility and recognition is the point that finally disabuses Coccio.[240] As he points out,

> Anything could be tolerable if at the end he who reads the things that are made by those who know judged with his ears and not with his nose. Oh, what a penance is the life of worthy minds torn apart by those who know only a couple of syllables and who can conjugate a couple of suffixes![241]

Only at this point is Coccio converted. From now on, he promises, he will follow the example of his interlocutors and court only the sciences.[242]

The model set for Coccio in the *Ragionamento delle corti* is that of the man of letters who has chosen Venetian freedom over the court. Such an example, moreover, does not preclude relationships with potentially useful connections, like with some rulers of Italian courts. Giustiniano's speech famously includes a list of "good" princes and courts that can consider themselves spared from the harsh judgment cast on the court in the previous pages.[243] To the figure of the resentful courtier featured in many satires on courts and courtiers, the *Ragionamento delle corti* opposes a figure who can maintain the right equilibrium between the search for patronage and the refusal of courtly service, who is capable of keeping good relationships with princes while simultaneously avoiding service at court. The *Ragionamento delle corti* formulates a condemnation of courtly life that does not also include condemnation of potentially useful connections but attempts to strike a balance between the rejection of courtly servitude and the association with powerful patrons.[244]

The court of heaven, the printer's garden

After dealing with all the existing types of courts, the *Ragionamento delle corti* ends with the image of the court of Jesus ("la Corte di Giesù"), praised as the only court that can be free of the vices of the courts of the world. This conclusion adds a nostalgic nuance to what is otherwise a caustic, often irreverent text, and easily calls to mind the equally visionary conclusion of Castiglione's *Book of the Courtier*.[245] The unexpected mystical turn of the satiric anti-court dialogue also needs to be linked to Aretino's contemporary attempts to establish a reputation for himself as a religious writer, following the publication in the mid-1530s of his first sacred works.

The conclusive frame of the *Ragionamento delle corti* signals the dialogue's otherness to courtly space by announcing the arrival of the Venetian typographer Francesco Marcolini, whose garden ("giardinetto"), with its quiet intimacy, has provided the speakers with a refuge from the late-summer sultriness as well as from the misery of courtly memories. The *Ragionamento delle corti*, in other words, leaves the readers not so much with the dream of a heavenly court as with the realistic picture of a consortium of free men – the courtier Piccardo now away from the scene, the host Marcolini presumably about to be informed of Coccio's successful conversion to anti-courtliness – sharing the benefits of intellectual exchange offered by the Venetian environment.

The setting in Marcolini's garden is also a way to underscore Aretino's connection to the printer himself and to the printing industry in general, and a way to emphasize the central role that the Venetian printing industry plays for the man of letters in the strategy of freedom from the court that the *Ragionamento delle corti* has outlined.[246] The years that saw the composition and publication of the *Ragionamento delle corti* are particularly important in Aretino's career, especially in relation to the image he was trying to build for himself. Shortly before the *Ragionamento delle corti*, Aretino had published the *Sei giornate*, a text that also includes elements of critiques of courts and courtiers.[247] The year 1540 (two years after the *Ragionamento delle corti* was published) saw the publication of the first two cantos of Aretino's unfinished mock-heroic poem *Orlandino*, a work that begins by deriding the courtly tradition of chivalric epic.[248] In the years around the creation of the *Ragionamento delle corti*, Aretino, it would seem, was conducting a general attack on courtliness and on its cultural products.

Most importantly, in 1538, the same year the *Ragionamento delle corti* was published, Aretino also launched a new enterprise with the publication of the first volume of his *Lettere*. Publishing an epistolary volume was a self-promotional move that allowed Aretino to present a carefully crafted image of himself. The image created, thanks to the presence among his correspondents of the most influential figures of the time, is that of a man who wants to be considered by those in power as an interlocutor, a mediator in delicate situations, and (faithful to his reputation as the "scourge of princes")[249] a judge of their reputations. The *Ragionamento delle corti* participates in this strategy precisely by countering the figure of the subjected courtier with that of an independent intellectual who aims to interact with those in power on his own terms. In addition, by including references to pivotal contemporary historical events such as the negotiations between France, Spain, and the papacy, the *Ragionamento delle corti* also testifies to Aretino's desire to take an active role in discussions involving the major political forces of the time.[250]

Throughout his epistolary collection, Aretino not only professes his relevance as a political interlocutor and judge of the powerful and boasts of the profits he can make, thanks to his connections. He also brags about his prodigality and how he squanders most of the money he receives. This candid confession of prodigality represents a precise self-fashioning strategy, a strategy that has a peculiar anti-court tone. Just as when Aretino adopts the mask of the satyr to underline his qualities of naturalness and truthfulness as opposed to courtly sophistication and duplicity,[251] when he insists on his prodigality, a characteristic that directly contrasts with the stinginess of the lords who are denounced in anti-court writings for neglecting their faithful servants,[252] Aretino wants to create for himself a persona that embodies anti-courtliness. At the end of his life, in his residence in Venice, Aretino becomes, in Larivaille's definition, a prince with no land ("principe senza terra") and even reaches the point of having himself portrayed on a medal, sitting on a throne while receiving gifts.[253] More precisely, one could say that he becomes an anti-prince whose lifestyle mirrors and defies the court at the same time, thus becoming the living embodiment of anti-courtliness.

The fate of the satirist

The *Ragionamento delle corti* had remarkable impact as a literary model. The tropes that it revived and reinterpreted – especially the notion of the court as the "hospice of hopes," where every expectation of success was destined to fail miserably – had a strong legacy in anti-court writings both in verse and in prose. Aretino's disciple Maffio Venier is the author of a *Satira contro la corte* in Venetian dialect that shows a strong influence of the anti-court topoi employed by Aretino.[254] Cesare Caporali's *La corte* directly quotes the *Ragionamento delle corti* by defining the court as the "public hospice of hopes" ("publico spedal delle speranze"),[255] while the pun *Corte/Morte* was heavily employed in verse satires and also appeared in prose works not directly centred on the court, such as Giuseppe Betussi's dialogue on love, *Raverta* (1544).[256] And yet, if the *Ragionamento delle corti* asserts itself as an influential model, the same cannot be said of the model of the man of letters embodied by its author. If Aretino was able to style himself as the "segretario del mondo,"[257] the generation of *literati* that came after him had to rely on a very different secretarial figure: the one theorized in treatises such as Battista Guarini's *Il segretario* that outline a figure whose only task is putting his skills at the service of his lord.

As the sixteenth century progressed, the fate of the anti-court satirist, and more generally of satire as a genre, became increasingly grim. As Danilo Romei has pointed out, as soon as satire became systematized and collections of satire began to enjoy wide dissemination, the production of satires began to decline.[258] Romei has identified the cause of this decline in the increased censorial control that followed the institution of the index of prohibited books, which, in its different versions published between 1559 and 1593, condemned the most important Italian satiric texts, including the works of Aretino.[259] As a result, works with the explicit title of *Satire* would rarely be published in the period from the mid-sixteenth century to the mid-seventeenth century. Writers continued to compose anti-court satires, such as two works by Vinciolo Vincioli and Iacopo Soldani, both titled *Sopra la corte*, proving the centrality of the theme in satiric production. Both works, however, as well as many other satirical works written in this period, would not be published until much later.[260]

One significant exception in the bleak panorama of late sixteenth-century satiric writings is represented by Cesare Caporali and his *Rime*, published in 1582, which include *capitoli* on the court. Caporali also explored anti-court themes in two more works, likewise published in 1582: the *Viaggio di Parnaso* and the *Avvisi di Parnaso*.[261] The *Viaggio di Parnaso* is styled as an imaginary trip on the part of the narrator, who, disappointed by the courts on earth, finds refuge on Mount Parnassus in the court of the god Apollo. Only there are the *literati* finally able to get the recognition denied them on earth, and are restored from the miseries suffered in the *tinelli*.[262] The *Avvisi di Parnaso* further develop the theme of the decadence of contemporary courts by employing the metaphor of the court as a woman already present in *La corte*, and by depicting the marriage of *Madonna Corte* with *Vituperio*.[263]

In Caporali's case, the causticity of his anti-court satire is contrasted by the good rapport that he was able to establish with the powerful and by his success as a courtier. In addition, it is also important to point out that while all of Caporali's comic works belong to the style of Bernesque poetry (and Francesco Berni is directly quoted as a point of reference for the author in the *Avvisi di Parnaso*),[264] Caporali's writings on the court are heavily influenced by Aretino's production, in particular the *Cortigiana* and the *Ragionamento delle corti*. The notion of the *Ragionamento delle corti* as a model for late sixteenth-century writings on courts and courtiers becomes particularly relevant when one considers the profoundly changed conditions of the courts of the time, and how this affected the opportunities available to men of letters. Such a different perspective is exemplified precisely in the contrast between the real – although idealized – civic heaven of the Venetian republic eulogized by Aretino in the *Ragionamento delle corti*, and the dream-like dimension of the escape to Mount Parnassus depicted in Caporali's *Avvisi di Parnaso*. The utterly fictional nature of Caporali's break from the court is a telling sign that the model of the man of letters offered by the *Ragionamento delle corti* was no longer a viable option.

The anti-courtier persona incarnated by Aretino – the man of letters who rejects the court, supports himself with his own writings, engages with princes from outside the court and on his own terms, and even styles himself, in his own residence, as an anti-prince – becomes an unattainable ideal. The anti-courtier model presented in later anti-court writings is hence bound to be something very different: no longer the irreverent public persona of the scourge of princes, but a private man who can retain his honesty and safeguard his liberty only by withdrawing into the private, simple world of a rural environment, be it a country villa or a secluded pasture.

Chapter Four

The Shepherd

Pastoral anti-courtliness

In Antonio Cammelli da Pistoia's play *Filostrato e Panfila* (1499),[1] the disenchanted courtier Tindaro decides to run away from the court immediately after having offered his support to the titular lovers as an act of rebellion against his prince, Panfila's tyrannical father. Tindaro's farewell to the treacherous environment of the court echoes the critiques of courts and courtiers found in many Renaissance satiric writings, ending with an eloquent "Be well, my friends, and you, Court, remain where you are; I run away from my death and from your snares."[2] The play offers no further hints as to where Tindaro may take refuge in his desperate flight from the corruption and subjection of the court; however, a reader of early modern anti-court texts might offer a plausible hypothesis regarding the character's fate. Someone like Tindaro – a product of court culture and yet extremely disappointed with it and in search of quiet and a long-lost genuineness – may have very well ended up in the pastoral world. The depiction of a rustic countryside that becomes a space of post-court recuperation and rediscovery of the values that were lost at court is prominent in the panorama of early modern Italian literature. The proem to the forty-fourth canto of the *Orlando Furioso*, for example, includes a reflection on friendship that contrasts the genuine relationships of a rustic environment to the fake interactions of the court:

> The bond of friendship tends to be better secured in the homes of the poor, and where there is misfortune and hardship, than it is amid the invidious wealth and luxury of royal courts and splendid palaces, full of snares and mistrust, where charity is extinct and friendship not to be found, other than counterfeit.[3]

Early modern literature also offers famous examples of former courtiers (fictional shepherds in pastoral dramas, or real-life autobiographical figures) lamenting the years they wasted at court before they took refuge in a world of pastoral simplicity. The shepherd who offers hospitality to the fugitive Erminia in Torquato Tasso's *Gerusalemme Liberata,* and the figure of Carino in Battista Guarini's *Pastor Fido* – to quote only two of the most famous cases – are eloquent illustrations of characters expressing regret for the time they spent fruitlessly at court prior to finding redemptive sanctuary in a pastoral dimension.

In early modern pastoral texts, shepherds are most often seen either professing their love for a recalcitrant nymph or despairing over her rejection. On the rare occasion when a shepherd is portrayed as happy, it is typically because he has recently returned to his native land after some long, unhappy years at court. The "happy shepherd" is, in other words, a former unhappy courtier.[4] The principal point of investigation of this chapter will be precisely this figure, the unhappy courtier turned happy shepherd, as well as his complement, the villa dweller, and the relationship between pastoral felicity and court-induced infelicity.

An investigation of anti-courtly sentiments in works that can be identified as belonging to the pastoral mode needs to also take into account the peculiar, oftentimes puzzling relationship between the pastoral and the world of the court.[5] Following a modern wave of studies on the topic, this chapter will refer to the pastoral as a mode rather than a genre, given that, as such studies have shown, pastoral elements (in tone, style, and themes) can be found across a wide variety of genres.[6] Similarly, this chapter will also employ a broad definition of pastoral, one that encompasses texts that refer to any green world characterized by a simple, homely, and rustic existence, lived in contact with nature, devoid of any pretence of elegance and sophistication, and alien to the complications that characterize life in urban settings.[7]

In spite of such an insistence on naturalness and the lack of cultivation, the early modern pastoral is also known for being a refined and erudite mode, frequently associated with court writers and a courtly public.[8] Works in the pastoral mode were authored by court writers for the enjoyment of the court: pastoral plays were presented in the most refined Renaissance courts, and pastoral texts in general often featured members of the court in disguise among their main characters. As Lisa Sampson has pointed out, part of the appeal of the pastoral mode for a courtly audience resided in the fact that pastoral texts "upheld a consistently courtly perspective, by re-creating an apparently remote, mythological Arcadian existence in which noble-minded shepherds and nymphs could interact in accordance with moral and courtly norms."[9] The anti-court stances uttered in pastoral texts, that is to say, stand in sharp contrast with the intrinsically courtly nature of the mode. Or – to approach the issue from an opposite and yet complementary point of view – the fascination of court society for the pastoral mode seems problematic, given that the primary feature of all the works that can be included in the "pastoral" category is precisely the opposition between the world of the countryside, on the one hand (embodied in the space and place of the villa and the shepherd's pasture), and that of the city and court, on the other, inevitably accompanied by praise of the former and contempt for the latter.

The villa versus the court

Aretino's civic anti-courtliness, explored in the previous chapter, founded on praise of the freedom of the Republic of Venice as the antidote to the servitude of the court, is an exception in the panorama of anti-courtly sentiments. The most common alternative setting to the court offered in early modern Italian writings is non-urban and based instead on praise of a rural setting. Classical verse satire set the model for opposing the corrupt and chaotic city environment with the quiet of the countryside. The qualities of rustic simplicity, naturalness, and genuineness are a trademark of the satiric persona, as discussed in the previous chapter, and accordingly, the satirist sees the countryside and rurality – places that can be incorporated within the pastoral green world – as his natural dimension. In early modern Italian literature, the satirist's search for a place of uncontaminated authenticity, commendation for the simple life in a rural green world, and rejection of the courtly lifestyle are combined in the genre of *capitoli* in praise of the villa. Such writings often take direct inspiration from classical poems (with Horace and Juvenal serving, again, as the most influential models)[10] that praised country life over the chaos and the corruption of the urban environment.

The villa is praised in satiric *capitoli* and in other texts depicting country life as the epitome of freedom and literary *otium*, a counterpoint to the subjection and many chores of the court. It corresponds to what the sixteenth-century Florentine writer Anton Francesco Doni, in his 1566 treatise, *Le ville*, defined as a country house of leisure ("podere di spasso").[11] In *Le ville* Doni distinguishes between five types of villas – which also include, interestingly, the lower-status dwellings of craftsmen and peasants (which are still praised as the setting of a purer and quieter life than that of the city). The "podere di spasso," which belongs to gentlemen, is the type of villa devoted to fishing, hunting, and similar pastimes, where if you want, you can behave freely ("se tu vuoi, puoi starti alla libera") and where for a short time all thought of the city can be left behind ("brevemente tutti i penseri della Città si gettano dietro alle spalle").[12] It is the place devoted to intellectual *otium*: "[T]his is the country house which is suited to the well educated, this is the way the *literati* choose it, and it should be a half-day's trip, and not more, away from the city."[13] The remark about the ideal distance of the "podere di spasso" from the city – distant enough, yet not too far – underlines the lingering connection between the kind of villa that is appropriate for *literati* and their urban manners. This villa must not be not completely wild, but instead a mix ("non avere in tutto del selvatico, ma misto"),[14] hinting at the complex relationship between the free informality of life in the villa and the persisting relevance of some aspects of courtliness.

While the villa is undeniably important as a foil to the sixteenth-century court, the revival of the myth of the villa as the place for intellectual *otium* actually began in fourteenth-century Italy and is usually credited to Petrarch, on account of his praise of a solitary life of contemplation in the quiet of the countryside in his *De vita solitaria*. Boccaccio's *Decameron* similarly presents a flattering picture of the countryside, where he has his brigade of young men and women escape the outbreak of the plague in Florence. Withdrawing to a villa located in the outskirts of Florence, they spend their time narrating stories, playing music, and engaging in other refined pastimes. In keeping the minds of the young people away from the squalor and brutality of a plague-ridden city, the villa of the *Decameron* thus assumes a salvific connotation.[15]

In investigating the history of the villa in both architectural and literary terms, James Ackerman has drawn attention to the villa as an ideology, a dream created by urban elites that focused on an idealized notion of the countryside and wilfully neglected the crudest aspects of the reality of country life. The villa, Ackerman points out, was a "myth or fantasy" invented by urban elites and rooted in their privilege.[16] Inaugurated in the fourteenth century by two extremely influential Tuscan writers, and supported by a renewed trend for building villas that similarly began in Florence in the same century, the revival of the myth of the villa spread to the rest of Italy and eventually to the rest of Europe, and persisted for a surprising amount of time, extending into the eighteenth century.[17] The villa as presented by fourteenth-century Italian literature was based on the classical notion of a space devoted to the pursuit of *otium*. Far from being simple leisure, *otium* was generally characterized in classical literature as time dedicated to intellectual enrichment. To the praise of *otium* as a noble intellectual pursuit, early modern texts on the villa also add an ethical component by praising country life as the choice of the moral man, who retreats to the villa in order to spurn the temptations of vice-ridden urban society.[18]

In addition, early modern texts on the villa almost inevitably conflate the city with the court, and descriptions of the evils of an urban environment mirror the picture of life at court presented by anti-court satires. The villa becomes the anti-court, the only antidote to courtly corruption. Life in the villa is the exact opposite of life at court, and once in the villa the many evils of the court can be left behind. The feeling conveyed is that one can start life anew. Early modern praise of the villa emphasizes precisely the intellectual and moral qualities of life in the country. According to Ackerman, however, one should make a distinction between early Renaissance encomia of country life and sixteenth- and seventeenth-century texts. Later texts on the villa, Ackerman says, "lack the morally elevated core" of classical models (such as Cicero and Pliny) upon which they still rely, instead representing the villa only as a "restorative relief from the evils, restrictions and responsibilities of the city." In Ackerman's opinion, authors of sixteenth- and seventeenth-century praise of the villa seem uninterested in looking for opportunities for self-improvement, to the point of appearing at times insensitive and antisocial.[19] While it is undoubtedly true that sixteenth- and seventeenth-century encomia of life in the villa often remain confined to an introspective dimension, focusing on the author's withdrawal into the intimacy of his countryside property, it should also be noted that such a withdrawal is part of a process of recovering a relationship with oneself in order to overcome the feeling of depersonalization that life at court often provoked. In addition, even while expressed from a private perspective, praise of the villa sometimes shows a search for a collective dimension of kindred spirits that can replace the corrupted, dystopian socialization of the court.

The depiction of villa life in early modern Italy

Like representations of the hellish life at court, early modern Italian depictions of the serene life of the villa were often written in the form of satiric *capitoli*. But before the popularization of the *capitolo* as the standard form of expression for the moral themes of satires, such themes appeared in fourteenth-century sonnets.[20] A telling example is the production of Niccolò da Correggio, whose work includes, in addition to the critiques of the court mentioned in the previous chapter, poems in praise of the villa where the life of the country is contrasted with the evils of the court. Correggio's poem "Chi semina fatiche e vòl quïete" juxtaposes the quiet of the villa with the disquiet of the court, where "you struggle for ten years, and then, if you enjoy for an hour / a small favour, you forget all evil / and you praise the court and the lord."[21] Even wild beasts in their dens – Correggio continues – live a quieter life than those who live at court, where men are "more in conflict among themselves than the wolf and the dog" ("più discordi tra lor che il lupo e il cane").[22]

In the sonnet "L'ozio già tanto disïato godo," Correggio further praises the villa while regretting the years lost in vain at court ("l'età persa vanamente in corte"). In commending the villa as the place for erudite *otium* and as devoid of the envy and vain ambitions of the court, Correggio additionally stresses how the villa is also the space for recuperating one's free will over the dominion of Fortuna that characterized the court: in the villa, unlike at court, free will reigns and not chance ("l'arbitrio regna, e non la sorte").[23] Similarly, the poem "Ne più ne men come a natura piace" presents country life as the only way to live according to the dictates of nature, and the only setting where it is possible to achieve real peace. Frustration over the unattainable goals of life at court is far removed, and one realizes that "sometimes one can find in a hut / more happiness than in the great courts / where, to gain high ranks, one struggles so much."[24] Most importantly, the author feels that his desires (which are reasonable and moderate) are no longer thwarted for no reason, but on the contrary, he states, "I am not denied what I desire" ("cosa ch'io cerchi aver, non mi si vieta").[25] Such liberty in one's will and desires needs to be regarded, in Correggio's opinion, as the most important attraction of life in the villa. Country life may be less rich in material goods, but for the wise man no riches are more valuable than freedom:

> And the more one becomes expert in this life
> he truly knows that it is more enjoyable
> to have free will in the middle of a desert
> than in the cities, where everyone is at each other's throat.[26]

Free will is celebrated as the only way to achieve happiness, and as something that can be granted only by a life of tranquillity away from the court. Correggio's reflection on the supremacy of free will in the villa paves the way for a broader definition of pastoral spaces as the only place where one can recover the sense of control over one's self that is lost in the dehumanizing environment of the court.

Similar stances are expressed in a *capitolo* written by the poet, philosopher, and heretic Panfilo Sasso (1455–1527). Sasso's *capitolo* 33, which also shows the strong influence of Horace, is structured as a response to an unnamed interlocutor who has tried to persuade the author to leave the dark caves ("oscure grotte") where he appears to have ensconced himself and return to the city, designated as the environment appropriate to humankind. In his reply, the author declares that he can find quiet only in a remote pastoral space. Sasso constructs his pastoral retreat in diametrical opposition to the court, a place where one is not forced to put up with envy, arrogance, fraud, and other vices, and where there is no need for the hypocrisy and flattery demanded by courtly manners. At court, where the just are considered evil, there is no place for freedom.[27]

Over the course of the sixteenth century, the villa continued to be the subject of writings that carry on classical literature's juxtaposition of the city and the country. More specifically, such writings disseminate the image of the villa as the quintessential anti-court. In Francesco Berni's sonnet 66, evocatively titled "His life in the villa and his life at court" ("Sua vita in villa e sua vita in corte," bearing the indication "Mugello, 1534"), the poet narrates how he goes on with his life after abandoning the service of Ippolito de' Medici and withdrawing to a villa "that has been mine for a thousand years" ("che mill'anni è stata mia").[28] Throughout the sonnet Berni displays self-deprecating humour in depicting how he is now employed in manual work such as laundry and cooking, to the point that one could say he has been turned from a courtier into an animal ("di cortigiano è fatto un animale").[29] Berni's defence of this apparently unworthy life for a man of his status assumes the form of a dream of independence and self-determination. The court has already taken away too much of his life – sixteen years of tribulations and struggles[30] – and given him nothing is return, which frees him from any obligations.

The dissemination of the topos contrasting the court and the villa in sixteenth-century Italian and European literature may also have been prompted by the 1539 publication of a very influential text that was later to undergo many reprints and translations: Antonio de Guevara's *Menosprecio de corte y alabanza de aldea* (Contempt of the court and praise of the small village). Guevara (1480?–1544) was a Spanish Franciscan monk well versed in topics related to courtly life, having previously published a portrait of the ideal prince titled *Relox de principes* (The diall of princes) in 1529, as well as an influential manual of court conduct whose popularity was to rival that of Castiglione's *Book of the Courtier*, the *Aviso de privados y doctrina de cortesanos* (Warning for favourites and advice to courtiers), published the same year as the *Menosprecio*.[31] The latter two texts were soon translated into Italian and combined in one volume with the title *Avviso de' favoriti e dottrina de' cortigiani, con la commendazione della villa* (and the subtitle *Dispregio delle corti e laude della villa*), which was reprinted a good number of times during the sixteenth century.[32] The subtitle of the Italian translation makes the structure at the core of the *Menosprecio*, and at the core of other texts that oppose the villa to the court, fully evident: praise of the villa is cast as the other side of the coin of contempt for the court. For this reason, as Pauline M. Smith has pointed out, the lack of realism that characterizes Guevara's – and, one should add, other writers' – representation of country life should not be considered a limitation of such writings. The focus of praise of the villa is, in fact, mainly the court, and the villa is praised in order to mark the distance separating the ideal of courtly life from the reality.[33] In addition, the symmetry of praise (for the villa) and blame (for the court) at work in texts like the *Menosprecio* and similar encomia of country life represents a significant structural innovation over the texts that limit themselves to critiquing the court. Texts that criticize the court by subjecting it to an unflattering comparison with the villa add to the *pars destruens* represented by the tradition of writings against courts and courtiers a *pars construens* represented precisely by enumerating the advantages of life in the villa.[34] Such a *pars construens* acquires different nuances in writings in praise of the villa, depending on the author's sensibility or on the cultural climate in which a given work was composed.

In Francesco Bolognetti's satires, the theme of the villa assumes a predominantly moral dimension. The villa becomes the site of an ethically uncompromised life, a place of purification that can restore a soul that has been forced to confront the manifold vices of the court. After having repeated the usual theme of the villa's otherness from typical courtly evils such as greed, envy, and ambition, Bolognetti states that when living in the villa, "one thinks / only of doing good, with a pure and quiet mind."[35] In the villa, Bolognetti declares, time is usefully spent reflecting on the brevity of human life and concentrating on the Kingdom of Heaven. All earthly values hence appear vain pursuits and are despised accordingly, while the glory of God occupies all thoughts.[36] In this sense, praise of the simplicity of life in the villa and rejection of the quest for fortune at court likewise becomes a call for a spiritual redemption. The influences of classical culture in the myth of the villa are in this case enriched by a new Christian dimension.[37]

If the *pars construens* of praise of the villa in Bolognetti's satires stresses the spiritual dimension, the temporal dimension, represented by the renewed ideal of intellectual *otium*, remains nevertheless central and in some cases is complemented by political tones. Alessandro Piccolomini's sonnets show the direct influence of Horace in praising the villa as symbolic of a calm and healthy life that is the opposite of the chaos and tumults of Rome,[38] while Luigi Alamanni's *Satire IX* ("A Thommasino Guadagni") couples imitation of Horace with political references. Alamanni's satire begins its commendation of rural life with a direct quote of Horace's "Beatus ille," designating as happy only he who is able to look past the upheavals of Fortuna and stay away from the residences of kings, where simulation and envy rule the day:

> Lucky is the one who on solitary shores
> far from the rough populace, under a naked sky
> lives happily outside of the big cities
> [...]
> hoping for nothing, fearing little.
> and holds Fortune and the goods that she guards
> in contempt, as short-lived and base,
> and dreads the royal thresholds, all surrounded
> by fake love, and by real envy,
> like Harpies, like Sirens.[39]

Only he who can forgo any ambition and delight in humble pleasures can eventually achieve true happiness. In the last lines of the satire this praise of the simple life is revealed to be voiced by a tyrant who seems to be looking for redemption, only to immediately go back to his old ways (and sentence to death two just men):

> These words, as though he wanted to change fate,
> sang the tyrant who oppressed Sicily;
> but the very next day he put to death
> the two best men who lived in Syracuse.[40]

This satire is usually interpreted as referring to the contemporary political climate in Florence. Alamanni was part of a group of intellectuals who actively opposed the authority of the Medici over Florence, and who, in 1522, attempted to assassinate the future Clement VII. The attempt failed, two of Alamanni's companions were executed, and the poet, sentenced to death as well, was forced to flee to France.[41] The tyrant who is trying to pass as a just man but ultimately reveals his true colours by killing two of the best men of his state is interpreted as being Clement VII, and it is hypothesized that the satire was written in the early months of Alamanni's exile.[42] The freedom of rural life praised by Alamanni therefore assumes a precise political meaning.

Alamanni's resolution to put words in praise of the villa in the mouth of the falsely repentant tyrant, and his decision to reveal the speaker's true identity and cruel actions at the end of the text has an unexpected effect on the satire's tone and on the meaning to be attributed to the topos of the villa. Once revealed as having been voiced by an unrepentant tyrant, the praise of life in the villa – its freedom, absence of material greed and ambition, and untainted peace – is invested with scepticism. How can the reader take such commendation of peacefulness, humility, and erudite *otium* seriously, knowing that it comes from an oppressor whose very next move was to have two outstanding citizens killed? In Alamanni's straightforwardly political satire, the withdrawal to the villa, with its consequent moral renovation and conversion to a purer form of life, is problematized in an original way.

According to Danilo Romei, the peculiar structure of the early modern Florentine territory – with its urban space surrounded by a belt of suburban villas – would result in a peculiar variation of the myth of the villa in seventeenth-century Florentine satiric writings. Such suburban villas became an alternative space for encounters and discussions, separate from those of the court and of academies that still gravitated to the court's area of influence. Praise of the villa thus develops into a more meaningful and concrete reprisal of a myth that could appear trite.[43] An equivalent renovation of the cliché (although with different nuances in different authors and social contexts) can be observed in another related literary genre – that of agricultural tracts.

Anti-courtliness and agricultural literature

Agricultural and agronomic literature, which often included pages stating the reasons why life in a countryside villa was preferable to life in the city, became increasingly popular in Italy toward the end of the sixteenth century. Alamanni himself contributed to the genre with a poem titled *La coltivazione* (1546). The most influential texts, however, are usually considered those authored by Northern Italian writers: the *Lettera nella quale rispondendo ad una di m. Hercole Perinato, egli celebra la villa, et lauda molto l'agricoltura* (1544) by the Ferrarese Alberto Lollio; *La villa* (1559) by Bartolomeo Taegio of Novara (who is also the author of a *Della vita pastorale* and the founder of an academy significantly named Accademia dei Pastori d'Agogna); *Le dieci giornate della vera agricoltura, e piaceri della villa* (1564)[44] by Agostino Gallo of Brescia; and *La nuova, vaga, et dilettevole villa* (1597) by Piacenza native Giuseppe Falcone. The four texts differ in perspective – being more or less close to classical authorities, or offering dissimilar interpretations of *otium* that stress intellectual commitment to varying degrees[45] – but all reflect relevant aspects of attitudes toward the countryside and the city/court in sixteenth-century Northern Italy.

It is not coincidental that all these texts were published in the mid-sixteenth century, when awareness of the political crisis in the Italian territory was intensely felt among Italian intellectuals, leading to a nostalgic reprisal of golden age mythology and a rediscovery of the villa as the space for preserving the cultural values of the *literati* in a period that rendered the model of the independent intellectual attempted by Aretino (the "prince without land") unattainable.[46] What is particularly relevant for the present analysis is that in agronomical literature, just as in satires in praise of the villa, the dominant sentiment is that of anti-courtliness. In Lollio's *Lettera* the villa is represented as the only place for the moral renovation – through the practice of intellectual *otium* – of a society that has been corrupted by a series of vices, the enumeration of which clearly mirrors what can be found in anti-court satires.[47] Lollio's text is introduced by a sonnet by Ercole Bentivoglio, in which the anti-court tone of praise of the villa is made explicit:

> In the tumid Courts, under the arrogant roofs
> of the City, among the haughty walls,
> reside envy, and biting disquiets,
> blind ambition, distressing thoughts:
> among the deep woods, and the wild paths
> lies the most serene and pure life
> in the Villas, in the Fields; a life that does not care
> for Jewels, Gold, Status, Castles, Empires.[48]

Similarly, Taegio's *La villa* – structured as a dialogue between a committed city dweller and a supporter of the villa, the latter being a spokesperson for the author – includes a straightforward anti-court section that enumerates the many evils found among courtiers. Taegio's affinity with satirical themes, especially those concerning anti-courtliness, is not surprising when one considers his close association with the satirist Giovanni Agostino Caccia.[49]

The opposition between the court and the villa, and pastoral themes in general, are present in Caccia's *Satire* as well. Particularly relevant in this regard is Caccia's *Satira VIII*, ("Al Signor Gian Filippo Cazza fiscale di Sua Maestà"), wherein the author invites the addressee to join him in the villa, where, in addition to partaking of the commonly quoted countryside pleasures, they will study the classics and Petrarch and the *Orlando Furioso* ("'il Petrarca, e 'l Furioso") and spend their time in contempt of those who pass their hours pursuing their ambition.[50] Similarly expressive are the satirical poems "Al signor Giacomo

Maria Stampa"[51] and "Al Torniello governator di Novara,"[52] where Caccia adopts a shepherd persona ("I am a shepherd, used to life in the woods")[53] and proclaims his otherness to urban environments and intrigues.

The relevance of the theme of praise of the villa for sixteenth-century satire becomes even more evident in light of Romei's claim that the final example of satiric writing to be published in the last thirty years of the sixteenth century, before the decline of the genre, is precisely a text devoted to the villa, Giovanni Boni's *Satira in lode della villa* (1577).[54] In keeping with the spirit of the genre, Boni's *Satira* revolves around the author's intention to abandon the court and all worldly aspirations, and withdraw to the quiet and simplicity of the villa.

Despite the occasional invitation to a like-minded friend to join the author in the delights of the countryside, the dominant dimension of life in the villa, as depicted in sixteenth-century Italian texts, appears to be one of solitude and withdrawal. This feature is not surprising when one considers that a major inspiration behind the early modern recuperation of the ideal of the villa was precisely Petrarch's treatise in praise of solitary life, *De vita solitaria*. The solitude of the villa seems to have, first of all, an essentially recuperative meaning: such isolation is needed to recover from the forced proximity of men of very different natures, the coerced and heavily ritualized interactions, and the constant peer rivalry that characterize life at court. Yet the escape from the court to take refuge in a pastoral space does not necessarily exclude the search for collectivity, when that collectivity is strictly and distinctly anti-courtly.

The pastoral community

Most satires on the villa focus on the author's search for quiet and on his private withdrawal from the chaos of city and court. As such, the predominant tone of these writings is often one of intimacy, almost a longing for solitude.[55] Yet there are significant examples of authors who express the desire for the company of a kindred soul, as evidenced by Caccia's satire addressed to Gian Filippo Cazza, where the satirist invites his addressee to join him and share in the pleasures of villa life.[56]

Other texts juxtaposing the court with the pastoral world introduce instead the theme of a pastoral community, whose accord is antithetical to the cut-throat competition among peers of the courtly world. Niccolò da Correggio's eclogue "Pasciute pecorelle" presents a view of pastoral life as a space where all desires are satisfied, so that there is nothing more to long for. Most importantly, it is a place where all shepherds coexist in fraternal harmony:

> There is never a grudge nor bitter word among us,
> everyone leads his fellow's herd
> and no shepherd complains about another;
> you will not see among us someone focused
> on his own gain, but only on the common good.[57]

This picture of accord in pastoral society is a complete reversal of court society as depicted by Tindaro in Pistoia's *Filostrato e Panfila*:

> One courtier distrusts another
> one drives another away
> and what makes one cry, makes the other laugh.[58]

Jacopo Sannazzaro's *Arcadia* (1480), which had a substantial influence on Italian pastoral writings, offers a similar view of community relationships among shepherds being impervious to conflict. Competition among shepherds is presented as friendly, and if any tension arises, everything is eventually resolved for the better and to everybody's enjoyment.[59] Sannazzaro's poem is pervaded by a sense of amused competition among the Arcadian shepherds, who engage in races and other demonstrations of athletic prowess. The Arcadian competition may resemble the theatricality of courtly society and the drive toward exhibiting one's abilities in front of one's peers, yet it counters it with the facility with which every conflict is harmoniously resolved. Pastoral society thus becomes a purified version of the courtly environment, one that similarly includes displays of excellence but is devoid of all its evils.[60]

This feature of the pastoral world – that it is both courtly and anti-courtly at the same time – became typical of the genre that put pastoral themes at the centre of court culture: the pastoral tragicomedy. As satire dwindled around the middle of the sixteenth century, the pastoral tragicomedy emerged as the genre that was destined to enjoy the most success with courtly audiences.

Courtliness and anti-courtliness in pastoral plays

Agostino Beccari's *Il sacrificio*, first performed in 1554 and printed the following year, is usually considered the first Italian pastoral tragicomedy. It was dedicated to members of the ducal family of Ferrara and performed in a courtly setting twice in 1554, at the Este palace of Schifanoia.[61] As noted by Sampson, Beccari's *Il sacrificio* and other examples of early pastoral plays, such as Alberto Lollio's *Aretusa* (first performed in 1563 and printed in 1564) and Agostino Argenti's *Lo sfortunato* (first performed in 1567 and printed in 1568), are notable precisely because "they upheld a consistently courtly perspective, by re-creating an apparently remote, mythological Arcadian existence in which noble-minded shepherds and nymphs could interact in accordance with moral and courtly norms."[62] Pastoral plays were not the first texts, however, to explore a connection between the court and the pastoral world. The transposition of courtly figures and norms of courtly behaviour in a pastoral setting was already at the centre of Baldassar Castiglione and Cesare Gonzaga's eclogue *Tirsi* (presented in 1508). The eclogue centres on praise for a goddess, under whose mask it is easy to recognize Duchess Elisabetta Gonzaga, and on the shepherds and nymphs devoted to her, who represent the duchess's entourage at the court of Urbino.[63] Despite the celebratory and reassuring pastoral setting, darker undertones related to dramatic contemporary historical events pervade the *Tirsi* in a manner not dissimilar to the way in which disquieting nuances pervade the *Book of the Courtier*.[64]

Such indirect references to disquieting elements of the idyllic pastoral atmosphere should not be regarded as surprising. On the contrary, the pastoral mode must be understood as, among other things, a way to safely deal with potentially troublesome topics. Quoting Renato Poggioli's analysis of the pastoral mode, Ann Rosalind Jones has referred to the pastoral as providing "a fantasy structure through which the poet resists the political and social constraints of their time."[65] The ability to translate the complex into the simple,[66] along with the opportunities for disguise typical of this mode,[67] render the pastoral an effective way to confront pressing social and political concerns that would otherwise be too risky to explore. This is particularly true in relation to the court and all its potential issues or shortcomings. It is not surprising, therefore, to notice that Argenti's *Lo sfortunato* features both a courtly tone and references to anti-courtly sentiments. The prologue is communicated as the reflections of an author who has lived both between woods and fields ("tra le selve e 'i campi") and within the best-decorated palaces ("tra i meglio adorni Palagi"), and who has judged the former and the latter ("giudicato ha questi, e quelli"). The play is presented as a demonstration, in front of an understanding public, of the fallacy of those who

> adorned, and clad in the richest cloaks,
> and living in the most luxurious homes
> believe they are happy, and call miserable
> those who reside in a humble home,

enjoying just what is given to them
by fate and by the frugal hand of Nature.[68]

The author, on the contrary, intends to

demonstrate how happy is the rough
pastoral state, how far removed
from the greedy and ambitious impulses
that make our life sombre and anxious,
and from ill envy, which erodes and gnaws away at
the heart of those who with false appearances
show a face that does not match their mind.[69]

The pastoral environment presented in the play, devoid of envy and greed, offers instead shepherds and nymphs living in a state of harmony. As pointed out by Sampson, *Lo sfortunato* is the play that reintroduces the contrast between the city and the court, on the one hand, and the pastoral world, on the other, which had been characteristic of the pastoral mode in classical literature.[70] In addition to the prologue, anti-courtly stances also make their appearance in *Lo sfortunato* in the words of one of its characters, Silvio, a shepherd. Sampson has also noticed the play's originality in presenting praise of pastoral simplicity and critique of courtly sophistication through Silvio, who refuses love and with it, everything sophisticated, stating his preference instead for the simple activities associated with a rustic life.[71]

A similar stance of refusing the life of the sophisticated *palagi* and all the constraints imposed by courtly norms is found in the prologue of the best-known pastoral play of the Italian Renaissance, Torquato Tasso's *Aminta* (1581), a work that also engages in a very complex relationship with courtliness and anti-courtliness.[72]

The anomaly of Tasso's pastoral writings

The *Aminta* begins with a declaration of impatience with the values of the city/court that echoes the prologue of Argenti's *Lo sfortunato,* with which it also shares a Ferrarese origins and setting.[73] According to Fabio Finotti, the anti-court critique in *Lo sfortunato* ultimately remains confined within the court, for despite the declarations in the prologue, the play does not propose any real alternative to the court apart from an imaginary setting such as the Arcadian one. In Finotti's opinion, this is manifest in the prologue itself, where anti-court speech is followed by the claim that the play and its happy ending are entirely designed to celebrate the majesty of the city and the splendour of the court.[74]

In the *Aminta*, however, the relationship between praise of the court and the utterance of anti-court sentiments is even more complex. In Tasso's play, in fact, critique of the court is presented in a very convincing manner, only to be immediately denied and, what is more, transformed into an occasion to praise the court of Ferrara and its duke, Alfonso II.

Written in 1573, and most likely performed for the Este court in the summer of the same year,[75] the *Aminta* was considered an example of a happy season in Tasso's life, before the dark years of the split with his patron, Duke Alfonso II d'Este, and his imprisonment in the hospital of Sant'Anna. The *Aminta* focuses on the love between a shepherd and a nymph, a love that is first tormented and then eventually resolved in a happy ending. The shepherd Aminta is in love with the nymph Silvia, who does not reciprocate, even though Aminta saves her from being raped by a satyr. After a few tragic developments, when both Aminta and Silvia are erroneously believed to be dead, Silvia realizes she loves Aminta. For a long time, the *Aminta* was interpreted as nothing more than an example of evasive literature, although a particularly successful one from a stylistic point of view. Revised interpretations of the pastoral mode in general, and of the *Aminta* in particular, that first appeared in the last decade of the twentieth century have begun highlighting the problematic issues that insinuate themselves between the elegant lines of the text and within its idyllic pastoral setting.[76] Such problematic issues verge mainly on the play's relationship with the world of the court.

The potential for anti-courtliness in the *Aminta* becomes manifest from its very first lines, in which a fugitive Cupid longs to break free from his mother Venus, who, vain and ambitious as she is, forces him to use his bow and arrow only in the courtly world. At the same time, the links between the *Aminta* and the courtly world – the very same court for whose entertainment it was conceived and performed – are evident and strong. Just like Castiglione's *Tirsi*, alongside characters of mere invention Tasso's *Aminta* features members of the Este court as shepherds and makes them easily recognizable under the pastoral disguise. Hence, from the very beginning it is evident that courtly and anti-courtly dimensions interact with each other throughout the play. The ambiguity in the interaction of courtly and anti-courtly elements in the *Aminta* is also reflected in its spatial ambiguity: the *Aminta* is not set in a remote Arcadia but in a "place of passage" ("luogo di passo") separating Ferrara's ducal palace and the Po River[77] – that is to say, in an in-between that simultaneously connects and separates the courtly and the non-courtly.

In addition to such thematic complications, the *Aminta* also has a complicated history in terms of its textual tradition. A relevant episode in the text that sees the shepherd Tirsi report the words of a character named Mopso is known for disappearing and reappearing again in the different editions of the play,[78] rendering any attempts to establish the exact nature of the text at the time of its first performance for the Este court particularly tortuous. Perhaps not surprisingly, given the ambiguous relationship of the *Aminta* with courtly values and the courtly space, the Mopso episode deals precisely with critique of the court. Set in the second scene of the first act, the Mopso episode is part of a dialogue between Tirsi and the titular character, where the subject of conversation moves quickly from matters of love to issues of courtliness and anti-courtliness. Mopso is first evoked by Aminta when he confides in Tirsi about his desperation, proceeding from the fact that the "wise Mopso" has predicted an unhappy ending for his love for Silvia. Tirsi reassures Aminta by questioning Mopso's reliability, not only in matters of the heart but also concerning more general issues:

> AMINTA: I have just cause for desperation: once wise Mopso spoke and he foretold my cruel, cruel fate. He understands the language of the birds, the powers of herbs and virtues of the springs.
>
> TIRSI: What Mopso do you speak of? Mopso who has honeyed words forever on his tongue while on his lips he wears a friendly grin and carries fraud within his breast and blades beneath his coat? Come on, for heaven's sake, for those unhappy, damned prophecies he sells to rash, imprudent men with grave and haughty airs, will never take effect. I'm telling you I know that for a fact. In fact, because he has predicted this, it makes me hope your love will have an end that's joyous and glad.[79]

Tirsi considers Mopso unreliable by virtue of the fallacious advice he himself received from Mopso about the court:

> TIRSI: [...] he [Mopso] replied: "Now you are going to the teeming town where sly and clever citizens abide and wicked courtiers who often make a jest, or laugh in cruel mockery at careless rustics such as we. But, son, be on your guard, and do not go too near a place where colored cloth and cloth of gold hang thick, and plumes and strange attires and modes; but guard above all else that destiny and young desire should never lead you to the shop of nothing-is. Ah! Flee the place, fly far away from that enchanted spot." "What place is this?" I asked; and he did add, "Magicians there abide and do enchant and veil the eyes and ears of those who come. What seems to be of diamonds and fine gold is glass and copper; and those silver arks, which you would think are full of treasures rare, are baskets full of empty bladder bags. Down there the walls are made with magic art; they speak and answer those who speak

> to them; they don't respond with half a word or phrase, as echo often answers in our wood, but they reply with words complete, complete, and even phrases others did not say. The stools, the tables, even every bench, the high-backed chairs, the bedsteads and the drapes, the objects of the bed- and living-rooms, they all have tongues and speech and always shout. There gossips go like dancing girls and weave intrigues; and if a mute man entered there, he'd chatter on although he'd rather not. But this is still the least ill that you could meet there: you could stay there forever changed to flint, to beasts, to water, or to fire; the water comes from tears, from sighs the fire." That's what he said, and I went forth with this fallacious vision of th' enchanted town; and, just as heaven willed that it should be, by chance I passed the place that he'd described. From there came forth, melodious and sweet, the mingled songs of sirens, swans, and nymphs, celestial siren sounds, such sounds they were, so soft and clear and full of fine delight, that all astonished, wondering and enjoying, I stopped for quite a time. Before the door, as if a guard of things so fine and rare, there was a man, magnanimous and strong, and I could not decide, how hard I looked, were he a cavalier or general, for with a smile both grave and so benign, he did invite me in with real grace – he so grand and fine, I, worthless, low. What did I hear? What did I see? I saw divinities; graceful, pretty nymphs; new Orfeos and Linuses, and more – Aurora, virgin dawn, without a cloud or veil, as she appears before the gods to strew the sun rays with gold and silver dew; and fertile Phoebus and the Muses, then I saw, illumining the scene; and there, among the Muses, Elpin sat; and then I felt myself become a greater man, infused with a new deity, and sang of wars and men, disdaining rustic shepherds' songs and lays. And if I then returned, as others asked, to these retreats, I've still retained a part of that proud spirit here; nor have I played my humble shepherd's pipes, as once I did, but with more sonorous and proud a voice I filled the forest with my trumpet tones. Then later Mopso heard me and he fixed me with his evil stare, and after I was hoarse and silent for a long, long time. The shepherds thus believed that I had been seen by the wolf, but it was really he, I've told you this so you will know how much the speech he makes is worthy of your trust, and just because he wants no one to hope, you should have hope.[80]

It is important to notice how in the words attributed to Mopso, Tasso makes deliberate use of the topoi of the anti-court tradition: wicked courtiers and their merciless jests and mockeries; the court as the "shop of nothing-is," or, more broadly, as the place of illusions, and as the realm of rumours and slander, where a man is transformed into something else. Tasso's reference to such topoi – which echo both the references to the world of the court as seen from the moon in Ariosto's *Orlando Furioso* and the much more explicit anti-court satire of Aretino's *Ragionamento delle corti* – shows his familiarity with the tradition of satires against courts and courtiers and demonstrates his potential inclination to compose a work of this kind. It is thus even more relevant that after offering a sample of his mastery of the genre of anti-court satire, Tasso decides to double back on it and convert the satire into a eulogy of the court of Duke Alfonso II d'Este.[81] Tirsi's tribute contrasts with the anti-court notions by referring to the court as a concert of sweet melodies and depicting it as heaven on earth, under the rule of a godlike prince. In addition, the court and the prince also have the merit of giving Tirsi a new, more elevated poetic voice.

It is quite accepted by the scholarly community that Tasso himself is hiding under the mask of Tirsi, and the identities of some of the other characters in the play are likewise generally agreed upon.[82] The identity of the mendacious Mopso, however, remains to be ascertained. Among the various hypotheses that have been proposed, the most popular one remains that of the Paduan *literatus* Sperone Speroni, who had been a mentor to Tasso before the two fell out in the 1570s on account of Speroni's harsh critiques of the cantos of the *Gerusalemme Liberata* that Tasso had sent him. The identification of Mopso with Speroni has been questioned, however, mainly because of the fluctuations between friendship and hostility in Tasso's relationship with Speroni during the years in which the play was revised and printed. Other figures of the Este court have thus been proposed as possible identities for Mopso.[83] In the absence of an unequivocal identification, it is useful to focus on what Mopso may represent in general terms. Claudio Gigante has introduced the notion that Mopso may stand for a type; specifically, Gigante proposes a reading of Mopso as the envious outsider, hypocritical scandalmonger, and evil counsellor.[84]

Building on the suggestion to move from a merely biographical reading of Mopso toward considering his value instead as a token for figures populating the society of the time, there is one more type that can be applied to Mopso, given that he is the source of criticism of the court. Mopso, in fact, can stand for the figure of the anti-court satirist. As can be inferred from Aminta and Tirsi's exchange, Mopso appears to present himself as a wise and moral man who does not refrain from providing advice to younger men who are trying to shape their future. Tirsi's references to Mopso's malevolent tongue (*lingua*) and to his habit of uttering prophecies (*pronostichi*) even recall a figure such as Aretino, who was known and feared precisely for the power of his *lingua* and for his habit of either flattering or blackmailing potential patrons through his *pronostichi*.[85] Tirsi's praise of the court that follows his own report of Mopso's words is an exercise in anti-satire, and also – since it is through Tirsi's voice that Mopso's anti-court satire is expressed – a gesture of self-censorship.[86] The exchange between Tirsi and Mopso (as reported by Tirsi to Aminta) both affirms and contradicts anti-courtly sentiments, and although the final image of the court is assumed to be positive, since it is Tirsi who has the last word, the reported exchange allows Tasso to present anti-court satire in an acceptable way, proceed to deny it, and yet leave it as a haunting presence over Tirsi's praising words. Through this process of affirming and denying opposing concepts, the picture of the court in the *Aminta* takes the form of an unresolved *disputatio in utramque partem*.

Sergio Zatti has argued for the presence in the *Aminta* of a "counterpoint technique" that gives an antithetical structure to the most ideologically charged moments of the text, eventually resulting in an "ideological relativism" and a multiplication of viewpoints that render any affirmations and denials reversible into each other.[87] A further example of this process of affirmation and denial is offered by the chorus immediately following Tirsi's confutation of Mopso, which centres on praise of the golden age as the time when men could live free from the constraints of *onore*:

> Oh, first fair age of gold,
> not just because streams ran
> with milk, and trees the honeyed dew distilled;
> nor that the earth did mold
> its fruit from unploughed land
> and serpents roamed no ire nor venom filled
> [...]
> but just because that vain
> abstraction, empty word,
> that erring idol of propriety –
> which was by folk, insane,
> as *Honor* since referred –
> which tyrannizes now society,
> mixed not anxiety
> within the happy joy
> of loving's faithful band;
> nor was its harsh command
> known by those souls who liberty employed,
> but nature's law of gold
> and joy, *do what pleases you*, was told.
> [...]

You, Honor, first you hid
the fount of love's delight,
denying drafts to slake the lover's thirst;
to lovely eyes you bid
restraint or even flight
to keep their beauties' charms in secrets cursed;
in nets you gathered first
their hair spread on the breeze;
sweet, wanton acts, so dear
you made coy and shy appear;
you stopped plain words, filled steps with modesties;
this, Honor, was your deed
that stole gifts that Love for us decreed.[88]

The centrality of honour – a fundamental concept for Renaissance court culture – in the lament against the constraints of the age, which are opposed to a pristine freedom in the chorus that concludes the first act, explains why such lines can be read as carrying anti-court implications.[89] Criticizing honour as tyrannical also entails extending the same criticism to the foundations of courtliness, and this position is reinforced by statements of frustration over the restraint imposed on speaking ("you stopped plain words") and over the artifice urged upon the body's natural activities ("filled steps with modesties"). In short, the honour that is recast in the *Aminta* as captivity because of its forced rules and control over speech and movement is nothing more than the basis for the courtly art par excellence – *sprezzatura*. Yet the *Aminta* also stages the risks involved with a rejection of those same values.

The rejection of *onore* in the first chorus is shortly thereafter contested through the appearance of a living embodiment of the rejection of the principles of courtliness. The second act of the play features a monologue by the satyr who attempted to violate Silvia, in which the satyr decries the corruption brought on by civilization and presents himself as the only one who, in his violent behaviour, lives according to nature.[90] In representing a life lived away from the rules imposed by *onore*, the satyr shows the risks of forfeiting the very rules that were lamented in the first chorus. In the satyr's monologue, Tasso exploits "the satirical possibilities" offered by such a figure,[91] which in the Renaissance were prompted by the association of satire with satyrs.[92] Speaking like a true satirist, the satyr presents himself as someone who lives in rustic simplicity and who opposes the uncouth naturalness of his persona to effeminate shepherds; his words recall the derision of the manicured appearance of courtiers in anti-court satires:

> This face of mine is ruddy-hued withal,
> my shoulders great and large, my sturdy arms
> robust and muscular, my chest is thick
> with hair, and these, my hairy thighs, are all
> an indication of virility
> and strength: I'll prove it if you don't believe.
> What would you have with tender little boys
> like these whose cheeks are scarcely flowered with
> the softest down? And who so artfully
> arrange their hair according to the mode?
> These men are feminine in semblance
> and in strength.[93]

The satyr also assumes the moral posture of a satirist by decrying the corruption of the present age:

> I am not ugly no; and you do not
> despise me for my shape, but just because
> I'm poor. Alas, for even villages
> do take the model of the cities' mode!
> And this is rightly called the golden age,
> since gold alone can conquer and can reign.[94]

The satyr's reference to the golden age myth that was also quoted in the chorus in act 1 is a denunciation of the present as an age of greed and corruption. What is striking in the satyr's satirical monologue is that in reprimanding the members of the pastoral community and denouncing the villages for mirroring the bad example set by the cities, it portrays the pastoral world as participating in the corruption of the city/court. If one is to give credence to the satyr, the pastoral space portrayed in the *Aminta* is not safe from the evils that affect cities and courts. By representing the pastoral idyll in his courtly pastoral play as not devoid of corruption, Tasso seems to imply that such a courtly pastoral is too similar to the court to offer any real alternatives to its evils.

In his rough naturalness, the satyr's function in the play is also to represent the embodiment of unbridled desire. Gigante has convincingly argued that the satyr is the counterpart of Aminta, who embodies instead a pure and refined form of love and is capable of exerting control over his sexual impulses.[95] In addition, Gigante has also argued for a connection between the satyr and Mopso, who becomes in turn Tirsi's mirror opposite.[96] Both figures indeed represent repressed impulses: if the satyr represents Aminta's sexual attraction to Silvia, Mopso stands for Tirsi/Tasso's attraction to anti-court satire, which is prudently dissimulated under his panegyric about Alfonso II's court. But the figure of the satyr, with his expression of uncouth genuineness and his critique of the contemporary age, also participates in conveying Tasso's temptation to write satirically. Through Mopso and the satyr, Tasso could indirectly experiment with a genre that he was never going to directly explore. Yet it is relevant that while staying away from openly satirical writing, Tasso's attitude toward the court would, in his subsequent production, move closer and closer to the view of the court expressed in anti-court satires. In this process, it is significant that the idyllic image of the Este court presented by Tirsi – as a place of magic, where one is surrounded by the harmony of celestial sirens – is reprised and denounced as a dangerous artificial illusion in the depiction of Armida's garden in the *Gerusalemme Liberata*.[97] The analogies between the pastoral eulogy of the Este court in the *Aminta* and the treacherous charms of the pastoral space represented by Armida's garden in the *Liberata* throw, in hindsight, a disquieting light on Tirsi's praise of the court and reposition Mopso's anti-court satirical words as the mark of a less naive view of the court.

In the *Gerusalemme Liberata*, Armida's artificial, corrupted impression of a pastoral world is counterbalanced by a genuine pastoral space, which also becomes the occasion for words condemning the court – and unlike in the *Aminta*, such critical words are not denied. The genuine pastoral is represented by the house of the shepherd – who, the reader soon learns, is a repentant former courtier who has turned to pastoral life – where the fugitive princess Erminia finds refuge after her failed attempt to reach the man she loves, Tancredi, and after she is chased by Christian knights. The shepherd's simple home also represents his "base poverty," which allows him immunity from the turmoil of war. Even he, however, was once tempted by the quest for honour and riches, and tried his fortune at court:

> There was a time when I was young and vain
> when all my longings were far otherwise.
> I held the life of shepherds in disdain
> and fled my native land for better skies.
> I lived in Memphis once, and in that reign
> was placed among the royal deputies,
> and though I was the keeper of the grounds

I saw the sins wherein the court abounds.
In my heart I stirred that ardent hope to climb,
so I bore servitude's indignities.
But after I had passed my manhood's prime,
and saw my bold hopes die, assurance cease,
I longed for the repose of this sweet time
and sighed for lost simplicity and peace.
I bid goodbye to the court and all its strife,
and in these woods have lived a happy life.[98]

As noted by Giorgio Bàrberi Squarotti, the focus of these words against the court is no longer the world of intrigue of the court, but the lost personal freedom of the shepherd-turned-courtier.[99] The shepherd's eventual return to his native countryside is an affirmation of personal freedom, much like the retreat to one's villa as praised by satirists. But Tasso's interpretation of the satiric topos of withdrawal to a world of pastoral tranquillity to regain mastery over oneself acquires a distinctive pessimistic tone when it involves those of a more elevated social condition than a groundskeeper. For these figures, their courtly persona seems inescapable.

Erminia's true nature – her belonging to the world of rich *palagi,* not to rustic simplicity – emerges from beneath her pastoral disguise. She may be dressed as a shepherdess, but her real courtly identity cannot be hidden:

The royal girl dressed in rustic clothes
and bound a homespun kerchief round her hair –
yet in her looks and motions nonetheless
she never really seemed a shepherdess.

Never could it be hid in simple garb
that sublime light of her nobility;
even when she was at her meanest chores
all her work shone through with majesty.[100]

Erminia herself is aware that such a world does not belong to her and plans to take refuge in the shepherd's house only until "good fortune come[s] again more readily"[101] and allows her to go back to her world. In a dialogue titled *Il padre di famiglia,* written during the dark years of his imprisonment in Sant'Anna, Tasso casts himself as an Erminia figure: a courtly gentleman "fleeing the wrath of princes and of fortune" who finds shelter in the self-sufficient tranquillity of a suburban villa. Just like the princess Erminia, the fugitive gentleman cannot help admiring the genuine and moral lifestyle of the father of the family but at the same time does not cease to be an outsider.[102]

If the *Aminta* is anomalous in its turning the anti-court topos into praise of the court, in blaming the constraints imposed by *onore*, and in hinting, through the figure of the satyr, at the dangers of a life lived according to the rejection of such constraints, the anomaly in the pastoral episode in the *Gerusalemme Liberata* lies in its disenchanted view of the illusion of an escape from the world of cities and courts for those who – by virtue of their birth and social position – are too closely involved with it.

The anti-court motif in later pastoral plays

Scholarly analysis has often remarked on *Aminta*'s influence on the evolution of pastoral drama in Italy. Such influence, however, does not extend to a legacy of the anti-court motifs expressed in the Mopso episode and in the chorus of the first act. As Domenico Chiodo has pointed out, imitations of the *Aminta* echo many elements of Tasso's pastoral, especially in relation to the chorus of act 1, but significantly leave out the discussion of *onore* while also avoiding any references to the unflattering image of the court conveyed by Mopso's words.[103] Tasso also censured his own anti-courtliness by changing the character of Erminia (renamed Nicea) and eliminating the pastoral anti-court episode in the *Gerusalemme Conquistata*. The character of Erminia and her brief adventure in the pastoral world nevertheless remained extremely popular and continued to inspire pastoral texts in the centuries that followed.[104]

A particularly relevant example of the return of the debate on the court that is associated with the encounter between Tasso's princess and the pastoral world is offered by the *Erminia*, a pastoral play authored by Eugenio Visdomini (a member of the Innominati academy) and most likely written in the 1580s.[105] Visdomini amplifies precisely the theme of Erminia's inescapable courtly nature. Visdomini's Erminia laments her annoyance with the humble pastoral life to the shepherd Doriolo, who has offered her refuge, and expresses her determination to go back to being what she once was ("quel ch'i fui").[106] Doriolo reprimands her by listing all the evils of the court: the greed, the envy, the flattery, and most of all the perennial uncertainty of the princely state, which often sees rulers succumb to the sudden mutations of fortune.[107] Erminia's reply is worthy of a late sixteenth-century manual of courtliness for introducing a distinction between the realms of tyrants – to which the arguments outlined by Doriolo may apply – and the realms of true and just kings, where all such evils cease to exist. Doriolo's reply, in turn, concedes that Erminia may be right as concerns the distinction between true kings and tyrants, and centres on praise of the pastoral as, once more, a space for autonomy and for the recovery of individual freedom, where one can be "to himself now master, now servant, now subject, now lord."[108] Erminia – who here plays the part of pro-court Tirsi reacting to Mopso – replies once again in defence of princely courts and the freedom of princes, whom she defines as the only ones who can change status at their will.[109] In Visdomini's play, Erminia is able to fulfil her love for Tancredi, and by converting to Christianity and marrying him she eventually is able to return to the world of princely courts. Visdomini's treatment of the theme of Erminia among the shepherds is notable for its heavily politicized tone, which can be explained through the influence of the political debates that were typical of the Innominati academy.[110] At the same time, the notion of the pastoral state as the only place where one can be master over oneself, despite being confuted by Erminia, is still present in the play, and this presence is testimony to the impact of such a concept on the imagination of the time.

Aside from the *Erminia*, where the contrast between the princess and the shepherd becomes the occasion for a debate about the nature of princes and their reigns, anti-courtly sentiments often appear in pastoral texts without the vehemence of the shepherd's words. The golden age topos of praise for the simple yet happy life led by shepherds, in contrast to the unhappiness of the rich cities, comes back in the prologues to Girolamo Vida's *Filliria* (1585) and Cristoforo Castelletti's *Amarilli* (1580).[111] In both cases, the golden age motif remains quite generic, without any direct references to courts and courtliness. Themes that can be defined as anti-court at large keep surfacing in pastoral texts authored in the 1580s. A 1587 reprint of Castelletti's *Amarilli* includes a brief passage warning against injuring faith in the pastoral space, since faith has taken refuge in the pastoral after running away from the clamour of the ambitious courts.[112] The *Danza di Venere* (first printed in 1584), a play written by an acquaintance of Tasso's, the Venetian Angelo Ingegneri, features a chorus of shepherds who sing the praises of pastoral society, presenting pastoral life as the only one that can offer quiet and self-sufficiency, and pastoral occupations as thus distinct from dangerous professions such as that of courtier.[113]

The topic of pastoral life as the only truly free life can also be found in Orlando Pescetti's *La regia pastorella* (1589), a play that, like the *Erminia*, features a princess in pastoral disguise (although in this case the princess is unaware of her royal heritage).[114] In *La regia pastorella*, however, the princess Partenia is reluctant to abandon the pastoral world and refuses the courtship of the prince Toano, who promises to make her a queen, on the basis that the simple life of shepherds is the only key to a serene mind. The pastoral world portrayed in *La regia pastorella* is a place where, as stated in the chorus to the third act, men do not suffer because of greed or ambition but only because of love.

In all the examples quoted above, however, references to the world of the court are sporadic. Only Battista Guarini's *Pastor Fido* offers an explicit opposition between the pastoral world and the court that is worthy of comparison with that found in Tasso's *Aminta* and *Gerusalemme Liberata*.

Anti-courtliness in Guarini's *Pastor Fido*

It is usually assumed that Guarini started working on his pastoral play, *Pastor Fido*, around 1580 or 1581, that is to say around the same time as the first edition of Tasso's *Aminta*. Set in remote Arcadia, the *Pastor Fido* tells the story of a cursed pastoral land, where every year a virgin needs to be sacrificed in order to placate the gods. The gods' wrath will be appeased only by the marriage of a nymph and a shepherd who descend from the Olympians. The nymph Amarilli (of Pan's bloodline) and the shepherd Silvio (a descendant of Hercules) are set to be married. But Silvio does not care for love, being devoted only to hunting, and Amarilli loves the shepherd Mirtillo, who reciprocates her affection.

Guarini's work on the text continued for a few years, during which the play circulated in manuscript form until its first printed edition in 1589 and its first authorized edition in 1602. Guarini, like Tasso, belonged to the Ferrarese courtly environment, and like Tasso experienced some ups and downs in his relationship with Duke Alfonso II d'Este, which – although not ending as dramatically as Tasso's imprisonment in Sant'Anna – led him to alternate employment between different courts. Guarini first left the Ferrara court in 1583, withdrew to his own villa, and yet kept contact with the court, undertaking diplomatic missions for Duke Alfonso. Between 1584 and 1585 Guarini was hired again by Duke Alfonso and employed as ducal secretary – a position that, if it allowed him stability, also involved a burden of administrative chores that took time and energy away from his intellectual endeavours.[115] Guarini's role at the Este court, in the way it required him to juggle literary work and administrative occupations, was more similar to Ariosto's experience than to Tasso's, who was initially hired by Alfonso under very advantageous conditions.[116]

The theme of the court is treated in the *Pastor Fido* through the character of the old shepherd Carino, Mirtillo's adoptive father, whose return to Arcadia and disclosure of Mirtillo's true lineage lead the play to its happy ending. Carino, like the shepherd met by Erminia in the *Gerusalemme Liberata*, has spent some time at court only to eventually return to the pastoral space after deep disillusionment with the courtly world. Carino confesses to being drawn to the court by the ambitions of his youth: "in youthful softness a poetic genius" made him feel constrained by his homeland and eager to look for more glory.[117] By characterizing Carino as an ambitious musical spirit, Guarini is identifying him, in pastoral terms, with the figure of a poet. Carino is neither the humble keeper of the grounds of the *Gerusalemme Liberata* nor a member of the princely elite like Erminia. His role as a poet puts him in relationship instead with figures such as Tirsi and Mopso in the *Aminta*. His final word on the court is entirely negative, thus distancing him from Tasso/Tirsi's reversal of the anti-court topos. Just like Tasso, however, Guarini gives proof of courtly prudence in his treatment of the episode, which appears to have been deleted from some manuscript versions of the play,[118] and was omitted from the 1598 performance of the play in front of the court of Mantua.[119] Carino's status as a poet has also allowed for identifying Carino with Guarini himself (as Tirsi is identified with Tasso). In spite of Guarini's attempts to insinuate doubts about the veracity of the complaints against the court expressed in the text,[120] the identification of Carino with Guarini is still largely accepted.

The early days of Carino's non-Arcadian experience were promising, as can be inferred from his narration of his serene days in "Elis" and in "Pisa," usually identified with the happy time that Guarini spent at the academy of the Eterei in Padua under the leadership of Scipione Gonzaga, the dedicatee of the *Pastor Fido*, who should be recognized in the figure of the "famous Egon."[121] Carino confesses to being guilty of ambition and recounts how it was his inability to be content with what he had that led him to move to "Argos and Mycene." The city of Argos in the *Pastor Fido* stands for the corruption of the urban and courtly environment. Argos – "wicked Argos," as the location is described in the text – is the homeland of Corisca, a corrupted nymph who is in love with Mirtillo while also being the lover of a different shepherd and the former lover of a lustful satyr, and who schemes to have Amarilli sentenced to death. Corisca is characterized as being entirely fake in her speech and appearance: she manipulates her words to get rid of her rival in love, and her beautiful hair turns out to be nothing but a wig. The misogynist stereotypes embodied by Corisca – her promiscuity, her deviousness, and her constant attempts to falsify reality – reinforce her otherness to the pastoral world and her connection to the city/court. In the corrupt environment of Argos, even Carino is unable to maintain his integrity, becoming – as he confesses upon his return to Arcadia – "an ardent vot'ry to an earthly deity."[122] The reference is of course to the relationship with the prince – in this case, Alfonso II d'Este – and to the courtly culture of subjection to and worship of the prince. The notion of the duke as an earthly deity – a deity whose worship is a heresy – gives perspective to the picture of Alfonso as a godlike figure presented in Tirsi's speech in *Aminta*.

This is the environment Carino eventually rejects in favour of a return to the pastoral world, and his rejection of the court is based first of all on the discovery that the supposed exceptionality of the court – its status as a congregation of the best among men – is nothing but fiction. As Carino declares to the shepherd Uranio, he found, in reality, the exact opposite:

> Persons of rank with courteous words that will
> be sparing in action, enemies to pity.
> A people calm in countenance and mild,
> yet deeper and more boisterous than the ocean.
> Men of mere outside, where you might descry
> love in the face, but envy in the mind.
> An upright look with a distorted soul;
> the more alluring, still the more perfidious.[123]

Carino's unhappiness at court was not the result of a lack of effort on his part. On the contrary, all his efforts to succeed were in vain:

> I wrote, I wept, I sang, I burned, I cooled,
> I fled, I stayed, I bore, in grief, in joy,
> now raised, now sunk, now slighted, now respected.
> And as the Delphic instrument of steel
> is to heroic works applied, and soon,
> to vile mechanic use, I feared no colors,
> nor was I shy of any undertaking.
> I aimed at all. Was nothing.[124]

In spite of attempting everything, Carino was eventually reduced to nothing. The reference may very well be to dissatisfaction because of insufficient rewards from the prince, and yet it is tempting to read this declaration of becoming nothing as hinting as well at the notion of a complete depersonalization caused by the court. Such a reading is reinforced by the following lines, where Carino states that he underwent a radical transformation, changing "my condition and my life, my thoughts / My morals; nay, I changed my very hair."[125]

In the remainder of his exchange with Uranio, Carino offers a picture of courtly life that matches the satirical image of the court as hell on earth. At court, virtues turn into vices and vices become virtues:

> to speak the truth, plain dealing, honest love,
> sincere compassion, faith inviolable,
> an innocence of hands and soul they deem
> the follies of a low and abject genius.
> A vain perfection to be ridiculed.
> To over-reach and lie and coz'n and steal,
> to plunder men beneath a mark of pity,
> to rise upon the ruin and the fall
> of others, to acquire a reputation
> by robbing them of theirs, are the best virtues
> which these insidious courtiers chiefly practice.[126]

At court everything is dominated by the "all-devouring famine of ambition,"[127] which holds nothing sacred: not valour, not law, not shame, not gratitude, nor respect for anything sacred. Also relevant is Carino's self-representation as other to the court's system of corruption. Carino's words here, just like Mopso's in the *Aminta*, are the words of a satirist. In terms that echo Ludovico Ariosto's *Satire*, Carino portrays himself as too honest to be part of the courtly world:

> Now I, who was unguarded and who lived
> a perfect stranger to their subtle arts,
> and had my thoughts engraved upon my forehead,
> my heart unveiled, you may with ease conceive
> was such an open and so fair a mark,
> I could not scape their unsuspected arrows.[128]

Similarly indebted to Ariosto is Carino's lament on the many cares ("cure") and plagues ("disagi") that negatively affected his literary work:

> from that very day
> wherein my Muse and I from Elis journeyed
> to Argos, if I had such to sing
> as I had cause to grieve, I should have sung
> my patron's feats in arms, his great renown.
> that he should not repine, the great Achilles
> had his fame blown through ye Meonian trumpet.
> And this my country famed for poet-swans,

> unfortunate should once again be crowned
> though my endeavours with distinguished laurel.
> But in this world (a too tyrannic age!)
> the drooping muse discouraged hangs her wings.
> The soaring swan requires an easy nest,
> a sky unclouded and sweet food, to sing.
> None climbs Parnassus with a load of cares.
> and he, who wrestles with contending fate,
> with all those plagues annexed to life, grows hoarse
> and scarce has voice enough to sing or speak.[129]

The legacy of Ariosto – in this case, of canto 34 of the *Orlando Furioso* – is present not only in the image of poets as swans but also in the ambivalence between the poet's profession of sincerity a few lines above and his willingness to lend his voice to the courtly art of praising a patron.[130]

This last passage above is also indicative of Guarini's ambivalence toward the world of the court and direct involvement with it. The *Pastor Fido*, on the one hand, includes an unapologetic anti-court passage that would be unthinkable in the *Aminta*, while presenting, on the other hand, a pastoral space that rewrites the opposition to the courtly space featured in the *Aminta* and instead integrates the courtly and the pastoral.[131] In addition, the *Pastor Fido* reverses the polemic against *onore* expressed in the *Aminta* (with all its implications concerning courtliness) and turns it into criticism of a fallacious notion of honour (honour as understood by the "folk, insane"),[132] which is at the root of greed and ambition, and praise of true honour, which is proclaimed the "king of kings" and therefore understood as the foundation of a just government.[133]

The same ambivalent attitude of both rejection and defence of courtliness comes into play in Guarini's attitude toward the topos of rejecting the court in favour of withdrawing to the villa. During his moments of harshest disillusionment with the court, Guarini himself devoted time to *otium* in Padua and in his villa in the Veneto.[134] His letters, then, and a comparison between the anti-court stances pronounced in the *Pastor Fido* and the vision expressed in Guarini's political text, *Trattato della politica libertà* (written in the late 1590s), offer testimony to the ongoing ambivalence that characterized his relationship to the world of the court. Despite the recurrence on numerous occasions in his epistolary production of a vision of the court as a stormy sea where shipwreck is almost inevitable, and despite the juxtaposition of such a vision with an image of private life as a safe haven,[135] Guarini's letters also offer proof of his unwillingness to completely renounce any involvement with the public sphere at large and with the courts in particular.

In a 1583 letter to Francesco Maria Vialardi, Guarini reveals the circumstances that led him to leave the court. Echoing the title of one of Tasso's dialogues, Guarini presents himself as a *padre di famiglia*, whose decision to leave the court was based on the recognition that in order to take care of the affairs of the court of his lord he was neglecting his own family and properties. The choice to leave also granted him a more comfortable lifestyle than that of a courtier, as well as more time to devote to his studies.[136] Yet while enumerating the joys of private life, Guarini does not completely rule out the option of one day returning to service at court, stating that he is not "pertinacious or bashful" to the point of refusing to return to public life if he were ever to encounter a more favourable fortune.[137] In the following pages of the letter, Guarini presents himself as a very committed courtier, one who is more interested in the good of his prince than in his own, while at the same time claiming to be wary of the court and ignorant of the courtly arts.[138]

An even more pronounced ambivalence toward the opposition between the court and private life can be found in a letter to Livio Passeri dated 1565. The letter, which opens Guarini's epistolary collection, is a lengthy reflection on private versus public life, presented – according to the typical Renaissance scheme – as a reply to a request coming from a less-experienced interlocutor on whether or not to accept a position at court. According to Elisabetta Selmi, the letter to Passeri, by virtue of its conspicuous position at the beginning of Guarini's volume of letters and its content, should be considered as written later than the declared date and interpreted as a fictional example more than as an authentic document.[139] In Guarini's letter to Passeri, contrary to other similar examples (such as Aretino's letter to Coccio), the speaker does not try to dissuade his interlocutor from entering the court. The picture of the court is bleak and the dominant tone of the advice is one of prudence and dissimulation in a manner very similar to Tasso's *Malpiglio*,[140] yet the choice of withdrawing to private life is presented as equally unsatisfactory and not immune to the dangers that affect those who enter the court. In Guarini's letter, the court is presented as a totalizing dimension, one that is inescapable even for those who decide to stay away from it, since in the end they will be subjected to the same sudden changes of fortune. In addition, the court is depicted as so pivotal to society that any gentleman, even he who has opted for private life, will find himself required to have contact with the courtly world.

The same tone of disbelief toward the prospects of freedom offered by withdrawing to private life is present in the *Trattato della politica libertà*. The text – which has been disregarded because of its flattering pro-Medici attitude – theorizes a rejection of the withdrawal to private life in favour of activism in the public sphere. As pointed out by Selmi, Guarini's *Trattato della politica libertà* can be considered a denunciation of an outdated model of courtiership and an attempt to rebuild a new relationship between the individual and the state. This call for renovation involves, in Selmi's opinion, the *Pastor Fido* as well, which should be read as carrying a similar civic message.[141]

It is important to underline how both political texts aimed at offering a new model of courtiership and pastoral texts that build an alternative to the world of the court struggle to completely free themselves from the courtly dimension. In Guarini's case, this effort becomes particularly relevant because his view of private life is still implicated with the world of the court – a notion of the court as invading the privacy of the villa. Even in pastoral works that do not depict similar interference of the court in the pastoral space, courts and courtliness remain pertinent in the survival of the ideal of a community of the noblest and most virtuous.

The redeemed court

In Ingegneri's *Danza di Venere*, the pastoral community is praised for its complete harmony: unlike any other society, its members live in total concord, devoid of any envy for each other, while the court is represented among the life choices to be avoided by those who want to achieve real contentment, courtiership being instead (together with professions such as merchant or sailor) only a source of danger, relentless and useless ambition, and greed.[142] Even in pastoral works that do not mention the court directly, the anti-court polemic appears indirectly through the representation of the pastoral community. The invasive presence of the court – direct or indirect – in pastoral works is not surprising when one considers that the pastoral mode could well become the ideal forum where the court poet could develop a representation of and reflection on court life, because, as Paul Alpers has pointed out, "shepherds fittingly represent those whose lives are determined by the actions of powerful men or by events and circumstances over which they have no control."[143]

Giuseppe Gerbino has further investigated the development and increasing importance of the pastoral genre in early modern literature by referring to the matter of self-representation. According to Gerbino, the figure of the shepherd needs to be understood as one of several models self-representation available to Renaissance court society. The oldest, traditional model of self-representation for men of the court was the chivalric knight. Although this option continued to exist in the sixteenth century, long after its loss of effective military and political value, its survival was just "a historical fantasy displaying all the essential element of an exoticized past,"[144] to be replaced by models of behaviour that were felt to be closer to the profile of the courtier. The second field of Renaissance self-representation was, according to Gerbino, the Petrarchan lover. Such a figure, however, was constructed as a private, introverted model, which would not entirely fit the collective structure of the court. Hence the pastoral ideal of the shepherd/lover emerged as the third, fundamental model for Renaissance self-representation – the only model that could transform the inwardness of the Petrarchan ideal into a collective voice, that of the pastoral community, needed to suit the demands of the networking structures of courtly collectivity. Such a model quickly challenged and successfully replaced the ideal of the chivalric hero, by virtue of meeting the demands of a court society that wanted to represent itself precisely as a collectivity of kindred spirits pursuing the spiritual elevation granted by love.[145]

The notion of the shepherd as a successful model of self-representation for courtly elites can be the basis for arguing one further reason – related to the proliferation of anti-court sentiments in Renaissance Italy, and to the connection between the pastoral and anti-courtliness – for the appeal of the pastoral to the courtly classes. The shepherd comes to embody, on the one hand, the qualities of the (ideal) courtier – a figure that, despite all the criticism, had not lost all its charm – and on the other hand, the naturalness, sincerity, and unsophistication advocated by anti-court satires. In the pastoral world, such a figure is part of a society that embodies precisely all the virtues of an ideal court society.

It is useful to recall here that pastoral society is depicted as a community of kindred spirits who spend their time pursuing the noblest activities of humankind, and who live in the cult of love, expressing their lovesickness through poetry and music. Shepherds are portrayed as engaging in friendly contest, intriguingly structured to mirror the competitiveness of the court yet depriving it of its innate aggressiveness. Pastoral writings reveal a world where there may be competition or disagreements, but where the ruthless rivalry among peers and the tricks and deceits of the courtly world have no place. Similarly, the beauty and elegance the of the pastoral environment are frequently praised for their total naturalness, their complete lack of artificiality or duplicity that could mask an ugly truth under a falsely beautiful appearance. The pastoral world and its community thus become a court society cleansed of all the intrinsic violence and deception of the court. This creates a further contradiction in the opposition between the image of the pastoral world as a natural and rustic environment, and the symbolic role of pastoral society as a polished and idealized version of the courtly one.

The unhappy courtier thus becomes a happy shepherd when, in running away from the court, he leaves behind the corruption and competition of its environment and finds in the green pastoral world a community of kindred souls sharing noble, elevated values – in short, what the court purports but fails to be. The courtier-turned-shepherd is cleansed of all the negativity associated with the courtier and becomes an ideal synthesis of the courtier as he should be and the anti-court satirist. In his naturalness and honesty, the satirist embodied the virtues that were felt to be most missing from the courtier, who in turn was seen as more and more cynical and corrupt. However, while the figure of the satirist might have worked well as an autobiographical persona for some court writers striving to proclaim their otherness from the contemporary decadence of court life, the satiric persona's quintessential otherness from the mainstream of society made it unsuitable as a self-fashioning model for the courtly environment. Court society needed a model that could inherit the legacy of Castiglione's ideal by trying again to salvage what remained of the ideology of the court as a congregation of noble spirits, living according to the dictates of chivalry and courtly love. The pastoral ideal of the unaffected and yet courteous shepherd, then, became the ideal utopian synthesis of the courtier's elegant sensibility and the anti-court satirist's artless genuineness, and thus imposed itself as the ultimate inspirational model for early modern court culture. One could even say that the untamed anti-court satirist is domesticated into a shepherd.

Nevertheless, it is important to underline that this association between anti-courtliness and the pastoral also entails one casualty: the satirist, and with him, satire. In a period when satire was declining, owing not only to a loss of interest in the genre but also to increased censorship and Inquisitorial pressure, the most controversial and potentially disruptive features of satire and the satirist were stigmatized and expelled through a figure that participated in pastoral naturalness and unsophistication but lacked the control of civilization and manners, and therefore was the nemesis of the courteous shepherd – the satyr. In a culture that saw satire and the satyr as etymologically linked – satire being the form of expression derived from satyrs – conflating some troublesome features of both the mythical figure and the popular genre would come quite naturally. Genuine but brutal, straightforward but uncivilized, the satyr concentrates in itself all the potentially disruptive aspects of satire, and rejection of the satyr from the pastoral community becomes a way to appease the anxieties related to the problematic nature of satire.

Anti-court satire together with its authorial figure, the satirist/satyr, are sacrificed on the altar of conciliation, mitigating anti-court feelings and retrieving courtly ideals. It is exactly this oxymoronic conciliation that makes the pastoral genre and its protagonist – the anti-court courtier-shepherd – the utopian synthesis of irreconcilable ideals. And this helps to explain the structural paradox of the pastoral becoming the preferred medium for the expression of anti-court feelings and the heir to anti-court writings, while simultaneously establishing itself as the ultimate courtly fashion.

Afterword

Anyone who searches the web in Italian for the word *cortigiano* (courtier/courtly) may be surprised by the results, especially as concerns the images associated with such a term. The first results to pop up may be portraits of refined, distinguished gentlemen whose clothes, posture, and facial expressions immediately convey an aura of elegance and good manners. Yet the same search will likely also produce alternative results. Among the Renaissance portraits, or Renaissance-inspired modern commercial images, something very different and rather controversial may also appear: photographs of journalists, celebrities, or other public personalities shown in the act of approaching some present-day politicians in a submissive and toadying manner.

The results of such a web search can be a useful reminder of the negative connotations still readily associated with the term *cortigiano*. In addition, the notion that *cortigiano* can be employed by modern Italian media to conjure images of flattery and corruption in the mind of the public is testimony to the persistence of the anti-court topoi that were so popular in the Italian Renaissance.

This book has investigated the emergence (or better, the re-emergence, based on examples already present to some extent in classical sources) and almost unstoppable dissemination of anti-court and anti-courtier sentiments at a time when courts stood at the centre of social, cultural, and political life. The sources analysed here, in their number and variety, and the survival of anti-court and anti-courtier topics to this day show that in spite of the court's centrality in early modern society and the aura of prestige that the court emanated as the fulcrum of culture and power, anti-courtly sentiments eventually prevailed. As the Renaissance progressed into the age of the *raison d'état* and of dissimulation, references to anti-court satires were incorporated in manuals of behaviour at court, as exemplified by works such as Pietro Andrea Canoniero's 1609 *Il perfetto cortegiano, et dell'ufizio del prencipe verso 'l cortegiano*. Canoniero's first book is a lengthy description of the "imperfect court" through citations from some of the most explicit anti-court passages to be found, in texts ranging from Lucian's *Imago vitae aulicae*, to Caporali's and Paterno's book-length satires, Aretino's *Ragionamento delle corti*, and Guarini's *Pastor Fido*. As similar texts show, confronting the inevitable negativity of the court becomes part of the training of any courtier.[1] Courts and courtiers also continue to be prominent satirical themes when the genre reappears after its decline in the second half of the sixteenth century.[2]

The first chapter of this study explored how in the period ranging from the sixteenth to the seventeenth centuries, depictions of strategies for survival at court became increasingly cynical, and closer in tone to the satirical depictions of the court analysed in the second and third chapters of this book. In both satiric and prescriptive texts, the courtier becomes an individual whose life is completely at the mercy of Fortuna. In a script by the renowned late sixteenth-century actor and playwright Francesco Andreini (1548–1624), which features Andreini's trademark character, Capitan Spavento, the life of the courtier is evoked precisely as the epitome of the triumph of Fortuna. The notoriously braggart captain boasts of having been married to none other than Lady Fortune herself, and, after a violent fight with her, of having thrown her out a window. Lady Fortune survives by falling into the arms of a poor wretch ("povero disgraziato") and rewards him by having him enter the court of a great prince, where all of a sudden and – it is implied – without any particular merit, he is raised to the highest honours. Courtly life is used here as the most easily recognizable example of a life lived, for better or for worse, in complete submission to the upheavals of fortune. In the struggle between virtue and fortune that represented a common theme of reflection in the Renaissance, the courtier appears to be only at the mercy of the latter. As pointed out by Capitan Spavento's wise servant, Trappola, the courtier has no recourse against the upheavals of fortune and the manifold evils of the court except to accept and endure everything with patience:

> Time, and patience enhance the Courtier, even though among Courtiers envy and hate have their reign, and those who know not how to endure it should leave the court.[3]

The notion of enduring troubles and evils with patience owes its Renaissance popularity to the combination of Christian and classical traditions.[4] Patience was a core virtue in the Christian tradition, often associated with the cardinal virtue of fortitude. Christian patience was considered the only solace for those living in hardship: although patience could not remove the evils that one had to suffer, it taught one how to withstand them. In the Renaissance, the Christian notion of patience was complemented with Stoic notions of patience, which emphasized calm in the face of adversity. As such, patience was also understood in the Renaissance as the only virtue that could triumph over Fortuna.[5] It is therefore not surprising to find texts that connect the topic of courtliness with that of patience. Celio Calcagnini's *De patientia, seu vita aulica commentatio* (On patience, or a commentary on courtly life), which first appeared in 1544, was translated into Italian and slightly reworked two years later by Lucio Paolo Rosello with the title *Dialogo de la vita dei cortegiani intitolato la patientia* (Dialogue on the life of courtiers, titled patience).[6] Depiction of the evils of the court became the starting point for a more general discussion involving issues of sincerity, simulation, and dissimulation in relation to matters of religious reform (both Calcagnini and Rosello held heretical beliefs).[7] Among these issues, however, patience – understood as the capacity to endure hardship and misfortune – is presented as the only viable remedy to the troubles of life at court.

The most interesting feature of patience as the main weapon of courtly life resides in the distance separating a courtly life inspired by patience from one inspired by *sprezzatura*. As Jon Snyder has already pointed out, the contrast between *sprezzatura* and patience is that the latter is not meant to provide any material advantage at court, being instead only an instrument for self-defence against the constant state of surveillance there.[8] Patience, together with dissimulation, becomes the sign of a scission between the public and the private persona of the courtier. The third and fourth chapters of this book have explored how satire and the satiric persona, on the one hand, and the pastoral dimension and mask of the shepherd, on the other, became a way to try to mend such a split in the fictional dimension of writing, at least. In his investigation of the invention of sincerity in the early modern period, John Jeffries Martin has identified in Michel de Montaigne's *Essays* the expression of a widespread need within courtly culture to provide a "comparatively honest or sincere account of oneself and of one's feelings."[9] The analysis of anti-courtly sentiments in satiric and pastoral writings in the third and fourth chapters of this book allows for these specific genres (or mode, in the case of the pastoral) to also be identified as works that offer poignant testimony to such a need.

The second and fourth chapters of this book have also pointed out that the search for escape – either real or fictional – from the world of the court is contrasted with feelings of lingering attraction for the court. Authors declare their intention to persuade readers to despise and ultimately abandon courtly life, but almost inevitably betray a continuing fascination with and deep attachment to the court system. As noted in the book's introduction, this feature of anti-court texts has often resulted in their dismissal by scholarship as trivial and unsophisticated. Examples in anti-court texts of wavering between opposite feelings of love and hate for the court have often puzzled scholars, and have reinforced readings of anti-court texts as pointless complaints that only assert the authors' inescapable dependence on the system that they criticize. Similarly puzzling to the modern reader is the lack in most anti-court text of calls for reformation of the court. Present-day sensibilities may find it odd that anti-court satires simply highlight the evils of court life without proposing any alternatives other than withdrawal to the private space of recuperation offered by the villa.[10] As a result, anti-court writings have been labelled futile outlets that carry no other meaning apart from confirming the enslavement of court *literati* to the political and economical power represented by the court.[11]

This book has aimed to call such a definition into question. Through an exploration of books on courts as well as writings against courts and courtiers, this book has shown that much more than providing a simple outlet was at stake in anti-court texts. Texts criticizing the court have been interpreted here as the instruments through which, in the age of progressive consolidation of absolutist powers, early modern intellectuals tried to come to terms with their increasing subordination. The perceived lack of political involvement of anti-court texts becomes less surprising if one reads them as only marginally reflecting on the court as a social institution and recognizes instead that these texts also focus on courtiers' interiority, and on the effect that the social environment created by a courtly institution has on the individual who experiences it. A major target of anti-court writings, that is to say, especially when they assume the form of first-person narrated satires, is not only the court as the dominant structure of early modern politics, but also – and with equal importance – the early modern self and its fashioning into a courtly (or anti-courtly) persona. Anti-court satires pinpoint the process of such self-fashioning, paying special attention to the perceived disappropriation of one's individuality and loss of self-determination that court life entails. By portraying the court as a dehumanizing environment, where individual needs and skills are suffocated by the rhythms and demands of a system that forces everyone to conform to its arbitrary rules, anti-court writings offer the clearest testimony to the crisis of the humanistic dream of the *homo faber*.

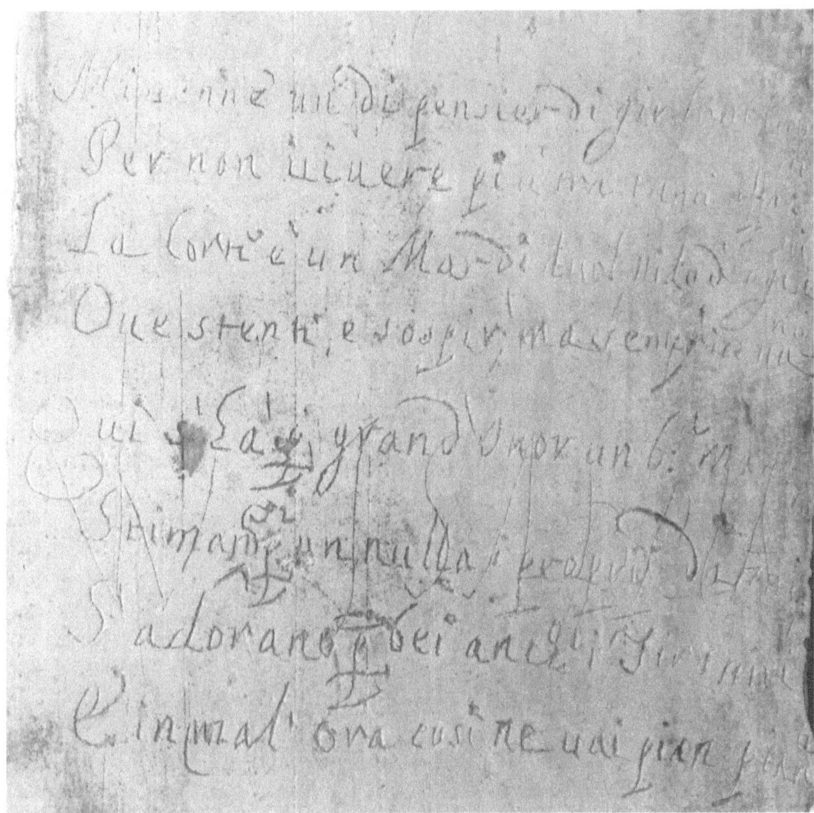

Figure 4. Ducal Palace of Urbino, etching on the jamb of the door that leads from the "Temple of the Muses" to the first-floor balcony.

In the spring of 2017, the ducal palace in Urbino hosted an ingenious exhibition. Historians and curators had looked closely at the walls of the palace, from the stables to the balconies, and uncovered a myriad of different inscriptions carved in the stone. Among the various engravings – which include portraits, symbols, sheet music, and love messages – they also discovered expressions of anti-courtly sentiments. The most explicit and most elaborate of such messages is etched into one of the jambs of the door that leads from the "Temple of the Muses" to the balcony. The inscription is a complaint in verse on the miseries of the court and the dream of escaping to faraway lands:

> A thought came to me of one day going away
> to avoid living among so many worries.

> The court is a sea of pain and a nest of treachery
> where one struggles and sighs, but always in vain.
> Here a modest tip is considered a great honour
> one's own losses are considered nothing
> even tyrants are venerated as gods
> and slowly you are led to your ruin.[12]

It is probably fair to assume that this writer's dream of running away from the court remained just a dream. And yet – as I hope this study has proven – as impracticable as it may have been, such a desire to leave the court should still be given serious consideration. This anonymous complaint carved into the walls of one of the most splendid palaces of the time exemplifies in the clearest way possible that anti-courtly sentiments were etched deeply into the very foundations of Renaissance court culture.

Notes

Introduction

1 cortigiano, s.m.

gentiluomo di corte: *Il Cortegiano*, titolo di un'opera dialogica di Baldassar Castiglione.

(fig.) adulatore, ipocrita intrigante.

Dizionario Garzanti della Lingua Italiana, www.garzantilinguistica.it; accessed 27 May 2019. Translation mine.

2 The term "courtier" (*corteggiano*) is present in the Italian version of Ambrogio Calepino's *Dictionarium* (see *Il dittionario di Ambrogio Calepino della lingua latina nella volgare brevemente ridotto*, lxv, v) with the definition "colui, che sta nella corte di qualche signore" (he who lives in the court of a given lord). It is also featured (as *cortigiano*) in the 1612 edition of the *Vocabolario degli Accademici della Crusca*, with the definition "che sta in Corte, serve Signori" ([he] who lives at Court, serves Lords). Intriguingly, a good number of the textual citations related to this term refer to negative views of courtiers. The most interesting occurrence of anti-courtliness in a dictionary that I have been able to find to date is in Domenico Nani Mirabelli's *Polyanthea*, where the verb *adulor* (to flatter, with words or gestures) is presented as possibly semantically related to *aula* (from the form *adaulor*), with the explanation that flattery happens most often at court ("quod hoc in aulis maxime fieri soleat"). See Mirabelli, *Polyanthea* (Savona: Francisco de Silva), 1503, xiir.

3 The bibliography on the early modern court is vast. For a general analysis, see Martines, *Power and Imagination*; Vasoli, *La cultura delle corti*; Dickens, *The Courts of Europe*; Bertelli, Cardini, and Zorzi, *Le corti italiane del Rinascimento*; Asch and Birke, *Princes, Patronage, and the Nobility*; Scaglione, *Knights at Court*; Chittolini, Molho, and Schiera, *Origini dello stato*; Cole, *La Renaissance dans les cours italiennes*; Muchembled,

"Manners, Courts, and Civility"; Fantoni, *The Court in Europe*. In addition, Norbert Elias's 1969 study, *The Court Society* (originally published as *Die höfische Gesellschaft* [n.p.: Neuwied Luchterhand, 1969]), remains an important point of reference for any analysis of the court although its premises have since been revised. For a discussion of Elias's theories on the court, see especially Duindam, *Myths of Power*.

4 Law, introduction to Law and Welch, "The Courts of Northern Italy in the Fifteenth Century," 354.

5 "Più che un luogo la corte è dunque un nodo concettuale, un mito (spesso proiettato in un passato inesistente), o un metaluogo letterario (al confine con l'*utopia* o con la *distopia*)." Vecchi Galli, "Corte medievale," 156. Unless otherwise noted, all translations into English are mine.

6 See chapter 3 of this book.

7 For a summary of critiques of the court in medieval Europe, see Jaeger, *The Origins of Courtliness*, 54–66; Anglo, "The Courtier"; Vecchi Galli, "Corte medievale." In spite of the numerous volumes that have been devoted to courts and courtliness in the Italian Renaissance, there is no comprehensive analysis of anti-courtly sentiments in Italy. Only two extensive studies have ever been dedicated to anti-court literature, both of which were published several decades ago and neither of which concentrates on the Italian context: Smith, *The Anti-Courtier Trend*; and Uhlig, *Hofkritik im England*, a study of anti-courtliness in Medieval and Renaissance England.

8 Pevere, "Introduzione."

9 On Guevara, see chapter 4 of this book.

10 "oggidì molte corti non sono altro che un collegio d'uomini depravati, una raunanza di volpi maliziose, un teatro di pessimi satelliti, una scuola di corruttissimi costumi, e un rifugio di disonestissime ribalderie. [...] L'invidie, le malevolenze, le detrazioni, gli offici cattivi, le passioni dell'animo, gli sdegni, l'ingiurie, gli oltraggi, le vendette, le vergogne tutte fanno ricapito in corte. Quivi la superbia s'inalza, l'alterezza si sublima, la boria vola in aere, la rapacità non ha freno, la libidine non ha ritegno, la perfidia non è corretta, la crapula gavaza, l'ira saltella, l'invidia si dimena, e tutti i vizi mantengono una abitazione, un albergo e un letto vergognoso dentro in corte. Quivi gli stupri, i rapimenti, gli adulteri, le fornicazioni, i puttanesimi, le ruffianie sono i giuochi e piaceri de' cortigiani e uomini nobili; dove è un naufragio di tutte le virtù, una oppressione di tutte le bontà; dove i semplici son beffati, i giusti perseguitati, i presontuosi e gli sfacciati son favoriti. Soli quivi van prosperando gli adulatori, i mormoratori, le spie, i referendari, gli accusatori, i calonniatori, i gaglioffi, le male lingue, i truffatori, gli inventori de' mali, i seminatori di zizania, e altra generazione di ribaldi [...]. Onde par che tutta la bestialità del mondo si sia raccolta

come in un corpo, nel gregge de' cortigiani [...]. Quivi si trovano i furiosi centauri, le perigliose Chimere, i pazzi satiri, le sporche arpie, le ribalde sirene, le Scille con due forme, le Meduse monstruose, i Protei vari, gli orrendi struzzi, gli ingordi griffoni, i terribili dragoni, e quanti strani e spaventosi mostri creò mai la natura contra sua voglia. Quivi ogni qualità di virtù patisce i suoi carnefici e tiranni. E, in somma, tutta la disgrazia e tutto il mal del mondo versa in corte." Garzoni, "De' cortigiani e delle donne di corte insieme," in *La piazza universale*, 852–3.

11 Alciato, *Emblemata*, 94.
12 Biagioli, *Galileo, Courtier*, 5.
13 Martin, "The Myth of Renaissance Individualism"; and Martin, *Myths of Renaissance Individualism*.
14 Martin, "Inventing Sincerity, Refashioning Prudence."
15 Burckhardt's theory of the individual was formulated in his well-known *The Civilization of the Renaissance in Italy* (*Die Kultur der Renaissance in Italien*, first published in 1860). On this point, see also chapter 3 of this book.
16 Greenblatt, *Renaissance Self-Fashioning*, 256.
17 On this point, see also Biow, *On the Importance of Being an Individual*, 3–4. For a notion of self-fashioning similarly based on Martin's suggestion that Renaissance individuals fashioned themselves in active terms, and which takes into account issues of gender as well, see Ross, *The Birth of Feminism*, 11–12, 317.
18 Martin, "Inventing Sincerity, Refashioning Prudence," 1322.
19 In *On the Importance of Being an Individual*, Biow has further expanded Greenblatt's and Martin's investigations of (male) identity by pointing out how both scholars refer to a notion of the self that is formed both by and in reaction to cultural constraints. According to Biow, in their different interpretations, Greenblatt and Martin have similarly focused on the first side of the dialectic, stressing the cultural forces that shape the self. By contrast, Biow concentrates on the opposite side of the dialectic, focusing on men who insisted on their own peculiarity and asserted themselves by underlining their own personalized voice or style (*On the Importance of Being an Individual*, 3–6). In a similar way, this study focuses on the struggle to affirm one's own individuality; in the case of the works and authors analysed here, this struggle was in reaction to a court society that was seen as dominated by the pressure to conform to such a degree that conformity became potentially de-individualizing.
20 "mettono a capo non in altro che nel sospiro verso la campagna e la vita rustica e la rinunzia alle ambizioni, ossia alla lotta sociale, e il contentarsi di poco." Croce, "Libri sulle corti," 198.
21 Many reasons can be suggested as to why Croce's disdain for anti-court literature has persisted for so long, but analysing those reasons are beyond the scope of the present study.

1. The Courtier

1 Martines, *Power and Imagination*, 218ff. On the evolution of Renaissance Italian courts, see also Gaeta, "Dal comune alla corte rinascimentale."

2 A brief sketch of the "invention" of the role of courtier in the Middle Ages, as well as of the novelty of the medieval concept of courtliness in relation to the theory of the "civilizing process" originating with Norbert Elias, can be found in Burke, *The Fortunes of the "Courtier,"* 12–18.

3 See Anglo, "The Courtier"; and Anglo, "Systematic Immorality."

4 "Però tra le altre cose che nate sono a' tempi oltre gli quali noi habbian notitia, e non molto da' nostri secoli lontani, veggiamo essere invalsa questa sorte d'huomini che noi chiamiamo corteggiani, della qual cosa molto per tutta Europa si fa professione. Ché, come da ogni tempo siano stati gli principi e gran signori da molti servitori obediti, e sempre n'habbiano avuti de' più cari e meno cari, ingegnosi alcuni, alcuni sciocchi, chi grati per il valere ne l'arme, chi nelle lettre, chi per la bellezza del corpo, molti per niuna di queste cause ma solo per una certa occulta conformità di natura, non è però forsi mai per lo adietro, se non da non molto tempo in qua, fattase tra gli huomini professione di questa corteggiania, per dire così, e riduttasi quasi in arte e desciplina, come hora si vede." Quoted in Motta, *Castiglione e il mito di Urbino*, 33–4.

5 Anglo, "Systematic Immorality," 580.

6 Anglo, "The Courtier," 36.

7 Berger, "Conspicuous Exclusion in Vermeer: An Essay in Renaissance Pastoral," in *Second World and Green World*," 442.

8 In considering the *Book of the Courtier* and not *Dello optimo cortesano* the first significant representative of its genre, I agree with Anglo's analysis, according to which Carafa's *Dello optimo cortesano* "offers no general prospect of the courtly profession," at least not in the way Castiglione's *Book of the Courtier* does.

9 On Carafa's life and career, see Gioachino Paparelli's introduction to Carafa, *Dello optimo cortesano*, 11–49; and Petrucci, "Carafa, Diomede."

10 "non se deve de nessuno oppresso né da povertà né da infirmità né de presonia havere maiore pietate che de sapio et bono homo soctoposto ad signore furioso ed temerario." Carafa, *Dello optimo cortesano*, 79.

11 "Et si bene uno signore li piaceno dicte gare et differentie de sua casa como se ne trovano de quelli non sulo li piace ma ce fa le opere dicendo che per dicte differentie non sape delle cose non sapperia et che l'uno per l'altro serveno meglio per le invidie." Carafa, *Dello optimo cortesano*, 87.

12 "che pare casa de angeli dove non sono tale nature de vivere: che l'altre sono vite infernali." Carafa, *Dello optimo cortesano*, 87.

13 "Et la prima cosa che lo iovene che delibera essere in corte se disponga et se sforzi et delibera servire in tale modo non haia da esse del numero generale ma con intentione non possendo essere lo primo, almeno volere essere de li secundi o terzi o quarti [...]. Et nota che in corte tanto so magiore le invidie, quanto se conosce sia disposto et sia virtuoso che non solo per ciò se have da guardare de fare male, ma de quello se potesse dire verisimile del male." Carafa, *Dello optimo cortesano*, 77.

14 "la gracia del Signore non ei mai consequita, fino tanto quanto te porterai in modo che quello signore non haia causa de desfavorirte." Carafa, *Dello optimo cortesano*, 104.

15 "amare et temere suo signore ad comparatione della inamorata." Carafa, *Dello optimo cortesano*, 119.

16 "sempre dare loco et cedere al suo Signore [...] chi con suo signore vole vincere ad ogni gioco che ioca ve dico che fa ad chi vence perde." Carafa, *Dello optimo cortesano*, 122. It is important to notice here that Carafa excludes surrendering to the lord in a matter that "would result in losing your honour" ("fosse ad mancamento de honore").

17 "sta ad presso ad un terrebele lione." Carafa, *Dello optimo cortesano*, 159.

18 Castiglione, *The Book of the Courtier*, ed. Javitch, II, i, 65. "Laudano i tempi passati e biasmano i presenti." Castiglione, *Il Libro del Cortegiano*, ed. Quondam, 117. All subsequent quotations in English are from the Javitch edition, with references to the Italian text in square brackets.

19 "Però come del resto, cosí parlano ancor delle corti, affermando quelle di che essi hanno memoria esser state molto piú eccellenti e piene di omini singulari, che non son quelle che oggidí veggiamo; e súbito che occorrono tai ragionamenti, cominciano ad estollere con infinite laudi i cortegiani del duca Filippo, o vero del duca Borso; e narrano i detti di Nicolò Piccinino; e ricordano che in quei tempi non si saria trovato, se non rarissime volte, che si fosse fatto un omicidio; e che non erano combattimenti, non insidie, non inganni, ma una certa bontà fidele ed amorevole tra tutti, una sicurtà leale; e che nelle corti allor regnavano tanti boni costumi, tanta onestà, che i cortegiani tutti erano come religiosi; e guai a quello che avesse detto una mala parola all'altro o fatto pur un segno men che onesto verso una donna; e per lo contrario dicono in questi tempi esser tutto l'opposito; e che non solamente tra i cortegiani è perduto quell'amor fraterno e quel viver costumato, ma che nelle corti non regnano altro che invidie e malivolenzie, mali costumi e dissolutissima vita in ogni sorte di vicii; le donne lascive senza vergogna, gli omini effemminati." Castiglione, *The Book of the Courtier*, II, ii, 67 [*Il Libro del Cortegiano*, 120–1].

20 "un'altra sorte de uomini, quali, per fare el filosofo, dannano tutte le corti in generale, e le presenti e le passate, e laudano la libertà, alla quale dicono

non potersi attendere stando in corte e servendo, come si fa, non meno all'ambizione e a mill'altri vizi, che agli propri signori. Ma a questi tali pensiamo avere dato risposta, facendo el nostro cortigiano sopra ogni altra cosa uomo da bene." Castiglione, *La seconda redazione del Cortegiano*, 84.

21 "E sogliono molti de questi così severi reprensori, ogni volta che possono intromettersi nelle corti, sommergersi totalmente in quelle passioni che essi in altrui biasmano, e quando tal vita per le lor proprie parole gli è rimproverata, alor mutano sentenzia e cominciano a disputare delle dignità de' signori e gran principi, e quegli affermano essere sacri et eletti da Dio, come dice Omero, e le lor grandezze e dominii de genti, le vittorie, la fama e gli triunfi essere cose c'hanno del divino; e poiché Iddio gli fa superiori agli altri uomini, essere ancor conveniente che ognuno gli onori e observi; et oltre gli altri argomenti che essi siano dalli cieli più estimati, allegano gli segni e prodigi, che spesso appareno al nascere e morire di quegli, e dicono Aristotele essere versato nella corte di Alessandro et avere quasi insegnato a Calistene, suo discipulo, di adularlo, Platone esser visso qualche volta come cortiggiano delli regi di Sicilia, e molt'altri filosofi, e questo perché conosceano nelle corti concorrer tanti nobili e varii ingegni, che non meno quivi che nelle scole imparar si potea. A questi adonque, poiché da se stessi se rispondano, non diremo altro, e bastandoci avere dimostrato le corti de' nostri tempi non essere di minor laude degne che quelle che tanto laudano gli vecchi, attenderemo agli ragionamenti avuti sopra il cortiggiano et alli nostri giuochi." Castiglione, *La seconda redazione del Cortegiano*, 84–5.

22 For an in-depth analysis of this point, see Quondam, "La forma del vivere," 15–18. On the contradictions in the *Book of the Courtier*, see also Wolfe, *Humanism, Machinery, and Renaissance Literature*, 33.

23 See Motta, *Castiglione e il mito di Urbino*.

24 Greene, "*Il Cortegiano* and the Choice of a Game."

25 Greene, "*Il Cortegiano* and the Choice of a Game," 7–9.

26 Rebhorn, *Courtly Performances*, 91–115.

27 Greene, "*Il Cortegiano* and the Choice of a Game," 1–3.

28 Greene, "*Il Cortegiano* and the Choice of a Game," 3.

29 Greene, "*Il Cortegiano* and the Choice of a Game," 3.

30 "everyone be allowed to speak out against those things which seem not right" ("in quelle cose che non pareranno convenienti sia licito a ciascun contradire"). Castiglione, *The Book of the Courtier*, I, xii, 19 [*Il Libro del Cortegiano*, 36].

31 "never was there concord of will or cordial love between brothers greater than that which was there among us all" ("mai non fu concordia di voluntà o amore cordiale tra fratelli maggior di quello, che quivi tra tutti era"). Castiglione, *The Book of the Courtier*, I, iv, 12 [*Il Libro del Cortegiano*, 22].

32 "di questi errori sono diverse cause; e tra l'altre la ostinazion dei signori, i quali, per voler far miracoli, talor si mettono a dar favore a chi par loro che meriti disfavore." Castiglione, *The Book of the Courtier*, I, xvi, 24 [*Il Libro del Cortegiano*, 44].

33 "nel cortegiano a me non par così necessaria questa nobilità; e s'io mi pensassi dir cosa che ad alcun di noi fusse nova, io addurrei molti i quali, nati di nobilissimo sangue, son stati pieni di vicii; e per lo contrario molti ignobili, che hanno con la virtù illustrato la posterità loro. E se è vero quello che voi diceste dianzi, cioè che in ogni cosa sia quella occulta forza del primo seme, noi tutti saremmo in una medesima condicione per aver avuto un medesimo principio, né più un che l'altro sarebbe nobile. Ma delle diversità nostre e gradi d'altezza e di bassezza credo io che siano molte altre cause: tra le quali estimo la fortuna esser precipua, perché in tutte le cose mondane la veggiamo dominare e quasi pigliarsi a gioco d'alzar spesso fin al cielo chi par a lei senza merito alcuno, e sepellir nell'abisso i più degni d'esser esaltati." Castiglione, *The Book of the Courtier*, I, xv, 22–3 [*Il Libro del Cortegiano*, 41–2].

34 "per aver adunque favore dai signori, non è miglior via che meritargli." Castiglione, *The Book of the Courtier*, II, xx, 83 [*Il Libro del Cortegiano*, 149].

35 See Pieri, "Colli, Vincenzo detto il Calmeta."

36 "'Prima che più avanti passate,' disse quivi Vincenzio Calmeta, 's'io ho ben inteso, parmi che dianzi abbiate detto che la miglior via per conseguir favori sia il meritargli; e che più presto dee il cortegiano aspettar che gli siano offerti, che prosuntuosamente ricercargli. Io dubito assai che questa regula sia poco al proposito e parmi che la esperienzia ci faccia molto ben chiari del contrario; perché oggidì pochissimi sono favoriti da' signori, eccetto i prosuntuosi; e so che voi potete esser bon testimonio d'alcuni, che, ritrovandosi in poca grazia dei lor prìncipi, solamente con la prosunzione si son loro fatti grati; ma quelli che per modestia siano ascesi, io per me non cognosco ed a voi ancor dò spacio di pensarvi, e credo che pochi ne trovarete.'" Castiglione, *The Book of the Courtier*, II, xxi, 83–4 [*Il Libro del Cortegiano*, 150].

37 "'Non dite così,' rispose allor messer Federico, 'perché questo sarebbe troppo chiaro argumento che i signori de' nostri tempi fossero tutti viciosi e mali; il che non è, perché pur se ne trovano alcuni di boni. Ma se 'l nostro cortegiano per sorte sua si troverà essere a servicio d'un che sia vicioso e maligno, sùbito che lo conosca, se ne levi, per non provar quello estremo affanno che senton tutti i boni che serveno ai mali.'" Castiglione, *The Book of the Courtier*, II, xxii, 85 [*Il Libro del Cortegiano*, 151].

38 "'Bisogna pregar Dio,' rispose il Calmeta, 'che ce gli dia boni, perché quando s'hanno è forza patirgli tali, quali sono; perché infiniti rispetti astringono chi è gentilomo, poi che ha cominciato a servire ad un

patrone, a non lasciarlo; ma la disgrazia consiste nel principio; e sono i cortegiani in questo caso alla condizion di que' mal avventurati uccelli, che nascono in trista valle.'" Castiglione, *The Book of the Courtier*, II, xxii, 85 [*Il Libro del Cortegiano*, 152].

39 For a detailed reading of the exchange between Calmeta and Federico, see Cox, *The Renaissance Dialogue*, 47–70.

40 "credo che possa con ragion e debba levarsi da quella servitù, che tra i boni sia per dargli vergogna." Castiglione, *The Book of the Courtier*, II, xxii, 85 [*Il Libro del Cortegiano*, 152].

41 Cox, *The Renaissance Dialogue*, 57.

42 Historical sources prove that Francesco Maria della Rovere was responsible for various crimes, including murder. On this and other historical data omitted from the *Book of the Courtier*, see Rebhorn, *Courtly Performances*, 55–6.

43 "Voglio adunque che 'l cortegiano, oltre lo aver fatto ed ogni dì far conoscere ad ognuno sé esser di quel valore che già avemo detto, si volti con tutti i pensieri e forze dell'animo suo ad amare e quasi adorare il principe a chi serve sopra ogni altra cosa; e le voglie sue e costumi e modi tutti indrizzi a compiacerlo." Castiglione, *The Book of the Courtier*, II, xviii, 80 [*Il Libro del Cortegiano*, 144].

44 "di questi cortegiani oggidì trovarannosi assai, perché mi pare che in poche parole ci abbiate dipinto un nobile adulatore." Castiglione, *The Book of the Courtier*, II, xviii, 80 [*Il Libro del Cortegiano*, 144].

45 "'Voi vi ingannate assai,' rispose messer Federico; 'perché gli adulatori non amano i signori né gli amici, il che io vi dico che voglio che sia principalmente nel nostro cortegiano; e 'l compiacere e secondar le voglie di quello a chi si serve si po far senza adulare, perché io intendo delle voglie che siano ragionevoli ed oneste, o vero di quelle che in sé non sono né bone né male.'" Castiglione, *The Book of the Courtier*, II, xvii, 80–1 [*Il Libro del Cortegiano*, 144].

46 "Disoneste e vituperose." Castiglione, *The Book of the Courtier*, II, xxiii, 85 [*Il Libro del Cortegiano*, 153].

47 "Molte cose paiono al primo aspetto bone, che sono male, e molte paiono male, e pur son bone." Castiglione, *The Book of the Courtier*, II, xxiii, 86 [*Il Libro del Cortegiano*, 153].

48 "è assai pericolosa cosa desviare dai comandamenti de' suoi maggiori, confidandosi più del giudicio di se stessi che di quegli ai quali ragionevolmente s'ha da ubedire." Castiglione, *The Book of the Courtier*, II, xxiv, 86 [*Il Libro del Cortegiano*, 154].

49 On this point, see Cox, *The Renaissance Dialogue*, 51–4.

50 See Berger, *Second World and Green World*. For a pastoral interpretation of Castiglione's Urbino, see also "The Nostalgic Courtier," in Rebhorn, *Courtly Performances*, 91–115.

51 Berger, *Second World and Green World*, 442.
52 Berger, *Second World and Green World*, 442.
53 Berger, *The Absence of Grace*, 10–12.
54 Berger, *The Absence of Grace*, 168.
55 Berger, *The Absence of Grace*, 164.
56 On the representation of nostalgic old men in the *Book of the Courtier*, see Kolsky, "Old Men in a New World: Morello da Ortona in the *Cortegiano*," in *Courts and Courtiers in Renaissance Northern Italy*, 330–47.
57 On the issue of despotism in the *Book of the Courtier*, see Javitch, "Il Cortegiano and the Constraints of Despotism," in Castiglione, *The Book of the Courtier*, 319–28.
58 Javitch has also argued that Ottaviano is the only speaker "who cannot appreciate the intrinsic value of beautiful manners"; see Javitch, *Poetry and Courtliness in Renaissance England*, 40.
59 "se con l'esser nobile, aggraziato e piacevole ed esperto in tanti esercizi il cortegiano non producesse altro frutto che l'esser tale per se stesso, non estimarei che per conseguir questa perfezion di cortegiania dovesse l'omo ragionevolmente mettervi tanto studio e fatica, quanto è necessario a chi la vole acquistare; anzi direi che molte di quelle condicioni che se gli sono attribuite, come il danzar, festeggiar, cantar e giocare, fossero leggerezze e vanità, ed in un omo di grado più tosto degne di biasimo che di laude." Castiglione, *The Book of the Courtier*, IV, iv, 209–10 [*Il Libro del Cortegiano*, 367–8].
60 "queste attillature, imprese, motti ed altre tai cose che appartengono ad intertenimenti di donne e d'amori, ancora che forse a molti altri paia il contrario, spesso non fanno altro che effeminar gli animi, corrumper la gioventù e ridurla a vita lascivissima; onde nascono poi questi effetti che 'l nome italiano è ridutto in obbrobrio." Castiglione, *The Book of the Courtier*, IV, iv, 210 [*Il Libro del Cortegiano*, 368]. This is a reference to the critiques voiced by Canossa in book I, xix. See chapter 2 of this book for an exploration of this point.
61 Castiglione, *The Book of the Courtier*, IV, x, 213 [*Il Libro del Cortegiano*, 374]. On the issue of the courtier's masculinity, see Milligan, "The Politics of Effeminacy in *Il Cortegiano*"; and chapter 2 of this book.
62 Castiglione, *The Book of the Courtier*, IV, ix, 213 [*Il Libro del Cortegiano*, 373].
63 "i signori, oltre al non intendere mai il vero di cosa alcuna, inebbriati da quella licenziosa libertà che porta seco il dominio e dalla abundanzia delle delizie, sommersi nei piaceri, tanto s'ingannano e tanto hanno l'animo corrotto, veggendosi sempre obediti e quasi adorati con tanta riverenzia e laude, senza mai non che riprensione ma pur contradizione, che da questa ignoranzia passano ad una estrema persuasion di se stessi, talmente che poi non ammettono consiglio né parer d'altri; e perché

credono che 'l saper regnare sia facilissima cosa e per conseguirla non bisogni altr'arte o disciplina che la sola forza, voltan l'animo e tutti i suoi pensieri a mantener quella potenzia che hanno, estimando che la vera felicità sia il poter ciò che si vole." Castiglione, *The Book of the Courtier*, IV, vii, 211 [*Il Libro del Cortegiano*, 370–1].

64 According to Eduardo Saccone, the *Book of the Courtier* comes to the point of transforming princes into sick and overdelicate children. See Saccone, "Grazia, Sprezzatura, Affettazione in *The Courtier*."

65 "i colossi che l'anno passato fur fatti a Roma il dì della festa di piazza d'Agone, che di fori mostravano similitudine di grandi omini e cavalli triunfanti e dentro erano pieni di stoppa e di strazzi." Castiglione, *The Book of the Courtier*, IV, vii, 212 [*Il Libro del Cortegiano*, 371]. On Ottaviano's depiction of contemporary princes, see Najemy, "Arms and Letters."

66 "quasi adornandola di frondi ombrose e spargendola di vaghi fiori, per temperar la noia del faticoso camino a chi è di forze debile; ed or con musica, or con arme e cavalli, or con versi, or con ragionamenti d'amore e con tutti que' modi che hanno detti questi signori, tener continuamente quell'animo occupato in piacere onesto, imprimendogli però ancora sempre, come ho detto, in compagnia di queste illecebre, qualche costume virtuoso ed ingannandolo con inganno salutifero; come i cauti medici, li quali spesso, volendo dar a' fanciulli infermi e troppo delicati medicina di sapore amaro, circondano l'orificio del vaso di qualche dolce liquore." Castiglione, *The Book of the Courtier*, IV, x, 213 [*Il Libro del Cortegiano*, 373–4].

67 On a similar note, Susan Gaylard has pointed out that Castiglione's courtier can be read as a successful counterpart to Cicero's orator: while Cicero's orator failed to secure the state through rhetoric, Castiglione's courtier, through tactics of morally justifiable deception, will be able to gain control over princes and ladies and proceed to build empires. See Gaylard, "Castiglione versus Cicero."

68 "la maggior parte di coloro, che sono introdutti nei ragionamenti, esser già morti." Castiglione, *The Book of the Courtier*, "To the Reverend and Illustrious Signor Don Michele de Silva, Bishop of Viseu," i, 3 [*Il Libro del Cortegiano*, 4].

69 "come un ritratto di pittura della corte d'Urbino." Castiglione, *The Book of the Courtier*, "To the Reverend and Illustrious Signor Don Michele de Silva, Bishop of Viseu," i, 4 [*Il Libro del Cortegiano*, 6].

70 "sempre la causa per la quale lo effetto è tale come egli è, non sia più tale che non è quello effetto; però bisogna che 'l cortegiano, per la instituzion del quale il principe ha da esser di tanta eccellenzia, sia più eccellente che quel principe; ed in questo modo sarà ancora di più dignità che 'l principe istesso, il che è inconvenientissimo." Castiglione, *The Book of the Courtier*, IV, xliv, 237 [*Il Libro del Cortegiano*, 416].

71 "le operazion delle quali esso per la grandezza sua facilmente po mettere in uso e farne abito; il che non po il cortegiano, per non aver modo d'operarle; e così il principe, indutto alla virtù dal cortegiano, po divenir più virtuoso che 'l cortegiano." Castiglione, *The Book of the Courtier*, IV, xlvi, 239 [*Il Libro del Cortegiano*, 419].

72 "poiché oggidì i prìncipi son tanto corrotti dalle male consuetudini e dalla ignoranzia e falsa persuasione di se stessi, e che tanto è difficile il dar loro notizia della verità ed indurgli alla virtù, e che gli omini con le bugie ed adulazioni e con così viciosi modi cercano d'entrar loro in grazia, il cortegiano, per mezzo di quelle gentil qualità che date gli hanno il conte Ludovico e messer Federico, po facilmente e deve procurar d'acquistarsi la benivolenzia ed adescar tanto l'animo del suo principe, che si faccia adito libero e sicuro di parlargli d'ogni cosa senza esser molesto." Castiglione, *The Book of the Courtier*, IV, ix, 213 [*Il Libro del Cortegiano*, 373–4].

73 "non ho detto che la instituzione del cortegiano debba esser la sola causa per la quale il principe sia tale; perché se esso non fosse inclinato da natura ed atto a poter essere, ogni cura e ricordo del cortegiano sarebbe indarno; come ancor indarno s'affaticaria ogni bono agricultore che si mettesse a cultivare e seminare d'ottimi grani l'arena sterile del mare, perché quella tal sterilità in quel loco è naturale [...]. Sono adunque molti prìncipi che sarian boni, se gli animi loro fossero ben cultivati; e di questi parlo io, non di quelli che sono come il paese sterile e tanto da natura alieni dai boni costumi, che non basta disciplina alcuna per indur l'anima loro al diritto camino." Castiglione, *The Book of the Courtier*, IV, xlv, 238 [*Il Libro del Cortegiano*, 418].

74 "Aristotile così ben conobbe la natura d'Alessandro e con destrezza così ben la secondò, che da lui fu amato ed onorato più che padre, onde, [...] lo formò nelle scienzie naturali e nelle virtù dell'animo talmente, che lo fece sapientissimo, fortissimo, continentissimo e vero filosofo morale, non solamente nelle parole ma negli effetti; [...] e di queste cose in Alessandro fu autore Aristotile, usando i modi di bon cortegiano; il che non seppe far Calistene, ancorché Aristotile glielo mostrasse; ché, per voler esser puro filosofo e così austero ministro della nuda verità, senza mescolarvi la cortegiania, perdé la vita e non giovò, anzi diede infamia ad Alessandro." Castiglione, *The Book of the Courtier*, IV, xlvii, 240–1 [*Il Libro del Cortegiano*, 423]. Aristotle famously lived at the court of Philip of Macedon, where he was the preceptor of the young Alexander.

75 See Faini, "Un sole 'docto e saggio.'"

76 For a celebration of Guidubaldo's virtues, see Castiglione, "Ad Henricum VII," in *Le Lettere*, 162–98.

77 "restò un dei più belli e disposti corpi del mondo deformato e guasto." Castiglione, *The Book of the Courtier*, I, iii, 11 [*Il Libro del Cortegiano*, 19–20].

78 As bluntly stated by Pietro Bembo in his *De Urbini ducibus liber*. The text has been recently published in a modern edition as *I duchi di Urbino*, ed. Marchesi.

79 "la sua condizione pareva più simile a quella dei morti, che a quella dei vivi." Bembo, *I duchi di Urbino*, 173.

80 Castiglione, *Il Libro del Cortegiano*, IV, xlvii, 422. For a detailed analysis of this topic, see Cox, "Tasso's *Malpiglio overo de la corte*."

81 "Per lo medesimo modo della cortegiania Platone formò Dione Siracusano; ed avendo poi trovato quel Dionisio tiranno come un libro tutto pieno di mende e d'errori e più presto bisognoso d'una universal litura che di mutazione o correzione alcuna, per non esser possibile levargli quella tintura della tirannide, della qual tanto tempo già era macchiato, non volse operarvi i modi della cortegiania, parendogli che dovessero esser tutti indarno. Il che ancora deve fare il nostro cortegiano, se per sorte si ritrova a servizio di principe di così mala natura, che sia inveterato nei vicii, come li tisici nella infirmità; perché in tal caso deve levarsi da quella servitù, per non portar biasimo delle male opere del suo signore, e per non sentir quella noia che senton tutti i boni che servono ai mali." Castiglione, *The Book of the Courtier*, IV, xlvii, 241 [*Il Libro del Cortegiano*, 423].

82 Cox, *The Renaissance Dialogue*, 59.

83 Cox, *The Renaissance Dialogue*, 59.

84 "vestirsi un'altra persona." Castiglione, *The Book of the Courtier*, II, xix, 82 [*Il Libro del Cortegiano*, 147].

85 Rebhorn, *Courtly Performances*, 25–6; Martin, *Myths of Renaissance Individualism*, 18, 35. See also Finucci, *The Manly Masquerade*.

86 Rebhorn, *Courtly Performances*, 25.

87 On the surveillance system of the court, see Webb, "All Is Not Fun and Games."

88 On the protean quality of Castiglione's courtier, see Rebhorn, *Courtly Performances*, 14, 29.

89 Saccone, "Grazia, Sprezzatura, Affettazione in *The Courtier*," 59–60; Javitch, "Il Cortegiano and the Constraints of Despotism," in Castiglione, *The Book of the Courtier*, 325.

90 Martin, *Myths of Renaissance Individualism*, 38. Martin singles out five different ways in which Renaissance individuals thought about the self (namely, the social or conforming self, the prudential self, the performative self, the porous self, and the sincere self). Martin explains the protean quality of the Renaissance self as its ability to shift between these five different identities. Manuals for behaviour at court played an important role in defining the social self and were fundamental in shaping the prudential self and the performing self, three selves that Martin considers deeply intertwined and interprets as testimonies to an "illusion of

control [...] over matters of self-presentation." Martin, *Myths of Renaissance Individualism*, 36. On Martin's notion of different Renaissance selves, see also chapter 3 of this book.

91 See chapter 3 for an in-depth exploration of this point.

92 For a detailed analysis of these points, see Gaeta, "Dal comune alla corte rinascimentale"; Rosa, "La Chiesa e gli stati regionali nell'età dell'assolutismo"; Snyder, *Dissimulation and the Culture of Secrecy in Early Modern Europe*, 108–9.

93 On the secretary, see Rosa, "La Chiesa e gli stati regionali nell'età dell'assolutismo," 301–3; Simonetta, *Rinascimento segreto*; Bolzoni, "Il segretario neoplatonico." On other early modern books of advice, see Fragnito, "La trattatistica cinque e seicentesca sulla corte cardinalizia"; and Nussdorfer, "Masculine Hierarchies in Roman Ecclesiastical Households."

94 Guarini, *Il segretario*, 58–9.

95 "Quello sappia fare della sua penna, che della sua persona faceva Proteo, in tutte le forme possibili tramutandola, et variandola secondo che ricerca il bisogno." Guarini, *Il segretario*, 65.

96 "Non basta, che 'l Secretario quanto alle parti dello 'ntelletto s'acconfaccia col suo padrone, se anche in quelle della volontà, et dei costumi non è conforme." Guarini, *Il segretario*, 81.

97 Elias, *The Court Society*.

98 Snyder, *Dissimulation and the Culture of Secrecy in Early Modern Europe*, 70.

99 Duindam, *Myths of Power*, 194–5.

100 Dionisotti, "La letteratura italiana nell'età del concilio di Trento," 187–8.

101 Muchembled, "Manners, Courts, and Civility."

102 Burke, *The Fortunes of the "Courtier,"* 118.

103 On this point, see Wolfe, *Humanism, Machinery, and Renaissance Literature*, 34.

104 "periglioso mare." Ducci, *Arte aulica*, 189.

105 Giraldi Cinzio, *L'uomo di corte*, 11.

106 Grimaldi Robio, *Discorsi*, A3*v*.

107 For an in-depth analysis of imitation of the *Book of the Courtier*, see Burke, *The Fortunes of the "Courtier,"* 81–98.

108 Anglo, "Systematic Immorality," 607.

109 On this point, see also Bàrberi Squarotti, *L'onore in corte*, 86.

110 Guazzo, *The civile conversation of M. Steeven Guazzo*. The Italian text is quoted from Guazzo, *La civil conversazione*, ed. Quondam.

111 For a summary of the different editions of *La civile conversazione*, see Javitch, "Rival Arts of Conduct," 179.

112 The later editions of the *Discorso* are: Venetia: a instantia di Pelegro de Grimaldi, author de l'opera, 1544; and Genoa: per Antonio Roccatagliata, 1583 and 1584.

113 *Discorso di M. Gio. Battista Giraldi Cinthio nobile ferrarese. Intorno a quello che si conuiene a giouane nobile & ben creato nel seruire vn gran principe*. The *Discorso* has also been published in a modern edition, edited by Walter Moretti; see Giraldi Cinzio, *L'uomo di corte*.
114 Tasso, *Il Malpiglio: A Dialogue on the Court (Il Malpiglio overo de la corte)*, in *Tasso's Dialogues*, ed. Trafton, 152–91. This edition contains both an English translation and the Italian text of *Il Malpiglio*.
115 Cesare Mozzarrelli, introduction to Commendone, *Discorso sopra la corte di Roma*, 9–39, 21.
116 Very little is known about Grimaldi Robio, aside from his birth in Chiavari. Grimaldi Robio was mainly a religious writer, and his only non-religious piece of work seems to be the *Discorsi*. For biographic information on Grimaldi Robio, see Soprani, *Li scrittori della Liguria*, 234.
117 On this point, see also Burke, *The Fortunes of the "Courtier,"* 119–24.
118 For a detailed analysis of the *Malpiglio* and its relationship to the *Book of the Courtier*, see Cox, "Tasso's *Malpiglio overo de la corte*"; Lucarelli, "Il nuovo *Libro del cortegiano*"; and Chiarelli, *"Una 'congregazione di uomini raccolti per onore'."* On Tasso's conflicted relationship with patronage, see also McCabe, *"Tasso: Patronage and Imprinsonment,"* in *"Ungainefull Arte,"* 135–46.
119 Tasso, *Il Malpiglio*, in *Tasso's Dialogues*, 155; "le corti si mutano a' tempi," 154.
120 For examples of this topos, see Giraldi Cinzio, *L'uomo di corte*, 11; Commendone, *Discorso sopra la corte di Roma*, 86; Ducci, *Arte aulica*, 189.
121 "che pare havervi sempremai avuta, et havervi oggidì più che mai, l'habitatione sua propria [...] desiderio, che ciascun vi si vede havere di esser tra primi nella gratia del lor Signore." Grimaldi Robio, *Discorsi*, A3*r*.
122 Grimaldi Robio, *Discorsi*, A3*v*.
123 Giraldi Cinzio, *L'uomo di corte*, 16–17.
124 Moretti, "Introduzione," in Giraldi Cinzio, *L'uomo di corte*, xi.
125 Moretti, "Introduzione," in Giraldi Cinzio, *L'uomo di corte*, xv.
126 On this point, see Javitch, "Rival Arts of Conduct," 182–3.
127 Guazzo, *La civil conversazione*, 173. The English translation omits the reference to losing one's vital spirits, describing Guglielmo only as "mortified" (p. 244).
128 See in particular the passage, already quoted above, in Castiglione, *The Book of the Courtier*, IV, x, 213.
129 Guazzo, *The civile conversation*, 2:112. "Io vorrei che non vi partiste punto dallo stile del diligente medico, il quale nonostante le ricette degli altri medici, non lascia di darne anch'egli una di sua mano all'infermo." Guazzo, *La civil conversazione*, 262.
130 Guazzo, *The civile conversation*, 2:112. "Io do per rimedio al corteggiano che essendo il principe [...] un dio terreno, non cessi di fargli sempre, come a cosa sacra, i dovuti onori [...]. Questo è il primo rimedio. Il secondo è

composto di due medicamenti ch'io ho ricavati dal ricettario di un valente filosofo, dell'uno de' quali o d'amendue volendosi servire il corteggiano, si conserverà lungamente la grazie del principe. I medicamenti sono l'astinenza o le vivande condite col zuccaro." Guazzo, *La civil conversazione*, 262.

131 Guazzo, *The civile conversation*, 2:112. "Il corteggian 'nanti al signore o taccia / o sia presto a dir cosa che gli piaccia." Guazzo, *La civil conversazione*, 262.

132 See Berger, *The Absence of Grace*, 10.

133 Giraldi Cinzio, *L'uomo di corte*, 24.

134 "chi disputa ne le corti e aspira in tutti i modi a la vittoria e con tutte le persone egualmente senza risguardo e senza considerazion di tempi e di luoghi, è piuttosto vago de la gloria che desidera il dialettico, che de l'onor cercato dal cortigiano, il qual non solamente ne le dispute, ma in tutte l'azioni de la vita dovrebbe contender, cedendo in quella guisa che fanno alcuni esperti lottatori, i quali piegandosi a quella parte dove li tira l'avversario, con questo pieghevole artificio più facilmente il gittano per terra." Tasso, *Il Malpiglio*, in *Tasso's Dialogues*, 183 [182].

135 Tasso seemed to have a particular interest in the works of Nifo. For a detailed analysis of this point, see Cox, "Rhetoric and Politics in Tasso's *Nifo*."

136 Although Nifo's sole explicit polemical target is Diomede Carafa, the reader senses that he is attacking Castiglione as well.

137 "recare piacere e diletto al suo principe, et massimamente dopo quelle faccende dalle quali e' si conosce esser stato affaticato." Nifo, *Il cortigiano del Sessa*, vii, 28*r*.

138 "si ricevono gli affabili nelle corti, et gli assentatori, et gli adulatori altresì, et i difficili si scacciano." Nifo, *De re aulica*, xv, 44*r*.

139 See also Trafton, introduction to *Il Malpiglio*, in *Tasso's Dialogues*, 1–13. A similar defensive concept of courtly behaviour is described in Lucio Paolo Rosello's dialogue on the court, *Dialogo de la vita de' cortegiani*, 15v–24*r*, a text that is a plagiarized version of Celio Calcagnini's 1544 *De patientia*. On both texts, see the afterword to this book.

140 See Caccamo, "Commendone, Giovanni Francesco."

141 Ducci, *Ars Aulica, or the Courtiers Arte*, trans. Blount. All further references in English are to this edition. The Italian text is cited from *Arte aulica di Lorenzo Ducci.*

142 On Fortuna and the court, see chapter 3 of this book.

143 "la virtù cortigiana non abbraccia tutte l'altre virtù: perché la virtù cortigiana è una certa virtù particolare mediante la quale l'huomo diviene cortigiano: et non ne seguita, che per la medesima virtù sia liberale, giusto, et forte." Nifo, *Il cortigiano del Sessa*, xii, 30*r*.

144 Grimaldi Robio, *Discorsi*, A3*r*.

145 "il rifugio di coloro, che poco vagliono, che rinversando sopra di lei, che niuna cosa è, o se pure è, è di niuna o picciolissima forza sopra di

noi, ove ci sappiamo ben reggere, le cagioni di tutte le loro avversità, e delle altrui prosperità, paionosi rimanere iscusati delle loro colpe." Grimaldi Robio, *Discorsi*, A4*r*. Interestingly, a similar point – concerning princes who blame Fortuna for their losses when they should blame only themselves – is made by Niccolò Machiavelli in chapter 24 of *Il principe.*

146 Langer, *Divine and Poetic Freedom in the Renaissance*, 62.

147 Ducci, *Ars Aulica*, 269. "gran Maestro nell'Arte Aulica." Ducci, *Arte aulica*, 184.

148 Ducci, *Ars Aulica*, 281–2. "le quali non per necessità, ma contingentemente, e quasi per fortuna conseguiscono il loro fine." Ducci, *Arte aulica*, 190–1.

149 Langer, *Divine and Poetic Freedom in the Renaissance*, 50.

150 De Certeau, *The Practice of Everyday Life*, 35–6.

151 De Certeau, *The Practice of Everyday Life*, 37.

152 Cox, *The Renaissance Dialogue*, 57.

153 Ducci, *Ars Aulica*, 195. "all'obligo della servitù tanto si condona, che si può se non honoratamente almeno senza nota d'infamia compiacere, e servire al suo principe in alcune cose, le quali in persona interamente libera senza censura, o biasimo non si comporterebbero." Ducci, *Arte aulica*, 136.

154 Contre les courtisans.

> Servir a la Court bien vestu,
> Manger du bon boire dautant,
> Estre de beau parler battu,
> Tout remply d'espoir qu'on attend,
> Rend le peu saige tres content:
> Comme un que en chaine d'or on lye:
> Dont jamais saillir ne pretend:
> Et treuve telle prison jolye.

Alciato, *Les emblems*, 241, emblem 111.

155

> Qui in Regum Principumve Aulis educunter & nutriuntur, hi quidem splendide vivunt, comedunt ac bibunt lautissime, vestiuntur magnifice, incedunt superbe, adeoque ut eorum felicissima videatur vita. Interim tamen sui iuris non sunt, nec ingenue liberi imo aureis vinculis colligati dici possunt, quos reprehendit Seneca inquiens, stulti esse compedes suas quamvis aureas amare, hinc Aulicorum conditio in proverbium abiit, Aureae compedes.

Andrea Alciato, *Emblematum libri II*, 184, emblem 111. This is a quotation from Erasmus's adagium *Aureae compedes*; see Ripa, *Iconologia*, 666.

156 Held, *Rembrandt's Aristotle*, 35. On the emblem of the courtier in stocks and with a golden chain around his neck, see also Muñoz Simonds, "Anti-Courtier Imagery in *Cymbeline*."

157 "perché la catena d'oro in cortesia ch'io ti mando non si convertisca in ferro di servitù." Doni, *Una nuova opinione del Doni*, c. 65*r*.

158 Javitch, "Rival Arts of Conduct," 195; Javitch, "The Philosopher of the Court," 121.

159 Guazzo, *The civile conversation*, 2:94. "che le catene e i ceppi di questi sono di ferro e di quelli d'oro." Guazzo, *La civil conversazione*, 249.

160 Guazzo, *The civile conversation*, 2:94. "i servitori vili sono nemici del patrone e della catena, e i nobili sono amici del patrone e nimici della catena." Guazzo, *La civil conversazione*, 249.

161 Guazzo, *The civile conversation*, 2:94–5. "quando attenderò a riposare in casa di mio padre, non sarò niente più di quel che siano i privati cittadini, e mi vedrò quasi inutile al mondo, e che per lo contrario presso a quel principe, a me tanto grazioso, mi passa per le mani ogn'ora con che giovare a infinite persone e acquistarmi altrettanti amici e farmi onorare dai più onorati della Corte. Onde trafitto da pungenti stimoli maledico l'indisposizione che non mi lascia star lungamente legato a questa catena d'oro a me sopramodo cara." Guazzo, *La civil conversazione*, 250.

2. The Lady

1 For an overview of the different phases of development of the third book of the *Book of the Courtier*, see, among others, Quondam, "*Questo povero Cortegiano*"; Motta, *Castiglione e il mito di Urbino*; Scarpati, "Osservazioni sul terzo libro del Cortegiano." The bibliography on the court lady as presented in the *Book of the Courtier* and on women in the *Book of the Courtier* is extensive; see, in particular, Saccaro Battisti, "La donna, le donne nel *Cortegiano*"; Chemello, "Donna di palazzo, moglie, cortigiana,"; Finucci, *The Lady Vanishes*; Freccero, "Politics and Aesthetics in Castiglione's *Il Cortegiano*"; Guidi, Piéjus, and Fiorato, *Images de la femme dans la litterature italienne*; Kelso, "The Lady at Court," in *Doctrine for the Lady of the Renaissance*, 210–65; Kolsky, "Women through Men's Eyes: The Third Book of *Il Cortegiano*," in *Courts and Courtiers in Renaissance Northern Italy*, 41–91; Zancan, "La donna e il cerchio nel *Cortegiano* di B. Castiglione."

2 Cox, "Seen but Not Heard."

3 Greene, "*Il Cortegiano* and the Choice of a Game," 12.

4 For in-depth treatment of all these points, see the introduction to Cox, *Women's Writing in Italy*, xi xxviii. On early modern women and the court, see also Welch, "Between Milan and Naples"; Welch, "Women as Patrons and Clients"; Clough, "Daughters and Wives of the Montefeltro";

McIver, "Matrons as Patrons"; Reiss and Wilkins, *Beyond Isabella*; Tomas, *The Medici Women*; Shemek, "In Continuous Expectation"; and Este, *Selected Letters*. Other relevant works on early modern women that take into account different social strata are Jones, *The Currency of Eros*; King, *Women of the Renaissance*; Campbell, *Literary Circles and Gender in Early Modern Europe*; Robin, *Publishing Women*; Ray, *Writing Gender in Women's Letter Collections*; and Ross, *The Birth of Feminism*.

5 For a thorough summary of all these scholarly theories, see Milligan, "The Politics of Effeminacy in *Il Cortegiano*"; and Moulton, "Castiglione: Love, Power, and Masculinity." On masculinity in early modern Italy, see also Finucci, *The Manly Masquerade*; Milligan, "Behaving Like a Man"; Nussdorfer, "Masculine Hierarchies in Roman Ecclesiastical Households"; and Biow, *On the Importance of Being an Individual*.

6 On this point, see Maclean, *The Renaissance Notion of Woman*.

7 On this point, see also Osborn, "The 'Discourse': Context and Historical Background," 11.

8 On women as patrons, see Manca, "Isabella's Mother"; Welch, "Women as Patrons and Clients"; and Gundersheimer, "Women, Learning and Power."

9 Javitch, *Poetry and Courtliness in Renaissance England*, 29; Richards, "'A Wanton Trade of Living?'"; Milligan, "The Politics of Effeminacy in *Il Cortegiano*."

10 Quint, "Courtier, Prince, Lady."

11 "molti sciocchi, i quali per essere prosuntuosi ed inetti si credono acquistar nome di bon cortegiano." Castiglione, *The Book of the Courtier*, I, xii, 19 [*Il Libro del Cortegiano*, 35].

12 It is also worth mentioning that Canossa is chosen as the first speaker precisely for his well-known contrarianism. In Emilia Pio's words, "You, Count, shall be the one to undertake this task the way messer Federico has said; not indeed because we think you so a good Courtier that you know what befits one, but because if you say everything contrarywise, as we hope you will do, the game will be the livelier" ("voi, Conte, sarete quello che averà questa impresa nel modo che ha detto messer Federico; non già perché ci paia che voi siate così bon cortegiano, che sappiate quel che si gli convenga, ma perché, dicendo ogni cosa al contrario, come speramo che farete, il gioco sarà più bello"). Castiglione, *The Book of the Courtier*, I, xiii, 20 [*Il Libro del Cortegiano*, 37].

13 "E di tal sorte voglio io che sia lo aspetto del nostro cortegiano, non così molle e feminile come si sforzano d'aver molti, che non solamente si crespano i capegli e spelano le ciglia, ma si strisciano con tutti que' modi che si faccian le più lascive e disoneste femine del mondo; e pare che nello andare, nello stare ed in ogni altro lor atto siano tanto teneri e

languidi, che le membra siano per staccarsi loro l'uno dall'altro; e pronunziano quelle parole così afflitte, che in quel punto par che lo spirito loro finisca; e quanto più si trovano con omini di grado, tanto più usano tai termini. Questi, poiché la natura, come essi mostrano desiderare di parere ed essere, non gli ha fatti femine, dovrebbono non come bone femine esser estimati, ma, come publiche meretrici, non solamente delle corti de' gran signori, ma del consorzio degli omini nobili esser cacciati." Castiglione, *The Book of the Courtier*, I, xix, 27 [*Il Libro del Cortegiano*, 50–1].

14 Aretino, *Lamento de uno cortigiano*, in *Operette politiche e satiriche*, 2:57, 53. On this text, see also Faini, "Un'opera dimenticata di Pietro Aretino."

15
> Io son un ch'a tocar pur con le dita
> Non degnavo i rubini e or la veste
> Da i bei pidochi ho riccamente ordita.
> Già per grandezza odiai pompose feste,
> Mi putiva il zibetto e ogni odore:
> Or con la vita comprerei la peste.

Aretino, *Lamento de uno cortigiano*, in *Operette politiche e satiriche*, 2:11–15.

16 On this point, see Milligan, "Masculinity and Machiavelli."

17 Breitenberg, *Anxious Masculinity in Early Modern England*. On similar issues, see also Finucci, *The Manly Masquerade*; and Rocke, *Forbidden Friendships*.

18 Milligan, "The Politics of Effeminacy in *Il Cortegiano*," 363. On the issue of masculinity and Italian subjugation to foreign powers, see also Milligan, "Behaving Like a Man"; and Gouwens, "Meanings of Masculinity in Paolo Giovio's Ischian Dialogues."

19 Aretino, *Lamento de uno cortigiano*, in *Operette politiche e satiriche*, 2:53–4.

20 Milligan, "The Politics of Effeminacy in *Il Cortegiano*," 346.

21 Gouwens, "Emasculation as Empowerment."

22 Castiglione, *The Book of the Courtier*, I, xxvi, 32 [*Il Libro del Cortegiano*, 59].

23 "Ma può far questo il ciel giovin perfetti / Che v'abbagli la corte in tal maniera / Che voi non conosciate i suoi difetti?" Aretino, *Lamento de uno cortigiano*, in *Operette politiche e satiriche*, 2:55.

24
> La corte si dipinge una Matrona
> Con viso asciutto, e chioma profumata
> Dura di schiena, e molle di persona
> La qual sen va d'un drappo verde ornata
> Benché attraverso, a guisa di Hercol tiene,
> Una gran pelle d'asino ammantata.
> Le pendon poi dal collo aspre catene
> Per propria dapocaggine o per male
> Che scior se le potrebbe, e uscir di pene.
> Ha di specchi, e scopette una Reale

Corona, e tien sedendo su la paglia,
Un piè in bordello, e l'altro a lo spedale.

Rime piacevoli di Cesare Caporali, del Mauro, e d'altri Auttori, 88. Caporali develops anti-court themes through the personification of the court as a woman in his *Avvisi di Parnaso* as well.

25 "Donna giovine, con bella acconciatura di testa, vestita di verde e di cangiante, con ambe le mani s'alzi il lembo della veste dinanzi, in modo che scuopra le ginocchia, portando nella veste alzata molte ghirlande di varie sorti di fiori, e con una di dette mani terrà anco de gli ami legati in filo di seta verde; averà a i piedi una statuetta di Mercurio, alla quale s'appoggiarà alquanto, et dall'altra banda un paro di ceppi di oro, overo i ferri che si sogliono mettere ad ambi li piedi, e che vi sieno con essi le catene parimente d'oro. Sarà la terra, ove si posa, sassosa, ma sparsa di molti fiori che dalla veste le cadano; ne' piedi averà le scarpe di piombo." Ripa, *Iconologia*, 122. Ripa's *Iconologia* was first printed in Rome in 1593, and later reprinted in numerous editions throughout the seventeenth century. All references here are to the modern edition edited by Sonia Mafei.

26 "lo tempo che vi ho consumato dal principio della mia fanciullezza sino a quest'ora." Ripa, *Iconologia*, 122.

27 "l'Encomio d'alcuni che dicono la corte esser gran maestà del vivere umano, sostegno della politezza, scala dell'eloquenza, teatro de gl'onori, scala delle grandezze, e campo aperto delle conversationi e dell'amicizie [...], che ogni cosa sa et ogni cosa intende [...] di tutte le cose più onorate et degne in tutta la fabrica del mondo, nel quale si fonda et afferma ogni nostro oprare et intendere." Ripa, *Iconologia*, 122.

28 "il che si mostra nelle ginocchia, ignude e vicine a mostrare le vergogne, e ne' ceppi che lo raffrenano e l'impediscono." Ripa, *Iconologia*, 123.

29 On this point, see duBois, "'The Devil's Gateway.'"

30 See, for example, Leon Battista Alberti's *Libri della famiglia*.

31 On this topic, see Faini, *Cosmologia macaronica*.

32 Faini, *Cosmologia macaronica*, 84.

33 Faini, *Cosmologia macaronica*, 167–220.

34 Tecta nitent aurum, muri, pavimenta, cadreghae,
strataque coltrinis variis, lectique parantur
argento, raso, samito, canzante, veluto.
Conspicit hic iuvenes circum scherzare puellas,
leggiadros motu, bellos, facieque galantos,
stringatos, agiles, semper saltare vedutos:
quos Baldus cernens cito iudicat esse diablos,
humanum vestisse caput, moresque virorum.
Quas gestent auri vestas, brettasque veluti,
praetereo, et calzas ostri, rensique camisas;

quin etiam petras pretiosas pono dacantum,
muschium, perfumos, zibetti vascula, namphas.
Sentit et ad nasum storacis, aquaeve rosadae
spiramenta, quibus sbrofatur saepe palazzus.
Florida porfidicos ornant spalleria muros,
in quibus adfixi dant specchi lumina circum.
Illic meschinae stant se doniare puellae,
imponuntque genis, fronti, colloque biaccas,
atque coralinos faciunt parere labrettos,
increspantque comas ferro, ciliique tosantur,
streppantur ve pili, strazzis stuppaque dedentrum
ingrossant humeros, slargantque ad pectora mammas,
ut, quam pensamus sembianzam Palladis esse,
sit saccus paiae, vel forma sit illa puvoni,
qui discazzandos ad osellos ponitur hortis.

Folengo, *Baldo*, XXIII, 538–62.

35 Non unquam regina fuit pomposior ista [...]
Longa sequit series hominum muschiata zibettis,
qui cortesanos se vantant esse tilatos,
quorum si videas mores rationis ochialo,
non homines maschios, sed dicas esse bagassas.
Cortesanus erat tunc verus tempore vecchio,
quum rex ille produs, rex ille bonissimus Artu,
egregiam tenuit chortem, tavolamque rotundam [...]
Tunc cortigiani facies fuit apta placendi,
et molzinandi rigidae praecordia damae,
quando lavabatur solo sudore celatae,
quando nigrabatur sabiis sub sole boiento.
Tempore sed nostro, pro dii, secloque dadessum,
non nisi perfumis variis et odore zibetti,
non nisi seu zazarae petenentur, sive tosentur,
brettis velluti, nec non scuofiotibus auri,
auri cordiculis, impresis atque medais,
millibus et frappis per calzas, perque giupones,
cercamus charum merdosi germen amoris.
En modo, dum celerem castigat Gelfora cocchium,
subsequitantque aliae vaccarum quinque carettae,
has veluti nymphas, divas, charasque madames,
cortesanelli sociant, illisque ragionant
nescio quos sognos, passata in nocte vedutos,
et portantinas properantes supra mulettas,
dente bachettinas vadunt rodendo politas,
mentitosque focos narrant, recitantque sonettos,
sat male stringatos, ac parlant mille baianas,
menchionasque suo dicunt in amore fusaras.
Baldus ab altano tumulo procul omnia visu
coeperat, et ridens ita raggionabat amicis:

"Cernite, compagni, de tantis millibus unum
non hominem video, non qui lignaminis ensem
disfodrare sciat, peius tirare stocatam.
Hi sunt, quos tantum manifestat barba viriles,
caetera conveniunt muliebribus apta conocchis."

Folengo, *Baldo*, XXIV, 48–96.

36 The reference can, of course, be read ironically, given that Arthur was cuckolded and betrayed.

37 See the sixth canto of Ariosto, *Orlando Furioso*.

38 Ariosto, *Orlando Furioso*, ed. Waldman, VII, viii, 61. "il più bel palazzo e 'l più giocondo [...], che mai fosse veduto al mondo." The Italian text is quoted from Ariosto, *Orlando Furioso*, ed. Ceserani and Zatti, 244. All subsequent quotations are from these editions, with page references to the Italian in square brackets.

39
Non tanto il bel palazzo era escellente,
perché vincesse ogn'altro di ricchezza,
quanto ch'avea la più piacevol gente
che fosse al mondo e di più gentilezza.
Poco era l'un da l'altro differente
e di fiorita etade e di bellezza:
sola di tutti Alcina era più bella,
sì come è bello il sol più d'ogni stella.

Ariosto, *Orlando Furioso*, VII, x, 61 [244].

40 For extensive analysis of Ruggiero in Alcina's realm and its allegorical implications, see Ascoli, *Ariosto's Bitter Harmony*.

41
non era in lui di sano altro che 'l nome;
corrotto tutto il resto, e più che mézzo.
Così Ruggier fu ritrovato, tanto
da l'esser suo mutato per incanto.

Ariosto, *Orlando Furioso*, VII, lv, 66 [259].

42 Ariosto, *Orlando Furioso*, VI, xxvii–liii, 53–6, [223–32].

43 Ariosto, *Orlando Furioso*, VI, l–li, 55–6, [231].

44 This complaint against the court is expressed with particular vehemence in Serafino Aquilano's sonnet "La corte è come el gioco del quadrelo"; see chapter 3 of this book, "Italian anti-court verse satire: early examples and leitmotifs."

45 On Armida's garden, and on Alcina and Armida in general, see Giamatti, *The Earthly Paradise and the Renaissance Epic*.

46 See canto 16, 10, of Tasso's *Gerusalemme Liberata*.

47 Tasso, *Jerusalem Delivered*, ed. and trans. Esolen, 16, 9, 301; "l'arte che tutto fa, nulla si scopre." The Italian text is quoted from Tasso, *Gerusalemme Liberata*, ed. Varese and Arbizzoni, 436. All subsequent references are to this edition.

48 Quint, "Courtier, Prince, Lady"; Martines, *Strong Words*, 14. The intertwining of courtliness and its power structures with courtly love has been previously explored from different point of views: see Kelly-Gadol, "Did Women Have a Renaissance?"; Freccero, "Politics and Aesthetics in Castiglione's *Il Cortegiano*"; Finucci, *The Lady Vanishes*; and Jordan, *Renaissance Feminism*.

49 Quint, "Courtier, Prince, Lady," 186.

50 "Tutti coloro c'hanno maledetta la corte, l'hanno parimente frequentata. E tutti coloro che la frequentano, la maledicono. [...] Egli è un costume degli innamorati, che quanto più maledicono, tanto più amano. Sono maledizzioni della lingua, non del cuore. Altrimenti lasceriano una volta quello, che biasimano sempre. Le maledittioni della Corte in bocca del Cortigiano sono maledittioni d'Amante, non d'Inimico." Peregrini, *Difesa del savio in corte*, 180.

51 Trafton, introduction to Tasso, *Il Malpiglio*, in *Tasso's Dialogues*, 10.

52 "Niuna maraviglia dunque è, signor Gianlorenzo, che voi siate invaghito di lei, che raccoglie il meglio, o quasi il meglio, non sol de' la città ma de' le provincie e de' regni, e, scegliendo il perfetto, s'alcuna cosa riceve di non perfetto, cerca d'aggiungerle perfezione." Tasso, *Il Malpiglio*, in *Tasso's Dialogues*, 187 [186].

53 According to Ian Moulton, this similarity contributed to making the masculinity of the courtier problematic, since love in early modern culture was seen as a feminine activity. Moulton, "Castiglione: Love, Power, and Masculinity," 130.

54 Quint, "Courtier, Prince, Lady," 185–6.

55 Ruggiero, *Machiavelli in Love*, 195.

56 Cox, *Women's Writing in Italy*, 44.

57 Ariosto, *Orlando Furioso*, VII, lv, 66 [232]. For a different interpretation of Ruggiero becoming just a name, see Ascoli, *Ariosto's Bitter Harmony*, 199–224.

58 Cox, *Women's Writing in Italy*, 167. On women and power at court in Italy, see Gundersheimer, "Women, Learning and Power"; King, *Women of the Renaissance*; Welch, "Between Milan and Naples" and "Women as Patrons and Clients"; Clough, "Daughters and Wives of the Montefeltro"; McIver, "Matrons as Patrons"; Shemek, "In Continuous Expectation"; Este, *Selected Letters*; and Tomas, *The Medici Women*.

59 Bandello, *La quarta parte de le novelle*, 55–74.

60 Quondam, *La conversazione*, 171–7.

61 Castiglione, *The Book of the Courtier*, III, 5, 151 [*Il Libro del Cortegiano*, 266]. It has also been suggested that the lady match her male counterpart in all the virtues and abilities that make him a proper courtier. Like the courtier, she needs to put such qualities to use in winning and maintaining

favour at court. Yet fundamental differences set them apart. According to Stephen Kolsky, one difference can be found in the greater importance given to court ladies' passive attributes, such as physical beauty, but the main dissimilarity concerns the final scope of each figure's respective courtiership. In Kolsky's opinion, "unlike the courtier, the *donna di palazzo* is not actively encouraged to pursue influence over the ruler, nor is it seen as the culmination of her skills." Kolsky, "Women through Men's Eyes: The Third Book of *Il Cortegiano*," in *Courts and Courtiers in Renaissance Northern Italy*, 66.

62 Ruggiero explains this disparity by referring to the "shared vision of the female body and its sexual dangers." Ruggiero, *Machiavelli in Love*, 198.

63 Outside of Italy, a clear picture of envy and rivalry among court ladies is offered by Christine de Pisan's *Le Tresor de la Cité des Dames* (1405); see Kelso, *Doctrine for the Lady of the Renaissance*, 233–5.

64 Somasco would also publish one of the key texts of seventeenth-century misogyny, Giuseppe Passi's *I donneschi difetti*. On Passi's text, see Cox, *Women's Writing in Italy*, 173–83.

65 "O malagevole mia fortuna, tu propriamente duplicato mi hai l'affanno [...]; cioè d'esser donzella di Corte, e d'esser Cortigiana d'Amore, le quali due servitù sono in miseria uguali: [...] se come donzella di corte son pagata d'ingratitudine, come inamorata di pianti e di dolori appagata mi trovo, se come donzella di corte invidiata sono, dall'altre mie pari, come inamorata son beffata e schernita dalle mie rivali. Se come donzella mi conviene servire alle Signore [...] come inamorata adorno l'amante mio d'infinite lodi, non accorgendomi l'imbrattar me stessa molte volte con infinito biasimo." Pascoli, *La pazzesca pazzia*, 243.

66 It is worth pointing out that the court where Gioseffo is mistreated is a Spanish court, not an Italian one, which may have recalled to the mind of the readers the theme of Italy's subjugation to foreigners.

67 "senz'alcuna custodia [...] senza padre e senza madre, sotto governo di donne di Corte, dove si sta sottoposta a mille pericoli, oltre il tormento delle pessime lingue delle cortigiane mormoranti, e cortigiani che giamai te finiscono." Pascoli, *La pazzesca pazzia*, 231.

68 Guasco's text has been published in a modern edition twice in its Italian version: as *Ragionamento a Donna Lavinia sua figliuola*, ed. Sanson; and as *Sotto il segno di Chirone*, ed. Giachino. It has also been translated into English by Peggy Osborn as *Discourse to Lady Lavinia His Daughter*. All references are to Sanson's edition. On the date of the text, see Sanson, in Guasco, *Ragionamento*, 68.

69 This has also been pointed out by Kelso, *Doctrine for the Lady of the Renaissance*, 216–17; and Osborn, "The 'Discourse': Context and Historical Background," 11–12.

70 For a detailed biography of Guasco, see Sanson, in Guasco, *Ragionamento*, 62–8.
71 For analysis of the *Ragionamento* in relation to other early modern conduct manuals, see Sanson, in Guasco, *Ragionamento*, 76–8. On its relationship with the third book of *Book of the Courtier* and with other writings on courts and courtiers, see Coller, "How to Succeed at Court"; and Ferrero, "Il *Ragionamento* di Annibale Guasco." On sixteenth-century manuals for women, see Zonta, *Trattati del Cinquecento sulla donna.*
72 The *Book of the Courtier* is one of the three books (together with Giovanni Della Casa's *Galateo* and Stefano Guazzo's *Civil conversazione*) that Guasco gives his daughter to take with her to court.
73 Guazzo, *Lettere del Signor Stefano Guazzo*, 33–4.
74 In Lavinia's foreword to the text, the printed edition of the *Ragionamento* is presented as her initiative. Due to Lavinia's young age, it is likely that either some older and more experienced lady-in-waiting, or even Annibale Guasco himself, may have decided to have it printed.
75 Guazzo, *Lettere del Signor Stefano Guazzo*, 33.
76 My translation. Guasco, *Ragionamento*, 135. The English edition does not translate this quote, but uses a different phrasing.
77 Guasco, *Discourse to Lady Lavinia*, 100. "Neanche gli orsi offendono chi s'atterra." Guasco, *Ragionamento*, 135.
78 In spite of underlining the presence of envy at court, Guasco does not deny the possibility for friendship among women at court, thus contrasting the most common picture offered by texts such as *La pazzesca pazzia.* On this point, see Coller, "How to Succeed at Court," 28.
79 Cox, introduction to *Women's Writing in Italy*, xiii–xiv. On women as writers, artists, and musicians in the Renaissance, see, among others, Robin, *Publishing Women*; Jacobs, *Defining the Renaissance Virtuosa*; Murphy, *Lavinia Fontana*; MacNeil, *Music and Women of the Commedia dell'Arte.*
80 Jacobs, *Defining the Renaissance Virtuosa*, 3–4.
81 On the *concerto delle donne*, see Newcomb, *The Madrigal at Ferrara*; and Durante and Martellotti, *Cronistoria delle dame principalissime di Margherita Gonzaga d'Este.* On its most famous member, Laura Peperara, see Durante and Martellotti, *Giovinetta peregrina.*
82 Newcomb, *The Madrigal at Ferrara*, 26.
83 Newcomb, *The Madrigal at Ferrara*, 7–8.
84 Nifo, *De re aulica*, 389.
85 Nifo, *De re aulica*, 395. On this point, see also Osborn, "The 'Discourse': Context and Historical Background," 11–12.
86 Coldagelli, "Brancaccio, Giulio Cesare." On Brancaccio, see also Wistreich, *Warrior, Courtier, Singer.*
87 Wistreich, *Warrior, Courtier, Singer*, 105.

88 Wistreich, *Warrior, Courtier, Singer*, 273; Coldagelli, "Brancaccio, Giulio Cesare."

89 On this letter, see Wistreich, *Warrior, Courtier, Singer*, 236.

90 "ché a questi tali meritamente si po dir quello, che una valorosa donna in una nobile compagnia piacevolmente disse ad uno, ch'io per ora nominar non voglio, il quale, essendo da lei, per onorarlo, invitato a danzare, e rifiutando esso e questo e lo udir musica e molti altri intertenimenti offertigli, sempre con dir così fatte novelluzze non esser suo mestiero, in ultimo, dicendo la donna, 'Qual è adunque il mestier vostro?,' rispose con un mal viso: 'Il combattere'; allora la donna sùbito: 'Crederei,' disse, 'che or che non siete alla guerra, né in termine de combattere, fosse bona cosa che vi faceste molto ben untare ed insieme con tutti i vostri arnesi da battaglia riporre in un armario finché bisognasse, per non ruginire più di quello che siate'; e così, con molte risa de' circunstanti, scornato lasciollo nella sua sciocca prosunzione." Castiglione, *The Book of the Courtier*, I, xvii, 25 [*Il Libro del Cortegiano*, 46].

91 Wistreich, *Warrior, Courtier, Singer*, 237.

92 Wistreich, *Warrior, Courtier, Singer*, 245.

93 The poems for Brancaccio are published in Tasso, *Le rime di Torquato Tasso*, 268–73.

94 Tasso, "Al signor Cesare Brancaccio," in *Le rime di Torquato Tasso*, 268.

95 Wistreich, *Warrior, Courtier, Singer*, 268–73.

96 Signore, Amor t'ha colto
Tra novelle sirene,
Quai non so s'udir mai le nostre arene.
Gli orecchi al suon, deh, chiudi,
Ed apri gli occhi al sonno.

Tasso, "A Giulio Cesare Brancaccio per il concerto de le dame a la corte di Ferrara," in *Le rime di Torquato Tasso*, 272.

97 fuga e oblio
Son più sicuri ove Amor canta o ride.
Fuggi; o t'inaspri tanto
Sdegno e n' sì dure tempre,
Che per dolcezza il cor non si distempre.

Tasso, "A Giulio Cesare Brancaccio per il concerto de le dame a la corte di Ferrara," in *Le rime di Torquato Tasso*, 272.

98 Gordon, *Monteverdi's Unruly Women*, 10–46. On these issues, see also Stras, *Women and Music in Sixteenth-Century Ferrara*, 58–9. For views of women's speech as unchaste, see also Ray, *Writing Gender in Women's Letter Collections*, 8–9.

99 Gordon, *Monteverdi's Unruly Women*, 41. On courtesans and music, see also Stras, *Women and Music in Sixteenth-Century Ferrara*, 59–62.

100 Shemek, "'Mi mostrano a dito tutti quanti,'" 49. On courtesans, see also Cohen, "Courtesans and Whores."
101 Speroni, *Orazione contra le cortigiane*, 220. For an analysis of this text, see Rosenthal, *The Honest Courtesan*, 25–9.
102 Chemello, "Donna di palazzo, moglie, cortigiana," 127.
103 See Rosenthal, *The Honest Courtesan*; and Shemek, "'Mi mostrano a dito tutti quanti.'"
104 See Rosenthal, "Satirizing the Courtesan," in *The Honest Courtesan*, 11–57; Shemek, "'Mi mostrano a dito tutti quanti'"; and Findlen, "Humanism, Politics and Pornography in Renaissance Italy."
105 On these issues, see Quaintance, *Textual Masculinity and the Exchange of Women in Renaissance Florence.*
106 Rosenthal, "Satirizing the Courtesan," in *The Honest Courtesan*, 30.
107 Rosenthal, epilogue to Aretino, *Dialogues*, 387–412.
108 "vuota di ogni bontà, e colma sempre di tutti i vizii, che possano essere in core umano indemoniato." Speroni, *Orazione contra le cortigiane*, 214.
109 "corte è albergo di cortesia, e cortesia è virtù, o non è senza virtù, anzi è composta di assai virtudi, come lo è lo elettro di ariento e d'oro; specialmente di liberalitade, e pietade, e discrezione, e modestia, tutte adunate prudentemente in coloro, che son famiglia di alcun signor valoroso." Speroni, *Orazione contra le cortigiane*, 214.
110 "la cortigiania delle peccatrici è in molti luoghi per tutta Italia, ove ora corte non ha; ma ben vi ha case e palazzi: ed ove ha principe e corte sua, già non son proprie de' cortigiani le meretrici, ma lor comuni e alla plebe." Sperone Speroni, *Orazione contra le cortigiane*, 220.
111 Pozzi, "Sperone Speroni: Nota introduttiva," in *Trattatisti del cinquecento*, 485.
112 Storey, *Carnal Commerce in Counter-Reformation Rome*, 67–8.
113 Aretino, *Ragionamento, Dialogo*, 176. All subsequent references are to this edition. On the relationship between courtesans and courtiers in Aretino's *Sei giornate*, see also Findlen, "Humanism, Politics and Pornography in Renaissance Italy"; and Paternoster, "'Le Sei Giornate' di Pietro Aretino.'"
114 "è di necessità che ci abbino dato anco il viso." Aretino, *Ragionamento, Dialogo*, 339.
115 "le puttane d'oggidì si simigliano ai cortigiani dal dì d'oggi, che per la divizia di loro stessi bisogna mariolare: altrimenti si moiano di stento." Aretino, *Ragionamento, Dialogo*, 338.
116 See, for example, statements like "E sappi che chi non usa [...] le astuzie che usano i cortigiani del mal tempo con i monsignori [...] gli diventa nimici." Aretino, *Ragionamento, Dialogo*, 244.
117 Aquilecchia, "Aretino's *Sei giornate*," 456.

118 Piccolomini, *La Raffaella*, 41. On the use of the terms *ingegno* and *arte* in *La Raffaella* in comparison with the use of the same terms in the *Book of the Courtier*, see Baldi, *Tradizione e parodia in Alessandro Piccolomini*, 153.
119 Cox, *The Renaissance Dialogue*, 57; see also chapter 1 of this book.
120 Aquilecchia explains such individualism by referring to Gucciardini's notion of *il particulare*. Aquilecchia, "Aretino's *Sei giornate*," 461.
121 Biondo's *Angitia* is briefly examined in Innamorati, "Ex tugurio Blondi"; and in Romano, "Michelangelo Biondo poligrafo e stampatore."
122 Stabile, "Biondo, Michelangelo"; Romano, "Michelangelo Biondo poligrafo e stampatore," 222.
123 Romano, "Michelangelo Biondo poligrafo e stampatore," 220. According to Romano, Biondo is most likely the "Biondello" of Aretino's *Ipocrito*.
124 This is also pointed out by Innamorati, "Ex tugurio Blondi," 14.
125 Aristeo (interpreted as a figure for Nifo or for Biondo himself) is the name of pastoral deity and represents wisdom. Angitia is the name of an ancient snake goddess, skilled in poisoning and witchcraft, and represents therefore a dangerously alluring charm. See Innamorati, "Ex tugurio Blondi," 16–17.
126 Biondo, *Angitia cortigiana*, Dii*r*–Dii*v*.
127 "non pensa ad altro che a fraude, inganni, doli, et stupri." Biondo, *Angitia cortigiana*, Eiii*v*.
128 "quei che sfacciatamente fanno professione del Cortegiano, sonno huomini li piu miseri, li più affliti li più sporchi li più sozzi et li più malfatti, i quali son a sembianza di quell muro, che novamente è ricoperto di calze biancha." Biondo, *Angitia cortigiana*, Eiv*v*.
129 "la peste universale, ruina inestricabile et indelebil machia de colui che ha a far seco." Biondo, *Angitia cortigiana*, Div*v*.
130 "quella caligine che oscura il vero et illumina il falso largamente." Biondo, *Angitia cortigiana*, Eii*v*.
131 "O quanto è misera la sorte del Cortigiano, benché anchor voi altre odo esser disgratiate, doppo che d'un medesimo nome sete ornate cul Cortegiano." Biondo, *Angitia cortigiana*, Div*v*–Ei*r*.
132 "nulla altra fortuna volge la rota de qual voi Cortigiana salvo el Cortegiano, et per contrario." Biondo, *Angitia cortigiana*, Ei*r*.
133 On Garzoni's "De' cortigiani e delle donne di corte insieme," see also the introduction to this book.
134 "di vagheggiare, di rubbare, di trappolare, d'incantare, di striare i suoi amatori, essendo [...] le arti delle donne solamente inganni, frodi, malie et vanità d'incanti." Garzoni, "De' cortigiani e delle donne di corte insieme," in *La piazza universale*, 854. The passages above are quotes from Agrippa's *De incertutidine et vanitate scientiarum* (see Paolo Cherchi's notes to the text).

135 Rosenthal, "Satirizing the Courtesan," in *The Honest Courtesan*, 31–3.
136 "è impossibile che chi si sottomette a ognuno, ami niuno." Aretino, *Ragionamento, Dialogo*, 154.
137 Shemek, "'Mi mostrano a dito tutti quanti,'" 50. In Shemek's opinion, these shaming rituals, as well as some anti-courtesan poems, served the purpose of diverting the gaze – and the shame – away from courtiers and converging it uniquely onto courtesans. "'Mi mostrano a dito tutti quanti,'" 62.
138 "mutato come la faccia d'una meretrice." Garzoni, "De' cortigiani e delle donne di corte insieme," in *La piazza universale*, 853. Again, the passage is taken from Agrippa's *De incertutidine et vanitate scientiarum*.
139

> Chi vuol sap[er] che cosa è stento e morte
> Legga me hora, intanto ch'io descrivo
> La miseria e pericol della Corte.
> Sepoltura e prigion dell'homo vivo
> È questa Circe, anzi trasforma l'homo
> Dall'esser proprio nel suo primo arrivo.
> [...]
> Proprio è la Corte come una puttana,
> Che par bella di fuora, e poscia dentro
> Parte non ha che si ritrovi sana.

Simeoni, *Della corte*, in *Satire alla berniesca*, 39.
140 On satires, courtesans, and syphilis, see Ugolini, "The Satirist's Purgatory."
141

> Ma diciam sol come cambiar ciascuno
> Fa questa Corte di costumi et pelo,
> O fia di vitii, o di virtù digiuno

Simeoni, *Della corte*, in *Satire alla berniesca*, 42.
142 "La Corte è piena d'invidie e d'inganni / con la fronte di rose et di viole." Simeoni, *Della corte*, in *Satire alla berniesca*, 45.

3. The Satirist

1 "Difficile est saturam non scribere," Juvenal, *Satire I*, 30.
2 On early modern Italian satires in general, see Corsaro, *La regola e la licenza*; Longhi, *Lusus*; Pelosi, *Satira barocca*; and especially Romei, "Ironia e irrisione."
3 Kernan, *The Cankered Muse*, 15–30.
4 Kernan, *The Cankered Muse*, 16.
5 Kernan, *The Cankered Muse*, 7–8.
6 Sandra Citroni Marchetti, "Quid Romae faciam?," 85. On the classical roots of early modern satire in general, see also Smith, *The Anti-Courtier Trend*, 13–21.

7 Burrow, "Roman Satire in the Sixteenth Century," 247.
8 On Lucian's legacy, see Marsh, *Lucian and the Latins.*
9 Smith, *The Anti-Courtier Trend*, 18.
10 Smith, *The Anti-Courtier Trend*, 19.
11 Lucan, *Pharsalia*, viii.
12 For an overview of anti-court sentiments in the Middle Ages, see Uhlig, *Hofkritik im England*; Cian, *La satira*, 52–3; Jaeger, *The Origins of Courtliness*, 58–9; Laura Kendrick, "Medieval Satire," in Ruben Quintero, *A Companion to Satire*, 52–69; Schreiner and Wenzel, *Hofkritik im Licht humanistischer Lebens-und Bildungsideale.*
13 See Jaeger, *The Origins of Courtliness*, 58.
14 Schreiner and Wenzel, *Hofkritik im Licht humanistischer Lebens-und Bildungsideale*, 3.
15 Kernan, *The Cankered Muse*, 42.
16 Kernan, *The Cankered Muse*, 50.
17 Kernan, *The Cankered Muse*, 50.
18 Piccolomini, *Aeneae Silvii De curialium miseriis epistola.* All subsequent references are to this edition. On the importance of *De curialium miseriis*, see Woodhouse, "Dal *De curialium miseriis* al *Libro del cortegiano* e oltre"; von Martels and Vanderjagt, *Pius II, 'el più expeditivo pontefice,'* 87–106; Uhlig, *Hofkritik im England*, 175–89; Schreiner and Wenzel, *Hofkritik im Licht humanistischer Lebens-und Bildungsideale*, 1–12.

On the relationship between Piccolomini's and Peter of Blois's anti-court writings, see Keith Sidwell, "Aeneas Silvius Piccolomini's *De curialium miseriis* and Peter of Blois," in von Martels and Vanderjagt, *Pius II, 'el più expeditivo pontefice,'* 87–106.
19 "Dantur honores in curiis non secundum mores atque virtutes, sed ut quisque ditior est atque potentior, eo magis honoratur." Piccolomini, *De curialium miseriis*, 29.
20 "Divitibus nonnumquam dari solent divitiae, sicut in mare feruntur aquae." Piccolomini, *De curialium miseriis*, 35; "Sunt qui se posse putant divitias cumulare principibus servientes, at hi ut divitias comparent, libertatem vendunt, nec tamen divitias assquuntur." Piccolomini, *De curialium miseriis*, 34.
21 On the figure of Sejanus in Ducci's *Ars Aulica*, see chapter 1 of this book, "Anti-courtliness and the *Book of the Courtier*'s epigones."
22 "Nulla dies est in qua mille res non videas quam tuum conturbent animum." Piccolomini, *De curialium miseriis*, 39.
23 "relinquamos hoc pelagus inquietum, nosque in aliam vitam redigamus." *Piccolomini, De curialium miseriis*, 68.
24 "Vale, vir, nisi ex curialibus unus esses, meo iudicio prudens." Piccolomini, *De curialium miseriis*, 69.

25 Woodhouse, "Dal *De curialium miseriis* al *Libro del cortegiano* e oltre," 424.
26 Celenza, *Renaissance Humanism.*
27 Celenza, *Renaissance Humanism*, 28.
28 According to Riccardo Fubini's biography on the author in the *Dizionario biografico degli italiani*, Castiglionchio did leave the court, while Celenza's biography states the opposite. See Fubini, "Castiglionchio, Lapo da, detto il Giovane."
29 Celenza highlights the bitter irony that suffuses Castiglionchio's dialogue, yet maintains that in the end Castiglionchio still believes in the court and in its potential to provide recognition to those who are worthy. Celenza, *Renaissance Humanism*, 56.
30 Celenza, *Renaissance Humanism*, 56.
31 W. Scott Blanchard, "Renaissance and Prose Satire: Italy and England," in Quintero, *A Companion to Satire*, 118. For a general overview of satire, see also Jones, "Satire, History, and Ideology," in *Satire in the Elizabethan Era*, 1–34.
32 Ejner J. Jensen, "Verse Satire in the English Renaissance," in Quintero, *A Companion to Satire*, 108.
33 Sansovino, *Sette libri di satire.*
34 Andini, *Satire di cinque poeti illustri.* The lack of information on Andini has led scholars to hypothesize that Mario degli Andini may be just a pen name for Lodovico Paterno.
35 See also Stella Galbiati, "Per una teoria della satira fra Quattro e Cinquecento."
36 Sansovino, *Sette libri di satire*, 2*r*.
37 "ritrar gli huomini dal vizio [...] indirizzandoli ai buoni ordini della natura." Sansovino, *Sette libri di satire*, 3*r*.
38 "i buoni hanno sempre avuto caro le cose Satirice, come quelle che non solo muovono, ma anche fanno effetto negli altrui cuori, percioche sì come son libere nella lor qualità, così ancho sono ardentissime riprenditrici nelle cose non buone." Sansovino, *Sette libri di satire*, 3*r*.
39 Andini, *Satire di cinque poeti illustri*, A2*r*.
40 "son Dei salvatici, et che s'allegrano delle lascivie, et che sono sfacciati. Laonde si come a nostri tempi è lecito introdur buffoni, pazzi, et gli ebbriachi da coloro che temono di ragionar liberamente a quali fanno dir ciò ch'essi vogliono esprimendo il concetto loro, così a quei tempi coloro che non avevano ardire di raccontare le bruttezze di quei tempi, introducevano i Satiri." Sansovino, "Discorso sulla materia della satira," in *Sette libri di satire*, n.p.
41 "imitante la natura: percioche basta al Satirico apertamente riprendere gli errori altrui senz'altro artificio." Sansovino, "Discorso sulla materia della satira," in *Sette libri di satire*, n.p.

42 "la verità nuda et aperta." Sansovino, "Discorso sulla materia della satira," in *Sette libri di satire*, n.p.
43 "i satirici non cominciano con invocation, o con maraviglia, ma o con sdegno o con qualch'altra maniera cosi fatta, quasi che essendo come provocati dalla moltitudine de vitij de gli huomini si muovino sdegnosamente, et con ira a riprenderle non potendo a un certo modo piu tacere." Sansovino, "Discorso sulla materia della satira," in *Sette libri di satire*. n.p.
44 "questi bizzarri intelletti hanno assai co' medici somiglianza, i quali col ferro, et col fuoco, o risvegliano le membra addormentate, over del tutto via troncano le già consumate, et guaste." Lodovico Paterno, "Lettera di M. Lodovico Paterno sopra la materia della satira," in Andini, *Satire di cinque poeti illustri*, A5*r*.
45 Ferroni, *Ariosto*, 89.
46 Michel Paoli, "'*Quale fu la prima satira che compose*': Storia vs. letteratura nelle satire ariostesche," in Berra, *Fra satire e rime ariostesche*, 48. On the *Satire* as a whole, see also Villa, "Ludovico Ariosto e la 'famiglia d'allegrezza piena'"; and Campeggiani, "Le *Satire*." On Ariosto's relationship with his patrons, see Masi, "The Nightingale in a Cage"; and McCabe, "Ariosto: Laureate or Poligrafo?," in "*Ungainefull Arte*," 123–34.
47 Floriani, *Il modello ariostesco*, 63. On the influence of Ariosto's *Satire* and their relationship with the Horatian model, see also Gasparini, "La satira del Cinquecento italiano."
48 Bologna, "*Satire* di Ludovico Ariosto," 198.
49 Bologna, "*Satire* di Ludovico Ariosto," 198.
50 Floriani, *Il modello ariostesco*, 53–4.
51 On Ariosto and the court, see Looney, "Corte."
52 Citroni Marchetti, "Quid Romae faciam?," 91.
53 Io desidero intendere da voi,
Alessandro fratel, compar mio Bagno,
s'in corte è ricordanza più di noi;
se più il signor me accusa; se compagno
per me si lieva e dice la cagione
per che, partendo gli altri, io qui rimagno;
o, tutti dotti ne la adulazione
(l'arte che più tra noi si studia e cole),
l'aiutate a biasmarme oltra ragione.
Pazzo chi al suo signor contradir vole,
se ben dicesse c'ha veduto il giorno
pieno di stelle e a mezzanotte il sole.
O ch'egli lodi, o voglia altrui far scorno,
di varie voci subito un concento
s'ode accordar di quanti n'ha dintorno;
e chi non ha per umiltà ardimento

la bocca aprir, con tutto il viso applaude
e par che voglia dir: – anch'io consento. –
Ma se in altro biasmarme, almen dar laude
dovete che, volendo io rimanere,
lo dissi a viso aperto e non con fraude.

Ariosto, *Satira I*, 1–21, in *The Satires of Ludovico Ariosto*, ed. Wiggins, 7. The Italian text is quoted from Ariosto, *Opere minori*, ed. Segre, 499–500. All further references are to these editions.

54 Dimmi or c'ho rotto il dosso e, se 'l ti piace,
dimmi ch'io sia una rózza, e dimmi peggio:
insomma esser non so se non verace.

Ariosto, *Satira III*, 10–12, 59 [*Opere minori*, 58].

55 Ariosto, *Satira III*, 115–50, 60–6 [*Opere minori*, 528–30].

56 On Ariosto's use of fables in the *Satire*, see Alessandra Villa, "Gli apologhi delle *Satire*," in Berra, *Fra satire e rime ariostesche*, 183–205.

57 Baldini, *Ludovico della tranquillità*. On this point, see also Bologna, "*Satire* di Ludovico Ariosto," 201–5; and Wiggins, introduction to Ariosto, *The Satires of Ludovico Ariosto*, ix–xxxvii.

58 "la corruzione della Corte [...] s'estende al mondo intero, specie quello interiore." Bologna, "*Satire* di Ludovico Ariosto," 199.

59 "impianto apologetico." Segre, "Premessa" to *Satire*, in Ariosto, *Opere minori*, ix.

60 "la difesa, e l'apologia, di un io che proprio dall'opposizione all'altro [...] trae certezza e definizione di sé." Eduardo Saccone, "Riflessione e invenzione," in Berra, *Fra satire e rime ariostesche*, 20.

61 "opposizione esplicita tra i diritti dell'io e le costrizioni imposte dai poteri contemporanei." Ferroni, *Ariosto*, 88. On the contrast between the *Satire* and the *Orlando Furioso*, see also Wiggins, introduction to Ariosto, *The Satires of Ludovico Ariosto*, xiii.

62 For my use of an "active" notion of self-fashioning, see introduction to this book.

63 Ariosto, *Satira I*, 85, 11 [*Opere minori*, 502].

64 Ariosto, *Satira I*, 225, 19 [*Opere minori*, 509].

65 Ariosto, *Satira I*, 150, 15 [*Opere minori*, 505].

66 Ariosto's *Satira I* was written in the last month of 1517, and *Satira III* at the beginning of 1518. Both works can therefore be supposed to have been read or circulated in manuscript form in 1518, the year when the manuscript of Castiglione's *Book of the Courtier* also began circulating. On the dates of the *Satire*'s composition, see Bologna, "*Satire* di Ludovico Ariosto," 200; on the circulation of the *Book of the Courtier*, see Burke, *The Fortunes of the "Courtier,"* 39.

67 "non vuol che laude sua da me composta / per opra degna di mercè si pona, / di mercè degno è l'ir correndo in posta." Ariosto, *Satira I*, 97–9, 11 [*Opere minori*, 503].

68
Il qual se vuol di calamo et inchiostro
di me servirsi, e non mi tòr da bomba,
digli: – Signore, il mio fratello è vostro. –
Io, stando qui, farò con chiara tromba
il suo nome sonar forse tanto alto
che tanto mai non si levò colomba.

Ariosto, *Satira I*, 226–31, 19 [*Opere minori*, 509].

69 Ariosto, *Satira III*, 39, 61 [*Opere minori*, 525].

70 See Ariosto, *Orlando Furioso*, XXXV, xx–xxiii, 424, [1225–6].

71 Augustus was not as august and beneficent as Virgil's clarion tones make him out to be – but his good taste in poetry compensates for the evil of his proscriptions. ("Non fu sì santo né benigno Augusto / come la tuba di Virgilio suona. / L'aver avuto in poesia buon gusto / la proscrizion iniqua gli perdona"). Ariosto, *Orlando Furioso*, XXXV, xxvi, 425, [1227].

72 On this point, see Jossa, "The Lies of Poets"; Ascoli, "Worthy of Faith?"; and Ugolini, "Self-Portraits of a Truthful Liar."

73 On the possible sources of Ariosto's *Satire*, see Godioli, "La prima satira di Ariosto"; and Floriani, *Il modello ariostesco*, 69–77. However, Bologna excludes from Ariosto's sources fifteenth- and sixteenth-century satirists such as Panfilo Sasso, Antonio Tebaldeo, Niccolò Lelio Cosmico, and Antonio Vinciguerra, considering the *Satire* more indebted to Petrarch's *Canzoniere* and Dante's *Commedia*. Bologna, "*Satire* di Ludovico Ariosto," 205.

74
Pascul de vizii, pocul di veneno
ospizio di dolor che hai nome corte
de invidie, odii e rancori arra, di morte
in ogni canto e insino al tecto pieno,
ben sparge el seme in arido terreno
quel che s'invecchia a le tue ingrate porte
e sempre vive a più infelice sorte
quel che più applaudi o che blandisci al seno.
Como l'aquila fai de la testude,
che in alto i levi e poi presto li abassi
e godi più che l'un l'altro delude.
In te, casa d'error, continuo stassi
tra l'acqua e 'l foco, el martello e l'incude:
che sien maledetti a te tutti i mie' passi.

Correggio, *Opere*, 156. The date of the composition of Correggio's poems cannot be determined with precision. According to Tissoni Benvenuti, the *terminus ante quem* is August 1508; see Correggio, *Opere*, 533. Anti-courtliness is a main theme of Correggio's lyrical production.

One meaningful example is offered by the sonnet "Gente mal nate, che a la flebil riva," where the court is depicted as hell on earth in tones reminiscent of Dante's *Inferno*. Dystopian depictions of the court are expressed in the sonnet "Ingrata patria, ove non ha bon stato" as well, and particularly in the *capitolo* "Chi semina fatiche e vòl quïete," wherein the poet states that to live at court one needs the same *astuzia* that is required for playing cards or dice. On this poem and its possible influence on Ariosto, see Godioli, "La prima satira di Ariosto." Anti-courtliness mixed with a pastoral tone is also the theme of "Le piagge erbose a i vili animaletti," "Selve dilecte, amiche piagge e rive," "L'ozio già tanto disiato godo," "Tu non sciai bene ancor con quanti dubii," and "Né più né men como a natura piace," which Vecchi Galli sees as possible inspiration for Ariosto's *Satire*; see Vecchi Galli, "Corte medievale," 165.

75 Invida corte, d'ogni ben nimica,
nuda di fede e colma d'impietate
scola di tradimenti e falsitate,
e d'ogni altra virtù priva e mendica.
 Terrestre inferno, e fonte di fatica
radice di miseria e adversitate,
rivo abondante de malignitate
et a lieta fortuna sempre ostica.
 Deh quando fia già mai, che giù del cielo
scendano di Vulcano i fieri dardi
ad aprir tante fraudi et tanti inganni?
 Ma s'io moro avanti il bianco pelo
spero vederte al fondo, benché tardi
con tuoi seguaci e perfidi tiranni.

Aquilano, *Le Rime*, 1:127.

76 Smith, *The Anti-Courtier Trend*, 30. Two sonnets are briefly analysed in Rossi, *Serafino Aquilano e la poesia cortigiana*, 84–5. Smith also quotes one more anti-court sonnet by Aquilano, "La corte è come el gioco del quadrelo," discussed below in this chapter.

77 Cian, *La satira*, 253.

78 Io ho provato che cosa è amore
e ho provato la doglia del dente;
morte ho sofferto di carnal parente
 e l'obedienza di frati menore;
molte altre doglie assai ho avute al core,
quali non son da dire a ogne gente;
febre mortale... Tutte son niente,
 com'è obedienza de star a signore.
S' tu me dicesti: – Dimme, come 'l sai? –,
io te respondo che l'aggio provato
e giorni e note ho tratto gran guai.

Così vorrei vedere scorticato
chi se diletta di aver signor mai.
Rengrazio Dio che fuor me n'ha cavato.

Antonio Beccari da Ferrara, in Sapegno, *Poeti minori del trecento*, 456.

79 On the *tinello* in anti-court writings, see Gigliucci, "'Qualis coena tamen!'"; and Gigliucci, "L'anti-festa del tinello."

80 Cenando, Fedel mio, iersera in corte,
m'apparecchiar Serafino e Galasso
una tovaglia lavata col grasso
che mostrava la mensa per le porte.
Poi le vivande che mi furon porte,
fu l'insalata mal condita, ahi lasso!
il pan peloso, più duro che sasso;
filava il vin, per la paura, forte.
La madre di Buezio avvolta a un osso
mi dieder prima, che del brodo puro
aveva ancor la cimatura addosso.
Diedi de' denti su quel cuoio duro,
(l'un era affaticato, e l'altro scosso,)
col culo al scanno e con li piedi al muro.
Allor dissi: – Io non curo
di questa imbandigion mangiarne troppa,
ch'io non son uso a pettinare stoppa. –
E poi volsi la groppa
e dissi, che chi è in corte è destinato
se non muor santo si muore disperato

Cammelli, *Rime*, 80. For other anti-court verse by Pistoia, see also the sonnet "Tornato in terra di promissione" (*Rime*, 77), a dystopian picture usually interpreted as referring to Rome and the papal court, and "Una donna fu già, che pregò Iddio" (*Rime*, 207), on the unreliability of the *signori*.

81 For detailed biographical information on each of these authors, see, respectively, Marti, "Beccari, Antonio"; De Robertis, "Cammelli, Antonio, detto il Pistoia"; Vigilante, "Ciminelli, Serafino"; and Farenga, "Correggio, Nicolò Postumo."

82 Quoted also in De Robertis, "Cammelli, Antonio, detto il Pistoia."

83 De Robertis, "Cammelli, Antonio, detto il Pistoia."

84 "il mio Signor più suole / stimare un rosignuol per l'armonia / che il barbaresco che portò il Messia." Cammelli, *Rime*, 75.

85 La corte è come el gioco del quadrelo
l'un caccia l'altro da seggio e partito,
non per ragion, ma sol per apitito
chi à dinari assai più che cervelo.
La sera vedrai sensa mantelo
un ragazon come un gufo smarito,

e la matin di seta e d'or vestito
tanto che tu dirai: non è più quelo.
  Quando è ben 'n alto fin dove pò andare
e' vien un for de villa e rompe el gazo
e fal giù de la rota trabucare,
  e ritornar come prima ragazi.
Com'è proverbio santo quell parlare:
ombra de gran signor, capel de pazo.

Aquilano, *Le Rime*, 1:128.

It is unclear what kind of game *quadrelo* was. In the anthology *Poesia italiana del Quattrocento*, the game is hypothesized to be a sort of *quattro cantoni* (four corners), a game where a player in the middle tries to take the spot of any of the other four players who stand at opposite corners. See *Poesia italiana del Quattrocento*, 252.

86 A copy of the game is held in the British Museum.

87 The play was most likely written and presented – intriguingly, in front of the court – in Ferrara in 1499. On this play, its representation at court, and the character of Tindaro, see also chapter 4 of this book.

88 "Pazzo è colui che se invecchia alla corte." Cammelli, *Rime*, 300.

89 "Io posso dir che 'l re m'abbia tradito / a tormi il tempo." Cammelli, *Rime*, 301.

90 Ariosto, *Satira I*, 57, 9 [*Opere minori*, 10].

91
Che cosa è Corte? Cortigiana avara
Che dà corti piaceri e lunghe pene
Teatro in cui si variano le scene
E a far più parti un personaggio impara.
  Reggia, che ha idea di fumo, e tempio, ed ara;
Galea, in cui sia ora e sempre in catene
Scala, per cui salire, e spesso avviene,
che unisca in un soggetto e trono, e bara.
  Ciecato un Belisario in Lei si vede;
Seneca estinto, ed in prigione arresta
Giuseppe il casto trarne a stento il piede
  Per lei sospese Aman forca funesta;
Vi entrò sol Pietro e vi perdé la fede
Parlò Giovanni, e vi lasciò la testa.

92 Vat. lat. 9199, 113*v*. The manuscript is part of a collection assembled by the late seventeenth- and early eighteenth-century scholar Francesco Cancellieri.

93 I thank Dario Brancato for his feedback on the handwriting style of the manuscript.

94 Kernan, *The Cankered Muse*, 7.

95 Vecchi Galli, "Corte medievale," 156.

96
Non così spesso si rimuta il Cielo
Nel più bel tempo di sua prima etade

O quando è mezzo tra la state e 'l gielo;
Come ora in alto surge, or basso cade
El Cortigiano, or di servi è fornito,
Et or lo trovi solo per le strade.
Oggi 'l vedrai di porpora vestito,
Doman di sacco, oggi pulito e grasso.
Doman rognoso, magro, e scolorito.
Oggi 'l vedrai col suo Signore a spasso
A par a par, doman chiuso in prigione,
E con vergogna della vita casso.

Simeoni, *Della corte*, in *Satire alla berniesca*, 42.

97 Fortuna, chi te pinse i crini in fronte,
nuda e fugace, già non prese errore:
chi non te liga mentre ti è in favore,
suo danno poi, se gli fai oltragio ed onte.
Lustrato hai tal che bruta l'acqua al fonte,
che 'l sol apresso a lui perde il splendore;
un grande privi poi tanto di onore,
ch'al eremo n'ha a star cum le man gionte.
Penso talor dove mantien' tuo segio:
s'io extimo in ciel, de lì alcun mal non vene;
se nel abisso, ognor daresti morte.
Vedendo poi che quando hai fatto il pegio,
a un miser, che pòi far, poi gli fai bene,
tua residenza altroe non è che in corte.

Correggio, *Opere*, 449.

98 On this point, see Skinner, *The Foundations of Modern Political Thought*, 94–9. On Fortuna, see also Pitkin, *Fortune Is a Woman*.

99 Skinner, *The Foundations of Modern Political Thought*, 98.

100 Santoro, *Fortuna, ragione e prudenza nella civiltà letteraria del Cinqucento*, 7–21; Skinner, *The Foundations of Modern Political Thought*, 186–9.

101 Skinner, *The Foundations of Modern Political Thought*, 186.

102 On the sixteenth-century notion of fortune, see Pitkin, *Fortune Is a Woman*.

103 "sarà poco grato ad un signore e [...] non gli arà sangue, e questo senza causa alcuna che si possa comprendere." Castiglione, *The Book of the Courtier*, II, xxxii, 93 [*Il Libro del Cortegiano*, 167]. I thank Victoria Kirkham for having brought this text to my attention.

104 "La corte avuto ha in presto / sedici anni da me d'affano e stento /et io da lei ducati quattrocento." Berni, *Rime*, 188.

105 Muovesi il Cortigian canuto e bianco
Da quel Tinello, ov'ha sua età fornita
E da quella famiglia sbigottita
Che vede il passo e'l tempo venir manco
E per poter un tratto alzare il fianco,
Senza stentare e assassinar la vita,

Quanto si può di ritornar s'aita
A' la sua casa, ancor che frusto e stanco
Quivi giunto gli manca ogni disio
Di più servire a' suoi giorni colui,
Che fallito anco un dì vedere spera:
Così, lasso ad ogn'hor vo' imparand'io,
A' le mie spese, e co' l'esempio altrui,
Che la Corte è una Morte aperta e vera.

Benucci, in Florence, BNCF, Ms. Magl. VII.779, fol. 108*r*.

106 For a detailed biography of Benucci, see Ballistreri, "Benucci, Lattanzio"; and Garullo, "Notizie sulla vita e sull'opera di Lattanzio Benucci 'giureconsulto sanese.'"

107 See n74, above.

108 Aretino, *Ragionamento delle corti*, in *Operette politiche e satiriche*, 1:78–162, 84; Paterno, *Satira III*, in Andini, *Satire di cinque poeti illustri*, 93*v*.

109 "in Corte / [...] ove la vita / è registrata al libro della Morte." Caporali's *capitoli* on the court were first published in 1582, and with the rest of his *Rime* enjoyed significant editorial success in the seventeenth century. See Romei, introduction to Caporali, *Capitoli*, 2–10; and Romei, "Ironia e irrisione," 30–1.

110 See chapter 2 of this book.

111 Paterno had served at the court of the Count of Lacerra. For biographical data on Paterno, see Boccia, "Paterno, Lodovico."

112 "s'appropria al vino / c'hoggi è qual hier, ma diman poi non tale." Paterno, *Satira III*, in Andini, *Satire di cinque poeti illustri*, 94*r*.

113 Non por fede ne' tuoi cari conservi
pensa, che quegli in te non pongan fede.
Sij doppio: in ciò sangue, ossa, carne et nervi
adopra, et petto, et mano, et lingua, et piede.
S'a me non credi, e più non ti conservi
Che se con mille combattessi a piede,
Ahi, quanto dapoi vecchio, e fuor di corte
Del tuo poco saver ti dorrà forte.
A te son que' nemici, a lor se' tu.
Fermati, et non cercarne, o frate, il quia.
La tavola rotonda, e 'l capo Artù
stansi oltra il campo, che mantiene Helia.

Paterno, *Satira III*, in Andini, *Satire di cinque poeti illustri*, 94*v*.

114 On this theme, see Ugolini, "Self-Portraits of a Truthful Liar."

115 For biographical information on Alamanni, see Weiss, "Alamanni, Luigi."

116 On Alamanni's satires, see Floriani, *Il modello ariostesco*, 95–123; Floriani, "Sulle satire di Luigi Alamanni"; and Tomasi, "Appunti sulla tradizione delle *satire* di Luigi Alamanni." The satires have been recently published in a modern edition, edited by Rossana Perri.

117 Sansovino, *Sette libri di satire*, 50; Andini, "Ai lettori," in *Satire di cinque poeti illustri*, A3*r*.

118 Floriani, *Il modello ariostesco*, 105–10; Perri, introduction to Alamanni, *Satire*, 23.

119 "Io non saprei, Sertin, pore in disparate / la verità, colui lodando ogni hora / che con più danno altrui dal ben si parte." Alamanni, *Satire*, 242.

120 Alamanni, *Satire*, 243.

121

El Libro parla.
Non per piacer a i rei, ne per dir male
Ma difender'el ben, scrivendo il vero,
M'ha partorito un cuor puro et sincero,
Il cui desio non è cosa mortale.
Quis vetat dicere verum?

Simeoni, *Satire alla berniesca*, n.p. On Simeoni's satires in general, see also Floriani, *Il modello ariostesco*, 175–83.

122 For biographical information on Fenaruolo, see Predari, *Raccolta dei poeti satirici italiani*, 70.

123

Io parlo sempre come qui si parla
e dico pane al pane, e vino al vino
[...]
Quando ch'io sudo, voglio dir ch'io sudo
quando ch'io tremo, voglio dir ch'io tremo,
e vo' dir cotto al cotto, e crudo al crudo.

Fenaruolo, *Satira terza*, in Sansovino, *Sette libri di satire*, 188*v*. "Dire pane al pane e vino al vino" and "dire cotto al cotto e crudo al crudo" are popular Italian sayings that mean to call things what they really are.

124 "quei divini / E magnifici titoli, che dare / Si soglion oggidì fin ai facchini." Caporali, *La corte: Parte seconda*, in *Capitoli*, 32–3.

125 "E con lor nacque a un patto il corteggiare
Che si giocò la libertà natia
E corruppe lo stil del favellare."

Caporali, *La corte: Parte seconda*, in *Capitoli*, 33.

126 "sarà tenuto savio il matto, / E matto il savio, perché il Signor vuole / Contro ogni legge di natura e patto."

Simeoni, *Della corte*, in *Satire alla berniesca*, 45.

127 "Scolare, Cortigian, Soldato e Prete." Allegri, "Al Signor Bernardetto Minerbetti," in *Rime e prose*, 88.

128 "E se pur mess'un tratto i pie' ne' ceppi / Della Corte, le dissi, Amica Addio." Allegri, "Al Signor Pandolfo Acciaiuoli," in *Rime e prose*, 76. Biographical information on Allegri is scarce. He was among the founders of the Florentine Accademia della Borra, whose members also included Cesare Caporali. For a biography of Allegri, see Asor Rosa, "Allegri, Alessandro."

129 Lo star in corte, e l'esser ammalato
Mi paion, come dir, frate' carnali
Tanto s'agguaglia l'uno all'altro stato.
[...]
E come quell ne va dal letto al cesso
A vomitar la cuccuma indigesta,
Per vari mezzi, quando gli è permesso,
Sfoga costui, che dentro ha chi la pesta;
Con sospiri, con lagrime, e parole
Segretamente quel, che lo molesta

Allegri, "Al Sig. Pandolfo Acciaiuoli," in *Rime e prose*, 78.

130 uno spedale
Ch'ognun raccoglie a suo post'è governa,
Dove non va, cred'io, chi non ha male
Nell'animo, o nel corpo.

Allegri, "Al Sig. Pandolfo Acciaiuoli," in *Rime e prose*, 94.

131 "la botte / D'oggi, non è qual fu quella d'Urbino." Allegri, "Al Sig. Pandolfo N.," in *Rime e prose*, 168.

132 "e dove troverete mai ch'il bianco / Stropicciandosi al nero non s'imbigi"? Allegri, "Al Sig. Pandolfo N.," in *Rime e prose*, 169.

133 Allegri, dedicatory letter "Al Sig. Bernardetto Minerbetti," in *Rime e prose*, 176.

134 "ricca di giudizi precisamente politici sulla curia romana [...] ma l'angolo visuale è rigorosamente privato, il registro rigorosamente psicologico." Floriani, *Il modello ariostesco*, 118.

135 Floriani, *Il modello ariostesco*, 123n29.

136 Doveva pur esser bello il secol d'oro
Trifon, che corteggiava ognun se stesso,
E si stava ciascun nel suo decoro,
Senz'aver altri cortigiani appresso
Se non due man, due piè, che facean tosto
Quanto da lor volere era commesso.

Caporali, *La corte: Parte seconda*, in *Capitoli*, 31. For Caporali's depiction of courtly servitude as slavery, see his *Viaggio di Parnaso*.

137 Un'altra cosa nella Corte veggio,
Qual perché importa la morte e la vita
Dell'uom, mi par di tutte l'altre peggio.
Questo è, ch'el dì, se la fame t'invita,
O di notte il dormir, questo né quella
Aran da te per tuo bisogno aita,
Se già non metti mano alla scarcella,
Perché fin ch'el Signor non ha mangiato
Non s'empion che di rabbia le budella.

Potresti ancor di sonno esser crepato,
Che se prima il Signor non va a dormire,
Saria vergogna averlo abbandonato:
Abbia poi male, e fosse da morire,
Dirà il Signor, pien d'ira e di disdegno,
Che così la fatica vuoi fuggire.

Simeoni, *Della corte*, in *Satire alla berniesca*, 45–6.

138 "È più dolce, cred'io, stare in segrete / Dove almen un s'abbioscia in sul pancone, / E dorme quanto il Sol gli fa la rete." Allegri, "Al Sig. Pandolfo N.," in *Rime e prose*, 173.

139 "Come, e quando mi par seggo, e mi rizzo, / Mettomi'n capo, e cavo la berretta, / Ed a mia posta m'addolcisco, e stizzo." Allegri, "Al Sig. Pandolfo Acciaiuoli," in *Rime e prose*, 76.

140 Voi mi direte: "Forse, tu ti scopri
un certo huomaccio di poca fatica:
meglio farai, se i tuoi difetti cuopri."
Per questo temo, e convien pur ch'io 'l dica
ch'io non sia troppo bon da star in corte
che la sincerità m'è troppo amica

Caccia, "Satira II," in *Satire, e capitoli piacevoli (1549)*, 84.

141 Direte forse: "Tu mi vai cercando
cotante cose, per non accordarti,
quand'io le vado molto ben pensando.
Ma sei in grande error, se pensi darti
tutti i tuoi agi stando ne le corti
e di ciò che vorreste accomodarti"
[...]
E io rispondo che più non m'attempo
a far patti con voi, e vi ringrazio,
ch'avertito m'avete sì per tempo.
Io son già de la corte più che sazio
né vo venir a far, sotto speranza
d'aver del ben, di me medesmo stratio.
Quel poco, o assai di vita, che m'avanza
vo' trapassar in libertate e 'n pace
ne la natia di me povera stanza;
et se debbo stentar, stentar mi piace
in casa mia, almen senz'esser schiavo
di chi del mal altrui si gode, e tace.

Caccia, "Satira II," in *Satire, e capitoli piacevoli (1549)*, 89–90.

142 Ma perché alquanto meglio me n'informi,
verrò a servitù un mese; e se m'aggrada,
starocci, se non vo' poter disciormi,
e indietro ritornar per la mia strada.

Caccia, "Satira II," in *Satire, e capitoli piacevoli (1549)*, 90.

143 Ser Cecco non può star senza la corte
e la corte non può senza ser Cecco;
e ser Cecco ha bisogno della corte
e la corte ha bisogno de ser Cecco.
Chi vol saper che cosa sia ser Cecco
pensi e contempli che cosa è la corte:
questo ser Cecco somiglia la corte
e questa corte somiglia ser Cecco.
E tanto tempo viverà la corte
quanto sarà la vita di ser Cecco,
perché è tutt'uno ser Cecco e la corte.

Berni, *Rime*, 83.

144 Francesco Benci of Assisi, papal secretary and uncle to Trifon Benci, the addressee of Caporali's *La corte*.

145 For a summary of critiques of Burckhardt's idea of the discovery of the individual, see Martin, "The Myth of Renaissance Individualism."

146 Martin, "The Myth of Renaissance Individualism," 210.

147 Martin, "Inventing Sincerity, Refashioning Prudence," 1322, 1326.

148 Martin, "Inventing Sincerity, Refashioning Prudence," 1322–3.

149 Martin, "The Myth of Renaissance Individualism," 210.

150 Martin, "The Myth of Renaissance Individualism," 217.

151 Martin, "The Myth of Renaissance Individualism," 217.

152 On this point, see Martin, "Inventing Sincerity, Refashioning Prudence," 1333–5.

153 For in-depth analysis of these issues, see Martin, "Inventing Sincerity, Refashioning Prudence."

154 Gigliucci, "'Qualis coena tamen!,'" 595; Smith, *The Anti-Courtier Trend*, 25.

155 On this point, see Gigliucci, "'Qualis coena tamen!'"

156 Domenichi, *Dialogo della corte*, in *Dialoghi*, 273–4.

157 "sbanditi da' veri uffici della vita." Domenichi, *Dialogo della corte*, in *Dialoghi*, 274.

158 "così poco sono io Signore, et padrone di me stesso, ch'io pendo tutto dal commandamento, et dalla voglia d'altri." Domenichi, *Dialogo della corte*, in *Dialoghi*, 275.

159 "non haver nessun luogo, ne tempo per se proprio? ogni cosa a voglia d'altrui? vivere alle tavole altrui? a ogni incontro del principe impallidire? arrossire? fuggire? alcune volta temere et stupire? simulare et dissimulare molte cose? tante volte piegar le ginocchia, et fare inchini? star quasi sempre a capo scoperto? ogni cosa fare da schiavo, et con umiltà? non esser mai Signor di se stesso?" Domenichi, *Dialogo della corte*, in *Dialoghi*, 275–6.

160 "non dire mai cose che tu voglia, ma solo che ti convenga? [...] disprezzar te stesso? havere ogni cosa in potere altrui? [...] et spesse volte contra la tua natura conformarti con gli altri?" Domenichi, *Dialogo della corte*, in *Dialoghi*, 276.

161 "Ma però ogniuno, che mette il collo sotto questo giogo, è di necessità, che prenda a imitare Alcibiade. Percioche si come egli visse d'altro modo in Athene, e in Lacedemone, e in Thracia, e in Persia, usando sempre diversi costumi secondo la qualità de' luoghi, cosi bisogna che un cortigiano, in ogni modo c'accomodi à costumi di coloro con cui vive, et ch'egli sia di natura mutabile a ogni patte; in tutte le cose doppio et astuto; e in somma, molto più vario, che non si favoleggia di Proteo." Domenichi, *Dialogo della corte*, in *Dialoghi*, 288.
162 On the protean quality of the courtier in Castiglione, see Rebhorn, *Courtly Performances*, 14, 29.
163 *Giamatti, "Proteus Unbound."*
164 *Giamatti, "Proteus Unbound,"* 442.
165 On this point, see Martin, "Inventing Sincerity, Refashioning Prudence," 1333, 1340.
166 Martin, "Inventing Sincerity, Refashioning Prudence," 1339, 1341.
167 Stella Galbiati, *Un poeta satirico del Cinquecento*, 14.
168 Stella Galbiati, *Un poeta satirico del Cinquecento*, 66.
169 Quondam, "La forma del vivere," 68.
170 "il luogo di una virtù davvero eccezionale, di una fortuna particolare, di una pratica eroica." Quondam, "La forma del vivere," 67.
171 Quondam, "La forma del vivere," 67.
172 Stella Galbiati, *Un poeta satirico del Cinquecento*, 14.
173 On Ariosto's experience in Garfagnana, see McCabe, *"Ungainefull Arte,"* 130–1.
174 On the literature dedicated to the villa, see chapter 4 of this book, "The villa versus the court."
175 Larivaille, *Pietro Aretino*, 131.
176 For a detailed biography of Aretino, see Larivaille, *Pietro Aretino*.
177 Larivaille, *Pietro Aretino*, 43–9.
178 On the history of Pasquino, and on Aretino's pasquinades, see Procaccioli, "Tu es Pasquillus in aeterno," 67–9; Romei, "Aretino e Pasquino"; Faini, introduction to Aretino, *Operette politiche e satiriche*, 2:9–24; Chiara Lastraioli, "'Pietro Aretino, bestial prophet' and Pasquino," in Faini and Ugolini, *Companion to Pietro Aretino*.
179 D'Onghia, "La 'Farza' è davvero di Pietro Aretino?"
180 Giovanni Aquilecchia, introduction to Aretino, *Cortigiana, Opera nova, Pronostico, Il testamento dell'elefante, Farza*, 375.
181 "gli è mal nemico ad chi lo acquiste." Aretino, *Farza*, in *Operette politiche e satiriche*, 2:48.
182 "Dio ne guarde ciascun da la sua lingua." Aretino, *Farza*, in *Operette politiche e satiriche*, 2:48.
183 Larivaille, *Pietro Aretino fra Rinascimento e Manierismo*, 69–70.
184 Larivaille, *Pietro Aretino*, 131.

185 Larivaille, *Pietro Aretino*, 84. For specific details of Aretino's life, see also Innamorati, "Aretino, Pietro."

186 At the time Aretino was still wanted dead in Rome, and Federico Gonzaga's reaction to the threats on Aretino's life is unclear. While supporting Aretino, he also sent letters to Rome declaring himself willing to have him assassinated. It is uncertain, however, whether he was actually willing to have Aretino killed or whether he was making false promises in an attempt to placate Aretino's enemies. For detailed discussion of this point, see Innamorati, "Pietro Aretino."

187 On Aretino and the Sack of Rome, see Catelli, "Pietro Aretino e il Sacco di Roma"; Catelli, "Una miriade di frammenti"; and Catelli, *Scherzar coi santi*; and Goethals, "Vanquished Bodies, Weaponized Words." On Venice as the new Rome, see also the poem "In laude di Venetia," in Aretino, *Scritti di Pietro Aretino nel Codice marciano It. XI 66 (6730)*, 40–4.

188 Waddington, *Aretino's Satyr*, xix.

189 Waddington, *Aretino's Satyr*, 34.

190 Waddington, *Aretino's Satyr*, xxi.

191 On the *Lamento de uno cortigiano*, see also chapter 2 of this book, "The courtier's anxious masculinity." The poem remained unknown until very recently, when it was rediscovered by Marco Faini, who has published it in a modern edition with a critical introduction in Aretino, *Operette politiche e satiriche*, vol. 2. See also Faini, "Un'opera dimenticata di Pietro Aretino." The text has numerous thematic and stylistic similarities to works composed by Aretino during his Roman years, and by members of his circle of friends and artistic partners, like the painter, writer, and actor Maestro Andrea Veneziano. More precisely, the *Lamento de uno cortigiano* may be considered part of a triptych including the *Lamento di una cortigiana ferrarese* (attributed to either Andrea or Aretino) and Andrea's *Purgatorio delle cortigiane di Roma*. Like the *Lamento di una cortigiana* and the *Purgatorio delle cortigiane*, the *Lamento de uno cortigiano* was most likely performed during Carnival festivities. On the *Lamento di una cortigiana ferrarese*, see Aquilecchia, "Per l'attribuzione e il testo del 'Lamento di una Cortigiana Ferrarese'"; and Shemek, "'Mi mostrano a dito tutti quanti.'" On the *Purgatorio delle cortigiane*, see Ugolini, "The Satirist's Purgatory."

192 Faini, "Un'opera dimenticata di Pietro Aretino."

193 On Aretino's relationship to courts and courtliness, and on this and other texts on the court by Aretino, see also Ugolini, "Pietro Aretino and the Court," in Faini and Ugolini, *Companion to Pietro Aretino*.

194 "O Sfacciate speranze della Corte
Favor briaco di volubil fume,
O vil, bugiarda et disonesta sorte."

Aretino, *Lamento de uno cortigiano*, vv. 1–3, in *Operette politiche e satiriche*, vol. 2.

195 Faini, "Un'opera dimenticata di Pietro Aretino," 76–7.

196 Mettetevi una Maschera su'l volto
Ch'ad ogni modo il Carnoval è giunto,
Il qual già fece ogniun pel gioco stolto
Mettete le comedie, e i pasti in punto:
Mandate per Trascin, che vi intrattenga
Et gettate hor cento scudi in un punto.
[...]
Hor voglio ir con questa sporta nuova
Poi cho detto la pistola, e'l vangelo
A comperar il Cavol, se si trova.

Aretino, *Lamento de uno cortigiano*, vv. 265–85, in *Operette politiche e satiriche*, vol. 2. "Trascin" refers to the poet Nicolò Campani, known as Strascino, who was a member of Leo X's court and who gained popularity for his comic verses.

197 On this point, see Ferroni, *Le voci dell'istrione*, 35–70; and Romano, "Appunti sui personaggi della *Cortigiana* (1525) dell'Aretino."

198 Aretino, *Cortigiana* (1525), in *Edizione nazionale delle opere di Pietro Aretino: Teatro*, 1:70. On this passage, see Ferroni, *Le voci dell'istrione*, 37. Christopher Cairns also proposes a reading of the *Cortigiana* as a parody of the *Book of the Courtier* for the first plot, and of Bembo's *Asolani* for the second plot. See Cairns, *Pietro Aretino and the Republic of Venice*, 36. On the *Cortigiana*, see also Waddington, "Introduction: *Cortigiana* (*La cortigiana*, 1525)," in *Pietro Aretino: Subverting the System*, 7–43.

199 Aretino, *Cortigiana* (1525), in *Edizione nazionale delle opere di Pietro Aretino: Teatro*, 1:120.

200 "quei cortigiani subalterni a cui Aretino si sente vicino." Ferroni, *Le voci dell'istrione*, 64.

201 "la Fortuna sete voi signori, voi signori sete la Fortuna, che da le stalle e da le staphe sulevate il vitio e la ignorantia, e alle stalle e alle staphe ponete la virtù." Aretino, *Cortigiana* (1525), in *Edizione nazionale delle opere di Pietro Aretino: Teatro*, 1:83.

202 Ferroni, *Le voci dell'istrione*, 66–7.

203 See, for example, the lines where Valerio tells the discontented Flaminio that the only available option for a courtier is to "take the vows of good fortune and to snatch up the best that man can get [...] However, one should not despair, because the profit of the courtly trade comes at an unexpected point." ("Votarsi ala buona fortuna e pigliare el meglio che l'omo può [...]. Né bisogna però disperarse, perché 'l guadagno dela mercantia cortigiana sta in un punto non aspettato.") Aretino, *Cortigiana* (1525), in *Edizione nazionale delle opere di Pietro Aretino: Teatro*, 1:114. I thank Bryan Brazeau for helping with the translation.

204 "[de]la natura di voi signori, che così facil credenza date agli asentatori e maligni, e senza odire il biasimato absente, sbandite ogni fedele giusto

omo dela gratia vostra," Aretino, *Cortigiana* (1525), in *Edizione nazionale delle opere di Pietro Aretino: Teatro,* 1:147.

205 "Ser Chemente" in Italian. I have attempted to render the pun in the original Italian on the second Medici pope's name: "Clemente" (Clement) becomes "Chemente," that is to say, "Che-mente," or "He-who-lies."

206

Sett'anni traditor ho via gettati,
con Leon quattro e tre con ser Chemente
e son fatto nemico de la gente
più per li lor che per mia peccati
e non ho pur d'intrata duo ducati
e son da men che non è Gian Manente,
onde nel culo, se ponete mente,
ho tutte le speranze de' papati.

Aretino, *Operette politiche e satiriche,* 2:89.

207 Shemek, "Aretino's *Marescalco.*"

208 See Catelli, "Pietro Aretino e il Sacco di Roma," 44; and Goethals, "Vanquished Bodies, Weaponized Words," 58.

209 The character's name is spelled "Flaminio'" in the first version of the *Cortigiana,* and "Flamminio" in the 1534 version.

210 "per eretica, per falsaria, per traditrice, per isfacciata, e per disonesta." Aretino, *Cortigiana* (1534), in *Edizione nazionale delle opere di Pietro Aretino: Teatro,* 1:289.

211 "virtù e costumi." Aretino, *Cortigiana* (1534), in *Edizione nazionale delle opere di Pietro Aretino: Teatro,* 1:259.

212 "nello Inferno è tormentata l'anima, e nella corte l'anima e 'l corpo." Aretino, *Cortigiana* (1534), in *Edizione nazionale delle opere di Pietro Aretino: Teatro,* 1:262.

213 "Io me ne andrò forse a Vinegia, ove sono già stato; et arrichirò la povertà mia con la sua libertade; che almeno ivi non è in arbitrio di niun favorito né di niuna favorita di assassinare i poverini; perché solamente in Vinegia la Giustitia tien pari le bilancie; ivi solo la paura della disgratia altrui non ti sforza ad adorare uno che ieri era un pidocchioso. E chi dubita del suo merito guardi in che maniera Iddio la essalta; e certamente ella è la Città Santa, et il Paradiso terrestre." Aretino, *Cortigiana* (1534), in *Edizione nazionale delle opere di Pietro Aretino: Teatro,* 1:284–5.

214 "addirittura cortigianesca." Larivaille, *Pietro Aretino,* 189.

215 "essendo avezzo tanti e tanti anni a servire, non posso star senza, mi risolvo andare nella corte di sua maestà." Aretino, *Cortigiana* (1534), in *Edizione nazionale delle opere di Pietro Aretino: Teatro,* 1:289.

216 Aretino, *Cortigiana* (1534), in *Edizione nazionale delle opere di Pietro Aretino: Teatro,* 1:283–90.

217 For Valerio's complaints, see Aretino, *Cortigiana* (1534), in *Edizione nazionale delle opere di Pietro Aretino: Teatro,* 1:304 and 317–18; for his

attachment to the court, his almost paradoxical defence of the court, and his acceptance of the nature of the *Signori*, see his exchange with Flamminio on pp. 288–9.

218 "Ma io, che ne la libertà di cotanto stato ho fornito d'imparare a essere libero, refuto la Corte in eterno, e qui faccio perpetuo tabernacolo a gli anni che mi avanzano, perché qui non ha luogo il tradimento, qui il favore non può far torto al diritto, qui non regna la crudeltà de le meretrici, qui non comanda l'insolenza de gli effeminati, qui non si ruba, qui non si sforza, e qui non si amazza." Aretino, "Al Serenissimo Andrea Gritti," in *Lettere,* 1:50.

219 On Aretino's chivalric poems, see Romei, introduction to Aretino, *Poemi cavallereschi,* in *Edizione nazionale delle opere di Pietro Aretino.*

220 Larivaille, *Pietro Aretino,* 138.

221 "praticare l'encomio stipendiato al riparo della minaccia sottintesa di Pasquino, tenuto in serbo come strumento di pressione sui mecenati ricalcitranti." Larivaille, *Pietro Aretino,* 142.

222 Waddington, "Pietro Aretino: The New Man of Letters," in *Pietro Aretino: Subverting the System,* 267.

223 On Marcolini, see Quondam, "Nel giardino del Marcolini."

224 On Aretino's debts to previous anti-court satires, see Crimi, introduction to Aretino, *Operette politiche e satiriche,* 1:9–49.

225 On the *Ragionamento delle corti,* see Quondam, "La scena della menzogna"; and Pevere, "Vita è il non andare in corte." The text has been recently edited by Giuseppe Crimi; see Aretino, *Operette politiche e satiriche,* vol. 1. All further references are to this edition.

226 See letters no. 254, "A M. Giovanni Agnello," no. 258, "Al Suo M. Ambrogio Eusebio," and no. 327, "A M. Francesco Coccio," in Aretino, *Lettere,* 1:352–4, 357–60, 452–3.

227 "tutte l'ore son l'ore de le mie volontà." "A M. Giovanni Agnello," in Aretino, *Lettere,* 1:353.

228 The Venetian *poligrafo* Lodovico Dolce (1508?–68) was a longtime collaborator of Aretino's. Information on Francesco Coccio is scarce, but he appears to have been originally from Umbria (Aretino, *Lettere,* 1:672) and to have worked with Aretino in Venice. Pietro Piccardo, the dedicatee of two of Aretino's letters, was a prelate and courtier whom Aretino seems to have particularly appreciated for his sense of humour (Aretino, *Lettere,* 1:692). Giovanni Giustiniano (or Giustiniani, or Giustinian) was originally from Candia, and was a translator of classical texts.

229 "La Corte, messeri miei, è spedale de le speranze, sepoltura de le vite, baila degli odii, razza de l'invidie, mantice de l'ambizioni, mercato de le menzogne, serraglio de i sospetti, carcere de le concordie, scola de le fraudi, patria de l'adulazione, paradiso de i vizi, inferno de le virtù,

purgatorio de le bontà, e limbo de le allegrezze." Aretino, *Ragionamento delle corti*, in *Operette politiche e satiriche*, 1:84.

230 Aretino, *Ragionamento delle corti*, in *Operette politiche e satiriche*, 1:88.

231 My reading of the *Ragionamento delle corti* differs on this point from that of Amedeo Quondam, who seems to consider Coccio already converted at the end of the first day of the dialogue, thanks to Piccardo's speech. See Quondam, "La scena della menzogna," 14.

232 Aretino, *Ragionamento delle corti*, in *Operette politiche e satiriche*, 1:91.

233 Aretino, *Ragionamento delle corti*, in *Operette politiche e satiriche*, 1:92–3.

234 "Now, believe me when I say that nobody [...] can teach you the ways of the court better than me because – even though I am close to sixty, I have a dozen years that come and go – like the years of a whore – and I use them depending on the women I love and the men I serve." ("Ora credetemi che niuno [...] può informarvi degli andamenti de la Corte meglio di me, perché io, se bene mi faccio di sessanta anni, ne ho una dozzina che va e viene, come quegli de le puttane e l'adopro secondo il proposito de le donne ch'io amo e de gli uomini che servo.") Aretino, *Ragionamento delle corti*, in *Operette politiche e satiriche*, 1:83–4.

235 "Chi vi tirasse un poco suso, confessareste in che modo avete trafugato de le unghie a la Corte l'entrata, di che godendone ne la incacate." Aretino, *Ragionamento delle corti*, in *Operette politiche e satiriche*, 1:93.

236 "io mi rimoverò da la oppenione de lo andare in Corte totalmente, o che metterò in opera la deliberazione in un tratto." Aretino, *Ragionamento delle corti*, in *Operette politiche e satiriche*, 1:121.

237 "adunque la Corte fa per me, se la contentezza si ritrae da l'operare." Aretino, *Ragionamento delle corti*, in *Operette politiche e satiriche*, 1:122.

238 Aretino, *Ragionamento delle corti*, in *Operette politiche e satiriche*, 1:143.

239 For a broader discussion of this point, see Quondam, "La scena della menzogna," 14.

240 On this point, see also Quondam, "La scena della menzogna," 13.

241 "Tutto si soffrirebbe a la fine se chi legge le cose che si fanno da chi pur sa giudicasse con le orecchie e non col naso. Che penitenzia è quella dei buoni ingegni lacerati dai conoscitori di due sillabe e dai fattori di due desinenze!" Aretino, *Ragionamento delle corti*, in *Operette politiche e satiriche*, 1:148.

242 As Dolce points out, "Dear sirs, I take great pleasure in my present state; having sought honor and greatness in courting the sciences, I am certain to obtain from their promises other seats, other Glory, other fame than those extracted from the Courts." ("Io, signori miei, provo un gran piacere ne lo stato che io sono, per avere posto gli onori e le grandezze nel corteggiare le scienze, sendo certo di ottenere da le loro promesse altri seggi, altre lodi, altra Gloria e altra fama che non si ritrae da le Corti.") Aretino, *Ragionamento delle corti*, in *Operette politiche e satiriche*, 1:148.

243 Aretino, *Ragionamento delle corti*, in *Operette politiche e satiriche*, 1:153–4.
244 As Quondam has pointed out, Giustiniano's speech also discloses a program: "The project-desire to manage the outside and the inside of the Court at the same time, to deal with the inside from the outside, from a position of autonomy and strength, and to be able thus to build his own 'freedom.'" ("Il progetto-desiderio di gestire contemporaneamente il fuori e il dentro della Corte, di trattare con il dentro da fuori, da una posizione di autonomia e forza, di poter così costruire la propria 'libertà.") Quondam, "La scena della menzogna," 16–17.
245 On the parallel between the conclusion of the *Ragionamento delle corti* and that of the *Book of the Courtier*, see Pevere, "Vita è il non andare in corte," 260. Pevere reads the conclusion of the dialogue as an escape into a dimension of ideal perfection that ultimately marks the defeat of the search for intellectual autonomy described in the dialogue.
246 See Quondam, "Nel giardino del Marcolini," where the setting of the dialogue is also described as a *locus amoenus*.
247 See chapter 2 of this book, "*Cortigiano, donna di corte, cortigiana.*"
248 On the *Orlandino* and the rest of Aretino's incomplete chivalric poems, see Aretino, *Poemi cavallereschi*.
249 "Flagello dei principi." The definition belongs to Ludovico Ariosto; see *Orlando Furioso*, XLVI, xiv, 558, [1591].
250 As pointed out by Crimi, introduction to Aretino, *Operette politiche e satiriche*, 1:16–22.
251 On the meaning of Aretino's self-presentation as a satyr, see Waddington, *Aretino's Satyr*, 34.
252 This is also pointed out by Larivaille, *Pietro Aretino*, 243.
253 Larivaille, *Pietro Aretino*, 355–6.
254 Venier, *Satira contro la corte*.
255 Caporali, *La corte*, in *Capitoli*, 13, v. 21
256 Betussi, *Il Raverta*, 77. On Betussi's reworking of the pun *Corte/Morte*, see Crimi, introduction to Aretino, *Operette politiche e satiriche*, 1:27.
257 The quote is from a letter to Francesco Alunno, dated 27 November 1537. Aretino, *Lettere*, no. 258, 1:355–7.
258 Romei, "Ironia e irrisione."
259 Romei, "Ricezione della poesia bernesca nel cinquecento."
260 On this topic, see Corsaro, "La poesia senza pubblico: Teoria, scrittura e diffusione della satira nel primo Seicento," in *La regola e la licenza*, 163–88; and Riga, "La satira italiana del Seicento."
261 Caporali can be considered the founder of the genre of the *avvisi di Parnaso* that would enjoy popularity in the following century, thanks to the works of writers such as Traiano Boccalini and Girolamo Brusoni, both of whom would also echo the anti-court elements present in Caporali's

Parnassian texts. On this topic, see Ciri, "Verso il Seicento"; and Romei, "Ironia e irrisione."

262 Caporali, *Il viaggio di Parnaso.*

263 Caporali, *Avvisi di Parnaso.*

264 On Bernesque poetry, and on its influence on Caporali, see Romei, "Ricezione della poesia bernesca nel Cinquecento"; Romei, "Ironia e irrisione"; and Ciri, "Verso il Seicento."

4. The Shepherd

1 On this play, see also chapter 3 of this book, "Italian anti-court verse satire: Early examples and leitmotifs."

2 "Valete, amici, e tu, corte, rimanti; / io fuggo la mia morte e la tua insidia." Cammelli, *Rime*, 320.

3 Spesso in poveri alberghi e in picciol tetti,
Ne le calamitadi e nei disagi,
Meglio s'aggiungon d'amicizia i petti,
Che fra ricchezze invidiose ed agi
De le piene d'insidie e di sospetti
Corti regali e splendidi palagi,
Ove la caritade è in tutto estinta,
Né si vede amicizia, se non finta.

Ariosto, *Orlando Furioso*, XLIV, i, 532, [1517].

In a lecture at the Accademia dell'Arcadia, Albert Russell Ascoli underlined how the position of this proem in the 1516 edition increased the text's critique of court culture. In the first edition of the poem, the passage above followed a celebration of friends and patrons from the courtly world, thus undermining such praise. Ascoli, "Che cosa c'è di nuovo nel *Furioso* del '16?" I thank Albert Russell Ascoli for sharing the text of the lecture with me and for giving me permission to cite it here.

4 For this definition, I am indebted to Susanne Wofford, who introduced the distinction between unhappy and happy shepherds and mentioned the latter's relationship to the court in a paper titled "The Nymph in the Woods Says No."

5 On this issue, see Clubb, "The Pastoral Play"; and Zatti, "Natura e potere nell'*Aminta.*"

6 For the definition of the pastoral as a mode rather than a genre, see Sampson, *Pastoral Drama*, 4; and, more extensively, Alpers, *What Is Pastoral?*, in particular chapter 2, "Mode and Genre."

7 For a definition of the pastoral and its scope, see Poggioli, *The Oaten Flute*; Empson, *Some Versions of Pastoral*; Loughrey, *The Pastoral Mode*; Ettin, *Literature and the Pastoral*; and Sampson, *Pastoral Drama*, esp. pp. 4–5.

8 On the pastoral and the court, see Sampson, *Pastoral Drama*, specifically the chapters dedicated to Torquato Tasso's *Aminta* and Battista Guarini's *Pastor Fido*; see also Denarosi, *L'accademia degli Innominati di Parma*, 345–90.
9 Sampson, *Pastoral Drama*, 28–9.
10 See Horace's satire II.vi, which features the tale of the city mouse and the country mouse, and Juvenal's third satire.
11 Doni, *Le ville*. See, for example, p. 92.
12 Doni, *Le ville*, 46.
13 "questo è quel podere che fa per i dotti, di questa manera se lo eleggono i letterati, et vuole essere una mezza giornata, et non più, lontano dalla Città." Doni, *Le ville*, 46.
14 Doni, *Le ville*, 46.
15 As pointed out by Roberto Bigazzi in "Un fragile paradiso," 16.
16 Ackerman, *The Villa*, 10. On villa literature, see also *La letteratura di villa e di villeggiatura*; and Fragnito, *In museo e in villa*.
17 Beck, introduction to Taegio, *La villa*, 1, 33; Ackerman, *The Villa*, 63–4.
18 On this point, see also Corsaro, "*Laus villae*," 170–2.
19 Ackerman, *The Villa*, 108.
20 Floriani, *Il modello ariostesco*, 37.
21 "dece anni stenti, e puoi se un'ora godi / d'un minimo favore, el mal ti scordi / e de la corte e del signor ti lodi." Correggio, *Opere*, 362.
22 Correggio, *Opere*, 362.
23 Correggio, *Opere*, 251.
24 "talor si trova sotto una capanna / magior felicità che in le gran corte / dove, per grado aver, tanto s'affanna." Correggio, *Opere*, 383.
25 Correggio, *Opere*, 382.
26 "E quanto più un di questa vita è experto,
Cognosce manifesto che più gode
Un libero voler dentro el deserto
Che in le cità, dove l'un l'altro rode."
Correggio, *Opere*, 384.
27 "La libertà, che ogni animo, ogni voglia / humana tempra e regge, in tutto è persa / che dove 'l iusto è mal, lei non ha spoglia" (Freedom, that governs and moderates every spirit / and every human will, is completely lost / because where justice itself is evil freedom cannot win). Sasso, *capitolo* 33, in *Opera del praeclarissimo poeta miser Pamphilo Sasso modenese*, hviii*v*. On Sasso's *capitolo* 33, see Floriani, *Il modello ariostesco*, 43–5 and 69–71, where Ariosto's debts to Sasso are also explored.
28 Berni, *Rime*, 188.
29 Berni, *Rime*, 188.

30 "sedici anni d'affanni e stento." For an analysis of this passage, see also chapter 3 of this book, "Courtly payoffs."

31 The bibliography on Antonio de Guevara is vast, and his works have been translated into numerous European languages since the sixteenth century. For a general overview of Guevara, see Jones, *Antonio de Guevara*; Chiong Rivero, *The Rise of Pseudo-Historical Fictions*; and Vosters, *Antonio de Guevara y Europa*. For Guevara's work on the court versus the villa and its influence on Italian literature, see Aguirre, "Antonio de Guevara's Corte-Aldea"; and especially Quondam, "Addio alla corte."

32 On the Italian translation of the *Menosprecio* and its publication history, see Quondam, "Addio alla corte," 22n2.

33 Smith, *The Anti-Courtier Trend*, 34.

34 This has already been noted by Quondam, in "Addio alla corte," 23–4. My perspective on praise of the villa differs slightly from Quondam's. While Quondam focuses on the contrast between praise of the villa and the persistence of the myth of the court, my reading focuses on an interpretation of pastoral spaces at large as a search for an alternative to the encompassing reality of the court.

35 "si pensa / solo al ben far con mente pura e queta." Bolognetti, *Satira III* ("Al Signor Pandolfo Rucellai"), in *Satire*.

36 Bolognetti, *Satira III*, in *Satire*. Bolognetti also praises live in the villa in his *Satira XIII* ("A Monsignor dalla Casa").

37 On this point, see Quondam, "Addio alla corte," 39. The villa as the locus of Christian renewal becomes particularly relevant in agricultural tracts originating in the area of Brescia; see Selmi, "Alberto Lollio e Agostino Gallo."

38 See in particular sonnet 16, "Al Dottor M. Iuan Paez: In lode de la vita de la villa," and sonnet 56, "A M. Giuliano Ardinghello: Sopra l'ambition de la corte di Roma," in Piccolomini, *I cento sonetti*. On the Horatian influences in Piccolomini's sonnets, see Refini, "Le 'gioconde favole' e il 'numeroso concento'."

39
> Beato quel che 'n solitarie rive
> lunge dal rozzo vulgo, al nudo cielo,
> fuor dall'ampie città contento vive
> [...]
> nulla sperando mai, temendo poco
> et la Fortuna e i ben che 'n guardia tiene,
> come fallaci e vil, si prende in gioco;
> e le soglie regai d'intorno piene
> di simulato amor, d'invidia vera,
> paventa quasi Harpye, quasi Sirene.

Alamanni, *Satire*, 225–6.

40 Così, quasi cangiar volesse sorte,
canto 'l tyranno che Sicilia oppresse;
ma l'altro giorno poi condusse a morte
i due miglior che Syracusa avesse.

Alamanni, *Satire*, 236.

41 On this episode and on Alamanni's exile in France, see Weiss, "Alamanni, Luigi"; and Alamanni, *Satire*, 222.

42 Alamanni, *Satire*, 222.

43 Romei, "La morale del savio: Introduzione alle *Satire* di Iacopo Soldani," in Soldani, *Satire*, xxi.

44 Gallo, *Le dieci giornate della vera agricoltura, e piaceri della villa*. Gallo's text was later expanded and republished as *Le tredici giornate della vera agricoltura* (1566), and finally as *Le vinti giornate della vera agricoltura* (1589).

45 For a comparison of these texts, see Ackerman, *The Villa*, 110–18; and Beck, introduction to Taegio, *La villa*, 15–16. On Taegio, see also Taegio, Borromeo, and Verri, *L'antico regime in villa*; and Lauterbach, "The Gardens of the Milanese 'Villeggiatura.'"

46 Stella Galbiati, *Un poeta satirico del Cinquecento*, 11–12.

47 Lollio, *Lettera*, 68*v*, 74*r–v*. On this point, see also Selmi, "Alberto Lollio e Agostino Gallo," 298–300. Lollio was also the author of a pastoral play titled *Aretusa*, performed in 1563 at the Este palace of Schifanoia and published in 1564.

48 Ne le tumide Corti, et tetti altieri
de la Città, tra le superbe mura
stassi l'invidia, et la mordace cura,
la cieca ambition, gli aspri pensieri:
tra i folti boschi, e gli horridi sentieri
siede la vita più tranquilla e pura
ne le Ville, e ne i Campi, che non cura
Gemme, Oro, Dignità, Castella, Imperi.

Lollio, *Lettera*, Aii.

49 On the relationship between Caccia and Taegio, see Caccia, *Satire, e capitoli piacevoli*, 351n1; and Stella Galbiati, *Un poeta satirico del Cinquecento*, 23. Caccia also wrote a sonnet in praise of Taegio that is featured in Taegio's *Le risposte di M. Bartolomeo Taegio*.

50 Caccia, *Satire, e capitoli piacevoli*, 145–56.

51 Caccia, *Rime*, no. 173, pp. 206–7.

52 Caccia, *Rime*, no. 176, pp. 211–12.

53 "Io son pastor, uso abitar in boschi." Caccia, *Rime*, 206.

54 Romei, "Poesia satirica e giocosa," 5.

55 An example can be found in Bolognetti's third satire, where life in the villa is praised as the pleasure of "solitary living" ("viver solitario").

56 See lines 58–165.

57 "Non mai fra nui rancore e aspre parole,
ognun guida l'armento del compagno
e l'un pastor dell'altro non si duole;
non molto intento al suo proprio guadagno,
si vede alcun fra noi, ma al commun bene."
Correggio, *Opere*, 343.

58 "l'un cortegian dell'altro non si fida
l'un scaccia ognora l'altro a poco a poco
di quel che un piange, par che un altro rida."
Cammelli, *Filostrato e Panfila*, in *Rime*, 301.

59 See, for example, chapter 11, where two shepherds argue over an athletic competition, only with every argument resolved peacefully at the end, while all the other shepherds laugh, delighted by what they have just seen.

60 These purified representations of court society in a pastoral form clearly abstain from acknowledging that sadness and death come to Arcadia as well.

61 Sampson, *Pastoral Drama*, 28.

62 Sampson, *Pastoral Drama*, 28–9. Beccari's *Il sacrificio*, Lollio's *Aretusa*, and Argenti's *Lo sfortunato* have been printed in a modern edition: see Pevere, *Favole*.

63 Castiglione and Gonzaga, *Tirsi*, in *Rime e Tirsi*. All further references are to this edition. On the *Tirsi*, see also Vela, "Il 'Tirsi' di Baldassar Castiglione e Cesare Gonzaga"; and Bigi, "Semplicità pastorale e grazia cortigiana nel *Tirsi*."

64 Castiglione and Gonzaga, *Tirsi*, in *Rime e Tirsi*, 188.

65 Jones, "Feminine Pastoral as Heroic Martyrdom," in *The Currency of Eros*, 123.

66 Empson, *Some Versions of Pastoral*, quoted in Jones, "Feminine Pastoral as Heroic Martyrdom," in *The Currency of Eros*, 124.

67 Pieri, "La pastorale," 276.

68 adorni, e cinti di più ricchi manti,
e d'albergando in più superbi tetti
credono esser felici, e chiaman tristi
quei, che fanno soggiorno in vile albergo
e che godono di quel, ch'a lor comparte
con parca mano la Natura, e il fato.

Argenti, *Lo sfortunato*, in Pevere, *Favole*, 207.

69 mostrar lo stato pastorale, e rozzo
quanto felice sia, quanto lontano
da quelle voglie ambitiose avare
onde fosco, e inquieto è il viver nostro
e dall'invidia rea, che lima, e rode
il core a quei che con mentite larve
mostran diverso dal pensiero il volto.

Argenti, *Lo sfortunato*, in Pevere, *Favole*, 207.

70 Sampson, *Pastoral Drama*, 43; Gigante, *Torquato Tasso*, 95.

71 Argenti, *Lo sfortunato*, 1, 4, in Pevere, *Favole*, 224–6; also quoted in Sampson, *Pastoral Drama*, 43.

72 For general analysis of *Aminta*, see Sampson, *Pastoral Drama*, 61–97; Gigante, *Torquato Tasso*, 95–123; Bruscagli, "*L'Aminta* e le pastorali ferraresi del '500"; and La Penna, "Note all'*Aminta* del Tasso."

73 On Argenti and *Lo sfortunato*, see Quattrucci, "Argenti, Agostino."

74 Finotti, *Retorica della diffrazione*, 346–7.

75 Sampson, *Pastoral Drama*, 63.

76 For a summary of the changes in the scholarly readings of *Aminta*, see Zatti, "Natura e potere nell'*Aminta*," 11–12.

77 Sampson, *Pastoral Drama*, 74.

78 On the history of the Mopso episode, see Sozzi, *Studi sul Tasso*, 44–9. Sozzi's analysis is quoted and further discussed in Chiodo, "Il 'supercilio' di Mopso non cela Speroni," 274.

79 AMINTA:
Giusta cagione
ho del mio disperar, che il saggio Mopso
mi predisse la mia cruda ventura,
Mopso ch'intende il parlar de gli augelli
e la virtù de l'erbe e de le fonti.
TIRSI:
Di qual Mopso tu dici? di quel Mopso
ch'ha ne la lingua melate parole,
e ne le labra un amichevol ghigno,
e la fraude nel seno, ed il rasoio
tien sotto il manto? Or su, sta di bon core,
che i sciaurati pronostichi infelici
ch'ei vende a' mal accorti con quel grave
suo supercilio non han mai effetto:
e per prova so io ciò che ti dico;
anzi da questo sol ch'ei t'ha predetto
mi giova di sperar felice fine
a l'amor tuo.

Aminta, act 1, scene 2, 44–5. The English text is quoted from Tasso, *Aminta*, ed. and trans. Jernigan and Jones. The Italian text is quoted from Tasso, *Opere*, ed. Sozzi, 2:319–20.

80 TIRSI:
[...] egli
così mi disse: – Andrai ne la gran terra,
ove gli astuti e scaltri cittadini
e i cortigian malvagi molte volte
prendonsi a gabbo, e fanno brutti scherni

di noi rustici incauti; però, figlio,
va su l'avviso, e non t'appressar troppo
ove sian drappi colorati e d'oro,
e penacchi e divise e foggie nove;
ma sopra tutto guarda che mal fato
o giovenil vaghezza non ti meni
al magazino de le ciancie: ah fuggi,
fuggi quell'incantato alloggiamento.
– Che luogo è questo? io chiesi; ed ei soggiunse:
– Quivi habitan le maghe, che incantando
fan traveder e traudir ciascuno.
Ciò che diamante sembra ed oro fino,
è vetro e rame; e quelle arche d'argento,
che stimaresti piene di tesoro,
sporte son piene di vesiche bugge.
Quivi le mura son fatte con arte,
che parlano e rispondono a i parlanti:
né già rispondon la parola mozza,
com'Eco suole ne le nostre selve
ma la replican tutta intiera intiera:
con giunta anco di quel ch'altri non disse.
I trespidi, le tavole e le panche,
le scranne, le lettiere, le cortine,
e gli arnesi di camera e di sala
han tutti lingua e voce: e gridan sempre.
Quivi le ciancie in forma di bambine
vanno trescando, e s'un muto v'entrasse,
un muto ciancerebbe a suo dispetto.
Ma questo è 'l minor mal che ti potesse
incontrar: tu potresti indi restarne
converso in selce, in fera, in acqua, o in foco:
acqua di pianto, e foco di sospiri. –
Così diss'egli: ed io n'andai con questo
fallace antiveder nella cittade;
e, come volse il Ciel benigno, a caso
passai per là dov'è il felice albergo.
Quivi uscian fuor voci canore e dolci
e di cigni e di ninfe e di sirene,
di sirene celesti; e n'uscian suoni
soavi e chiari; e tant'altro diletto,
ch'attonito godendo ed ammirando
mi fermai buona pezza. Era su l'uscio,
quasi per guardia de le cose belle,
uom d'aspetto magnanimo e robusto,
di cui, per quanto intesi, in dubbio stassi
s'egli sia miglior duce o cavaliero;
che, con fronte benigna insieme e grave,

con regal cortesia invitò dentro,
ei grande e 'n pregio, me negletto e basso.
Oh che sentii? che vidi allora? Io vidi
celesti dee, ninfe leggiadre e belle,
novi Lini ed Orfei; ed oltre ancora,
senza vel, senza nube, e quale e quanta
a gl'immortali appar, vergine Aurora
sparger d'argento e d'or ruggiade e raggi;
e fecondando illuminar d'intorno
vidi Febo, e le Muse; e fra le Muse
Elpin seder accolto; ed in quel punto
sentii me far di me stesso maggiore
pien di nova virtù, pieno di nova
deitade, e cantai guerre et herroi,
sdegnando pastoral ruvido carme.
E se ben poi (come altrui piacque) feci
ritorno a queste selve, io pur ritenni
parte di quello spirto: né già suona
la mia sampogna umil come soleva:
ma di voce più altera e più sonora,
emula de le trombe, empie le selve.
Udimmi Mopso poscia: e con maligno
guardo mirando affascinommi: ond'io
roco divenni, e poi gran tempo tacqui:
quando i pastor credean ch'io fossi stato
visto dal lupo, e 'l lupo era costui.
Questo t'ho detto, acciò che sappi quanto
il parlar di costui di fede è degno:
e déi bene sperar, sol perché ei vuole
che nulla speri.

Tasso, *Aminta*, act 1, scene 2, 44–51 [*Opere*, 2:320–3].

81 Clubb, "The Pastoral Play," 69.

82 Elpin and Batto are understood as representing Giovan Battista Pigna and (probably) Battista Guarini, respectively, while the nymph Licori is associated with Lucrezia Bendidio. See Gigante, *Torquato Tasso*, 100.

83 For a summary of the various hypotheses concerning Mopso's identity, see Gigante, *Torquato Tasso*, 117–19; and Chiodo, "Il 'supercilio' di Mopso non cela Speroni."

84 Gigante, *Torquato Tasso*, 119.

85 See Larivaille, *Pietro Aretino*, 52–7; and Catelli, "Una miriade di frammenti," 6–7.

86 A similar act of self-censorship is evident in the composition of Tasso's *Malpiglio*. From a letter dated 27 June 1584, addressed to his friend Curzio Ardizio, we know that Ardizio had invited Tasso to write "a few stanzas on the court" ("alcune stanze sovra la corte"; Tasso, *Le lettere*, 2:278). And from Tasso's reply, which centres on the idea that both his feelings

and his rationality dissuade him from writing any criticism of the court: "not only the feelings in my heart, but reason as well dissuades me from writing blame of the court" ("non solo l'affetto de l'animo, ma la ragione ancora mi dissuade da lo scrivere in biasimo de la corte"; Tasso, *Le lettere*, 2:278), one can easily infer that what Ardizio expected from Tasso was a work of anti-court satire. Instead of writing the satire requested, however, Tasso shortly thereafter composed his masterpiece of courtly prudence, *Il Malpiglio*. On the relationship between the letter to Curzio and the composition of *Malpiglio*, see Cox, "Tasso's *Malpiglio overo de la corte*"; and Chiarelli, "Una 'congregazione di uomini raccolti per onore'."

87 Zatti, "Natura e potere nell'*Aminta*," 15.

88
O bella età de l'oro,
non già perché di latte
sen' corse il fiume e stillò mele il bosco;
non perché i frutti loro
dier da l'aratro intatte
le terre, e gli angui errâr senz'ira o tosco;
[...]
ma sol perché quel vano
nome senza soggetto,
quell'idolo d'errori, idol d'inganno,
quel che dal volgo insano
onor poscia fu detto,
che di nostra natura 'l feo tiranno,
non mischiava il suo affanno
fra le liete dolcezze
de l'amoroso gregge;
né fu sua dura legge
nota a quell'alme in libertate avvezze,
ma legge aurea e felice
che natura scolpì: *S'ei piace, ei lice.*
[...]
Tu prima, Onor, velasti
la fonte de i diletti,
negando l'onde a l'amorosa sete;
tu a' begli occhi insegnasti
di starne in sé ristretti,
e tener lor bellezze altrui secrete;
tu raccogliesti in rete
le chiome a l'aura sparte;
tu i dolci atti lascivi
festi ritrosi e schivi;
a i detti il fren ponesti, a i passi l'arte:
opra è tua sola, o Onore,
che furto sia quel che fu don d'Amore.

Tasso, *Aminta*, act 1, scene 2, 50–5 [*Opere*, 2:323–5].

89 *Onore* is also invoked as the distinctive character of the courtly milieu in the *Malpiglio*, where the court is defined as "a gathering for the sake of honour" ("La corte dunque è congregazion d'uomini raccolti per onore"; Tasso, *Il Malpiglio*, in *Tasso's Dialogues*, 164–5). On this point, see also Bàrberi Squarotti, "Il forestiero in corte," in *L'onore in corte*, 90–109.

90 The contrast between the chorus and the satyr's monologue is also pointed out by Zatti, "Natura e potere nell'*Aminta*," 15–16.

91 Sampson, *Pastoral Drama*, 77.

92 See chapter 3 of this book, "Satire/satirist/satyr."

93

> Questa mia faccia di color sanguigno,
> queste mie spalle larghe, e queste braccia
> torose e nerborute, e questo petto
> setoso, e queste mie velate coscie
> son di virilità, di robustezza
> indicio; e, se no 'l credi, fanne prova.
> Che vuoi tu far di questi tenerelli,
> che di molle lanugine fiorite
> hanno a pena le guancie? e che con arte
> dispongono i capelli in ordinanza?
> Femine nel sembiante e ne le forze
> sono costoro.

Tasso, *Aminta*, act 2, scene 1, 60–1 [*Opere*, 2:328].

94

> Non sono io brutto, no, né tu mi sprezzi
> perché sì fatto io sia, ma solamente
> perché povero sono: ahi, che le ville
> seguon l'essempio de le gran cittadi;
> e veramente il secol d'oro è questo,
> poiché sol vince l'oro e regna l'oro.

Tasso, *Aminta*, act 2, scene 1, 60–1 [*Opere*, 2:328].

95 See the first scene in act 2, when Aminta is presented with an opportunity to use violence on Silvia who has been tied to a tree by the satyr, and instead frees her and even lowers his eyes to respect her modesty.

96 Gigante, *Torquato Tasso*, 119–21.

97 See chapter 2 of this book, "Women, anti-feminism, and anti-courtliness in the Italian Renaissance." On the connections between *Aminta* and Armida's garden, see also Sampson, *Pastoral Drama*, 89.

98

> Tempo già fu, quando piú l'uom vaneggia
> ne l'età prima, ch'ebbi altro desio
> e disdegnai di pasturar la greggia;
> e fuggii dal paese a me natio,
> e vissi in Menfi un tempo, e ne la reggia
> fra i ministri del re fui posto anch'io,
> e benché fossi guardian de gli orti

vidi e conobbi pur l'inique corti.
Pur lusingato da speranza ardita
soffrii lunga stagion ciò che piú spiace;
ma poi ch'insieme con l'età fiorita
mancò la speme e la baldanza audace,
piansi i riposi di quest'umil vita
e sospirai la mia perduta pace,
e dissi; "O corte, a Dio." Cosí, a gli amici
boschi tornando, ho tratto i dí felici.

See canto 7, 12–13, in Tasso, *Jerusalem Delivered*, 136 [*Gerusalemme Liberata*, 206].

99 Bàrberi Squarotti, *Fine dell'idillio*, 180.

100 La fanciulla regal di rozze spoglie
s'ammanta, e cinge al crin ruvido velo;
ma nel moto de gli occhi e de le membra
non già di boschi abitatrice sembra.
Non copre abito vil la nobil luce
e quanto è in lei d'altero e di gentile,
e fuor la maestà regia traluce
per gli atti ancor de l'essercizio umile.

Tasso, *Jerusalem Delivered*, 7, 17–18, 137 [*Gerusalemme Liberata*, 207–8]. On this passage, see also Bàrberi Squarotti, who defines Erminia's pastoral disguise as a "masquerade" that ends any bucolic illusions. Bàrberi Squarotti, *Fine dell'idillio*, 182–3.

101 Tasso, *Jerusalem Delivered*, 7, 14, 136. "Insino a tanto almen farne soggiorno / ch'agevoli fortuna il suo ritorno" [*Gerusalemme Liberata*, 207].

102 "Fuggo sdegno di principe e di fortuna." Tasso, *Il padre di famiglia*, in *Tasso's Dialogues*, 48–9. Interestingly, the conclusion of the dialogue features a comparison between private households, such as that of the *padre di famiglia*, and princely households, and mentions the possibility that one of the *padre di famiglia*'s sons may one day decide to enter the court; yet the discussion of courts and of princely households is left out, with the justification that those who intend to enter the court can find appropriate instruction in Aristotle's books and in day-to-day experience.

103 Chiodo, "Tra l'*Aminta* e il *Pastor Fido*," 566.

104 On the legacy of Tasso's Erminia in pastoral texts, see Sampson, *Pastoral Drama*, 201, 235n25.

105 Denarosi, "L'*Erminia* di Eugenio Visdomini," 30. Denarosi's article also includes a transcription of the recovered manuscript of the play. On Visdomini's *Erminia*, see also Denarosi, *L'accademia degli Innominati di Parma*, 351–2.

106 Denarosi, "L'*Erminia* di Eugenio Visdomini," 78.

107 Denarosi, "L'*Erminia* di Eugenio Visdomini," 78–80.

108 "a se stesso ora padrone, or servo, or suddito, or signore." Denarosi, "L'*Erminia* di Eugenio Visdomini," 81.

109 Denarosi, "L'*Erminia* di Eugenio Visdomini," 81–2.

110 Denarosi, "L'*Erminia* di Eugenio Visdomini," 33.

111 On both plays, see Sampson, *Pastoral Drama*, 99–100.

112

> la fé, c'abbandonando
> i romor de le corti ambitiose
> ne l'amico silentio ricovrossi
> de' più secreti boscherecci horrori.

Castelletti, *Amarilli, pastorale* (1587), C6*v*.

113 Ingegneri, *Danza di Venere*, 113–17.

114 Pescetti's *La regia pastorella* has been published in a modern edition, edited by Lorenzo Carpanè.

115 For a biography of Guarini, and for details on his troubled relationship with Duke Alfonso II d'Este, see Selmi, "Guarini, Battista."

116 On Tasso's conditions at the beginning of his employment at the Este court, see Sampson, *Pastoral Drama*, 62.

117 Guarini, *The Faithful Shepherd*, act 5, scene 1, 84; 151. "Musico spirto in giovanil vaghezza." Guarini, *Il Pastor Fido*, 233.

118 Molinari, "Per il *Pastor Fido* di Battista Guarini," 183–4.

119 Sampson, "The Mantuan Performance of Guarini's *Pastor Fido*," 73.

120 Sampson, *Pastoral Drama*, 147.

121 Sampson, *Pastoral Drama*, 147.

122 Guarini, *The Faithful Shepherd*, act 5, scene 1, 104, 150. "Adorator di deità terrena." Guarini, *Il Pastor Fido*, 234. I have amended Sheridan's translation of "earthly Goddess" to "earthly deity" to keep the non-gendered meaning of the original Italian. Sheridan's translation seems to imply that the "earthly Goddess" was a female beloved, thus losing the anti-courtly nuance of the original text. For a reading of the "earthly deity" as the prince, see Selmi's notes to the text in Guarini, *Il Pastor Fido*, 440.

123

> Gente di nome e di parlar cortese,
> ma d'opre scarsa e di pietà nemica;
> gente placida in vista e mansüeta,
> ma piú del cupo mar tumida e fèra;
> gente sol d'apparenza in cui se miri
> viso di carità, mente d'invidia
> poi trovi, e 'n dritto sguardo animo bieco,
> e minor fede allor che piú lusinga.

Guarini, *The Faithful Shepherd*, act 5, scene 1, 136–43, 151. Guarini, *Il Pastor Fido*, 234–5.

124 Scrissi, piansi, cantai, arsi, gelai,
corsi, stetti, sostenni, or tristo or lieto,
or alto or basso, or vilipeso or caro,
e come il ferro delfico, stromento
or d'impresa sublime, or d'opra vile,
non temei risco e non schivai fatica.
Tutto fei, nulla fui.

Guarini, *The Faithful Shepherd*, act 5, scene 1, 109–15, 151. Guarini, *Il Pastor Fido*, 234.

125 Guarini, *The Faithful Shepherd*, act 5, scene 1, 115–16, 151. "Per cangiar loco, / stato, vita, pensier, costumi e pelo." Guarini, *Il Pastor Fido*, 234.

126 Quel ch'altrove è virtú, quivi è difetto:
dir vero, oprar non torto, amar non finto,
pietà sincera, invïolabil fede,
e di core e di man vita innocente,
stiman d'animo vil, di basso ingegno,
sciocchezza e vanità degna di riso.
L'ingannare, il mentir, la frode, il furto
e la rapina di pietà vestita,
crescer col danno e precipizio altrui
e far a sé de l'altrui biasmo onore,
son le virtú di quella gente infida.

Guarini, *The Faithful Shepherd*, act 5, scene 1, 144–54, 151–2. Guarini, *Il Pastor Fido*, 235.

On these lines, see also Selmi, *Classici e moderni*, 165.

127 Guarini, *The Faithful Shepherd*, act 5, scene 1, 162, 152. "Fame d'avere." Guarini, *Il Pastor Fido*, 235.

128 Or io, ch'incauto e di lor arti ignaro
sempre mi vissi, e portai scritto in fronte
il mio pensiero e disvelato il core,
tu puoi pensar s'a non sospetti strali
d'invida gente fui scoperto segno.

Guarini, *The Faithful Shepherd*, act 5, scene 1, 164–8, 152. Guarini, *Il Pastor Fido*, 235.

129 se da quel dí, che meco
passò la musa mia d'Elide in Argo,
avessi avuto di cantar tant'agio,
quanta cagion di lagrimar sempr'ebbi,
con sí sublime stil forse cantato
avrei del mio signor l'armi e gli onori,
ch'or non avria de la meonia tromba
da invidiar Achille; e la mia patria,
madre di cigni sfortunati, andrebbe
già per me cinta del secondo alloro
Ma oggi è fatta (oh secolo inumano!)

l'arte del poetar troppo infelice.
Lieto nido, èsca dolce, aura cortese
bramano i cigni; e non si va in Parnaso
con le cure mordaci. E chi pur garre
sempre col suo destino e col disagio,
vien roco, e perde il canto e la favella.

Guarini, *The Faithful Shepherd*, act 5, scene 1, 171–87, 152–3. Guarini, *Il Pastor Fido*, 235–6.

130 On the same ambivalence in Ariosto, see Ugolini, "Self-Portraits of a Truthful Liar."

131 On Guarini's conflation of courtly and pastoral space, see Sampson, *Pastoral Drama*, 143.

132 Tasso, *Aminta*, act 1, scene 2, 50.

133 Guarini, *Il Pastor Fido*, act 4, scene 9, 1407–61. On the different interpretations of honour in *Aminta* and the *Pastor Fido*, see Chiodo, "'Soavi Licor' e 'succhi amari,'" 121–4.

134 Selmi, "Guarini, Battista."

135 On the contrast between the court as a sea and the haven of private life in Guarini's letters, see Avellini, "'Pelago' e 'porto.'"

136 Guarini, "Al Signor Francesco Maria Vialardi," in *Lettere*, 59–63.

137 "Con tutto ciò non sono così pertinace, o ritroso, che quantunque io mi sia incamminato a questa vita privata, non fussi per dar volta, e tornare alla pubblica, se più cortese, e men pericolosa fortuna mi scorgesse il sentiero." Guarini, "Al Signor Francesco Maria Vialardi," in *Lettere*, 61.

138 Guarini, "Al Signor Francesco Maria Vialardi," in *Lettere*, 63.

139 Selmi, *Classici e moderni*, 212.

140 On the similarities with the *Malpiglio*, see also Selmi, *Classici e moderni*, 213.

141 Selmi, *Classici e moderni*, 214.

142 See act 2, 6. Ingegneri, *Danza di Venere*, 113–17.

143 Alpers, *What Is Pastoral?*, 162.

144 Gerbino, *Music and the Myth of Arcadia*, 246.

145 Gerbino, *Music and the Myth of Arcadia*, 247.

Afterword

1 According to Paolo Cherchi, beginning in the 1540s one can notice the emergence of a "third wave" of writings on courts that adopt an attitude between vituperation and idealization of the court. See Cherchi's introduction to Gilio, *Dialogo del letterato cortigiano*, 10.

2 As can be testified to by the frequent occurrence of anti-courtly themes in Salvator Rosa's satiric writings; see Rosa, *Satire*.

3 "Il Tempo, e la pacienza aggrandisce il Cortegiano, ancor che trà loro Cortegiani l'odio, e l'invidia habbia il suo Regno, e chi non sà sopportare s'allontani dalla Corte." Andreini, "Nono Ragionamento," in *La seconda parte delle bravure del capitano Spavento*, 21*r*. I thank Sarah G. Ross for having brought this text to my attention. Francesco's wife, Isabella Andreini, also authored writings against the court. See Andreini, *Del servir in corte, and Delle lodi della villa*, in *Lettere d'Isabella Andreini*, 70r and 138r–40v. I thank Caterina Mongiat Farina and Paola De Santo for the information about Isabella Andreini's letters.

4 On the notion of patience in the Renaissance, see Schiffhorst, *The Triumph of Patience*.

5 On this topic, see Schiffhorst, *The Triumph of Patience*, 22.

6 On both texts, see Cherchi, "Leonardo Fioravanti e Antonio de Guevara"; Ray, "Lucio Paolo Rosello's Dialogue on 'La vita de' Cortigiani'"; and Vagnoni, "Il plagio del *De patientia*."

7 See Vagnoni, "Il plagio del *De patientia*," 347, 355; and Snyder, *Dissimulation and the Culture of Secrecy in Early Modern Europe*, 81–2.

8 Snyder, *Dissimulation and the Culture of Secrecy in Early Modern Europe*, 83–4.

9 Martin, "Inventing Sincerity, Refashioning Prudence," 1335.

10 Even Aretino's satirical writings on the court, the only writings that juxtapose the court with the opposite political reality of the Venetian republic, base their support of Venetian republicanism not on broad notions of politics but on the private notion of intellectual autonomy more commonly associated, in other writings, with the villa.

11 See the discussion concerning Benedetto Croce's "Libri sulle corti" in the introduction to this book.

12

Mi venne un di pensier di gir lontano
Per non vivere più tra tanti affanni
La corte è mar di duol, nido d'inganni
Ove stenti, e sospir, ma sempr'in vano
Qui si hà per grand'onor un bona mano
Stimansi per un nulla i propri danni
S'adorano per dei anch'i tiranni
E in mal'ora così ne vai pian piano.

Sarti, *La pietra racconta*, 80.

Bibliography

Primary Sources

Alamanni, Luigi. *Satire*. Edited by Rossana Perri. Florence: Franco Cesati Editore, 2013.

Alciato, Andrea. *Emblemata*. Lyon: Macé Bonhomme for Guillaume Rouille, 1551. https://www.emblems.arts.gla.ac.uk/alciato/. Accessed 26 Feburary 2019.

– *Emblematum libri II*. Lyon: Jean de Tournes and Guillaume Gazeau, 1556. https://www.emblems.arts.gla.ac.uk/alciato/. Accessed 26 Feburary 2019.

– *Les emblems*. Paris: Chrestien Wechel, 1542. https://www.emblems.arts.gla.ac.uk/alciato/. Accessed 26 Feburary 2019.

Allegri, Alessandro. *Rime e prose di Alessandro Allegri Accademico Fiorentino: Riviste, ed Aggiunte*. Amsterdam: sine nomine, 1754.

Andini, Mario degli. *Satire di cinque poeti illustri*. Venetia: per Gio. Andrea Valvassori, 1565.

Andreini, Francesco. *La seconda parte delle bravure del capitano Spavento*. Venetia: Appresso Vincenzo Somasco, 1618.

Andreini, Isabella. *Lettere d'Isabella Andreini*. Venetia: Appresso Marc'Antonio Zaltieri, 1607.

Aquilano, Serafino. *Le Rime di Serafino de' Ciminelli dall'Aquila*. Edited by Mario Meneghini. 2 vols. Bologna: Romagnoli-Dall'Acqua, 1894.

Aretino, Pietro. *Cortigiana, Opera nova, Pronostico, Il testamento dell'elefante, Farza*. Edited by Angelo Romano. Milan: Rizzoli, 1989.

– *Dialogues*. Translated by Raymond Rosenthal. New York: Marsilio, 1994.

– *Edizione nazionale delle opere di Pietro Aretino: Teatro*. Tomo 1, *Cortigiana* (1525 e 1534). Edited by Paolo Trovato and Federico Della Corte. Rome: Salerno, 2010.

– *Lettere*. Edited by Paolo Procaccioli. 6 vols. Rome: Salerno, 1997.

– *Operette politiche e satiriche*. Vol. 1, edited by Giuseppe Crimi. Rome: Salerno Editrice, 2013.

– *Operette politiche e satiriche*. Vol. 2, edited by Marco Faini. Rome: Salerno Editrice, 2012.

– *Poemi cavallereschi*. Edited by Danilo Romei. Rome: Salerno Editrice, 1995.

– *Ragionamento, Dialogo*. Milan: Garzanti, 2005.

– *Scritti di Pietro Aretino nel Codice marciano It. XI 66 (6730)*. Edited by Danilo Romei. Florence: Cesati, 1987.

Ariosto, Ludovico. *Opere minori*. Edited by Cesare Segre. Milan: Ricciardi, 1954.

– *Orlando Furioso*. Edited and translated by Guido Waldman. Oxford: Oxford University Press, 1983.

– *Orlando Furioso*. Edited by Remo Ceserani and Sergio Zatti. Turin: UTET, 2015.

– *Satire*. Edited by Cesare Segre.Turin: Einaudi, 1987.

– *The Satires of Ludovico Ariosto: A Renaissance Autobiography*. Edited by Peter DeSa Wiggins. Athens: Ohio University Press, 1976.

Baldini, Antonio. *Ludovico della tranquillità: Divagazioni ariostesche*. Bologna: Zanichelli, 1933.

Bandello, Matteo. *La quarta parte de le novelle*. Edited by Delmo Maestri. Alessandria: Edizioni dell'Orso, 1996.

Bembo, Pietro. *I duchi di Urbino*. Edited by Valentina Marchesi. Bologna: Emil, 2010.

Benucci, Lattanzio. *Muovesi il Cortigian canuto et bianco*. Florence, BNCF, Ms. Magl. VII.779.

Berni, Francesco. *Rime*. Edited by Danilo Romei. Milan: Mursia, 1985.

Betussi, Giuseppe. *Il Raverta*. Milan: Daelli, 1864.

Biondo, Michelangelo. *Angitia cortigiana: De natura del cortigiano*. Roma: per Antonio Blado, 1540.

Bolognetti, Francesco. *Satire*. Rome: Biblioteca Italiana, 2004. http://www.bibliotecaitaliana.it/indice/visualizza_scheda/bibit000607. Accessed 13 February 2015.

Caccia, Giovanni Agostino. *Rime*. Edited by Benedict Buono. Milan: Lampi di Stampa, 2010.

– *Satire, e capitoli piacevoli (1549): Con un'appendice di testi inediti di Bartolomeo Taegio*. Edited by Benedict Buono. Milan: Lampi di Stampa, 2013.

Calcagnini, Celio. *De patientia, seu vita aulica commentatio Caelii Calcagnini ad Lodovicum Balneum*. In Celio Calcagnini, *Opera aliquot*, 400–4. Basileae: Froben, 1544.

Calepino, Ambrogio. *Il dittionario di Ambrogio Calepino della lingua latina nella volgare brevemente ridotto*. Venice: A San Luca al segno del Diamante, 1552.

Cammelli da Pistoia, Antonio. *Rime edite ed inedite di Antonio Cammelli detto il Pistoia*. Edited by Antonio Cappelli and Severino Ferrari. Livorno: Francesco Vigo Editore, 1884.

Canoniero, Pietro Andrea. *Il perfetto cortegiano, et dell'ufizio del prencipe verso 'l cortegiano*. Roma: per Bartolomeo Zannetti, 1609.

Caporali, Cesare. *Avvisi di Parnaso*. In *Rime piacevoli di Cesare Caporali Accademico degl'Insensati di Perugia detto lo Stemperato*, 2:146–70. Firenze: presso Giuseppe Becherini, 1820.

– *Capitoli: Con le osservazioni di Carlo caporali suo nipote. Nuovamente messi in luce per cura di mastro Stoppino filologo maccheronico.* Banca Dati "Nuovo Rinascimento," 22 February 2015. http://www.nuovorinascimento.org/n-rinasc/testi/pdf/caporali/capitoli.pdf. Accessed 14 November 2017.
– *Il viaggio di Parnaso.* Edited by Norberto Cacciaglia. Perugia: Guerra, 1993.
Carafa, Diomede. *Dello optimo cortesano.* Edited by Gioachino Paparelli. Salerno: Beta, 1971.
Castelletti, Cristoforo. *Amarilli, pastorale.* Ascoli: Giuseppe de gl'Angeli, 1580.
– *Amarilli, pastorale.* Vinegia: Presso Giovan Battista Sessa, et fratelli, 1587.
Castiglione, Baldassar. *The Book of the Courtier.* Edited by Daniel Javitch. New York and London: Norton, 2002.
– *Il Libro del Cortegiano.* Edited by Amedeo Quondam. Milan: Garzanti, 2000.
– *La seconda redazione del Cortegiano di Baldassarre Castiglione.* Edited by Ghino Ghinassi. Florence: Sansoni, 1968.
– *Le Lettere.* Edited by Guido La Rocca. Verona: Mondadori, 1978.
Castiglione, Baldassar, and Cesare Gonzaga. *Rime e Tirsi.* Edited by Giacomo Vagni. Bologna: I libri di Emil, 2015.
Commendone, Giovan Francesco. *Discorso sopra la corte di Roma.* Edited by Cesare Mozzarelli. Rome: Bulzoni, 1996.
Correggio, Nicolò da. *Opere.* Edited by Antonia Tissoni Benvenuti. Bari: Laterza, 1969.
Domenichi, Ludovico. *Dialoghi di M. Lodovico Domenichi; cioè dell'amore, della vera nobiltà, de' rimedi d'amore, dell'imprese, dell'amor fraterno, della fortuna, et della stampa.* Vinegia: appresso Gabriel Giolito de' Ferrari, 1562.
– *La donna di corte.* Lucca: per il Busdrago, 1564.
Doni, Antonfrancesco. *Le ville.* Edited by Ugo Bellocchi. Modena: Aedes Muratoriana, 1969.
– *Una nuova opinione del Doni circa all'imprese amorose et militari.* Florence, Biblioteca Nazionale Centrale, ms. N.A. 267.
Ducci, Lorenzo. *Ars Aulica, or the Courtiers Arte.* Translated by Edward Blount. London: Melch. Bradwood for Edward Blount, 1607.
– *Arte aulica di Lorenzo Ducci: Nella quale s'insegna il modo, che deve tenere il Cortigiano per divenire possessore della gratia del suo Principe.* Ferrara: appresso Vittorio Baldini, 1601.
Este, Isabella d'. *Selected Letters.* Edited and translated by Deanna Shemek. Toronto: Iter Press; Tempe: Arizona Center for Medieval and Renaissance Studies, 2017.
Falcone, Giuseppe. *La nuova, vaga, et dilettevole villa.* Pavia: appresso Andrea Viani, 1599.
Folengo, Teofilo. *Baldo.* Translated by Ann E. Mullaney. I Tatti Renaissance Library. Cambridge, MA, and London, England: Harvard University Press, 2008.

Gallo, Agostino. *Le dieci giornate della vera agricoltura, e piaceri della villa.* Brescia: appresso Lodovico di Sabbio, 1564.

– *Le tredici giornate della vera agricoltura, e piaceri della villa.* Venetia: presso Nicolò Beuilacqua, 1566.

– *Le vinti giornate della vera agricoltura, e piaceri della villa.* Venetia: appresso Gratioso Percaccino, 1569.

Garzoni, Tomaso. *La piazza universale di tutte le professioni del mondo.* Edited by Paolo Cherchi and Beatrice Collina. Turin: Einaudi, 1996.

Gilio, Giovanni Andrea. *Dialogo del letterato cortigiano.* Edited by Paolo Cherchi. Ravenna: Longo, 2002.

Giraldi Cinzio, Giovan Battista. *L'uomo di corte: Discorso intorno a quello che si conviene a giovane e nobile e ben creato nel servire un gran principe.* Edited by Walter Moretti. Modena: Mucchi, 1989.

Grimaldi Robio, Pellegro. *Discorsi ne' quali si ragiona compiutamente di quanto far debbono i gentilhuomini ne' seruigi de lor signori per acquistarsi la gratia loro.* Genoa: per Antonio Roccatagliata, 1583.

Guarini, Battista. *The Faithful Shepherd: A Translation of Battista Guarini's Il Pastor Fido by Dr. Thomas Sheridan.* Edited by Robert Hogan and Edward A. Nickerson. Newark: University of Delaware Press; London and Toronto: Associated University Presses, 1989.

– *Il Pastor Fido.* Edited by Elisabetta Selmi. Venice: Marsilio, 1999.

– *Il segretario.* Venetia: Appresso Ruberto Megietti, 1600.

– *Lettere.* Venetia: Presso Giovan Battista Ciotti, 1615.

Guasco, Annibal. *Discourse to Lady Lavinia His Daughter.* Edited and translated by Peggy Osborn. Chicago: University of Chicago Press, 2003.

– *Ragionamento a Donna Lavinia sua figliuola.* Edited by Helena Sanson. *Letteratura Italiana Antica* 11 (2010): 61–140.

– *Sotto il segno di Chirone.* Edited by Luisella Giachino. Turin: Nino Aragno Editore, 2012.

Guazzo, Stefano. *The civile conversation of M. Steeven Guazzo, the first three books translated by George Pettie, anno 1581, and the fourth by Barth. Young, anno 1586. With an Introduction by Sir Edward Sullivan.* 2 vols. London: Constable and Co. Ltd; New York: Alfred A. Knopf, 1925.

– *La civil conversazione.* Edited by Amedeo Quondam. Modena: Franco Cosimo Panini Editore, 1993.

– *Lettere del Signor Stefano Guazzo, Gentilhuomo di Casale di Monferrato.* Vinegia: Presso Barezzo Barezzi, 1592.

Ingegneri, Angelo. *Danza di Venere.* Edited by Roberto Puggioni. Rome: Bulzoni, 2002.

Lollio, Alberto. *Lettera nella quale rispondendo ad una di m. Hercole Perinato, egli celebra la villa, et lauda molto l'agricoltura.* Vinetia: Appresso Gabriel Giolito de' Ferrari, 1544.

Mirabelli, Domenico Nani. *Polyanthea*. Savona: Francisco de Silva, 1503.

Nifo, Agostino. *De re aulica ad Phausinam libri duo per Augustinum Niphum medicem*. Neapoli: Ioannes Antonius de caneto papiensis excudebat, 1534.

– *Il cortigiano del Sessa*. Genoa: appò Antonio Belloni, 1560.

Pascoli, Gabriele. *La pazzesca pazzia degli uomini e delle donne di corte*. Venetia: appresso Giulio Somasco, 1592.

Peregrini, Matteo. *Che al savio è convenevole il corteggiare. Libri III*. Bologna: per Nicolò Tebaldini, 1624.

– *Difesa del savio in corte*. Edited by Gian Luigi Beti and Sandra Saccone. Lecce: Argo, 2009.

Pescetti, Orlando. *La regia pastorella*. Edited by Lorenzo Carpanè. Bologna: CLUEB, 2012.

Pevere, Fulvio, ed. *Favole*. Turin: RES, 1999.

Piccolomini, Alessandro. *I cento sonetti*. Edited by Franco Tomasi. Geneva: Droz, 2015.

– *La Raffaella, ovvero Dialogo della bella creanza delle donne*. Rome: Salerno, 2001.

Piccolomini, Enea Silvio. *Aeneae Silvii De curialium miseriis epistola*. Edited by Wilfred P. Mustard. Baltimore: Johns Hopkins University Press, 1928.

Rime piacevoli di Cesare Caporali, del Mauro, e d'altri Auttori. Ferrara: per Benedetto Mamarello, 1590.

Ripa, Cesare. *Iconologia*. Edited by Sonia Maffei. Turin: Einaudi, 2012.

Rosa, Salvator. *Satire*. Edited by Danilo Romei. Milan: Mursia, 1995.

Rosello, Lucio Paolo. *Dialogo de la vita de' cortegiani, intitolato la patientia*. In *Due dialoghi*, 15*v*–24*r*. Venetia: per Comin Trino da Monferrato, 1549.

Sannazzaro, Jacopo. *Arcadia*. Edited by Francesco Erspamer. Milan: Mursia, 1990.

Sansovino, Francesco. *Sette libri di satire di Lodovico Ariosto, Hercole Bentivogli, Luigi Alamanni, Pietro Nelli, Antonio Vinciguerra, Francesco Sansovino, e d'altri scrittori: Con un discorso in materia della satira; Di nuovo raccolti per Francesco Sansovino*. Venetia: appresso Francesco Sasovino et C., 1560.

Sasso, Panfilo. *Opera del praeclarissimo poeta miser Pamphilo Sasso modenese: Sonetti. CCCC.VII; Capituli. XXXVIII; Egloge. V*. Venetiis: per Guilielmum de Fontaneto de Monferrrato, 1519.

Simeoni, Gabriello. *Satire alla berniesca*. Turino: pro Martino Cravotto, 1549.

Soldani, Iacopo. *Satire*. Edited by Danilo Romei. Florence: Società Editrice Fiorentina, 2012.

Soprani, Raffaele. *Li scrittori della Liguria e particolarmente della maritima*. Genova: per Pietro Giovanni Calenzani, 1667.

Speroni, Sperone. *Orazione contra le cortigiane*. In *Opere di M. Sperone Speroni degli Alvarotti tratte da' mss. originali: Tomo quinto*, 191–244. Venezia: appresso Domenico Occhi, 1750.

Taegio, Bartolomeo. *La villa*. Edited and translated by Thomas E. Beck. Philadelphia: University of Pennsylvania Press, 2011.

– *Le risposte di M. Bartolomeo Taegio, Giureconsulto del Collegio di Melano.* Novara: Appresso Francesco e Giacomo Sesalli, 1554.

Taegio, Bartolomeo, Federico Borromeo, and Pietro Verri. *L'antico regime in villa: Con tre testi milanesi.* Edited by Cesare Mozzarelli. Rome: Bulzoni, 2004.

Tasso, Torquato. *Aminta.* In *Opere*, edited by Bortolo Tommaso Sozzi, 2:295–389. Turin: UTET, 1981.

– *Aminta.* Edited and translated by Charles Jernigan and Irene Marchegiani Jones. New York: Italica, 2000.

– *Gerusalemme Liberata.* Edited by Claudio Varese and Guido Arbizzoni. Milan: Mursia, 1983.

– *Jerusalem Delivered.* Edited and translated by Anthony M. Esolen. Baltimore and London: Johns Hopkins University Press, 2000.

– *Le lettere disposte per ordine di tempo ed illustrate da Cesare Guasti.* Florence: Le Monnier, 1854.

– *Le rime di Torquato Tasso: Edizione critica su i manoscritti e le antiche stampe.* Edited by Angelo Solerti. Bologna: Romagnoli Dall'Acqua, 1900.

– *Tasso's Dialogues: A Selection, with the Discourse on the Art of the Dialogue.* Edited by Dain A. Trafton. Hanover, NH: Dartmouth College in conjunction with English Literary Renaissance, 1973.

Venier, Maffio. *Satira contro la corte.* In *Poesie diverse*, edited by Attilio Carminati, 224–32. Venice: Corbo e Fiore, 2001.

Vida, Girolamo. *Filliria, favola boscareccia.* Padova: Appresso Gioanni Cantoni, 1585.

Vincioli, Vinciolo. *Satira sopra la corte.* In *Raccolta dei poeti satirici italiani*, edited by Giulio Carcano, 3:255–60. Turin: Ferrero e Franco, 1853.

Vocabolario degli Accademici della Crusca. Venezia: Appresso Giovanni Alberti, 1612. http://vocabolario.sns.it/html/index.html. Accessed 28 February 2019.

Secondary Sources

Ackerman, James. *The Villa: Form and Ideology of Country Houses.* London: Thames and Hudson, 1990.

Aguirre, J.M. "Antonio de Guevara's Corte-Aldea: A Model for All Seasons." *Neophilologus* 65, no. 4 (1981): 536–47.

Alpers, Paul. *What Is Pastoral?* Chicago: University of Chicago Press, 1996.

Anglo, Sydney. "The Courtier: The Renaissance and Changing Ideals." In *The Courts of Europe: Politics, Patronage and Royalty*, edited by A.G. Dickens, 33–53. New York: McGraw-Hill, 1977.

– "Systematic Immorality: The Courtier's Art." In *Machiavelli: The First Century; Studies in Enthusiasm, Hostility, and Irrelevance*, 573–679. Oxford: Oxford University Press, 2005.

Aquilecchia, Giovanni. "Aretino's *Sei giornate*: Literary Parody and Social Reality." In *Women in Italian Renaissance Culture and Society*, edited by Letizia Panizza, 453–62. Oxford: Legenda, 2000.

– "Per l'attribuzione e il testo del 'Lamento di una Cortigiana Ferrarese.'" In *Schede di italianistica*, 127–51. Turin: Einaudi, 1976.

Asch, Ronald G., and Adolf M. Birke, eds. *Princes, Patronage, and the Nobility: The Court at the Beginning of the Modern Age, c. 1450–1650*. London, Oxford, and New York: German Historical Institute London, 1991.

Ascoli, Albert Russell. *Ariosto's Bitter Harmony: Crisis and Evasion in the Italian Renaissance*. Princeton, NJ: Princeton University Press, 1987.

– "Che cosa c'è di nuovo nel *Furioso* del '16?" Lecture given at the Accademia dell'Arcadia on June 9, 2017. Cited by permission of the author.

– "Worthy of Faith? Authors Readers in Early Modernity." In *The Renaissance World*, edited by John Jeffries Martin, 435–51. New York and London: Routledge, 2007.

Asor Rosa, Alberto. "Allegri, Alessandro." In *Dizionario biografico degli italiani*, vol. 2. Rome: Istituto dell'Enciclopedia italiana, 1960. http://www.treccani.it/enciclopedia/alessandro-allegri_(Dizionario-Biografico)/. Accessed 14 November 2017.

Avellini, Luisa. "'Pelago' e 'porto': La corte e il cortigiano nell'epistolario del Guarini." In *La corte e lo spazio: Ferrara estense*, edited by Giuseppe Papagno and Amedeo Quondam, 683–96. Rome: Bulzoni, 1982.

Baldi, Andrea. *Tradizione e parodia in Alessandro Piccolomini*. Lucca: Pacini Fazzi, 2001.

Ballistreri, Gianni. "Benucci, Lattanzio." In *Dizionario biografico degli italiani*, vol. 8. Rome: Istituto dell'Enciclopedia italiana, 1966. http://www.treccani.it/enciclopedia/lattanzio-benucci_(Dizionario-Biografico)/. Accessed 14 November 2017.

Bàrberi Squarotti, Giorgio. *Fine dell'idillio: Da Dante a Marino*. Genoa: Monferrato, 1978.

– *L'onore in corte: Dal Castiglione al Tasso*. Milan: Angeli, 1986.

Berger, Harry, Jr. *The Absence of Grace: Sprezzatura and Suspicion in Two Renaissance Courtesy Books*. Stanford, CA: Stanford University Press, 2000.

– *Second World and Green World: Studies in Renaissance Fiction-Making*. Berkeley and Los Angeles: University of California Press, 1988.

Berra, Claudia, ed. *Fra satire e rime ariostesche*. Milan: Cisalpino, 2000.

Bertelli, Sergio, Franco Cardini, and Elvira Gambero Zorzi, eds. *Le corti italiane del Rinascimento*. Milan: Mondadori, 1985.

Biagioli, Mario. *Galileo, Courtier: The Practice of Science in the Culture of Absolutism*. Chicago: University of Chicago Press, 1994.

Bigazzi, Roberto. "Un fragile paradiso: La villa nella tradizione europea." In *La letteratura di villa e di villeggiatura: Atti del convegno di Parma 29 settembre–1 ottobre 2003*, 15–32. Rome: Salerno Editrice, 2004.

Bigi, Emilio. "Semplicità pastorale e grazia cortigiana nel *Tirsi*." In *Poesia latina e volgare nel Rinascimento italiano*, 341–70. Naples: Morano, 1989.

Biow, Douglas. *On the Importance of Being an Individual in Renaissance Italy: Men, Their Professions, and Their Beards*. Philadelphia: University of Pennsylvania Press, 2015.

Boccia, Carmine. "Paterno, Lodovico." In *Dizionario biografico degli italiani*, vol. 81. Rome: Istituto dell'Enciclopedia italiana, 2014. http://www.treccani.it/enciclopedia/lodovico-paterno_(Dizionario-Biografico)/. Accessed 14 November 2017.

Bologna, Corrado. "*Satire* di Ludovico Ariosto." In *Letteratura italiana: Le opere*, edited by Alberto Asor Rosa. Vol. 2, *Dal Cinquecento al Settecento*, 181–218. Turin: Einaudi, 1992.

Bolzoni, Lina. "Il segretario neoplatonico." In *La corte e il Cortegiano*, vol. 2, edited by Adirano Prosperi, 133–69. Rome: Bulzoni, 1980.

Breitenberg, Mark. *Anxious Masculinity in Early Modern England*. Cambridge: Cambridge University Press, 1996.

Bruscagli, Renato. "*L'Aminta* e le pastorali ferraresi del '500." In *Studi di filologia e critica offerti dagli allievi a Lanfranco Caretti*, 1:279–318. Rome: Salerno Editrice, 1985.

Burke, Peter. *The Fortunes of the "Courtier": The European Reception of Castiglione's "Cortegiano."* University Park: Pennsylvania State University Press, 1995.

Burrow, Colin. "Roman Satire in the Sixteenth Century." In *The Cambridge Companion to Roman Satire*, edited by Kirk Freudenburg, 243–60. Cambridge: Cambridge University Press, 2005.

Caccamo, Domenico. "Commendone, Giovanni Francesco." *Dizionario biografico degli italiani*, vol. 27. Rome: Istituto dell'Enciclopedia italiana, 1982. http://www.treccani.it/enciclopedia/giovanni-francesco-commendone_(Dizionario-Biografico). Accessed 14 November 2017.

Cairns, Christopher. *Pietro Aretino and the Republic of Venice: Researches on Aretino and His Circle in Venice, 1527–1556*. Florence: Olschki, 1985.

Campbell, Julie D. *Literary Circles and Gender in Early Modern Europe: A Cross-Cultural Approach*. Aldershot, UK: Ashgate, 2006.

Campeggiani, Ida. "Le *Satire*." In *L'ultimo Ariosto: Dalle "Satire" ai frammenti autografi*, 31–118. Pisa: Edizioni della Normale, 2017.

Catelli, Nicola. "Pietro Aretino e il Sacco di Roma." *Campi immaginabili* 32–3 (2005): 1–2, 22–5.

– *Scherzar coi santi: Prospettive comiche sul Sacco di Roma*. Parma: Uninova, 2008.

– "Una miriade di frammenti: Note su Pietro Aretino e il Sacco di Roma." In *L'elmo di Mambrino: Nove saggi di letteratura*, edited by Giovanni Ronchini and Andrea Torre, 5–17. Lucca: Maria Pacini Fazzi Editore, 2006.

Celenza, Christopher. *Renaissance Humanism and the Papal Curia: Lapo da Castiglionchio the Younger's "De curiae commodis."* Ann Arbor: University of Michigan Press, 1999.

Chemello, Adriana. "Donna di palazzo, moglie, cortigiana." In *La corte e il "Cortegiano,"* vol. 2, edited by Adriano Prosperi, 113–32. Rome: Bulzoni, 1980.

Cherchi, Paolo. "Leonardo Fioravanti e Antonio de Guevara." *Esperienze letterarie* 22 (1995): 13–35.

Chiarelli, Angelo. "Una 'congregazione di uomini raccolti per onore': Tentativi di aggiornamento della teoria cortigiana nella dialogistica e nella prosa tassiana." *La Rassegna della letteratura italiana* 121, no. 1 (2017): 34–43.

Chiodo, Domenico. "Il 'supercilio' di Mopso non cela Speroni: Alle radici di un equivoco, con qualche riflessione." *Giornale storico della letteratura italiana* 177 (2000): 273–82.

– "'Soavi Licor' e 'succhi amari': Guarini e Baldi emuli del Tasso." *Lettere italiane* 45, no. 1 (1993): 116–28.

– "Tra l'*Aminta* e il *Pastor Fido*." *Italianistica: Rivista di letteratura italiana* 24, nos. 2–3 (May 1995): 559–75.

Chiong Rivero, Horacio. *The Rise of Pseudo-Historical Fictions: Fray Antonio de Guevara's Novelizations*. New York: Peter Lang, 2004.

Chittolini, Aldo, Anthony Molho, and Pierangelo Schiera, eds. *Origini dello stato: Processi di formazione statale in Italia fra medioevo ed età moderna*. Bologna: Il Mulino, 1994.

Cian, Vittorio. *La satira*. Vol. 1. Milan: Vallardi, 1923.

Ciri, Filippo. "Verso il Seicento: Cesare Caporali." In *Autorità, modelli e antimodelli nella cultura artistica e letteraria tra Riforma e Controriforma: Atti del seminario internazionale di studi Urbino-Sassocorvaro, 9–11 novembre 2006*, edited by Antonio Corsaro, Harald Hendrix, and Paolo Procaccioli, 213–24. Manziana: Vecchiarelli, 2007.

Citroni Marchetti, Sandra. "Quid Romae faciam? Mentiri nescio: Il motivo del rifiuto giovenaliano della arti indegne nella tradizione della satira regolare italiana e francese." *Rivista di letterature moderne e comparate* 33, no. 2 (1980): 85–121.

Clough, Cecil H. "Daughters and Wives of the Montefeltro: Outstanding Bluestockings of the Quattrocento." *Renaissance Studies* 10, no. 1 (1996): 31–55.

Clubb, Louise George. "The Pastoral Play: Conflations of Country, Court and City." In *Il teatro italiano del Rinascimento*, edited by Maristella De Panizza Lorch, 65–73. Milan: Edizione di Comunità, 1980.

Cohen, Elizabeth S. "Courtesans and Whores: Words and Behavior in Roman Streets." *Women's Studies* 19 (1991): 201–8.

Coldagelli, Umberto. "Brancaccio, Giulio Cesare." In *Dizionario biografico degli italiani*, vol. 13. Rome: Istituto dell'Enciclopedia italiana, 1971. http://www.

treccani.it/enciclopedia/giulio-cesare-brancaccio_(Dizionario-Biografico)/. Accessed 14 November 2017.

Cole, Allison. *La Renaissance dans les cours italiennes*. Paris: Flammarion, 1995.

Coller, Alexandra. "How to Succeed at Court: Guasco's Advice to His Daughter Lavinia and Renaissance Manuals of Conduct." *California Italian Studies* 4, no. 2 (2013): 1–31.

Corsaro, Antonio. *La regola e la licenza: Studi sulla poesia satirica e burlesca fra Cinque e Seicento*. Manziana: Vecchiarelli, 1999.

– "*Laus villae*: Scritti e vicende di prelati umanisti prima e dopo il Concilio." In *La letteratura di villa e di villeggiatura: Atti del convegno di Parma 29 settembre–1 ottobre 2003*, 169–204. Rome: Salerno Editrice, 2004.

Cox, Virginia. *The Renaissance Dialogue*. Cambridge: Cambridge University Press, 1992.

– "Rhetoric and Politics in Tasso's *Nifo*." *Studi secenteschi* 30 (1989): 3–98.

– "Seen but Not Heard: The Role of Women Speakers in Cinquecento Literary Dialogue." In *Women in Italian Renaissance Culture and Society*, edited by Letizia Panizza, 385–400. Oxford: Legenda, 2000.

– "Tasso's *Malpiglio overo de la corte*: *The Courtier* Revisited." *Modern Language Review* 90, no. 4 (October 1995): 897–918.

– *Women's Writing in Italy, 1450–1600*. Baltimore: Johns Hopkins University Press, 2008.

Croce, Benedetto. "Libri sulle corti." In *Poeti e scrittori del pieno e tardo Rinascimento*, 198–207. Bari: Laterza, 1958–70.

de Certeau, Michel. *The Practice of Everyday Life*. Berkeley: University of California Press, 1988.

Denarosi, Lucia. *L'accademia degli Innominati di Parma*. Florence: Società Editrice Fiorentina, 2003.

– "L'*Erminia* di Eugenio Visdomini." *Schifanoia* 24–5 (2003): 29–122.

De Robertis, Domenico. "Cammelli, Antonio, detto il Pistoia." In *Dizionario biografico degli italiani*, vol. 17. Rome: Istituto dell'Enciclopedia italiana, 1974. http://www.treccani.it/enciclopedia/cammelli-antonio-detto-il-pistoia_(Dizionario-Biografico)/. Accessed 14 November 2017.

Dickens, A.G. *The Courts of Europe: Politics, Patronage, and Royalty 1400–1800*. New York: Greenwich House, 1984.

Dionisotti, Carlo. "La letteratura italiana nell'età del concilio di Trento." In *Geografia e storia della letteratura italiana*, 183–204. Turin: Einaudi, 1967.

D'Onghia, Luca. "La 'Farza' è davvero di Pietro Aretino? Note linguistiche su un testo d'incerta attribuzione." *Scaffale aperto: Rivista di italianistica* 4 (2013): 115–37.

duBois, Page Ann. "'The Devil's Gateway': Women's Bodies and the Earthly Paradise." *Women's Studies* 7 (1980): 43–58.

Duindam, Jeroen. *Myths of Power: Norbert Elias and the Early Modern European Court*. Amsterdam: Amsterdam University Press, 1995.

Durante, Elio, and Anna Martellotti. *Cronistoria delle dame principalissime di Margherita Gonzaga d'Este*. Florence: SPES, 1989.

– *Giovinetta peregrina: La vera storia di Laura Peperara*. Florence: Olschki, 2010.

Elias, Norbert. *The Court Society*. Translated by Edmund Jephcott. Oxford: Blackwell; New York: Pantheon Books, 1973.

Empson, William. *Some Versions of Pastoral*. London: Chatto & Windus, 1935.

Ettin, Andrew. *Literature and the Pastoral*. New Haven, CT: Yale University Press, 1984.

Faini, Marco. *Cosmologia macaronica: L'universo malinconico del "Baldus" di Teofilo Folengo*. Manziana: Vecchiarelli, 2010.

– "Un'opera dimenticata di Pietro Aretino: Il *Lamento de uno cortigiano*." *Filologia e critica* 32 (2008): 75–93.

– "Un sole 'docto e saggio': Aspetti del mito di Guidubaldo da Montefeltro." *Humanistica* 3, no. 1 (2008): 35–43.

Faini, Marco, and Paola Ugolini, eds. *Companion to Pietro Aretino*. Leiden: Brill, forthcoming.

Fantoni, Marcello, ed. *The Court in Europe*. Rome: Bulzoni, 2012.

Farenga, Paola. "Correggio, Nicolò Postumo." In *Dizionario biografico degli italiani*, vol. 29. Rome: Istituto dell'Enciclopedia italiana, 1983. http://www.treccani.it/enciclopedia/niccolo-postumo-correggio_(Dizionario-Biografico)/. Accessed 14 November 2017.

Ferrero, Bruno. "Il *Ragionamento* di Annibale Guasco: Una lettera d'*institutio* all'ombra della *Civil conversazione*." In *Stefano Guazzo e Casale tra Cinque e Seicento*, edited by Daniela Ferrari, 357–74. Rome: Bulzoni, 1997.

Ferroni, Giulio. *Ariosto*. Rome: Salerno Editrice, 2008.

– *Le voci dell'istrione: Pietro Aretino e la dissoluzione del teatro*. Naples: Liguori, 1977.

Findlen, Paula. "Humanism, Politics and Pornography in Renaissance Italy." In *The Invention of Pornography, 1500–1800: Obscenity and the Origins of Modernity*, edited by Lynn Hunt, 49–108. New York: Zone Books, 1993.

Finotti, Fabio. *Retorica della diffrazione: Bembo, Aretino, Giulio Romano e Tasso; Letteratura e scena cortigiana*. Florence: Olschki, 2004.

Finucci, Valeria. *The Lady Vanishes: Subjectivity and Representation in Castiglione and Ariosto*. Stanford, CA: Stanford University Press, 1992.

– *The Manly Masquerade: Masculinity, Paternity, and Castration in the Italian Renaissance*. Durham, NC: Duke University Press, 2003.

Floriani, Piero. *Il modello ariostesco: La satira classicista nel Cinquecento*. Rome: Bulzoni, 1988.

"Sulle satire di Luigi Alamanni." *Giornale storico della letteratura italiana* 161 (1984): 30–59.

Foà, Simona. "Ducci, Lorenzo." In *Dizionario biografico degli italiani*, vol. 41. Rome: Istituto dell'Enciclopedia italiana, 1992. http://www.treccani.it/enciclopedia/lorenzo-ducci_(Dizionario-Biografico)/. Accessed 14 November 2017.

Fragnito, Gligliola. *In museo e in villa: Saggi sul Rinascimento perduto*.Venice: Arsenale, 1988.

– "La trattatistica cinque e seicentesca sulla corte cardinalizia." *Annali dell'istituto storico italo-germanico in Trento* 17 (1991): 135–85.

Freccero, Carla. "Politics and Aesthetics in Castiglione's *Il Cortegiano*: Book III and the Discourse on Women." In *Creative Imitation: New Essays on Renaissance Literature in Honor of Thomas M. Greene*, edited by Thomas M. Greene and David Quint, 259–79. Binghamton, NY: Medieval and Renaissance Texts and Studies, 1992.

Fubini, Riccardo. "Castiglionchio, Lapo da, detto il Giovane." In *Dizionario biografico degli italiani*, vol. 22. Rome: Istituto dell'Enciclopedia italiana, 1979. http://www.treccani.it/enciclopedia/castiglionchio-lapo-da-detto-il-giovane_(Dizionario-Biografico)/. Accessed 14 November 2017.

Gaeta, Franco. "Dal comune alla corte rinascimentale." In *Letteratura italiana*. Edited by Alberto Asor Rosa. Vol. 1, *Il letterato e le istituzioni*, 149–255. Turin: Einaudi, 1982.

Garullo, Maria Antonietta. "Notizie sulla vita e sull'opera di Lattanzio Benucci 'giureconsulto sanese.'" *Scaffale aperto: Rivista di italianistica* 5 (2014): 9–48.

Gasparini, Patrizia. "La satira del Cinquecento italiano." In *La satira in versi: Storia di un genere letterario europeo*, edited by Giancarlo Alfano, 119–42. Rome: Carocci, 2015.

Gaylard, Susan. "Castiglione versus Cicero." *Italian Culture* 27, no. 2 (September 2009): 81–98.

Gerbino, Giuseppe. *Music and the Myth of Arcadia in Renaissance Italy*. Cambridge: Cambridge University Press, 2009.

Giamatti, A. Bartlett. *The Earthly Paradise and the Renaissance Epic*. Princeton, NJ: Princeton University Press, 1966.

– "Proteus Unbound: Some Versions of the Sea God in the Renaissance." In *The Disciplines of Criticism*, edited by Peter Demetz, Thomas Greene, and Lowry Nelson Jr, 437–75. New Haven, CT: Yale University Press, 1968.

Gigante, Claudio. *Torquato Tasso*. Rome: Salerno Editrice, 2007.

Gigliucci, Roberto. "L'anti-festa del tinello: Un *topos* anti-rinascimentale." In *Patrimonium in festa: Cortei, tornei, artifici e feste alla fine del Medioevo (secoli 15–16)*, edited by Anna Modigliani, 149–82. Orte Viterbo: Centro di studi per il patrimonio di S. Pietro in Tuscia, 2000.

– "'Qualis coena tamen!' Il topos anticortigiano del tinello." *Lettere italiane* 50, no. 4 (1998): 587–605.

Godioli, Alberto. "La prima satira di Ariosto e la poesia delle corti padane." *Italianistica: Rivista di letteratura italiana* 39, no. 2 (May–August 2010): 115–27.

Goethals, Jessica. "Vanquished Bodies, Weaponized Words: Pietro Aretino's Conflicting Portraits of the Sexes and the Sack of Rome." *I Tatti Studies in the Italian Renaissance* 17, no. 1 (Spring 2014): 55–78.

Gordon, Bonnie. *Monteverdi's Unruly Women: The Power of Song in Early Modern Italy*. Cambridge: Cambridge University Press, 2004.

Gouwens, Kenneth. "Emasculation as Empowerment: Lessons of Beaver Lore for Two Italian Humanists." *European Review of History: Revue européenne d'histoire* 22, no. 4 (2015): 536–62.

– "Meanings of Masculinity in Paolo Giovio's Ischian Dialogues." *I Tatti Studies in the Italian Renaissance* 17, no. 1 (Spring 2014): 79–101.

Greenblatt, Stephen. *Renaissance Self-Fashioning: From More to Shakespeare*. Chicago: University of Chicago Press, 1980.

Greene, Thomas. "*Il Cortegiano* and the Choice of a Game." In *Castiglione: The Ideal and the Real in Renaissance Culture*, edited by R.W. Hanning and D. Rosand, 1–15. New Haven, CT: Yale University Press, 1983.

Guidi, José, Marie-Françoise Piéjus, Adelin-Charles Fiorato, eds. *Images de la femme dans la litterature italienne de la Renaissance: Préjugés misogynes et aspirations nouvelles; Castiglione Piccolomini Bandello*. Paris: Université de la Sourbonne Nouvelle, 1980.

Gundersheimer, Werner L. "Women, Learning and Power: Eleonora of Aragon and the Court of Ferrara." In *Beyond Their Sex: Learned Women of the European Past*, edited by Patricia H. Labalme, 43–65. New York: New York University Press, 1980.

Hanning, R.W., and D. Rosand, eds. *Castiglione: The Ideal and the Real in Renaissance Culture*. New Haven, CT: Yale University Press, 1983.

Held, Julius S. *Rembrandt's Aristotle*. Princeton, NJ: Princeton University Press, 1969.

Innamorati, Giuliano. "Aretino, Pietro." In *Dizionario biografico degli italiani*, vol. 4. Rome: Istituto dell'Enciclopedia italiana, 1962. http://www.treccani.it/enciclopedia/pietro-aretino_(Dizionario-Biografico)/. Accessed 14 November 2017.

– "Ex tugurio Blondi." *Paragone: Letteratura* 36 (1985): 10–37.

Jacobs, Fredrika. *Defining the Renaissance Virtuosa: Women Artists and the Language of Art History and Criticism*. Cambridge: Cambridge University Press, 1997.

Jaeger, C. Stephen. *The Origins of Courtliness: Civilizing Trends and the Formation of Courtly Ideals, 939–1210*. Philadelphia: University of Pennsylvania Press, 1985.

Javitch, Daniel. "The Philosopher of the Court: A French Satire Misunderstood." *Comparative Literature* 23, no. 2 (Spring 1971): 97–124.

– *Poetry and Courtliness in Renaissance England*. Princeton, NJ: Princeton University Press, 1978.

– "Rival Arts of Conduct in Elizabethan England: Guazzo's *Civile Conversation* and Castiglione's *Courtier*." *Yearbook of Italian Studies* (1971): 178–98.

Jones, Ann Rosalind. *The Currency of Eros: Women's Love Lyric in Europe, 1540–1620*. Bloomington and Indianapolis: Indiana University Press.

Jones, Joseph Ramon. *Antonio de Guevara*. Boston: Twayne, 1975.

Jones, William. *Satire in the Elizabethan Era*. New York and London: Routledge, 2017.

Jordan, Constance. *Renaissance Feminism*. Ithaca, NY, and London: Cornell University Press, 1999.

Jossa, Stefano. "The Lies of Poets: Literature as Fiction in the Italian Renaissance." In *Renaissance Studies in Honor of Joseph Connors*, edited by Machtelt Israëls and Louis A. Waldman, 565–74. Cambridge, MA: Harvard University Press, 2013.

Kelly-Gadol, Joan. "Did Women Have a Renaissance?" In *The Book of the Courtier*, edited by Daniel Javitch, 340–52. New York and London: W.W. Norton, 2002.

Kelso, Ruth. *Doctrine for the Lady of the Renaissance*. Urbana and Chicago: University of Illinois Press, 1956.

Kernan, Alvin. *The Cankered Muse: Satire of the English Renaissance*. New Haven, CT: Yale University Press, 1962.

King, Margaret. *Women of the Renaissance*. Chicago: University of Chicago Press, 1990.

Kolsky, Stephen. *Courts and Courtiers in Renaissance Northern Italy*. Aldershot, UK: Ashgate; Burlington, VT: Variorum, 2003.

La letteratura di villa e di villeggiatura: Atti del convegno di Parma 29 settembre–1 ottobre 2003. Rome: Salerno Editrice, 2004.

Langer, Ulrich. *Divine and Poetic Freedom in the Renaissance: Nominalist Theology and Literature in France and Italy*. Princeton, NJ: Princeton University Press, 1990.

La Penna, Antonio. "Note all'*Aminta* del Tasso." In *Omaggio a Gianfranco Folena*, edited by Pier Vincenzo Mengaldo et al., 2:1171–82. Padua: Programma, 1993.

Larivaille, Paul. *Pietro Aretino*. Rome: Salerno Editrice, 1997.

– *Pietro Aretino fra Rinascimento e Manierismo*. Rome: Bulzoni, 1980.

Lauterbach, Iris. "The Gardens of the Milanese 'Villeggiatura' in the Mid-Seventeenth Century." In *The Italian Gardens: Art, Design, and Culture*, edited by John Dixon Hunt, 127–59. Cambridge: Cambridge University Press, 1996.

Law, John E., and Evelyn S. Welch, eds. "The Courts of Northern Italy in the Fifteenth Century." *Renaissance Studies* 3, no. 4 (December 1989): 353–6.

Longhi, Silvia. *Lusus: Il capitolo burlesco nel Cinquecento*. Padua: Editrice Antenore, 1983.

Looney, Dennis. "Corte." In *Lessico critico dell'Orlando Furioso*, edited by Annalisa Izzo, 41–60. Rome: Carocci, 2017.

Loughrey, Bryan. *The Pastoral Mode: A Casebook*. London: Palgrave Macmillan, 1984.

Lucarelli, Massimo. "Il nuovo *Libro del cortegiano*: Una lettura del 'Malpiglio' di Tasso." *Studi tassiani* 52 (2004): 7–22.

Maclean, Ian. *The Renaissance Notion of Woman*. Cambridge: Cambridge University Press, 1980.

MacNeil, Anne. *Music and Women of the Commedia dell'Arte*. Oxford: Oxford University Press, 2003.

Manca, Joseph. "Isabella's Mother: Aspects of the Art Patronage of Eleonora d'Aragona, Duchess of Ferrara." *Aurora* 4 (2003): 79–94.

Marsh, David. *Lucian and the Latins: Humor and Humanism in the Renaissance*. Ann Arbor: University of Michigan Press, 1998.

Marti, Mario. "Beccari, Antonio." In *Dizionario biografico degli italiani*, vol. 7. Rome: Istituto dell'Enciclopedia italiana, 1970. http://www.treccani.it/enciclopedia/antonio-beccari_(Dizionario-Biografico)/. Accessed 14 November 2017.

Martin, John Jeffries. "Inventing Sincerity, Refashioning Prudence: The Discovery of the Individual in Renaissance Europe." *The American Historical Review* 102, no. 5 (December 1997): 1309–42.

– "The Myth of Renaissance Individualism." In *A Companion to the Worlds of the Renaissance*, edited by Guido Ruggiero, 208–24. Oxford: Blackwell Publishing, 2002.

– *Myths of Renaissance Individualism*. Basingstoke, UK: Palgrave Macmillan, 2004.

Martines, Lauro. *Power and Imagination: City-States in Renaissance Italy*. Baltimore: Johns Hopkins University Press, 1979.

– *Strong Words: Writing and Social Strain in the Italian Renaissance*. Baltimore: Johns Hopkins University Press, 2001.

Masi, Giorgio. "The Nightingale in a Cage: Ariosto and the Este Court." In *Ariosto Today: Contemporary Perspectives*, edited by Donald Beecher, Massimo Ciavolella, and Roberto Fedi, 71–92. Toronto: University of Toronto Press, 2003.

McCabe, Richard A. *"Ungainefull Arte": Poetry, Patronage, and Print in the Early Modern Era*. Oxford: Oxford University Press, 2016.

McIver, Katherine A. "Matrons as Patrons: Power and Influence in the Courts of Northern Italy in the Renaissance." *Artibus et historiae* 22, no. 43 (2001): 75–98.

Milligan, Gerry. "Behaving Like a Man: Perfomed Masculinities in *Gl'ingannati*." *Forum Italicum* 41, no. 1 (2007): 23–42.

– "Masculinity and Machiavelli: How to Avoid Effeminacy, Perform Manliness, and Be Wary of the Author." In *Seeking Real Truths: Multidisciplinary Perspectives on Machiavelli*, edited by Patricia Vilches and Gerald Seaman, 149–72. Leiden: Brill, 2007.

– "The Politics of Effeminacy in *Il Cortegiano*." *Italica* 83, nos. 3–4 (Fall–Winter 2006): 345–66.

Molinari, Carla. "Per il *Pastor Fido* di Battista Guarini." *Studi di filologia italiana* 43 (1985): 161–238.

Motta, Uberto. *Castiglione e il mito di Urbino: Studi sulla elaborazione del Cortegiano*. Milan: Vita e pensiero, 2003.

Moulton, Ian Frederick. "Castiglione: Love, Power, and Masculinity." In *The Poetics of Masculinity in Early Modern Italy and Spain*, edited by Gerry Milligan and Jane Tylus, 119–42. Toronto: Centre for Reformation and Renaissance Studies, 2010.

Muchembled, Robert. "Manners, Courts, and Civility." In *A Companion to the Worlds of the Renaissance*, edited by Guido Ruggiero, 156–72. Oxford: Blackwell, 2002.

Muñoz Simonds, Peggy. "Anti-Courtier Imagery in *Cymbeline*." In *Myth, Emblem, and Music in Shakespeare's Cymbeline: An Iconographic Reconstruction*, 170–97. Newark: University of Delaware Press, 1992.

Murphy, Caroline. *Lavinia Fontana: A Painter and Her Patrons in Sixteenth-Century Bologna*. New Haven, CT: Yale University Press, 2003.

Najemy, John M. "Arms and Letters: The Crisis of Courtly Culture in the Wars of Italy." In *Italy and the European Powers: The Impact of War, 1500–1530*, edited by Christine Shaw, 207–38. Leiden and Boston: Brill, 2006.

Newcomb, Anthony. *The Madrigal at Ferrara, 1579–1597*. Vol. 1. Princeton, NJ: Princeton University Press, 1980.

Nussdorfer, Laurie. "Masculine Hierarchies in Roman Ecclesiastical Households." *European Review of History: Revue européenne d'histoire* 22, no. 4 (2015): 620–42.

Osborn, Peggy. "The 'Discourse': Context and Historical Background." In *Discourse to Lady Lavinia His Daughter*, by Annibal Guasco, 1–38. Chicago: University of Chicago Press, 2003.

Ossola, Carlo, and Adriano Prosperi, eds. *La corte e il "Cortegiano."* 2 vols. Rome: Bulzoni, 1980.

Paternoster, Annick. "'Le Sei Giornate' di Pietro Aretino: L'urbanitas parodiata." In *Traités de savoir-vivre italiens*, edited by Alain Montandon, 225–36. Clermont-Ferrand: Association des publications de la Faculté des Lettres et des Sciences Humaines de Clermont-Ferrand, 1993.

Pelosi, Olimpia. *Satira barocca e teorie sul genere dal Cinque all'Ottocento*. Naples: Federico and Ardia, 1991.

Petrucci, Franca. "Carafa, Diomede." In *Dizionario biografico degli italiani*, vol. 19. Rome: Istituto dell'Enciclopedia italiana, 1976. http://www.treccani.it/enciclopedia/diomede-carafa_(Dizionario-Biografico)/. Accessed 14 November 2017.

Pevere, Fulvio. "Introduzione." In *Ragionamento delle corti*, by Pietro Aretino, 5–39. Milan: Mursia, 1995.

– "Vita è il non andare in corte: Il *Ragionamento delle corti* di Pietro Aretino." *Critica letteraria* 20 (1992): 237–60.

Pieri, Marzia. "La pastorale." In *Manuale di letteratura italiana: Storia per generi e problemi*. Edited by Franco Brioschi and Costanzo Di Girolamo. Vol. 2, *Dal Cinquecento alla metà del Settecento*, 271–92. Turin: Bollati Boringhieri, 1993.

Pieri, Marzio. "Colli, Vincenzo detto il Calmeta." In *Dizionario biografico degli italiani*, vol. 27. Rome: Istituto dell'Enciclopedia italiana, 1982. http://www.treccani.it/enciclopedia/colli-vincenzo-detto-il-calmeta_(Dizionario-Biografico)/. Accessed 14 November 2017.

Pitkin, Hannah. *Fortune Is a Woman: Gender and Politics in the Thought of Niccolò Machiavelli*. Chicago: University of Chicago Press, 1984.

Poesia italiana del Quattrocento. Edited by Carlo Oliva. Milan: Garzanti, 1978.

Poggioli, Renato. *The Oaten Flute*. Cambridge, MA: Harvard University Press, 1975.

Pozzi, Mario. *Trattatisti del Cinquecento. Tomo I*. Milan and Naples: Ricciardi, 1978.

Predari, Francesco. *Raccolta dei poeti satirici italiani: Premessovi un discorso intorno alla satira ed all'ufficio morale di essa di Giulio Carcano*. Vol. 2. Turin: Dalla Società Editrice della Biblioteca dei Comuni Italiani, 1835.

Procaccioli, Paolo. "Tu es Pasquillus in aeterno: Aretino non romano e la maschera di Pasquino." In *Ex marmore: Pasquini, pasquinisti, pasquinate nell'europa moderna; Atti del colloquio internazionale, Lecce-Otranto, 17–19 novembre 2005*, edited by Chrysa Damianaki, Paolo Procaccioli, and Angelo Romano, 67–96. Manziana: Vecchiarelli, 2006.

Quaintance, Courtney. *Textual Masculinity and the Exchange of Women in Renaissance Florence*. Toronto: University of Toronto Press, 2015.

Quattrucci, Mario. "Argenti, Agostino." In *Dizionario biografico degli italiani*, vol. 4. Rome: Istituto dell'Enciclopedia italiana, 1962. http://www.treccani.it/enciclopedia/agostino-argenti_(Dizionario-Biografico)/. Accessed 14 November 2017.

Quint, David. "Courtier, Prince, Lady: The Design of the *Book of the Courtier*." *Italian Quarterly* 37, nos. 143–6 (2000): 185–95.

Quintero, Ruben, ed. *A Companion to Satire: Ancient and Modern*. Oxford: Blackwell Publishing, 2007.

Quondam, Amedeo. "Addio alla corte: Il *Menosprecio* di Antonio de Guevara." In *Studi sul manierismo letterario, per Riccardo Scrivano*, edited by Nicola Longo, 21–67. Rome: Bulzoni, 2000.

– *La conversazione: Un modello italiano*. Rome: Donzelli, 2007.

– "La forma del vivere: Schede per l'analisi del discorso cortigiano." In *La corte e il Cortegiano*, vol. 2, edited by Adriano Prosperi, 15–68. Rome: Bulzoni, 1980.

– "La scena della menzogna: Corte e cortigiano nel 'Ragionamento' di Pietro Aretino." *Psicon* 3, nos. 8–9 (1976): 4–24.

– "Nel giardino del Marcolini: Un editore veneziano tra Aretino e Doni." *Giornale storico della letteratura italiana* 157, no. 497 (1980): 75–116.

– *"Questo povero Cortegiano": Castiglione, il libro, la storia*. Rome: Bulzoni, 2000.

Ray, Meredith K. "Lucio Paolo Rosello's Dialogue on 'La vita de' Cortigiani': A Case of Renaissance Plagiarism." In *Sondaggi sulla riscrittura del Cinquecento*, edited by Paolo Cherchi, 96–119. Ravenna: Longo, 1998.

– *Writing Gender in Women's Letter Collections of the Italian Renaissance*. Toronto: University of Toronto Press, 2009.

Rebhorn, Wayne. *Courtly Performances: Masking and Festivity in Castiglione's "Book of the Courtier."* Detroit: Wayne State University Press, 1978.

Refini, Eugenio. "Le 'gioconde favole' e il 'numeroso concento': Alessandro Piccolomini interprete e imitatore di Orazio nei *Cento Sonetti* (1549)." *Italique* 10 (2007): 17–45.

Reiss, Sheryl E., and David G. Wilkins, eds. *Beyond Isabella: Secular Women Patrons of Art in Renaissance Italy*. Kirksville, MO: Truman State University Press, 2001.

Richards, Jennifer. "'A Wanton Trade of Living?' Rhetoric, Effeminacy, and the Early Modern Courtier." *Criticism: A Quarterly for Literature and the Arts* 42, no. 2 (Spring 2000): 185–206.

Riga, Pietro Giulio. "La satira italiana del Seicento." In *La satira in versi: Storia di un genere letterario europeo*, edited by Giancarlo Alfano, 163–82. Rome: Carocci, 2015.

Robin, Diana. *Publishing Women: Salons, the Presses, and the Counter-Reformation in Sixteenth-Century Italy*. Chicago: University of Chicago Press, 2007.

Rocke, Michael. *Forbidden Friendships*. Oxford: Oxford University Press, 1996.

Romano, Angelo. "Appunti sui personaggi della *Cortigiana* (1525) dell'Aretino." In *Scenery, Set and Staging in the Italian Renaissance*, edited by Christopher Cairns, 121–36. Lewiston, NY: Edwin Mellen Press, 1996.

– "Michelangelo Biondo poligrafo e stampatore." In *Officine del nuovo: Sodalizi fra letterati, artisti ed editori nella cultura italiana fra Riforma e Controriforma; Atti del simposio internazionale, Utrecht, 8–10 novembre 2007*, edited by Harald Hendrix and Paolo Procaccioli, 217–41. Manziana: Vecchiarelli, 2008.

Romei, Danilo. "Aretino e Pasquino." Banca dati "Nuovo Rinascimento," 28 July 2009. http://www.nuovorinascimento.org/n-rinasc/saggi/pdf/romei/aretpasq.pdf. Accessed 14 November 2017.

– "Ironia e irrisione." In *Storia letteraria d'Italia*. Vol. 7, *Il Cinquecento*, edited by Giovanni Da Pozzo, 1658–9. Padua: Piccin Nuova Libreria, 2007.

– "Poesia satirica e giocosa nell'ultimo trentennio del Cinquecento." Banca dati "Nuovo Rinascimento," 21 August 1988. http://www.nuovorinascimento.org/n-rinasc/saggi/pdf/romei/cinquec.pdf. Accessed 1 April 2015.

– "Ricezione della poesia bernesca nel Cinquecento." In *Il poeta e il suo pubblico: Lettura e commento dei testi lirici nel Cinquecento*, edited by Massimo

Danzi and Roberto Leporatti, 273–91. Travaux d'Humanisme et Renaissance 482. Geneva: Librairie Droz, 2012.
Rosa, Mario. "La Chiesa e gli stati regionali nell'età dell'assolutismo." In *Letteratura italiana*. Edited by Alberto Asor Rosa. Vol. 1, *Il letterato e le istituzioni*, 257–389. Turin: Einaudi, 1982.
Rosenthal, Margaret. *The Honest Courtesan: Veronica Franco, Citizen and Writer in Sixteenth-Century Venice*. Chicago: University of Chicago Press, 1992.
Ross, Sarah G. *The Birth of Feminism: Woman as Intellect in Renaissance Italy and England*. Cambridge, MA: Harvard University Press, 2009.
Rossi, Antonio. *Serafino Aquilano e la poesia cortigiana*. Brescia: Morcelliana, 1980.
Ruggiero, Guido. *Machiavelli in Love: Sex, Self, and Society in the Italian Renaissance*. Baltimore: Johns Hopkins University Press, 2007.
Saccaro Battisti, Giuseppa. "La donna, le donne nel *Cortegiano*." In *La corte e il "Cortegiano,"* vol. 1, edited by Carlo Ossola, 219–49. Rome: Bulzoni, 1980.
Saccone, Eduardo. "Grazia, Sprezzatura, Affettazione in *The Courtier*." In *Castiglione: The Ideal and the Real in Renaissance Culture*, edited by R.W. Hanning and D. Rosand, 45–67. New Haven, CT: Yale University Press, 1983.
Sampson, Lisa. "The Mantuan Performance of Guarini's *Pastor Fido* and Representations of Courtly Identity." *Modern Language Review* 98, no. 1 (January 2003): 65–83.
– *Pastoral Drama in Early Modern Italy*. Oxford: Legenda, 2006.
Santoro, Mario. *Fortuna, ragione e prudenza nella civiltà letteraria del Cinqucento*. Naples: Liguori, 1966.
Sapegno, Natalino. *Poeti minori del Trecento*. Milan: Ricciardi, 1952.
Sarti, Raffaella. *La pietra racconta: Un palazzo da leggere*. Urbino: Stibu, 2017.
Scaglione, Aldo. *Knights at Court: Courtliness, Chivalry and Courtesy from Ottonian Germany to the Italian Renaissance*. Berkeley: University of California Press, 1991.
Scarpati, Claudio. "Osservazioni sul terzo libro del *Cortegiano*." *Aevum* 3 (1992): 519–37.
Schiffhorst, Gerald J. *The Triumph of Patience: Medieval and Renaissance Studies*. Orlando: University Presses of Florida, 1978.
Schreiner, Klaus, and Ernst Wenzel, eds., *Hofkritik im Licht humanistischer Lebens- und Bildungsideale: Enea Silvio Piccolomini, De miseriis curialium (1444), Über das Elend der Hofleute, und Vlrichi de Hvtten, Equitis Germani Aula dialogus (1518), Aula, eines deutschen Ritters Dialog über den Hof*. Leiden: Brill, 2012.
Selmi, Elizabetta. "Alberto Lollio e Agostino Gallo." In *Agostino Gallo nella cultura del Cinquecento: Atti del convegno, Brescia, 23–24 ottobre 1987*, edited by Maurizio Pegrari, 271–314. Brescia: Edizioni del Moretto, 1988.

– *Classici e moderni nell'officina del "Pastor Fido."* Alessandria: Edizioni dell'Orso, 2002.
– "Guarini, Battista." In *Dizionario biografico degli italiani*, vol. 60. Rome: Istituto dell'Enciclopedia italiana, 2003. http://www.treccani.it/enciclopedia/battista-guarini_(Dizionario-Biografico)/. Accessed 14 November 2017.
Shemek, Deanna. "Aretino's *Marescalco*: Marriage Woes and the Duke of Mantua." *Renaissance Studies* 16, no. 3 (2002): 366–80.
– "In Continuous Expectation: Isabella d'Este's Epistolary Desire." In *Phaethon's Children: The Este Court and Its Culture in Early Modern Ferrara*, edited by Deanna Shemek and Dennis Looney, 269–300. Tempe: Arizona Center for Medieval and Renaissance Studies, 2005.
– "'Mi mostrano a dito tutti quanti': Disease, Deixis, and Disfiguration in the *Lamento di una cortigiana ferrarese*." In *Medusa's Gaze: Essays on Gender, Literature, and Aesthetics in the Italian Renaissance in Honor of Robert J. Rodini*, edited by Paul A. Ferrara, Eugenio Giusti, and Jane Tylus, 49–64. Italiana 11. Lafayette, IN: Bodighera, 2004.
Simonetta, Marcello. *Rinascimento segreto: Il mondo del segretario da Petrarca a Machiavelli*. Milan: Franco Angeli, 2004.
Skinner, Quentin. *The Foundations of Modern Political Thought*. Vol. 1, *The Renaissance*. Cambridge: Cambridge University Press, 1978.
Smith, Pauline. *The Anti-Courtier Trend in Sixteenth-Century French Literature*. Geneva: Droz, 1966.
Snyder, Jon R. *Dissimulation and the Culture of Secrecy in Early Modern Europe*. Berkeley: University of California Press, 2009.
Sozzi, B. T. *Studi sul Tasso*. Pisa: Nistri-Lischi, 1954.
Stabile, Giorgio. "Biondo, Michelangelo." In *Dizionario biografico degli italiani*, vol. 10. Rome: Istituto dell'Enciclopedia italiana, 1968. http://www.treccani.it/enciclopedia/michelangelo-biondo_(Dizionario-Biografico)/. Accessed 14 November 2017.
Stella Galbiati, Giuseppina. "Per una teoria della satira fra Quattro e Cinquecento." *Italianistica* 16, no. 1 (1987): 9–37.
– *Un poeta satirico del Cinquecento: Giovanni Agostino Caccia*. Pisa: Giardini, 1991.
Storey, Tessa. *Carnal Commerce in Counter-Reformation Rome*. Cambridge: Cambridge University Press, 2008.
Stras, Laurie. *Women and Music in Sixteenth-Century Ferrara*. Cambridge: Cambridge University Press, 2018.
Tomas, Natalie R. *The Medici Women: Gender and Power in Renaissance Florence*. Aldershot, UK: Ashgate, 2003.
Tomasi, Franco. "Appunti sulla tradizione delle *satire* di Luigi Alamanni." *Italique* 4 (2001): 31–59.

Ugolini, Paola. "The Satirist's Purgatory: 'Il Purgatorio delle Cortigiane' and the Writer's Discontent." *Italian Studies* 64, no. 1 (Spring 2009): 1–19.

– "Self-Portraits of a Truthful Liar: Satire, Truth-Telling, and Courtliness in Ludovico Ariosto's *Satire* and *Orlando Furioso*." In "Comedy, Satire, Paradox, and the Plurality of Discourses in Cinquecento Italy," edited by Stefano Jossa and Ambra Moroncini. Special issue, *Renaissance and Reformation/ Renaissance et Réforme* 40, no. 1 (Winter/Hiver 2017): 143–60.

Uhlig, Claus. *Hofkritik im England des Mittelalters und der Renaissance: Studien zu einem Gemeinplatz der Europäischen Moralistik*. Berlin, New York: de Gruyter, 1973.

Vagnoni, Debora. "Il plagio del *De patientia* di Celio Calcagnini nel secondo dei *Due dialoghi* di Lucio Paolo Rosello." In *Furto e plagio nella letteratura del classicismo*, edited by Roberto Gigliucci, 347–55. Rome: Bulzoni, 1998.

Vasoli, Cesare. *La cultura delle corti*. Bologna: Cappelli, 1980.

Vecchi Galli, Paola. "Corte medievale." In *Luoghi della letteratura italiana*, edited by Gian Mario Anselmi, 155–70. Milan: Mondadori, 2003.

Vela, Claudia. "Il 'Tirsi' di Baldassar Castiglione e Cesare Gonzaga." In *La poesia pastorale nel Rinascimento*, edited by Stefano Carrai, 245–92. Padua: Antenore, 1998.

Vigilante, Magda. "Ciminelli, Serafino." In *Dizionario biografico degli italiani*, vol. 25. Rome: Istituto dell'Enciclopedia italiana, 1981. http://www.treccani.it/enciclopedia/serafino-ciminelli_(Dizionario-Biografico)/. Accessed 14 November 2017.

Villa, Claudia. "Ludovico Ariosto e la 'famiglia d'allegrezza piena,' con una riflessione sul progetto delle *Satire*." *Giornale storico della letteratura italiana* 185, no. 4 (2008): 510–35.

von Martels, Z.R.W.M., and Arie Johan Vanderjagt, eds. *Pius II, 'el più expeditivo pontefice': Selected Studies on Aeneas Silvius Piccolomini (1405–1464)*. Leiden and Boston: Brill, 2003.

Vosters, Simon A. *Antonio de Guevara y Europa*. Salamanca: Ediciones Universidad Salamanca, 2009.

Waddington, Raymond B. *Aretino's Satyr: Sexuality, Satire, and Self-Projection in Sixteenth-Century Literature and Art*. Toronto: University of Toronto Press, 2004.

– *Pietro Aretino: Subverting the System in Renaissance Italy*. Aldershot, UK; Burlington, VT: Ashgate, 2013.

Webb, Jennifer D. "All Is Not Fun and Games: Conversation, Play, and Surveillance at the Montefeltro Court in Urbino." *Renaissance Studies* 26, no. 3 (2011): 417–40.

Weiss, Robert. "Alamanni, Luigi." In *Dizionario biografico degli italiani*, vol. 1. Rome: Istituto dell'Enciclopedia italiana, 1960. http://www.treccani.it/enciclopedia/luigi-alamanni_(Dizionario-Biografico)/. Accessed 14 November 2017.

Welch, Evelyn. "Between Milan and Naples: Ippolita Maria Sforza, Duchess of Calabria." In *The French Descent into Renaissance Italy, 1494–95: Antecedents and Effects*, edited by David Abulafia, 123–36. Aldershot, UK: Ashgate, 1995.

– "Women as Patrons and Clients in the Courts of Quattrocento Italy." In *A History of Women's Writing in Italy*, edited by Letizia Panizza and Sharon Woods, 18–34. Cambridge: Cambridge University Press, 2000.

Wistreich, Richard. *Warrior, Courtier, Singer: Giulio Cesare Brancaccio and the Performance of Identity in the Late Sixteenth Century*. Aldershot, UK: Ashgate, 2007.

Wofford, Susanne. "The Nymph in the Woods Says No: Tasso's Silvia, Spenser's Belpheobe, Cervantes's Marcela, and the Influence of Italian Pastoral Drama on Epic." Paper given at the Renaissance Society of America conference, 2014.

Wolfe, Jessica. *Humanism, Machinery, and Renaissance Literature*. Cambridge: Cambridge University Press, 2004.

Woodhouse, John R. "Dal *De curialium miseriis* al *Libro del cortegiano* e oltre." In *Il sogno di Pio II e il viaggio da Roma a Mantova: Atti del convegno internazionale, Mantova, 13–15 aprile 2002*, edited by A. Calzona, F.P. Fiore, A. Tenenti, C. Vasoli, 423–41. Florence: Olschki, 2003.

Zancan, Marina. "La donna e il cerchio nel *Cortegiano* di B. Castiglione: Le funzioni del femminile nell'immagine di corte." In *Nel cerchio della luna: Figure di donna in alcuni testi del XVI secolo*, edited by Marina Zancan, 13–56. Turin: Marsilio, 1983.

Zatti, Sergio. "Natura e potere nell'*Aminta*." In *Torquato Tasso quattrocento anni dopo: Atti del convegno di Rende, 24–25 maggio 1996*, edited by Antonio Daniele and Walter Lupi, 11–24. Soveria Mannelli: Rubbettino, 1997.

Zonta, Giuseppe. *Trattati del Cinquecento sulla donna*. Bari: Latserza, 1913.

Index

Page numbers in italics refer to figures.

Accademia dei Pastori d'Agogna, 154
Achilles, 174
Ackerman, James, 148, 149; on the myth of the villa, 148, 149
Adrian VI, Pope, 128, 129; death of, 129; election of, 128
adulterer, 78
adulteress, 79
adultery, 7
advice, 10, 13, 16, 27, 34, 35, 36, 37, 43, 44, 62, 63, 87, 88, 90, 113, 128, 131, 161, 163, 176. *See also* conduct manuals
Aeneid, 59
affabilitas, 41
agricultural literature, 154–5, 239n37; and anti-courtliness, 155; in Northern Italy, 154; similarities to anti-court satires, 155
Alamanni, Luigi, 113–14, 152–4; contemporary criticism of, 114; forced to flee to France, 153
Alciato, Andrea: *In aulicos*, 7, 8, 45–7, 48
Alcibiades, 123
Alcina (*Orlando Furioso*), 59, 61–2, 65, 121
Alessandria, 69
Alessandro (*Satire*, Ariosto), 96, 98
Alexander the Great, 17, 30, 31
Alfonso II, Duke. *See* Este, Alfonso II d', Duke
Alfonso d'Aragona, King, 15; court of, 15
Allegory of the New Testament (Vermeer), 24–5
Allegri, Alessandro, 116, 118; *Rime piacevoli*, 116; on courtly malaise, 116
Alpers, Paul, 177
"Al signor Giacomo Maria Stampa" (Caccia), 155–6
"Al Signor Gian Filippo Cazza fiscale di Sua Maestà" (Caccia), 155, 156
"Al Torniello governator di Novara" (Caccia), 156
Aman, 106
Amarilli (Castelletti), 170
Amarilli (*Pastor Fido*), 171, 172
ambition, 3, 5, 6, 11, 12, 17, 34, 36, 42, 45, 68, 84, 85, 87, 88–9, 90, 91, 127, 130, 135, 137, 139, 150, 152, 153, 154, 155, 159, 160, 170, 171, 172, 174, 175, 177
Aminta (*Aminta*), 160, 161, 163, 164, 166, 167, 246n95
Aminta (Tasso), 159–69, 171, 172, 173, 174, 175; anti-court topoi in, 162–3; "counterpoint technique" in, 164;

different editions of, 161; echo of Argenti's *Lo sfortunato*, 159; first edition of, 171; influence of on pastoral drama in Italy, 169; on honour as constraint, 164–5, 169; picture of the court in as a *disputatio in utramque partem*, 164; relationship between praise of the court and anti-courtliness in, 160–1, 163, 166, 169. *See also names of individual characters*
anatomy, female, 75
Andini, Mario degli, 93, 114; on the literary and moral value of satire, 93; as possible pen name for Lodovico Paterno, 217n34; *Satire di cinque poeti illustri*, 93, 112
Andreini, Francesco, 182
Andreini, Isabella, 251n3
androgyne, myth of, 79–80
Angitia (*Angitia cortigiana*), 79, 80, 214n125
Angitia cortigiana (Biondo), 79–80, 81
Anglo, Sydney, 13, 14
animal metaphors, 7, 22, 31, 70, 97, 100, 101, 104, 105, 150, 151, 162, 174, 175
Annibale (*Ragionamento a Donna Lavinia*), 69
Annibale Magnocavalli (*Civile conversation*). *See* Magnocavalli, Annibale
anti-court critique. *See* anti-courtliness
anti-court discourse. *See* anti-courtliness
anti-courtesan critique, 76–9, 82–3; courtiers' use of to distinguish themselves from courtesans, 76, 215n137; mirroring anti-courtier critique, 80
anti-courtier critique: in the Middle Ages, 87; mirroring anti-courtesan critique, 80
anti-courtliness, 3–12, 73, 79, 87, 125–7; 2017 exhibition in Urbino revealing inscriptions of, 185–6; and analogies between the language of love and the language of patronage, 63; and the *Book of the Courtier*, 14, 19–20, 23, 24–32; connection to anti-feminism, 52, 53, 57, 67, 71; genres of, 6, 7, *8*, 88, 94, 125, 137, 163; as language for expressing discontent, 108–9, 125; legacy of, 10, 15–16, 181–2; media of, 6; and retaliation, 108; social function, 125–7; topoi of, 5, 6, 7, 14, 20, 38, 41, 42, 94, 97, 101, 102, 105, 106, 112, 138, 139, 142, 151, 162–3, 168, 169, 170, 172, 175, 181
anti-courtly sentiment. *See* anti-courtliness
anti-court writings. *See* anti-courtliness
anti-feminism, 51, 59, 76, 79; connection to anti-courtliness, 52, 53, 57, 67, 71
Apollo. *See* Phoebus Apollo
Aquilano, Serafino, 101, 103, 104, 105, 106; "Dimmi Menandro mio, deh dimmi sozio," 104; "Invidia corte, d'ogni ben nimica," 101; on the court as a game of *quadrelo*, 104, 105
Arcadia, 18, 146–7, 157, 158, 159, 160, 171–2; court of Urbino as, 18; and death, 241n60. *See also* pastoral setting; villa
Arcadia (Sannazzaro), 157
Ardizio, Curzio: letter from Torquato Tasso, 244–5n86
Aretino, Pietro, 11, 46, 54, 55, 56, 76–9, 81, 103, 112, 127–38, 140–3, 147, 155, 163–4, 176, 182; as *acerrimus virtutum ac vitiorum*

demonstrator, 129; ambition of, 127, 128, 130, 135, 141; as an anti-prince, 142, 143–4; in Arezzo, 128; assassination attempt on, 129, 231n186; in Bologna, 128; civic anti-courtliness of, 147; and connection to printing industry, 136, 140–1; as counsellor, 128, 129; golden chain received from King Francis I, 46; hope to join the court of King Francis I, 135; included on index of prohibited books, 142; influence on Cesare Caporali, 142, 143; as judge of the powerful, 141; in Florence, 128; letter to Francesco Coccio, 137, 176; *malalingua* of, 46; in Mantua, 128, 129, 133–4; medal portrait of, 142; as model of an independent intellectual, 136, 141, 142, 144, 155; and Pasquino, 127, 128, 136; Petrarchan poems by, 127; play on Clement VII's name, 133, 233n205; as *poligrafo*, 136; as political interlocutor, 141; possible authorship of the *Lamento di una cortigiana ferrarese*, 231n191; praise of Venice, 129, 134–5, 137, 140, 143, 147, 251n10; as a prince with no land, 142, 155; prodigality of, 141; in Reggio Emilia, 129; rhyme *Corte/sorte*, 130; in Rome, 127, 128, 129, 130; sacred works of, 140; as satyr, 129–30, 141; as scourge of princes, 46, 127, 141, 144; as "segretario del mondo," 142; self-fashioning of, 129–30, 133, 140, 141, 142, 143–4; success of, 136; in Venice, 79, 127, 128, 129, 134–7, 141, 142, 234n228. *See also specific titles and names of individual characters*

Aretusa (Lollio), 158; performed at Schifanoia, 240n47

Arezzo, 127, 128, 136

Argenti, Agostino: *Lo sfortunato*, 158–9

Argos, symbolism of in the *Pastor Fido*, 172, 174

Ariosto, Ludovico, 11, 59, 73, 95–101, 106, 113, 114, 117, 119, 126–7, 163, 171, 174, 175; defining Pietro Aretino the "scourge of princes," 236n249; as satirical persona, 96–100, 126; sources for, 220n73. *See also specific titles and names of individual characters*

Aristeo (*Angitia cortigiana*), 79, 80, 214n125

Aristotle, 247n102: as courtier-counsellor to Alexander the Great, 17, 30, 32; theories on men, 56; theories on women, 51, 52

Armida (*Gerusalemme Liberata*), 59, 61, 62, 64, 65, 74, 124, 167

arrogance, 7, 27, 72, 151, 155

Ars aulica (Ducci), 36, 42, 43–4, 45; popularity of in England, 36

Arte aulica. See *Ars aulica* (Ducci)

Arthur, King, 60, 61, 113, 208n36

Ascoli, Albert Russell, 237n3

Astolfo (*Orlando Furioso*), 62

astuzia, 220–1n74

Athens, 123

Atlante (*Orlando Furioso*), 62

Augustus, 220n71

Aurora, 162

authenticity, 122, 147

autonomy, 33–4, 118, 119–20, 126, 170, 251n10. *See also* freedom; free will; mastery over oneself

Aviso de favoriti (Guevara), 6

Aviso de privados y doctrina de cortesanos (Guevara), 151–2

Avvisi di Parnaso (Caporali), 143, 205–6n24; Bernesque style of, 143;

marriage of *Madonna Corte* with *Vituperio*, 143
avvisi di Parnaso as genre, 236–7n261
Avviso de' favoriti e dottrina de' cortigiani, con la commendazione della villa (Guevara), 151–2

Babel, the court as, 131
Bagno (*Satire*, Ariosto), 96
Baldus (Folengo), 51, 59–61. *See also names of individual characters*
Bandello, Matteo: *Novelle*, 51, 66. *See also names of individual characters*
Barcelona, 67
Barros, Alonso de, 105; *Filosofia cortesana*, 105
Battista (*Discorsi*), 37
Batto (*Aminta*), 244n82
"Beatus ille" (Horace), 153
Beccari, Agostino, *Il sacrificio*, 157–8
Beccari da Ferrara, Antonio, 102, 103, 106; "Io ho provato che cosa è amore," 102
beffa, 133
Belisarius, 106
Belloni, Francesco, 36
Bembo, Pietro (*Book of the Courtier*), 19, 31
Benci, Francesco, 229n144
Benci, Trifon, 117, 229n144
Bendidio, Lucrezia, 244n82
Bentivoglio, Ercole, 155
Benucci, Lattanzio, 111–12; pun *Corte/Morte*, 112
Berger, Harry, Jr, 14, 24–5
Berni, Francesco, 111, 120, 143, 151; animal metaphor in, 151; "Sua vita in villa e sua vita in corte," 151
betrayal, 101, 105, 108, 133, 136, 208n36. *See also* treachery
Betussi, Giuseppe, 142; *Raverta*, 142
Biagioli, Mario, 9
Biandrate di San Giorgio, Cardinal Giovan Francesco, 37
Biondo, Michelangelo, 79, 214n125; *Angitia cortigiana: De natura del cortigiano*, 79–80, 81
Blanchard, W. Scott, 92; on the public nature of satire, 92
Blois, Peter of, 87–8
Blount, Edward, 36
Boccaccio, 105, 148; *Decameron*, 105, 148
Boccalini, Traiano, 236–7n261
body metaphors, 57, 75, 113, 116–17, 165
body of the courtier, 7, *8*, 53–4, 56, 60, 81, 106, 113, 117–18. *See also* manicured appearance of the courtier
Bologna, 128
Bolognetti, Francesco, 152
Boni, Giovanni, 156; *Satira in lode della villa*, 156
Book of the Courtier, The (Castiglione), 3, 7–8, 13–14, 15, 16–41, 43, 45, 50–6, 60–1, 64–5, 66, 68, 69, 70, 72–3, 78, 79, 94, 98, 111, 116, 124, 128, 132, 140, 151, 158; absence of urgency in compared to other texts, 37; and anti-courtliness, 14, 19–20, 23, 24–32; compared to Aretino's *Sei giornate*, 78–9; on the courtier's role in leading the prince to virtue, 26–31; on the court lady, 50–1, 64, 65, 66; epigones of and their differences, 35–45; "feminine enclosed space" in, 50; first book, 53, 72–3; first book compared to second book of, 22–3; fourth book, 25–32, 36, 51, 52, 69, 70, 94; games in, 19, 53; on the irrationality of princely favor, 14, 111; as manual for courtiers, 8, 13–14; as manual

for the court lady, 50; model of the courtier seen as an unattainable ideal, 8, 37–8; on the need for caution in dealing with the prince, 28, 29–30, 31; parodies of, 78–9, 128, 131–2; presenting the first positive image of the courtier, 14; on princes, 13–14, 20–3, 25, 26–31; *prima redazione* of, 13–14; on the protean nature of the courtier, 32–3, 124; second book of, 16–17, 21, 22–3, 32, 45; *seconda redazione* of, 16, 17, 32; success of, 13, 35; *terza redazione* of, 13, 16, 17, 25, 32; third book of, 50, 53, 65; as utopian representation of the court, 18, 28. *See also* Castiglione, Baldassar
Borgia, Cesare, 19
Bradamante (*Orlando Furioso*), 62
Brancaccio, Giulio Cesare, 71, 72–4, 75; as singer, 71, 72–4; as soldier, 72, 73
Brescia, 115, 154
brothel, 57
Brusoni, Girolamo, 236–7n261
buffoon, 6, 84, 93, 124
Burckhardt, Jacob, 9, 92, 121; and the discovery of the individual, 9, 121
Burke, Peter, 35
Burgundy, Duchess of (*Novelle*), 66

Caccia, Giovanni Agostino, 119–20, 125, 127, 155–6; "Al signor Giacomo Maria Stampa," 155–6; "Al Signor Gian Filippo Cazza fiscale di Sua Maestà," 155, 156; "Al Torniello governator di Novara," 156; *Satire e capitoli piacevoli*, 119–20, 125, 155–6; shepherd persona of, 156
Calandro (*Farza*), 128
Calcagnini, Celio, 183; *De patientia, seu vita aulica commentatio*, 183
Calisthenes, 17, 30, 31
Calmeta, Vincenzo (*Book of the Courtier*), 21–2, 25, 31
Cammelli, Antonio. *See* Pistoia, il
Campani, Nicolò, 232n196
Canoniero, Pietro Andrea, 181–2; *Il perfetto cortegiano, et dell'ufizio del prencipe verso 'l cortegiano*, 181–2
Canossa, Ludovico da (*Book of the Courtier*), 20, 22, 23, 29, 53, 54, 60, 204n12
Canzoniere (Petrarch), 220n73
Capitan Spavento, 182
capitolo satirico. *See* satire
Caporali, Cesare, 11, 57, 82, 97, 112, 115, 118, 142, 143, 182; Aretino's influence on, 142, 143; Bernesque style of, 143; on being one's own courtier and *Signore*, 117–18; on the birth of courtliness, courtly language, and courtiership, 115; on the court as a woman, 57, 82; as founder of the *avvisi di Parnaso* genre, 236–7n261; on the golden age, 115, 118; on the link between *Morte* and *Corte*, 112; member of the Accademia della Borra, 226n128; success as a courtier, 143. *See also specific titles*
captain: as model of masculinity, 54
captivity, the court as, 7, 46–9, 58, 61, 65, 82, 90, 97, 118, 123, 137, 165. *See also* chains
Carafa, Diomede, 15; *Dello optimo cortesano*, 15–16, 22
Carino (*Pastor Fido*), 146, 171–5; as Guarini, 172; as poet, 172; as satirist, 174
Carlo (*Gerusalemme Liberata*), 62, 74
Carlo (*Novelle*), 66
Carlo Emanuele of Savoy, 69
Carnival, 130, 131, 133, 231n191

Castelletti, Cristoforo, 170; *Amarilli*, 170
Castiglionchio, Lapo da, 91–2, 217nn28–9; *De curiae commodis*, 91–2
Castiglione, Baldassar, 3, 7–8, 13, 14, 15, 17, 18, 20, 25, 26, 28, 31, 34, 37, 66, 76, 98, 116, 124, 128, 158, 179; and anti-courtliness, 14–15, 16; courtier figure of as a successful counterpart to Cicero's orator, 196n67; on the protean nature of the courtier, 32–3, 124; and self-censorship, 16; *Tirsi*, 158, 160. See also *Book of the Courtier, The*; *sprezzatura*
Castus (*Dialogo della corte*), 122
Caterina, the Infanta of Spain, 69, 70
Cazza, Gian Filippo, 155, 156
Celenza, Christopher, 91
chains, 57, 74, 90, 106; golden, 46–9, *47*, *48*, 57; gift of a golden chain to Aretino from King Francis I, 46
"chameleon-like character" of the court, 4
changeable nature of the court, 38, 58, 62. *See also* court: changing the nature of those with whom it comes into contact
changeable nature of the courtier, 10, 17, 32–3, 34, 56, 81, 90, 122–5, 173
chaos, 147, 152, 156
chastity, 69, 75, 76, 106
Che al savio è convenevole il corteggiare (Peregrini), 36
Chemello, Adriana, 76
"Chi semina fatiche e vòl quïete" (Correggio), 149–50
Chigi, Agostino, 127
chimera, 7, 90
Chiodo, Domenico, 169
Christianity, 167, 170; conversion to, 170; the court as the antithesis to the ideals of, 59, 88, 89; and the myth of the villa, 152; values of, 87, 88, 108, 182–3
Cian, Vittorio, 102
Cicero, 149, 196n67. *See also* orator, Roman
Circe, 82, 97, 112, 124
city: compared to a pastoral setting, 147–51, 154, 155, 156, 159, 166, 172; conflated with the court, 149, 154, 155, 156, 159, 166, 172; as disfigured after a princely court's visit, 81; and morality, 77; and satire, 92, 93
"civil conversation," 66
civil conversazione, La. See *Civile conversation*
Civile conversation (Guazzo), 36, 37, 39–40, 47–9; on the connection between courtliness and illness, 39–40; rivalling the popularity of the *Book of the Courtier*, 36
Clement VII (pope), 113, 129, 133, 134, 153; Aretino's play on his name, 133, 233n205; as Cardinal Giulio de' Medici, 113, 128, 153; election of, 129
clergy, 87, 88, 108
Coccio, Francesco, 137, 234n228; letter from Pietro Aretino, 137, 176
Coccio, Francesco (*Ragionamento delle corti*), 137, 138–40
collectivity, 121, 156, 178; and the pastoral setting, 156, 170; and the villa, 149, 155, 156
coltivazione, La (Alamanni), 154
Commendone, Giovanni Francesco, 36, 37, 42; *Discorso sopra la corte di Roma*, 36, 37
competition: at court, 15–16, 38, 39, 40, 42, 66, 70, 84, 104–5, 106, 109, 112, 156, 179; among courtiers, 15–16, 39, 40–1, 42, 66, 70, 104–5,

118; between courtiers and court ladies, 71; among court ladies, 66; among shepherds, friendly, 157, 178, 241n59
complaints about the court, 5, 6, 14, 19, 57, 72, 73, 88, 99–100, 101, 107, 117, 125, 135, 185–6
concerto delle donne, 71–2, 73, 74, 75
conclave of 1522 (that elected Pope Adrian VI), 128
conduct manuals, 6, 8, 10, 32, 33–5, 36–45, 68–9, 70, 75, 78, 91, 92, 112–13, 126, 151–2, 169, 181–2, 198n90; and new producers of and audience for such works, 34–5
conformity: at court, 11, 34, 45, 95, 123, 184, 189n19
Contra clericos aulicos (Damian), 87
Corisca (*Pastor Fido*), 172
Correggio, court of, 103
Correggio, Niccolò Postumo da, 101, 103, 104, 109–10, 112, 149–50, 156–7; animal metaphors in, 150; anti-courtliness as a main theme of, 220–1n74; "Chi semina fatiche e vòl quïete," 149–50; "L'ozio già tanto disïato godo," 150; "Ne più ne men come a natura piace," 150; "Pasciute pecorelle," 156–7; "Pascul de vizii, pocul di veneno," 101, 102, 104, 106, 112; pastoral tone in, 220–1n74
corruption, 16–17, 21, 30, 36, 45, 59, 61, 62, 86, 92, 107, 108, 128, 145, 147, 155, 165, 166, 172, 181; of language, 115. *See also* court: as corrupt; court: as corrupting
corte: the term, 75, 77, 87; *Corte/Morte* rhyme, 112, 142; *Corte/sorte* rhyme, 130
corte, La (Caporali), 57, 82, 97, 112, 115, 117–18, 142; Aretino's *Ragionamento* as a model for, 142; on the link between *Morte* and *Corte*, 112
Cortegiano, Il. See *Book of the Courtier, The*
cortigiana, the term, 75–6, 77, 80
Cortigiana (Aretino), 128, 131–2, 143; dual meaning of title, 132; first version (1525), 131–2, 134, 135, 233n209; as parody of the *Book of the Courtier*, 128, 131–2; second version of (1534), 134–5, 233n209. *See also names of individual characters*
cortigiano, the term, 75, 77, 80, 181
cortigiano del Sessa, Il (Nifo), 36
Cosimo I, 82
Cosmico, Niccolò Lelio, 220n73
countryside. *See* pastoral setting
court: as abstract notion, 5, 108; as anonymous archetype, 108; attractiveness of, despite its evils, 47, 49, 53, 58, 63, 88, 91, 98, 126, 137–8, 183; changing the nature of those with whom it comes into contact, 61, 62, 81, 82, 90, 97, 109, 112, 162, 173; as corrupt, 26, 27, 29, 45, 59, 61, 80, 82–3, 89, 90, 172; as corrupting, 45, 59, 67, 82, 83, 84, 87, 94, 97, 101, 106, 107, 112, 116, 149, 174, 179; as courtesan, 106–7; and development of specialized bureaucracy, 33–4; as diseased, 82–3; as disfiguring, 81, 82; as feminized space, 74; forcing men of different natures to live side by side, 38, 42, 85, 138, 156; as group of people or society, 4, 10, 18, 33, 34, 52, 55, 66, 78, 81, 94, 147, 157, 177, 178, 179; as inescapable, 46–8, 91, 168, 169, 176, 177, 184; infatuation with, 63–4; as illusion, 56, 58, 61, 89–90, 105, 107, 123, 131,

161–2, 167, 174, 178; as institution, 5, 13, 56, 84, 117, 184; as location, 4; meaning of, 4; mythical character of, 5; as needing medical help, 39, 94; of the past compared with those of the Renaissance, 4, 16–17; role in the emergence of women as protagonists, 51; symbolic value of, 5; as toxic, 112
court, writings on: biographical elements of, 5, 15, 21, 36–7, 39, 58, 64, 88, 103, 107, 111, 112, 113, 125, 146, 225n111
courtesan, 75–82, 132; changeable nature of, 81; the court as a, 106–7; and the courtier, 75, 76–81; and the court lady, 75–6, 80; as diseased, 82; and greed, 80, 81; and love, 76, 81; and music, 75; as performer or spectacle, 75, 81; as "public woman," 81; rejection of chastity, 75; as shameless, 81; subjection of, 76. See also *cortigiana*, the term
courtesy, 79, 81; relation to "court," 77
courtier: as aggregate of vices, 14; characteristics of, 3, 5, 7, 13–14, 85, 181; and courtesans, 75, 76–81; definitions of, 3, 187n2; as devoted to his prince, 23, 81; as different from the court secretary, 34; as doctor, 27–8, 30, 39; as entertainer, 28, 33, 41; as flatterer, 3, 7, 23, 41, 108; and fraternal love, 16; frustration of, 150; judgment of, 23–4; as lover of the court or prince, 63, 64; nobility of, 7, 20; as performer, 10, 15, 33, 51, 76, 81; as professional, 13–14, 42; as "public man," 81; resentment of toward figures in power, 66, 67; scission between the public and private persona of, 183; as "scaled-down version of the omnicompetent Renaissance prince," 14; as shameless, 81; in stocks, *8*; success of, 16, 124; as tactical not strategic, 44; turned satirist, 86, 94–5, 96, 97, 98–9; turned shepherd, 146, 167–8, 179; as "unhappy bird," 22. See also *cortigiano*, the term; courtier-counsellor
courtier-counsellor, 7, 25–33, 34, 36, 81, 128
court lady: aligned with the prince, 64; as advisor, 66; and "civil conversation," 66; and courtesans, 75–6, 80; compared to the courtier, 209–10n61; as judge of men's behaviour, 51, 64–5; in a position of power, 64, 67; position at court as beneficial to her family, 69; relationship to the courtier, 50, 64–5; satire of, 10; service at court, 67; as sirens, 73, 74, 75; as sought after at court, 71; structural core of the court, 65; success at court, 70, 71; training of, 68–70. See also *virtuosa*; women
courtliness: and "civil conversation," 66; effect on the courtier's sense of self, 117, 120, 123, 184; as illness or malaise, 39–40, 115–17; "negative theology" of, 43, 44. *See also* court; courtier
courtly arts: as feminizing, 52
courtly language, 6, 63, 113–15; analogous to language of patronage, 63; compared to the language of satire, 96, 105, 113–15; as distorted communication, 6, 109, 113–15
Cox, Virginia, 22, 32, 41, 45, 65
Croce, Benedetto, 11; critique of anti-court writings, 11

cultural production, the court as a site of, 51, 52
Cupid, 160
curia (term), 87. *See also* papal court

Damian, Peter, 87; *Contra clericos aulicos*, 87
dancing, 26, 59, 73, 162; as problematic for masculinity, 55, 75, 81
Dante, 95; *Commedia*, 220n73; *Inferno*, 220–1n74; as a model for Ariosto's *Satire*, 95
Danza di Venere (Ingegneri), 170, 177
d'Aragona, Tullia, 77
d'Arco, Livia, 71
death, in Arcadia, 241n60
Death, the court as, 111–12
Decameron (Boccaccio), 105, 148
deceit, 5, 6, 16, 19, 26, 27, 28, 44, 56, 62, 67, 78, 80, 83, 96, 101, 113, 124, 138, 178. *See also* duplicity
De Certeau, Michel, 44
"De' cortigiani e delle donne di corte insieme" (Garzoni), 80–1
De curiae commodis (Castiglionchio), 91–2; analysis of the court's effects on the five senses, 91
De curialium miseriis epistola (Piccolomini, Enea Silvio), 43, 87, 88–91, 101, 102, 126; analysis of the court's effects on the five senses, 91; description of courtiers' meals, 102; "homeopathic" function, 91; introduction of secular tone to anti-court satire, 101; as transition from medieval anti-court writing to early modern anti-court writing, 89
Della corte (Simeoni), 82, 83, 97, 109, 112
della Rovere, Francesco Maria, 22–3, 25, 31, 194n42
Della vita pastorale (Taegio), 154
Dello optimo cortesano (Carafa), 15–16, 22
de Magistris, Giovanni Lazzaro. *See* Serapica
"De muliere aulica" (Nifo), 51–2
De nugis curialium (Map), 88
De patientia, seu vita aulica commentatio (Calcagnini), 183
depersonalization: and the court, 11, 65, 94, 98–9, 112, 119, 120, 149, 150, 173, 184, 189n19
De re aulica (Nifo), 36, 41, 42, 51, 68, 72; notion of *affabilitas*, 41; notion of *virtù cortigiana*, 42
De Silva, Miguel, 28
despotism, 23, 25, 28, 40, 43, 44. *See also* tyranny
De vita solitaria (Petrarch), 148, 156
Dialogo de la vita dei cortegiani intitolato la patientia (Rosello), 183
Dialogo della corte (Domenichi), 122–4; compared to the *Book of the Courtier*, 124. *See also names of individual characters*
dieci giornate della vera agricoltura, e piaceri della villa, Le (Gallo), 154
Difesa del savio in corte (Peregrini), 63
discontent, 17, 39, 43, 51, 53, 73, 88, 98, 106, 109, 127
Discorsi ne' quali si ragiona compiutamente di quanto far debbono i gentilhuomini ne' seruigi dei loro signori per acquistarsi la gratia loro (Grimaldi Robio), 36, 37, 38, 42–3. *See also names of individual characters*
Discorso intorno a quello che si conviene a giovane e nobile e ben creato nel servire un gran principe (Giraldi Cinzio), 36, 37, 38–9, 40; on courtiers as "new Momuses,"

38–9; frontispiece of the emblem of the Hydra, 39; motto *Virescit vulnere virtus*, 39; notion of *gentile ironia*, 40
Discorso sopra la corte di Roma (Commendone), 36, 37
"Discorso sulla materia della satire" (Sansovino), 92–4
Dion of Syracuse, 31
Dionisotti, Carlo, 34
Dionysius of Syracuse, 31
discontent as illness or malaise, courtier's, 39–40, 51, 94–5, 116
disputatio in utramque partem, 164
dissimulation, 40, 78, 122, 123, 176, 181, 183
Dizionario Garzanti della Lingua Italiana, 3
Dolce, Lodovico, 234n228
Dolce, Lodovico (*Ragionamento delle corti*), 137, 139
Domenichi, Ludovico, 51, 68, 122; *Dialogo della corte*, 122–4; *La donna di corte*, 51–2, 68–9
Doni, Anton Francesco, 46, 147–8; *Le ville*, 147–8; *Nuova opinione*, 46; on the types of villas, 147–8
donna di corte: as alternative to "*cortigiana*," 75–6. *See also* court lady
donna di corte, La (Domenichi), 51–2, 68–9
donna di palazzo: as alternative to "*cortigiana*," 75. *See also* court lady
Doriolo (*Erminia*), 169–70
Ducci, Lorenzo, 36, 37, 42, 43, 45; *Ars aulica*, 36, 42, 43–4, 45
Duchess of Burgundy (*Novelle*), 66
duplicity, 80, 95, 96, 113, 124, 141, 178. *See also* deceit
dystopia, 5, 65; the court as, 6–7, 101, 102, 108, 149, 220–1n74
effeminacy, 17, 26, 51, 53–5, 57, 60, 84, 136, 165, 166, 209n53
Egon (*Pastor Fido*), 172
elegance, 7, 26, 46, 53, 55, 56, 58, 59, 76, 90, 123, 146, 178, 179, 181
Elias, Norbert, 34, 51
Elijah, 113
Elisabetta, Duchess. *See* Gonzaga, Duchess Elisabetta
Elpin, 162, 244n82
emasculating effect of the court, 10, 51, 52, 56–7
emblems, books of, 7
Emilia Pio (*Book of the Courtier*). *See* Pio, Emilia
Encomium Moriae (Erasmus), 87
England, 87
envy, 5, 12, 38, 41, 42, 83, 101, 106, 137, 138, 150, 151, 152, 153, 155, 159, 169, 173, 177, 182; at court, 7, 15–16, 38, 41–2, 43, 66, 67, 70, 137, 138, 151, 153, 155, 173; among courtiers, 15–16, 42; among court ladies, 67, 70; between courtiers and court ladies, 71
Envy, 38
Erasmus, 87; *Encomium Moriae*, 87
Erminia: (*Erminia*), 169–79; (*Gerusalemme Liberata*), 146, 167, 168, 169, 171, 172; renamed Nicea in the *Gerusalemme Conquistata*, 169
Erminia (Visdomini), 169–79; politicized tone of, 170. *See also names of individual characters*
Essays (Montaigne), 183
Este, Alfonso II d', Duke, 41, 71, 72, 73, 97, 160, 163, 167, 171, 173. *See also* Ferrara
Este, Cardinal Ippolito d', 96, 98, 99; unworthiness of as patron, 99. *See also* Ferrara

Eterei, academy of, 172
etymological link between "satyr" and "satire"/"satirist," 93–4, 129, 165, 179
evils of the court, 4, 6–7, 16–17, 41, 45, 54, 65–6, 67, 90, 106, 136, 137–8, 152, 169

Faini, Marco, 130
Falcone, Giuseppe, 154; *La nuova, vaga, et dilettevole villa*, 154
Farza (anonymous), 127–8. *See also names of individual characters*
fathers, 30, 49, 62, 63, 68, 70, 88, 145, 168–9, 171, 176; benefitting from daughter's position at court, 69; concerns for daughters at court, 68–9; households of compared to princely households, 247n102; service at court as neglect of his family, 176
favour, of the prince or at court, 4, 15, 16, 20, 28, 36, 38, 39, 40, 42, 43, 58, 63, 64, 68, 70, 85, 88, 105, 108, 110, 111, 112, 134, 136, 210–11n61; irrationality of, 14, 38, 53, 104, 115, 132
Federico Fregoso (*Book of the Courtier*). *See* Fregoso, Federico
femininity, 61, 71, 74, 75, 76, 209n53
Fenaruolo, Girolamo, 115
Ferrara, 36–7, 39, 71–2, 74, 75, 95, 101, 103, 107, 108, 157, 159, 160, 171, 223n87; *concerto delle donne*, 71–2, 73; Schifanoia palace, 157–8, 240n47
Ferroni, Giulio, 98, 132
Filliria (Vida), 170
Filosofia cortesana (Barros), 105
Filostrato (*Filostrato e Panfila*), 105
Filostrato e Panfila (Pistoia, il), 105, 145, 157; presented at the court of Ferrara, 223n87. *See also names of individual characters*
Finotti, Fabio, 159
flagello dei principi, 127, 236n249. *See also* Aretino: as scourge of princes
Flam(m)inio, 132, 134–5, 233n209
flattery, 78, 80, 86, 87, 96, 114, 115, 118, 163, 181; at court, 3, 6, 7, 17, 23, 29, 38, 41, 45, 80, 90, 100, 106, 108, 113, 118, 132, 137, 151, 169
Florence, 71, 82, 128, 148, 153, 154; plague in, 148; variation on the myth of the villa, 154
Floriani, Piero, 95, 117
flowers, 27, 56, 57, 58, 59, 83, 114
Folengo, Teofilo, 51, 59–61; *Baldus*, 51, 59–61
foreign occupation of the Italian peninsula, anxiety related to, 11, 55
Forestiero Napolitano (*Malpiglio*), 37, 38, 63, 64, 70; as Tasso's alter ego, 37
fortitude, 56, 182
Fortuna, 6, 20, 42–3, 62, 80, 84, 92, 96, 104, 108, 109–11, 130, 131, 132, 139, 150, 153, 167, 168, 169, 176, 182, 183; in battle against *virtù*, 42; as conquerable, 43; as the product of a prince who is both absolute and fickle, 43
fortune, 86, 127, 152. *See also* Fortuna
Fra Serafino (*Book of the Courtier*), 19
France, 82, 112, 113, 114, 129, 135, 141; invasion of Italy, 110; negotiations with Spain and the papacy, 141
Francis I, King, 46, 82, 135; gift of a golden chain to Pietro Aretino, 46
fraud, 78, 80, 83, 101, 151, 161
freedom, 9, 29, 97, 100, 114, 115, 120, 122, 136, 140, 141, 144, 160, 164, 165, 170, 176; and the court, 7, 17, 46, 57, 102, 107, 115, 118, 119, 123, 126, 151,

170; and the pastoral setting, 147, 150, 153, 168, 170, 176; Venice as the site or symbol of, 76, 127, 129, 134–5, 136, 137, 140, 147, 251n10; and the villa, 147, 148, 150, 154, 168, 251n10. *See also* autonomy; free will; mastery over oneself

free will, 137, 150; and the pastoral setting, 150, 170; and the villa, 150

Fregoso, Federico (*Book of the Courtier*), 19, 21, 22, 23, 25, 29, 31, 32, 54, 204n12

Fregoso, Ottaviano (*Book of the Courtier*), 19, 25–32, 51, 52, 94, 195n58; as critic of the court system, 26; as future Doge of Genoa, 26

friendship, 58, 145; among men, 67, 68, 122; among women at court, 211n78

futility: of battling Fortuna, 92; of complaining about the court, 125, 184; of life at court, 102, 105, 109, 133, 146, 150, 173, 186

Galenic view of women, 72

Galilei, Galileo, 9

Gallo, Agostino, 154; *Le dieci giornate della vera agricoltura, e piaceri della villa*, 154

Game of the Goose, 105

games, 7, 90, 131, 222–3n85; in the *Book of the Courtier*, 18, 19, 53; the court as a, 104–5

Ganymede, 54

Garfagnana, 127

garlands. *See* flowers

Garzoni, Tomaso, 6–7, 80–1; *La piazza universale di tutte le professioni del mondo*, 6–7, 80–1

Gelfora, 59–60, 61, 65

gender, 11, 75; roles, 5, 55, 64, 67, 71, 72; gender shaming, 55, 61

Genoa, 26; Republic of Genoa, 26

Gerbino, Giuseppe, 177–8; on models of self-representation in the Renaissance, 177–8

Gerusalemme Conquistata (Tasso), 169; Erminia of the *Gerusalemme Liberata* renamed Nicea, 169

Gerusalemme Liberata (Tasso), 59, 61, 62, 74, 146, 163, 167, 169, 171, 172; as inspiration for pastoral texts, 169; pastoral episode in, 167, 168–9. *See also names of individual characters*

Giamatti, A. Bartlett, 124; on the figure of Proteus in the Renaissance, 124

Gian Manente, 133

Gigante, Claudio, 163, 166–7; reading of Mopso from Tasso's *Aminta*, 163; on the role of the satyr in Tasso's *Aminta*, 166–7

Gioseffo (*La pazzesca pazzia*), 67, 68, 210n66

Giovanlorenzo Malpiglio (*Malpiglio*). *See* Malpiglio, Giovanlorenzo

Giovanni dalle Bande Nere, 129; death of, 129

Giraldi Cinzio, Giovan Battista, 36–7, 38, 39, 40; humiliation at the court of Ferrara, 39; notion of *gentile ironia*, 40; son, Lucio Olimpio, 37. See also *Discorso intorno a quello che si conviene a giovane e nobile e ben creato nel servire un gran principe*

Giuliano de' Medici (*Book of the Courtier*). *See* Medici, Giuliano de' (*Book of the Courtier*)

Giustiniano, Giovanni, 234n228

Giustiniano, Giovanni (*Ragionamento delle corti*), 137, 138, 139, 140

gluttony, 7, 91

God, 15, 17, 21, 89, 102, 128, 135, 152
golden age, 115, 117–18, 134, 155, 164, 166, 170
Gouwens, Kenneth, 55
Gonzaga, Cesare, 158; *Tirsi*, 158
Gonzaga, Cesare (*Book of the Courtier*), 19, 65
Gonzaga, Duchess Elisabetta, 158
Gonzaga, Duchess Elisabetta (*Book of the Courtier*), 19, 22, 55, 66
Gonzaga, Duke Federico, 128, 133–4, 136; and the assassination attempt on Pietro Aretino, 231n186
Gonzaga, Margherita, 71
Gonzaga, Scipione, 172
Gonzaga, Duke Vincenzo, 42
good examples of courts, 15, 16, 61, 139, 140
Gordon, Bonnie, 75
grazia, 14, 124
greed, 7, 80, 81, 104, 106, 107, 152, 154, 159, 166, 169, 171, 175, 177
Greenblatt, Stephen, 8–10
Greene, Thomas, 18, 19
Gregorio (*La pazzesca pazzia*), 67–8
Grimaldi Robio, Pellegro, 36, 38, 42–3, 200n116; *Discorsi ne' quali si ragiona compiutamente di quanto far debbono i gentilhuomini ne' seruigi dei loro signori per acquistarsi la gratia loro*, 36, 37, 42–3
Grimaldi Robio, Pierfrancesco (*Discorsi*), 37
Gritti, Doge Andrea, 136
Guarini, Battista, 34, 142, 171–2, 175–7; as character in Tasso's *Aminta*, 244n82; as *padre di famiglia*, 176; letter to Francesco Maria Vialardi, 176; letter to Livio Passeri, 176; letters of, 175, 176; personal villa of, 171, 175; service to Duke Alfonso II d'Este, 171. *See also specific titles and names of individual characters*
Guarini, Laura, 71
Guasco, Annibale (Annibal), 68–71, 211n74; on friendship among women at court, 211n78; letter from Stefano Guazzo, 70; *Ragionamento a Donna Lavinia sua figliuola, della maniera del governarsi ella in Corte; andando per Dama alla Serenissima Infante Donna Caterina, Duchessa di Savoia*, 68–70; *The Book of the Courtier* as a model for, 68, 69
Guazzo, Guglielmo (*Civile conversation*), 37, 39–40, 48–9; withdrawal from society as a disavowal of court life, 39
Guazzo, Stefano, 36, 37, 47, 70; *Civile conversation*, 36, 37, 47–9; letter to Annibale Guasco, 70; opinion of *Ragionamento a Donna Lavinia* (Guasco), 70
Guevara, Antonio de, 6, 151–2; *Aviso de favoriti*, 6; *Aviso de privados y doctrina de cortesanos*, 151–2; *Avviso de' favoriti e dottrina de' cortigiani, con la commendazione della villa: Dispregio delle corti e laude della villa*, 151–2; *Menosprecio de corte y alabanza de aldea*, 151–2; *Relox de principes*, 151
Guglielmo Guazzo (*Civile conversation*). *See* Guazzo, Guglielmo
Guinevere, 61

Haich, Ioannes, 88
happiness, 27, 46, 88, 90, 102, 139, 158; in the pastoral setting compared to unhappiness at court, 11, 146, 150, 153, 159, 167–8, 170, 179

harlot, 7, 54, 57, 77, 81; the court as, 10; the courtier as, 60; effeminate men as, 54, 60
harmony, 16, 18, 19, 24, 25, 31, 66, 167; and the pastoral setting, 157, 159, 177
harpies, 7, 153
Hate, 38
Heaven, Kingdom of, 152
Held, Julius S., 46
hell on earth, the court as, 3, 6, 21, 66, 88, 101, 106, 107, 108, 134, 135, 138, 149, 174, 220–1n74
Henry II, King, 88
Hercules, 39, 45, 57, 171; the courtier as, 39, 45
Homer, 17
homines novi, 34
homo faber, 184
honour, 58, 67, 69, 89, 164–5, 175, 246n89; as constraint, 164–5, 169; as tyrannical, 164–5
Horace, 86, 95, 99, 114, 147, 150, 152–3; as a model for Ariosto's *Satire*, 95
hospice or hospital, 57, 101, 116, 137, 160, 168, 171; the court as, 116, 137, 142; "of hopes," 142; of Sant'Anna, 41, 42, 160, 168, 171
humility, 69, 70, 88, 123, 154; as defence against envy, 70
Hungary, 96, 98
Hydra, the court as, 39
hypocrisy, 3, 36, 96, 108, 151, 163

Iconologia (Ripa), 57–8
Imago vitae aulicae (Lucian), 182
In aulicos (Alciato), 7, *8*, 45–7, *47*, *48*; editions of, 46
index of prohibited books, 142
individual, concept of the, 9–10, 121–2; relationship with the state, 177
individuality, 119, 120–2, 124–5, 126; court life as threat to, 90, 120–1, 122, 125, 184, 189n19; courtliness's effect on, 117, 120, 184; and satire, 11, 86, 95, 119. *See also* self, sense of
Ingegneri, Angelo, 170; *Danza di Venere*, 170, 177
Innominati academy, 169, 170
Inquisition, 77, 179
intellectual: and the court, 10, 85, 99, 100, 184; and subordination, 184; role of, 11, 85, 100
interiority, 97, 98, 121, 184
"Invidia corte, d'ogni ben nimica" (Aquilano), 101–2
"Io ho provato che cosa è amore" (Beccari da Ferrara), 102
Italy: feminization of, 53; invasions of, 110; Northern, 154; political crisis in the sixteenth century, 155; subjugation of, 53, 55, 210n66

Jacobs, Fredrika, 71
Javitch, Daniel, 48
jealousy at court. *See* envy
Jensen, Ejner J., 92
jester, 6
Jesus, court of, 140
John, Saint (*Orlando Furioso*), 100
John the Baptist, 106
John of Salisbury, 87
Jones, Ann Rosalind, 158
Joseph, 106
justice, 29
Justice, 134
Juvenal, 84, 86, 95, 96, 102, 114, 147; as a model for Ariosto's *Satire*, 95

Kelly-Gadol, Joan, 50
Kernan, Alvin, 85, 88
knight, as a model of self-representation for men of the court, 177–8

Lacedaemon, 124
Lady Court, 58
Lady Folly, 6
Lady Fortune, 182
Lamento de uno cortigiano già favorito in palazzo, et hora in grandissima calamità (Aretino), 54, 55, 56, 130–1, 136; performed during Carnival, 231n191; recent rediscovery of, 231n186; rhyme *Corte/sorte*, 130; universal quality of protagonist, 131
Lamento di una cortigiana ferrarese (Aretino/Veneziano), 231n191
Langer, Ulrich, 43, 44
language of love poetry and of patronage, analogies between, 63, 64
Lario, Andrea (*Dialogo della corte*), 122–3
Larivaille, Paul, 127, 135, 136, 142
lasciviousness, 17, 58, 93. *See also* lust
laudatio temporis acti, 25
Laura (*Cortigiana*), 132
Lavinia (*Ragionamento a Donna Lavinia*), 68–70, 71, 211n74
Leo X (pope), 37, 127, 128, 131, 133, 134; death of, 131
"Lettera di M. Lodovico Paterno sopra la materia della satira" (Paterno), 92–3, 94
Lettera nella quale rispondendo ad una di m. Hercole Perinato, egli celebra la villa, et lauda molto l'agricoltura (Lollio), 154, 155
Lettere (Aretino), 141; as self-promotion, 141
liberality, 29
libro del Cortegiano, Il. See *Book of the Courtier*
Licori, 244n82
life at court: compared to private life, 88, 123; compared to the villa, 149–50; of the courtier, 118–20; futility of, 102, 105, 109, 133, 146, 150, 173, 186
life of the courtier compared to the life of a prisoner, 118
Linus, 162
literati, 34–5, 73, 85, 95, 99, 104, 106, 107, 126, 128, 136, 137, 140, 143, 148, 155, 163, 184; social role similar to that of the doctor, 94
Lollio, Alberto, 154, 155, 240n47; *Aretusa*, 158, 240n47; *Lettera nella quale rispondendo ad una di m. Hercole Perinato, egli celebra la villa, et lauda molto l'agricoltura*, 154, 155
Lomellini, Piero Battista, 37
Longchamps, Nigel of, 87, 88
Love, 74, 165
love, 171; as ally of tyrannical courtly power, 67; and the courtesan, 76; and courtliness, 62, 76; and the court lady, 76; for the lady, 62–3; of the courtier for the prince, 63; as problematic for the courtier's masculinity, 209n53
love poetry, language of as similar to the language of patronage, 63, 64
Lucan, 87; *Pharsalia*, 87
Lucian, 87, 102; *Imago vitae aulicae*, 182
Lucio Olimpio, 37
lust, 7, 91, 172. *See also* lasciviousness

Maco da Coe (*Cortigiana*), 132
Maecenus, 86, 99
Maestro Andrea (*Cortigiana*), 132
magnanimity, 29, 162
Magnocavalli, Annibale (*Civile conversation*), 39–40, 48
makeup, 59–60, 80
Malaguzzi, Annibale, 97
malaise, 11, 51, 94, 95, 115–17
malfrancese, 82

Malpiglio, Giovanlorenzo (*Malpiglio*), 37, 63–4, 70
Malpiglio, overo de la corte (Tasso), 36, 37, 38, 40–1, 42, 63–4, 70, 176; as the "new *Book of the Courtier*," 38, 41; on honour, 246n89; on the interaction between peers as a wrestling match, 40–1, 70; irony in, 63, 64. *See also names of individual characters*
Malpiglio, Vincenzo (*Malpiglio*), 37, 38, 63
manhood. *See* masculinity
manicured appearance of the courtier, 5, 53–4, 55, 56, 60, 123, 165, 166. *See also* body of the courtier
Mantua, 37, 42, 71, 103, 108, 128, 129, 133, 134, 136, 172. *See also* Gonzaga, Duke Federico
Manuzio, Aldo, 35
Map, Walter, 87, 88; *De nugis curialium*, 88
Marchese del Vasto, 37
Marcolini, Francesco, 136
Marcolini, Francesco (*Ragionamento delle corti*), 140
Marescalco, Il (Aretino), 133–4
Marfisa disperata (Aretino), 136
Margarita (*Raffaella*), 78
marriage, 69, 73, 75, 79, 95, 133, 171; of *Madonna Corte* with *Vituperio*, 143
Martial, 102
Martin, John Jeffries, 9–10, 33, 121, 183; and the different kinds of early modern self, 121–2, 198–9n90; on the "layered quality" of the early modern self, 121; on the myth of Renaissance individualism, 9; on the need for sincerity in courtly culture, 183; on the "protean" nature of the Renaissance self, 33
Martines, Lauro, 13, 63
masculinity, 5, 10, 52, 53–7, 61, 64, 67, 72–3; anxiety about, 53–7, 209n53; characteristics of, 55–6; the court as a threat to, 52, 74; the courtier as a model of, 54, 56, 178; love as problematic for, 209n53; military ineptitude as lack of, 60–1; and models of self-representation, 177–8; prince as a model of, 54; women's presence as a threat to, 57. *See also* men
mastery over oneself, 46, 90, 117–18, 123, 137, 168, 170. *See also* autonomy; freedom; free will
matron, 80; the court as a, 57, 82
Medici, rule over Florence, 113, 153
Medici, Giovanni de'. *See* Giovanni dalle Bande Nere
Medici, Giuliano de' (*Book of the Courtier*), 28–9, 51
Medici, Cardinal Giulio de', 113, 128, 129, 153; as Pope Clement VII, 113, 129, 133, 134, 153; assassination attempt on, 113, 153; election to pope, 129
Medici, Ippolito de', 151
Medusa, 7
Melissa (*Orlando Furioso*), 62
Memphis, 167
men: Aristotle's theories on, 56; as prisoners of women, 59
Menosprecio de corte y alabanza de aldea (Guevara), 151–2; innovation of compared to other texts that critique the court, 152
Mercury, 57
meretriciousness, 79, 80, 81, 82, 83, 138
Middle Ages, 4, 87, 121
Milligan, Gerry, 55
Mirtillo (*Pastor Fido*), 171, 172
Misaulus (*Dialogo della corte*), 122

misogyny, 10, 51, 52, 53, 56–7, 65, 76, 79, 80, 82, 106, 133, 172
modesty, 21, 69, 77, 246n95
Molza, Tarquinia, 71
Momus, myth of, 38–9
mondo alla rovescia, the court as a, 6, 59, 65, 72, 88, 101, 115, 138, 174
monk, the courtier as a, 16
Montaigne, Michel de, 183; *Essays*, 183
Montefeltro, Guidubaldo I da, 22, 30–1, 32; as the new Alexander, 30; problems with gout, 30–1
Mopso, 161–2, 163–4, 167, 169, 170, 172, 174; as mask of Sperone Speroni, 163; a satirist, 163; as a type, 163
moralistic tradition, medieval, 5
morality, 23, 77, 121; and the court, 36, 82–3, 84, 89, 106, 173; and the courtesan, 76, 78, 79, 80; and the courtier, 22, 23, 24, 26, 28, 32, 42, 44, 45, 78, 80, 116; and the pastoral setting, 146–7, 149, 152, 154, 155, 158, 163, 166, 169; and the prince, 30; and satire, 79, 82, 86, 93, 94, 95, 107, 149, 166; and the *virtuoso*, 71
Moretti, Walter, 39
Movesi il vecchierel canuto et bianco (Petrarch), 111–12
Mozzarelli, Cesare, 37
Muchembled, Richard, 35
murder, 16, 134, 136, 194n42
Muses, 162, 174, 175, 185
musicians, 71, 104; as professional, public performers, 73
mutability. *See* changeable nature of the courtier
Mycene, symbolism of in the *Pastor Fido*, 172
myth of the androgyne, 79–80
myth of the villa, 148, 149; Christian dimension to, 152; Florentine variation on, 154

Nanna (*Sei giornate*), 78, 81, 82
Naples, 15, 79, 104, 112
Napoli, Pietro da (*Book of the Courtier*), 23
narcissism, 56
"Ne più ne men come a natura piace" (Correggio), 150
Newcomb, Anthony, 71
New Historicism, 9
Nifo, Agostino, 36, 37, 41, 42, 69, 72, 79, 214n125; "De muliere aulica," 51–2; *De re aulica*, 36, 41, 42, 51, 68, 72; *Il cortegiano del Sessa*, 36
Nigel of Longchamps, 87, 88
nobility, 6, 7, 26, 34, 42, 48, 72, 73, 75, 91, 103, 122, 168; of the courtier, 20, 49, 56, 73
Northern Italy and agricultural literature, 154
nostalgia, 8, 16, 17, 25, 28, 38, 140, 155
Novara, 154, 156
Novelle (Bandello), 51, 66
Nuova opinione (Doni), 46
nuova, vaga, et dilettevole villa, La (Falcone), 154
nymphs, 60, 146, 158, 159, 160, 162, 171, 172

onore. *See* honour
orator, Roman: as failed compared to Castiglione's courtier, 196n67; as model of masculinity, 54
Orfeos, 162
Orlandino (Aretino), 141
Orlando Furioso (Ariosto), 59, 61–2, 98, 100, 136, 145, 155, 163, 175; animal metaphors in, 100; compared to the *Satire*, 98; on friendship as tenuous at court, 145. *See also names of individual characters*
Orazione contra le cortigiane (Speroni), 76–8

otium, 99, 126, 147, 148–9, 152, 154, 155, 175; as leading to moral renovation, 155; and the pastoral setting, 147, 148–9; and the villa, 148–9, 150, 155
Ottaviano Fregoso (*Book of the Courtier*). *See* Fregoso, Ottaviano
"ozio già tanto disïato godo, L'" (Correggio), 150

padre di famiglia, Il (Tasso), 168–9, 247n102
Padua, 77, 172, 175; and the academy of the Eterei, 172
Pallavicino, Gasparo (*Book of the Courtier*), 19, 20, 25, 51
Pan, 171
Panfila (*Filostrato e Panfila*), 105, 145
Panfilia (*La pazzesca pazzia*), 67, 68
panoptical control, the court as a system of, 33
papacy, negotiations with France and Spain, 141
papal court, 77, 78, 79, 87, 88, 89, 101, 107, 108, 117, 127, 128, 133, 134, 137; and corruption, 107, 108, 128, 129, 134; as negative paradigm, 108; pro-France party within, 129; pro-Spain party within, 129; as whore, 128, 129
Parabolano (*Cortigiana*), 132
Parnassus, Mount, 143, 175
pars construens, 152
pars destruens, 152
Partenia (*La regia pastorella*), 170
"Pasciute pecorelle" (Correggio), 156–7
Pascoli da Ravenna, Gabriele, 66–7; *La pazzesca pazzia degl'huomini e donne di corte innamorati, ovvero il cortigiano disperato*, 66–8
"Pascul de vizii, pocul de veneno" (Correggio), 112
pasquinade, 54, 88, 128
Pasquino, 127, 128, 136
Passeri, Livio, 176; letter from Battista Guarini, 176
Pastor Fido (Guarini), 146, 171–7, 182; animal metaphor in, 174–5; different versions of, 172; on honour, 175; marriage in, 171; misogynist stereotypes in, 172; as opposition between the pastoral world and the court, 171; setting in Arcadia, 171, 172; virgin sacrifice in, 171. *See also names of individual characters*
pastoral drama, 6, 10, 146, 169
pastoral genre. *See* pastoral mode
pastoral mode, 146, 147, 158, 159, 160, 177; anti-court stance of, 147; characteristics of, 146; connection to anti-courtliness, 178; definition of, 146; genres of, 157; opportunities for disguise provided by, 158; popularity of leading to decline of satire, 179–80
pastoral setting, 11, 18, 144, 145–80; as alternative setting to the court, 147; as both idealization and critique of the court, 11, 175; as choice of the moral man, 149; as community, 156, 157, 179; in drama, 10; as fantasy structure, 158; life in as superior to life in the city or at court, 147; as participating in the corruption of the city/court, 166; as peaceful, 150, 168, 170; as purified version of the courtly environment, 157, 179; in relation to the court, 11, 145, 146–7, 157, 166, 167–8, 171, 177; as recuperative or restorative, 145, 170; as remedy to split between courtier's public and

private persona, 183; as sanctuary, 146; as site of simplicity, 146, 159, 168. *See also* Arcadia; collectivity; nymphs; shepherd; villa
pastoral tragicomedy, 157; first Italian example of, 157
pasture. *See* pastoral setting
Paterno, Lodovico, 92–3, 94, 112, 113, 182; "Lettera di M. Lodovico Paterno sopra la materia della satira," 92–3, 94; Mario degli Andini as possible pen name for, 217n34; *Satira III*, 112–13
patience, 56, 182–3; combination in the Renaissance of the Christian notion with the Stoic notion, 183; connection to courtliness, 183; in contrast to *sprezzatura*, 183; in enduring life at court, 182–3; as instrument for self-defence, 183; as remedy to troubles of life at court, 183; as sign of a scission between the public and private persona of the courtier, 183
patronage, 22, 35, 41, 51, 52, 65, 71, 76, 86, 88, 96, 97, 100, 104, 119, 127, 128, 133, 136, 138, 140, 160, 163, 174, 175; decline of in classical times, 86; language of as similar to the language of love, 63, 64; and prostitution, 76
La pazzesca pazzia degl'huomini e donne di corte innamorati, ovvero il cortigiano disperato (Pascoli da Ravenna), 66–8. *See also names of individual characters*
peace and peacefulness, 32, 66, 120, 137, 150, 154, 168
Peperara, Laura, 71
Peregrini, Matteo, 36; *Che al savio è convenevole il corteggiare*, 36; *Difesa del savio in corte*, 63
perfetto cortegiano, et dell'ufizio del prencipe verso 'l cortegiano, Il (Canoniero), 181–2
performance, 10, 15, 33, 44, 51, 59, 73, 75, 81; role of in achieving success at court, 34
performances of writings on the court, 130, 133–4, 157–8, 160, 161, 172, 231n191, 240n47
Persia, 124
Pescetti, Orlando, 170; *La regia pastorella*, 170–1
Peter, Saint, 106
Peter of Blois, 87–8
Petrarch, 111, 148, 155, 156; *Canzoniere*, 220n73; *De vita solitaria*, 148, 156; *Movesi il vecchierel canuto et bianco*, 111–12
Petrarchan conventions, 49, 53, 127, 178
Petrarchan lover, as model of self-representation for men in the Renaissance, 178
Pharsalia (Lucan), 87
philosopher, figure of the, 9, 17, 28
Phoebus Apollo, 74, 143, 162
piazza universale di tutte le professioni del mondo, La (Garzoni), 6–7, 80–1
Piccardo, Pietro, 234n228
Piccardo, Pietro (*Ragionamento delle corti*), 137–9, 140
Piccolomini, Alessandro, 152; *La Raffaella, ovvero Dialogo della bella creanza delle donne*, 78–9
Piccolomini, Enea Silvio, 43, 87, 101, 102, 126; *De curialium miseriis epistola*, 87, 88–92, 101, 102, 126; introduction of secular tone to anti-court satire, 101
Pietro da Napoli (*Book of the Courtier*). *See* Napoli, Pietro da
Pigna, Giovan Battista, 39, 244n82

Pio, Emilia (*Book of the Courtier*), 19, 55, 66, 204n12
Pippa (*Sei giornate*), 78
Pistoia, il, 103, 104, 105, 106, 157; *Filostrato e Panfila*, 105, 145, 157; "Questi signor fan come piace a loro," 104. *See also names of individual characters*
plague, 148
Plato: as courtier to the kings of Sicily, 17, 31, 32; myth of the androgyne, 79–80; *Symposium*, 79
Pliny, 149
Poggioli, Renato, 158
Policraticus (Salisbury), 87
poligrafo, 136, 137
politics, 11, 12, 110, 114, 117, 141, 152, 153, 154, 155, 158, 170, 175, 181, 184; the court as the site of political power, 4, 5, 13, 51, 52, 108, 184; gender and political conscience, 55; women and political influence, 50–1, 65, 70. See also *Trattato della politica libertà*
Po River, 160
Porzio, Camillo, 93
prestige, 5, 135, 136, 181; of women, 71
prince: and unmanliness, 27; arrogance of, 27; characteristics of, 16; as corrupted by praise and flattery, 27, 29; evil or wicked, 15, 21, 22, 31, 102; fickleness, capriciousness, or whimsicality of, 16, 20, 29, 38, 42, 43, 53, 62, 90, 94, 96, 104, 108, 110, 132; good, 15, 140, 169; judgment of, 20; lead to virtue by the courtier, 26–31; praise of, 17; "salutary deception" of, 26–30; service to as golden chains, *8*, 46–9, *47*, *48*, 57; stinginess of, 141; as strategic not tactical, 44; as "terrible lion," 16; as unrewarding, 67, 89, 98, 105, 108, 132, 133, 138, 139, 173. *See also* despotism; tyranny
princely favour. *See* favour
printing industry, role for *literatus*, 140–1
printing press, 136
private life, compared to life at court, 88, 96, 144, 175, 176
pronostichi, 163–4
prostitutes, 75, 76, 78, 136; and crisis of traditional morals, 79. *See also* courtesan
prostitution, 77; and patronage, 76
protean nature of courtier, 10, 32–3, 122–5
protean nature of the Renaissance self, 33, 198n90; discomfort with, 33
Protestant Reformation, 79
Proteus, 7, 34, 123–4; court secretary as, 34; and individuality, 124–5; as positive and negative figure, 124
prudence, 9, 23, 40, 41–2, 63, 91, 121, 122, 172, 176
Purgatorio delle cortigiane di Roma (Veneziano), 231n191

quadrelo, 104, 222–3n85
querelle des femmes, 50, 51
Quint, David, 52–3, 63, 64; on anti-feminism in the *Book of the Courtier* as critique of the prince, 52–3; on court lady being aligned with the prince, 64; on similarities between the language of courtly love and the language of patronage, 63, 64
Quondam, Amedeo, 126; on the social function of anti-court writings, 126

Raffaella (*Raffaella*), 78
Raffaella, ovvero Dialogo della bella creanza delle donne, La (Piccolomini,

Alessandro), 78–9. *See also names of individual characters*
Ragazzoni, Vettor, 115
Ragionamento a Donna Lavinia sua figliuola, della maniera del governarsi ella in Corte; andando per Dama alla Serenissima Infante Donna Caterina, Duchessa di Savoia (Guasco), 68–70. *See also names of individual characters*
Ragionamento delle corti (Aretino), 103, 112, 134, 135, 136–43, 163, 182; compared to the *Book of the Courtier*, 140; on the evils of the court, 137–8; garden setting of, 140; impact as literary model, 142; on the link between *Morte* and *Corte*, 112; list of "good" princes and courts, 140; as a rethinking of anti-court satire, 137; tropes of, 142; uniqueness of, 137
Raimondi, Marcantonio, 129; prints of Giulio Romano's *I modi*, 129
rape, 7, 80, 136, 160, 165
Ravenna, 68
Raverta (Betussi), 142
Rebhorn, Wayne, 18, 33
Reformation, 79
Reggio Emilia, 129
regia pastorella, La (Pescetti), 170–1. *See also names of individual characters*
religious reform, 183
Relox de principes (Guevara), 151
Renaissance courts, differences between, 107–8
respect, 17, 28, 66, 75, 76, 122, 127, 134, 139, 173, 174, 246n95
revenge, 7, 67, 105, 133
Rigoletto (Verdi), 3
Rime (Caporali), 143
Rime piacevoli (Allegri), 116
Rinaldo (*Gerusalemme Liberata*), 61, 62, 63–4, 74
Ripa, Cesare, 57–8; *Iconologia*, 57–8
rivalry, 12, 15, 66, 67, 71, 112, 156, 172, 178
Romano, Giulio, 129; *I modi*, 129
Rome, 27, 37, 42, 71, 76, 78, 79, 84, 87, 104, 107, 108, 112, 127, 128, 129, 130, 131, 132, 152; Inquisition of, 77, 179; Sack of, 79, 129, 134. *See also* papal court
Romei, Danilo, 142, 156
Rosello, Lucio Paolo, 183; *Dialogo de la vita dei cortegiani intitolato la patientia*, 183
Rosenthal, Margaret, 76, 80
Rosso (*Cortigiana*), 132
ruffiane, 76, 78
Ruggiero (*Orlando Furioso*), 61–2, 65
Ruggiero, Guido, 64–5
rural environment. *See* pastoral setting

Saccone, Eduardo, 97
Sack of Rome, 79, 129, 134
sacrificio, Il (Beccari), 157–8
Salisbury, John of, 87; considered founder of medieval anti-court satire, 87; *Policraticus*, 87
"salutary deception" of the prince, 26–30
salvation, 89, 148
Sampson, Lisa, 146, 158, 159
Sannazzaro, Jacopo, 157; *Arcadia*, 157
Sansovino, Francesco, 92, 93, 94, 114, 115; "Discorso sulla materia della satira," 92; on the literary and moral value of satire, 93; *Sette libri di satire*, 92, 115
Sant'Anna hospital, 41, 42, 160, 168, 171
Santoro, Mario, 110

Sardo, Francesco (*Dialogo della corte*), 122–3
Sasso, Panfilo, 150–1, 220n73; *capitolo*, 33, 150–1
Satira III (Paterno), 112–13; on the link between *Morte* and *Corte*, 112
Satira contro la corte (Venier), 142
Satira in lode della villa (Boni), 156
satire, 84, 152; and agricultural literature, 155; as alternative to the corrupt court, 84; anti-courtesan, 76–9, 82–3; appeal of for writers, 92; of the *Book of the Courtier*, 78; *capitolo* form, 57, 82, 84, 95, 100, 106, 115, 116, 119–20, 143, 147, 149, 150–1, 221; as casualty of the pastoral, 179–80; classical and medieval sources/models, 86–8; common features in, 85–6, 93, 94, 107, 109, 178; common targets of, 93, 108; of the court, 6, 10, 11, 35, 36, 48, 52, 65, 84–144; of the courtier, 13, 54, 55, 56, 82, 85; courtiers' use of to distinguish themselves from courtesans, 76, 215n137; decline of, 142–3, 156, 157, 179–80, 182; as defence of the self, 98, 122, 126; early modern compared with medieval, 89; in England, 87–8; Greek, 5, 86, 87; and honesty, 122; included on the index of prohibited books, 142; language of compared to courtly language, 96, 105, 113–15; Latin/Roman, 5, 84, 86–7; literary and moral value of, 93; medieval, 87, 88; as outlet for frustration, 85, 95, 108–9; as payback, 85; political, 117; private and psychological dimension of, 117; public nature of, 92; reemergence of, 182; as remedy to split between courtier's public and private persona, 183; and retaliation, 108; topoi of, 95, 98, 106, 107, 109, 112. *See also* etymological link between "satyr" and "satire"/"satirist"
Satire (Alamanni), 114, 152–4
Satire (Ariosto), 73, 95–100, 113, 119, 174; animal metaphors in, 97, 100; Ariosto's satirical persona in, 96–100; circulating at the same time as Castiglione's *Book of the Courtier*, 219n66; compared to the *Orlando Furioso*, 98; as defence of the poet's self and value, 97, 98, 99; as foundation or model of early modern Italian prose satire, 95, 98, 100; models for, 95; possible sources for, 220n73; *Satira I*, 96, 99, 113; *Satira II*, 117; *Satira III*, 96, 97, 100, 113; satiric persona in, 97–8, 119; themes of, 95, 98, 106. *See also names of individual characters*
Satire alla berniesca (Simeoni), 114
Satire di cinque poeti illustri (Andini), 93, 112
Satire e capitoli piacevoli (Caccia), 119–20, 125, 155–6
satirical eulogy, 87
satirist, 83, 84; as alternative model to courtier, 10, 49, 85, 95, 98, 126; as casualty of the pastoral, 179–80; common features of, 85–6, 93, 107, 109, 147; decline of, 142–3, 179; as former courtier, 46, 86, 94–5, 98; as genuine and sincere, 11, 83, 85, 98; as inherently unable to adapt to life at court, 114–15; as model of rectitude, 84, 93, 94; as motivated by rage or disdain over the vices of humankind, 94; pastoral setting as the natural dimension of, 147; persona of as remedy to split

between courtier's public and private persona, 183; as poetic device or persona, 46, 85, 88, 98, 100, 147; and self-fashioning, 86, 95, 126–8; social importance of, 94; social role similar to that of the doctor, 94; as speaker of the truth, 83, 85, 94, 96, 97, 105, 107, 113, 114, 129, 130, 141, 174; as unsuitable to courtly environment, 179. *See also* etymological link between "satyr" and "satire"/"satirist"
satyr, 93, 94, 129–30, 160, 172, 179; lasciviousness of, 93, 166; opposed to the effeminate shepherd, 165; sexuality of, 130; truthfulness of, 130, 165. *See also* etymological link between "satyr" and "satire"/"satirist"
satyr (*Aminta*), 160, 165–7, 169, 246n95; as satirist, 165–6
Savorgnan, Gerolamo, 37
Savoy, court of, 69. *See also* Caterina, the Infanta of Spain
Schifanoia palace, 157–8, 240n47
Scylla, 7
secretary, role of at court, 34; protean qualities of, 34
seductress, 57
Segre, Cesare, 97
segretario, Il (Guarini), 34, 142
Sei giornate (Aretino), 76–7, 78–9, 81, 82, 141; as parody of the *Book of the Courtier*, 78–9. *See also names of individual characters*
Sejanus, 43, 90
self, sense of, 8–10, 11, 32–3, 90, 97, 98, 117, 184, 189n19; court and courtliness's effect on, 117, 120–1, 123; courtliness as a distortion of the self, 98–9; in the early modern period, 33, 121–2, 123, 125, 126, 198–9n90; and gender roles, 64–5; as protean, 33
self-censorship: by Castiglione, 16; by Tasso, 164, 244–5n86
self-fashioning, 8–10, 11, 32–3, 85, 86, 97, 98, 126, 129, 130, 141, 174, 177–8, 184; courtliness as a distortion of the self, 98–9
selfhood. *See* self, sense of
self-presentation. *See* self-fashioning
self-representation. *See* self-fashioning
self-sufficiency, 18, 168, 170
Selmi, Elisabetta, 176, 177
Sempronio (*Cortigiana*), 132, 134
Seneca, 46, 106
senses, effect of the court on, 90, 91
Serapica, 130–1
Sertini, Tommaso, 114
service to the prince, 13–14, 15–16, 21–3, 31, 42, 63, 89, 99, 102, 123, 140; as golden chains, 46–9, 57; as neglect of family, 176; as servitude, 46, 127, 140, 147, 168
servility, 3, 5, 87
servitude, 46, 67, 98, 123, 126, 127, 129, 135, 140, 147, 168
Sette libri di satire (Sansovino), 92
sfortunato, Lo (Argenti), 158–9. *See also names of individual characters*
Sforza, Cardinal Ascanio, 104
Shemek, Deanna, 81, 133
shepherd, 10, 11, 128, 146–7, 156, 157, 158, 159, 160, 162, 167–8, 169, 170–3, 177–80, 183; as alternative model to courtier, 10; as combination of the courtier and the satirist, 178–9, 180; as community, 157; as effeminate, 165; as former courtier, 146, 167–8, 179; and fraternal harmony, 157, 159; and friendly competition, 157,

178, 241n59; as happy, 146, 167, 170, 179; as lover, 178; mask of as insufficient to hide nobility, 168–9; as model of self-representation for men, 177–8; as performer, 157; persona as legacy of Castiglione's ideal, 179; persona as remedy to split between courtier's public and private persona, 183
shepherd (*Gerusalemme Liberata*), 167–8
shipwreck, 7, 35, 38, 44, 85, 90, 175
shoes made of lead, 57
Sicily, 17, 153; court of, 17
Signore, being one's own, 117–18. *See also* prince
Silvano (*Farza*), 128
Silvia (*Aminta*), 160, 161, 165, 167, 246n95
Silvio (*Lo sfortunato*), 159
Silvio (*Pastor Fido*), 171
Simeoni, Gabriello, 82, 83, 97, 112, 118; *Della corte*, 82, 83, 97, 109, 112, 118; *Satire alla berniesca*, 114
sincerity, 9, 23, 83, 87, 107, 114, 115, 119, 121, 122, 124, 174, 175, 183; as antithetical to life at court, 122; and individuality, 122, 124–5; and satire, 100, 114, 119, 122, 124, 129; and the shepherd, 178
singers, 71, 74; as controversial, 73, 75; as public performers, 73
Sir Cecco (Francesco Benci), 120
sirens, 7, 73, 74, 75, 153, 162, 167
slander, 66, 105, 114, 115, 162
Slander, 38
Smith, Pauline M., 87, 102, 152
Snyder, Jon, 183
social climbing, 6, 34, 42, 84, 87, 106, 168
social mobility, 11, 34, 76, 89, 91, 92, 130, 139
Soldani, Iacopo, 143; *Sopra la corte*, 143
soldier, 51, 61, 62, 71, 72, 73, 116, 124; as courtier's former profession, 52, 60–1, 62, 72–3; as model of masculinity, 54
solitude, 156; need for as a disavowal of court life, 39; and the villa, 156
Somasco, Giulio, 66
Sonetti lussuriosi (Aretino), 129
Sopra la corte (Soldani), 143
Sopra la corte (Vincioli), 143
sorceress, 57, 62, 112, 124
Spain, 129, 210n66; Caterina, the Infanta, 69, 70; negotiations with France and the papacy, 141
speculum principis, 26
Speroni, Sperone, 76–7; critique of the *Gerusalemme Liberata*, 163; *Dialoghi*, 77; *Dialogo d'amore*, 77; on differences between courtesans and courtiers, 77; *Orazione contra le cortigiane*, 76–8; as possible character in Tasso's *Aminta*, 163
sprezzatura, 25, 33, 38, 40, 62, 130, 165, 183; as an art of self-defence, 38, 40; in contrast to patience, 183; as a "figuration of anxiety," 25; as ironic behaviour, 33, 40
squalor, 6, 88, 90, 148
Squarotti, Giorgio Bàrberi, 168
Stampa, Gian Maria, 155–6
stealing, 78, 80, 105, 111, 136, 174
Stella Galbiati, Giuseppina, 125, 126
stocks, 7, *8*, 46, *47*, *48*
stormy sea, the court as a, 35, 38, 44, 85, 90, 91, 105, 175, 186
stultitia, 89
"Sua vita in villa e sua vita in corte" (Berni), 151
subjection of the courtier, 5, 11, 76, 90, 123, 132, 141, 145, 147; to

female authority figures, 55; to the prince, 15, 55, 73, 125, 173
subjectivity. *See* self, sense of
sycophants, 3, 27, 41, 84, 96, 100
Symposium (Plato), 79
syphilis, 82
Syracuse, 31, 153

Taegio, Bartolomeo, 154, 155; affinity with satirical themes, 155; *Della vita pastorale*, 154; founder of the Accademia dei Pastori d'Agogna, 154; *La villa*, 154, 155
Tancredi (*Erminia*), 170; (*Gerusalemme Liberata*), 167
Tasso, Torquato, 36–7, 41–2, 64, 70, 73, 74–5, 159–61, 162–4, 165, 166, 167, 168–9, 170, 171, 172, 176; as Erminia figure, 168–9; Forestiero Napolitano character as alter ego of, 37; imprisonment in the hospital Sant'Anna, 41, 42, 160, 168, 171; initial hiring by Duke Alfonso II d'Este, 171; letter to Curzio Ardizio, 244–5n86; poems to Giulio Cesare Brancaccio, 73–5; and self-censorship, 169, 244–5n86; as Tirsi, 163, 167, 172, as a wandering pilgrim, 74. *See also specific titles and names of individual characters*
Tebaldeo, Antonio, 220n73
theatre, the court as a, 6, 10, 33, 44, 58, 106, 107, 157
Thrace, 124
Tiberius, 43
Tindaro (*Filostrato e Panfila*), 105, 145, 157
tinello, 88, 90, 102, 103, 111, 118, 119, 143
Tirsi, 160, 161 2, 163 4, 167, 170, 172, 173; as mask of the author, 163, 167, 172
Tirsi (Castiglione), 158, 160
Toano (*La regia pastorella*), 170
translatio Romae, 129
Trappola, 182
Trascin, 131, 232n196
Trattato della politica libertà (Guarini), 175, 176–7; civic message of, 177; pro-Medici attitude of, 176
treachery, 80, 105, 145, 167, 186. *See also* betrayal
Trifone. *See* Benci, Trifon
triviality, 28, 32, 52, 119; courtier's risk of, 26
truth and truthfulness, 27, 29, 30, 31, 41, 100, 105, 114, 138, 174, 178; and satire, 94, 100, 114. *See also* satirist: as speaker of the truth
Turin, 69. *See also* Caterina, the Infanta, of Spain
tyranny, 7, 16, 20, 31, 67, 86, 102, 114, 132, 145, 153, 154, 169–70, 175, 186; of honour, 164–5. *See also* despotism

Ubaldo (*Gerusalemme Liberata*), 62, 74
Umbricius, 86
unhappiness at court, 4, 6, 22, 67, 80, 88, 91, 101, 105, 125, 146, 173, 179
Unico Aretino (*Book of the Courtier*), 19
Uranio (*Pastor Fido*), 173, 174
Urbino, 18–19, 24, 25, 28, 32, 116, 158, 185; 2017 exhibition at the ducal palace in, 185–6; as a civic Arcadia, 18; duchess of (*see* Gonzaga, Duchess Elisabetta); duke of (*see* Montefeltro, Guidubaldo I da); as a maternal space, 18, 19; as space for the construction of the ideal courtier, 18 19
utopia, 5, 11, 108, 179, 180; the court as a, 18, 28, 59, 108

Valerio (*Cortigiana*), 132, 133, 134, 135
vanity, 54, 124
Vecchi Galli, Paola, 5
Veneziano, Maestro Andrea, 231n191; *Lamento di una cortigiana ferrarese*, 231n191; *Purgatorio delle cortigiane di Roma*, 231n191
Venice, 42, 76, 79, 127, 128, 129, 134–6, 142, 143; as antithesis to the court and its evils, 136; as civic heaven, 143; as Heaven on earth, 135; as the Holy City, 135; as the new Rome, 129; publishing/printing industry of, 66, 76, 140–1; as site or symbol of freedom, 76, 127, 129, 134–5, 136, 137, 140, 147, 251n10; as Virgin, 129
Venier, Lorenzo, 76
Venier, Maffio, 76, 142; *Satira contra la corte*, 142
Venom, 38
Venus, 160
Verdi, Giuseppe, 3; *Rigoletto*, 3
Vermeer, 24, 25; *Allegory of the New Testament*, 24–5
Viaggio di Parnaso (Caporali), 143
Vialardi, Francesco Maria, 176; letter from Battista Guarini, 176
vice: the court as the seat of, 5, 6–7, 16, 85, 88, 101, 137; turned to virtue at court, 174
Vida, Girolamo, 170; *Filliria*, 170
villa, 49, 144, 147–56; as anti-court or antidote to courtly corruption, 149, 151; compared to the court, 148, 149–50, 151; depictions of in *capitolo* form, 147, 149, 150–1; depictions of in sonnet form, 149; Florentine variation on the myth of, 154; ideal distance from the court, 148; myth of in the eighteenth century, 148, 149; myth of in the seventeenth century, 148, 149, 154; myth of in the sixteenth century, 148, 149; and peacefulness, 152; Petrarchan model for, 156; as recuperative or restorative, 149, 152, 156, 184; as sanctuary, 148; as site of moral renovation, 154, 155, 239n37; as site of withdrawal, 156; and spiritual redemption, 152. *See also* collectivity; pastoral setting; solitude
villa dweller, 146
villa, La (Taegio), 154, 155
ville, Le (Doni), 147–8
Vincenzo Malpiglio (*Malpiglio*). *See* Malpiglio, Vincenzo
Vinciguerra, Antonio, 220n73
Vincioli, Vinciolo, 143; *Sopra la corte*, 143
Virescit vulnere virtus, 39
Virgil, 220n71
virtù. *See* virtue
virtue: the court as the seat of, 16; courtier's role in leading the prince to, 26–31; "courtly," 42, 43; as defence against Fortuna, 42, 43, 110–11; turned to vice at court, 174
virtues: Christian, 88, 182; feminine, 69, 71, 76
virtuosa: figure of, 71–2; term, 71
virtuoso, figure of, 71
Visdomini, Eugenio, 169–70; *Erminia*, 169–70, 171; membership in Innominati academy, 169
voice, sexualized vision of, 75
Vulcan, 101

Waddington, Raymond B., 129–30; on parallel between Aretino as satyr and Castiglione's *sprezzatura*, 130

wantonness, 53, 66, 84, 165
warrior. *See* soldier
whore, 78; and the court, 81, 82–3; the court as a, 82–3, 128, 129; the courtier as a, 78
Wistreich, Richard, 74
Wickedness, 38
wine, 90, 102, 103, 113, 115, 119
witch, 59, 60, 61, 65; the court as a, 53, 58–62
witchcraft, 214n125
withdrawal, 39, 119, 127, 144, 148, 149, 151, 154, 156, 168, 175, 176, 184
Wofford, Susanne, 237n4
woman, the court as a, 10, 49, 56–8, 62–3, 64, 65, 82, 143
women: ability to shame men into action, 55; as advisors, 51, 66; Aristotle's theories on, 51, 52; as artists, 51, 71; as audience for male courtiers, 51, 65, 71; as consumers of cultural artefacts, 51; as dangerous or a threat, 57, 58–9, 74; as enforcers of a "civilizing process," 51; as an effeminizing presence, 51, 73, 74; Galenic view of, 72; as judges of men's behaviour, 51, 64–5; as interlocutors, 50, 71; magical powers of, 59; use of makeup, 59–60; as musicians, 71; as patrons of the arts, 51, 52, 65; as perpetual children, 72; in a position of power, 64, 65, 67; presence at court, 52, 57, 61, 64, 65, 71, 72; as protagonists, 51; as regents of state, 51, 52, 66; as rivals of men, 71; role of in the early modern period, 50, 72; as sirens, 73, 74, 75; wantonness of, 84; as weak in body and mind, 65; as writers, 51, 71. *See also* court lady; *querelle des femmes*
Woodhouse, John, 91

Zatti, Sergio, 164; on a "counterpoint technique" in Tasso's *Aminta,* 164

www.ingramcontent.com/pod-product-compliance
Lightning Source LLC
LaVergne TN
LVHW090152080826
844660LV00013B/773/J

* 9 7 8 1 4 8 7 5 0 5 4 4 8 *